SUPERVISION IN THOUGHT AND ACTION

SUPERVISION IN THOUGHT AND ACTION

THIRD EDITION

William H. Lucio
John D. McNeil

Graduate School of Education
University of California, Los Angeles

McGRAW-HILL
BOOK COMPANY

New York   St. Louis   San Francisco   Auckland   Bogotá   Düsseldorf
Johannesburg   London   Madrid   Mexico   Montreal   New Delhi
Panama   Paris   São Paulo   Singapore   Sydney   Tokyo   Toronto

SUPERVISION IN THOUGHT AND ACTION

Copyright © 1979 by McGraw-Hill, Inc. All rights reserved.
Formerly published under the title of SUPERVISION: A SYNTHESIS OF
THOUGHT AND ACTION, copyright © 1969, 1962 by McGraw-Hill, Inc.

1 2 3 4 5 6 7 8 9 0   DODO   7 8 3 2 1 0 9 8

This book was set in Optima by BookTech, Inc. (ECU).
The editors were Eric M. Munson and James B. Armstrong;
the cover was designed by Rafael Hernandez;
the production supervisor was Donna Piligra.
R. R. Donnelley & Sons Company was printer and binder.

Library of Congress Cataloging in Publication Data

Lucio, William H.
  Supervision in thought and action.

  Earlier ed. published under title: Supervision:
a synthesis of thought and action.
  Includes indexes.
  1. School supervision.   I. McNeil, John D.,
joint author.   II. Title.
LB2805.L76   1979   371.2   78-19140
ISBN 0-07-038952-7

90588

CONTENTS

PREFACE

When people grow impatient with flaws in their schools and in their children or their children's teachers, a different emphasis in supervision is required. As the demands on pupils' minds become more vigorous, students of supervision must address themselves to the task of shaping the process and content of supervision with both ideals and reality. This textbook is written on the assumption that students of supervision—superintendents, principals, teachers, coordinators, and curriculum workers, as well as those in preparation for leadership positions in the schools—have responsibility for exploring, surveying, and mapping new terrain in supervision. Grasping and influencing the forces which affect our thinking and behaving are new requirements to which supervision must accommodate its technique. Supervision cannot survive on concepts that produce little or no social benefit.

The reader is reminded that this is a textbook drawing upon a number of treatises. It is not a monograph dealing in depth with a small corner of the field of supervision, nor does it attempt to place facts and principles into any one particular system. Our constant target has been to beckon students of supervision into new paths in order to determine why certain procedures are superior to others for given purposes. As a result of reading this book, it is hoped that supervisors will respond to an environment of uncertainty with better choices, because interpretation rather than prescription is featured. We expect the thoughtful reader to regard all suggestions for appropriate action in this book as an invitation to question and adapt. This is not to say that the authors do not seek to evoke a certain kind and quality of response. On the contrary, there is a deliberate attempt to make a case for three beliefs regarding supervision:

1. We believe that supervision requires a super vision—a superior perspective attained by special preparation and position. We argue, for example, that a supervisor's education and responsibilities can provide maximum differentiation of conditions and alternatives, bringing a larger view of the instructional mission and process. To the extent that persons are confined to a particular situation and have only a partial or distorted view of teaching and its ends, they are not supervisors. As a prerequisite to supervision we would require possession of a methodology which respects (a) the learner, (b) disciplined approaches to knowledge, and (c) social conditions. We believe that supervisors must be statesmen, able to give direction beyond merely ministering to an organization's equilibrium. To this end, the notion of the supervising statesman is a recurring theme in this text.

2. We believe that a raison d'etre for teachers and supervisors is to promote desired and desirable changes in learners and that those accepting responsibility for such a task must be held accountable. We believe that the observation of results of instructional practice for both immediate and long-term consequences is consistent with the premise that supervision is itself a process of discovering what values are worthwhile and proper for instructional objectives. To those accepting responsibility for supervision we offer data and propositions from a number of disciplines as instruments for (a) defining situations, (b) suggesting promising avenues for experimentation, and (c) making more intelligent educational decisions. We do not regard theories from organized disciplines as fixed rules for practice in unique situations. This point of view is represented by the schema A Visual Concept of Supervision.

3. We are committed to supervisory methods of reason and practical intelligence. The method of reason requires the formulation of explicit purposes to be fulfilled by schools and expects the main energies of all concerned to be directed and dedicated in accordance with these purposes. The method of practical intelligence permits all to judge the relevance of purposes and the attainment of objectives. It is necessary to ensure that (a) formulated purposes do not become idols which limit freedom, (b) purposes are reinterpreted through judgment of their consequences by those affected, and (c) those who are expected to invest their energies can be committed to purposes and conduct themselves appropriately.

While this book aims at a realistic conception of what constitutes supervision and suggests ways to do better the things that are now necessary, everything that ought to be known about supervision has not been put into this book.

Part One presents changing views of supervision and the varied roles associated with supervisory positions. It sets the stage for a systematic treatment of human and technical factors associated with successful supervision.

Part Two aims at giving the reader insight into observing and interpreting supervisory situations. Research from many sources is used to help the supervisor translate practical supervisory procedures into their theoretical equivalents: to know not merely as a matter of brute fact that certain arrangements work, but to know how and why they work.

Part Three seeks to put the reader in control of conditions which potentially can effect better human relations and increase supervisory efficacy. Elements in human relations—such as supervisors' and teachers' perceptions of each other, communication processes, ways of working toward change, and supervisory behavior as related to learning—are discussed.

Part Four focuses on those supervisory skills applicable to the appraising and improving of teacher performance and on ways of conducting in-school research. A series of alternative views for curriculum improvement and development is presented to help give direction for decisions about what and how to teach. Readers' appropriation of the subject matter of this section will improve personal scholarship and help them to be more conscious of inquiry and method in supervision.

The planning of this book was a cooperative venture from its inception. Each author contributed suggestions and materials to chapters written by the other. Responsibility for the writing and content of chapters, however, has been placed: W. H. L. for Chapters 7 through 12; J. D. M. for Chapters 1 through 6 and 13.

WILLIAM H. LUCIO

JOHN D. McNEIL

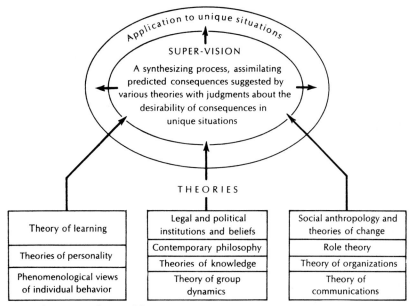

A visual concept of supervision.

PART ONE

THE NATURE OF SUPERVISION

An interesting thing is happening with respect to the term "supervision." Many people are reluctant to use it. Euphemisms—management, planning, consultation, coordination, evaluation, and the like—are appearing in ever greater numbers. By gradual stages the central meaning of the word itself is changing, perhaps more in the direction of pejoration than amelioration.

One possible reason for this change is that supervision itself is changing. Another reason is that the term does not stand for the same things to all who use it. Moreover, supervision calls up in every individual an emotional as well as a purely intellectual concept.

Our purpose in Part One is to explain and interpret what supervision has meant, what it now means, and what it is likely to mean in the future. We do this, not as an exercise in linguistics, but as basic orientation for studying this vital activity and for knowing the many dimensions of supervision so that supervisors—both those with experience and those in preparation—can make wise choices regarding their supervisory roles.

CHAPTER 1

A HISTORICAL PERSPECTIVE OF SUPERVISION

Historical knowledge gives insight into the nature of supervision, for we are wedded in our practice to the thought of other eras. Such a perspective also focuses attention upon what is going on today under the name of supervision. Briefly, the history of modern school supervision shows that in the first quarter of the century supervision was, in general, dominated by a classical view of people and institutions. Teachers were regarded as instruments that should be closely supervised to ensure that they mechanically carried out the methods of procedure determined by administrative and special supervisors. In the second quarter of the century supervision was conceived as the practice of human relations. This view endowed teachers with feelings and motives but often gave less attention to their properties as reasoning beings. Presently, there are demands for a supplementary approach which will recognize the importance of both mechanism and morale, yet stress cognition in its process. By stressing cognition, we mean helping supervisors and teachers develop the intellectual content of their tasks, acquiring the theories with which to relate particular consequences to the conditions which produce these consequences.

SUPERVISION BY ADMINISTRATIVE OFFICERS

Supervisory control of American public schools was originally vested in local or religious officers and special committees of laypeople with power to visit and inspect schools. In the eighteenth century it was common for official committees not only to become familiar with the methods used in teaching but to "inquire of their proficiency," giving examinations to check on the work. These committees were less interested in improving deficient teachers than in dismissing them. Early in the nineteenth century the powers and duties of the committees or boards were placed in such positions as "acting visitor," "school clerk," or "superintendent of schools," and upgrading the work of teachers became a recognized function.[1] Eventually, these positions were filled by professional educators. By 1870, there were twenty-nine superintendents of schools serving as executive officers, with the supervising of instruction as one of their duties, in which the improvement of weak teachers' deficiencies was sought more than rejections. Supervision by administrative officers long remained a primary method for the improvement of teachers, although variations in the method were great. A turn-of-the-century view of supervision was expressed as follows:[2]

> In visits for personal inspection and suggestion, I am generous in praise of the good things which I see, and criticize only when I believe my criticism will be received in the right spirit and will probably work improvement. I gave up years ago all criticism for the sake of freeing myself from responsibility. Often I refrain from direct criticism and talk to the principal of the school concerning the teacher's faults. I am reaching the conclusion that I would better always consult the principal before making criticism of any kind. The reason for this will be appreciated by every experienced superintendent.
>
> The best method of helping teachers is, I believe, by example. The superintendent or principal should be always at his post of duty, and always within call of every teacher to assist her in any possible way. Early and late, in season and out of season, school days and holidays, it should be known that he is trying to do all that his time and strength will permit to promote the interests of the schools. He must always say "Come"; must study harder and work more hours than his teachers; must set a pace which his best teachers find impossible to follow. Otherwise, he should resign and let some one who will do more and better work take his place.

---

1. Fred C. Ayer and A. S. Barr, *The Organization of Supervision*, D. Appleton & Company, Inc., New York, 1928, pp. 7–37.
2. National Society for the Scientific Study of Education, *The Relation of Superintendents and Principals to the Training and Professional Improvement of Their Teachers*, Seventh Yearbook, part I, The University of Chicago Press, Chicago, 1908, p. 18.

The school principalship lagged behind the superintendency in the assumption of a supervisory role, presumably because of the principal's own teaching and clerical duties. Although in 1857 certain principals in Boston were released from part of their teaching to assist teachers, the innovation did not spread rapidly. The position of supervising principal did not become well known until the twentieth century.

Supervision of rural schools under the direction of the county superintendent began early in the twentieth century, with supervisors appointed to improve administration as well as instruction. A concrete example of the work of one early rural supervisor is seen in this outline:[3]

1. Installed individual drinking cups in several schools.
2. Had sanitary water jar, or cooler, placed in several schools.
3. Secured the analysis of the drinking water in a large number of schools, with the result that in four cases out of five the water was condemned.
4. In all but one school had window boards installed for ventilating purposes.
5. Had the stoves jacketed in most of the schools.
6. Secured medical inspection of the pupils.
7. Readjusted the seating of the pupils with reference to health and comfort.
8. Emphasized the importance of better hygienic conditions and placed a copy of Dr. Allen's Health Rules in every school.
9. Distributed among the schools four hundred ninety-nine supplementary readers for the individual grades.
10. Enforced the state course of study.
11. Helped the teachers in their efforts to use modern methods and devices of teaching.
12. Encouraged picture study in all schools.
13. Secured the exchange of pupils' compositions with other school children in Oregon and in other states.
14. Assisted boards of education in securing and retaining capable teachers.
15. Persuaded boards to supply better school equipment.
16. Directed the work of the Teachers' Reading Circle and encouraged many teachers to attend summer schools.
17. Supplied teachers with lists of helpful state and government publications.
18. Held twenty-five public meetings and at ten of these gave stereopticon lectures.

3. L. J. Hanifan, "District Supervision," in *The Supervision of Rural Schools,* Twelfth Yearbook, part II, National Society for the Study of Education, The University of Chicago Press, Chicago, 1913, pp. 23–24.

19. Helped the pupils plan for vocational work during the summer vacation.

SUPERVISION BY SPECIALISTS

By the turn of the century, a number of new subjects, such as music, drawing, manual training, home economics, and physical education, became part of the curriculum as the result of changing social conditions and the efforts of such pressure groups as organized mothers. Inasmuch as superintendents and teachers were not prepared to teach these new subjects, special teachers and general supervisors were engaged to conduct the classes and to assist regular teachers. Shortly thereafter, a number of cities organized special supervisory departments to provide leadership in connection with language, mathematics, social studies, and science as well as the special subjects.

Problems of authority, function, and procedures arose with the expansion of two kinds of supervisory officers—administrators and specialists. These questions were commonly asked: "How should school supervision be differentiated from school administration?" "Is supervision the overseeing, inspection, and enforcement of regulations?" "Whose instructions should teachers follow?" In general, supervision was seen as that aspect of administration specifically concerned with raising instruction to a certain standard of performance.

Lowry in 1908 placed responsibility for the policy of instruction upon the principal. "Whether in the regular or in the special subjects (responsibility) should be his and not that of the visiting supervisor, no matter how expert she may be in her particular line."[4] Lowry conceived the principal as releasing the unexpressed talent of the teachers and the supervisor as working with the principal rather than with teachers directly.

The assumption that teachers were best helped and changed by direction from above was implicit in most of the practice of the day. The way this direction was to be carried out, however, differed according to the qualifications of the individual teacher. Van Sickle's interesting scheme for the treatment of different kinds of teachers by the supervisor not only reflects this differentiation, but also indicates the rising level of professional preparation among teachers:[5]

1. Superior teachers who need no stimulation other than their own ideals of excellence: By the fine standard of work which they maintain and by their student-like habits they might, under favorable conditions, set the pace for the entire teaching force. At the present

4. National Society for the Scientific Study of Education, *The Relation of Superintendents and Principals to the Training and Professional Improvement of Their Teachers,* Seventh Yearbook, part II, The University of Chicago Press, Chicago, 1908, p. 19.
5. Ibid., p. 21.

time, this group is a large one. With this group, supervision is chiefly concerned in gaining their cooperation in working out the problems and in bringing their influences to bear on other teachers in tactful ways.

2. Teachers possessing a good degree of executive ability and adequate scholarship of the book-learning variety, who resist change because they honestly believe the old ways are better: They are patriotic defenders of the views and traditions and practices in which they were reared. The greater number of these will as strongly support the new when fully convinced of its advantages; but in the absence of positive orders they resist proposed changes until absolutely conclusive demonstration is furnished in a concrete way. Supervision must confidently accept these conditions and furnish demonstration.

3. Teachers lacking adequate scholarship or practical skill or both, self-conscious and timid, because unacquainted with standards of work and valid guiding principles, desirous of avoiding observation, doing their work in a more or less perfunctory and fortuitous way: Supervision needs to give these teachers courage by an exhibition of standards plainly within their reach and by personal work in their own classrooms.

4. Teachers lacking adequate scholarship or practical skill or both, but not conscious of this lack and therefore unaware of any need of assistance: Some form of positive direction is here necessary in the first stages of supervision.

5. Teachers yet in the early years of their service: Supervision should be able to concern itself chiefly in keeping these teachers in class 1 so far as their personal attitude is concerned. There will, of course, always be differences among them in scholarship and personal power, but all should have guidance in kind and quantity adapted to prevent any of them, even the weakest, from developing the characteristics of class 2, class 3, or class 4. If these new recruits are to be able to lead children to be open-minded, to hold opinions tentatively, to be sure but not too sure, to be willing to give both sides of a question a hearing before reaching a final conclusion, they must keep themselves open-minded. To aid them in doing this, supervision will keep itself free from dogmatism even in dealing with the youngest teachers.

Teachers of class 1, class 2, and class 5 are willing to have their work seen and valued by competent and trusted supervisors. People who know how to do a thing, or who sincerely think they know how, or who sincerely wish to learn how, are neither afraid nor reluctant to have their work seen by any fair-minded person. Supervisors must be both skillful and fair-minded, and their work must prove that supervision means help.

THE SCIENCE OF SUPERVISION

By 1913 the world of material production saw the possibilities of "scientific management," and school leaders were proposing the application of organizational principles to school supervision.[6] These principles called for clear definition of educational ends and coordination of all who work to attain them. The "best" methods of teaching were to be found, and the use of these methods was to be enforced on teachers. The qualifications of teachers were to be specifically defined, and it was the job of supervisors to see that all met these standard qualifications. Supervisors were to keep teachers supplied with detailed instructions and the materials and appliances to be used. They would, of course, place incentives before teachers in order to stimulate desirable efforts.

Scientific management proposed to alter the personal relations between supervisors and teachers. Instead of the supervisors directing the methods of the teachers in a personal and arbitrary manner, the primary task of the scientific supervisor was to discover educational "laws" and apply them through the labors of the teacher. The teacher would be expected to find the controlling scientific law through cooperation with the supervisor. Neither was to be personally over the other, for both were under the law of science. The supervisory staff would keep teachers up to standard (1) by involving the labors of teachers in the social concerns of the community (thereby widening and renewing teachers' vistas while releasing them from dreary chores at school which dwarf their humanity) and (2) by offering incentives in the form of salary, promotion, and social recognition, as well as appealing to their motives for social service.

Scientific supervision was partly a protest movement against the confusion of goals and practices existing at the time.

"At present, the chief difficulty is that there are no standards to work to. Schools are simply grinding away without any goal in view. They move in the right direction—they move in the wrong direction. Without a goal their efforts are relatively random, feeble, inefficient. The pupil does not know what to aim at; the teacher does not know how much to require; the principal does not know how high the teacher is aiming; the superintendent has no means of knowing the standards of either teacher or principal. The whole situation represents the jellyfish stage of organization and direction."[7] In place of teachers using every conceivable method and every kind of material in their trial-and-error experimentation with children, the movement anticipated Public Law 531. This law made possible the national curriculum projects of the 1960s in recommending that the then U.S.

6. Franklin Bobbitt, in *The Supervision of City Schools*, Twelfth Yearbook, part I, National Society for the Study of Education, The University of Chicago Press, Chicago, 1913, pp. 7–96.
7. Ibid., p. 40.

Bureau of Education coordinate cooperative efforts of expert staffs in school systems and communities in analyzing the relative efficacy of methods.

It was contended that although conscientious supervisors earnestly desired to share tasks with teachers, they found themselves unable to do so because of the dearth of scientifically formulated information on what constituted the best control of the various factors of method. Supervisors had opinions, but others of equal ability had neutralizing opinions. When supervisors turned to the literature of the profession for guidance, they found more conflicting opinions.

To those representing the scientific movement, there was but one avenue of escape from the condition of relative helplessness in the ability to direct and supervise: research and measurement. The earlier assumption that supervisors could judge the work of teachers by noting the extent to which classroom practices followed general principles was declared false. These so-called educational principles were criticized as being of poor help when one tried to apply them to a concrete task. Their use was of little value in seeking answers to such problems as these: At what age shall addition combinations be taught? What amount of time per week should be devoted to the practice of particular skills? Under what conditions should teachers make use of concrete problems and abstract examples? What is the relative value of appeal to vocational or civic motives?

It was the supervisory staff which was to have the largest share in the work of determining proper methods. The burden of finding the best methods was too great and too complex to be laid on the shoulders of teachers. Teachers were expected to be specialists in the practice that would produce "the product"; supervisors were to specialize in the science relating to the process. Supervisors were to (1) discover best procedures in the performance of particular educational tasks and (2) give these best methods to the teachers for their guidance.

Instruments for measuring outcomes and setting standards were promised. Courtis, for example, tentatively determined measuring scales for arithmetical ability. These scales measured the accuracy and amount of work that could be performed within a given time. Using these measurements, Courtis developed norms for setting expectations in mathematical operations for pupils in grades three through eight. It was held that clear expectation would help teachers judge themselves and their methods. Further, teachers would receive help in proportion to need and recognition in proportion to merit.[8]

8. S. A. Courtis, "Standard Scores in Arithmetic," *Elementary School Teacher,* vol. 12,

Under scientific management, children, rather than the machinery of education, were to become the center of educational consciousness. The focus was to remain on ends: development of the pupil. Manipulation of process was to be the means. Diverse standards for pupils of varying abilities were recommended. It was assumed that once pupils knew what was expected of them, the teaching problem was to teach them how to study, and to provide stimulations that would produce the desired effort. There is a striking similarity between the educational views of leaders in the early scientific movement and the views of persons currently associated with instructional technology.[9] Both imply that the effort expended by teachers in carrying students passively along can be dispensed with: that pupils can be made to walk and bear their own burdens with their own strength and gain further strength thereby. Both hold that the time saved by pupil and teacher under systematic methods of instruction can be expended more profitably. Then as now the science of education was concerned with the determination of the amount and sequence of presentation in accordance with the individual differences of the learner and a wide variety of social conditions.

SUPERVISION AS DEMOCRATIC HUMAN RELATIONS

The late 1920s saw further protest against imposition of curriculum and method by personal authority of administrative officers. Writers began to conceive of supervision as guidance rather than inspection. Kyte's *How to Supervise* defined supervision as "the maximum development of the teacher into the most professionally efficient person she is capable of becoming."[10] Teachers were presumed professionally efficient when competent in self-analysis, self-criticism, and self-improvement. In practice, however, the standards for teaching procedures were still determined at higher levels and transmitted to teachers as supervisors gave commendations and condemnations following visits to classrooms and demonstrations.

Related to the economic and social transformations of the depression and war years were spirited pleas for a kind of supervision which would embrace the ideals of a democratic order. Instead of emphasis upon tradition—the leader and the led—supervision became associated with precepts respecting human personality and encouraging wide participation in the formulation of policy. Those who

pp. 127–137, November 1911.
9. Eva L. Baker, "The Technology of Instructional Development," *Second Handbook of Research on Teaching,* Robert M. W. Travers (ed.), Rand McNally and Co., Chicago, 1973, pp. 245–286.
10. George C. Kyte, *How to Supervise,* Houghton Mifflin Company, Boston, 1930, p. 45.

opposed the imposition of courses of study and methods planned by upper levels were committed to a philosophy of situational relativism; that is, there were no absolutes, and "correct" procedures depended upon particular circumstances. Gestalt psychology supplied theory and Lewin supplied evidence to support the social supervision desired. Such psychology placed emphasis upon the relation of the concrete individual to the concrete situation, in contrast to former modes of thought which saw the characteristics of the individual as independent of a particular situation. Lewin's work in the study of motivation drew additional attention to the social factors in supervision. His interest and research in such problems as conflict in industry, morale in time of war, and the enlightenment of prejudiced groups[11] had much influence on supervisory practice. His studies also stimulated the growth of action research and group dynamics, which became useful tools to accompany the growing concept that the supervisor was a cooperating member of a total group studying a particular teaching-learning situation. Special responsibilities of the supervisor (increasingly called consultant at this time) included setting a relaxed atmosphere and obtaining wide participation.[12] The improvement of the entire staff rather than of teachers alone became a goal to be reached through cooperative attack upon a commonly

11. Kurt Lewin, *Resolving Social Conflicts,* Harper & Row, Publishers, Incorporated, New York, 1948.
12. Kimball Wiles, *Supervision for Better Schools,* Prentice-Hall, Inc., Englewood Cliffs, N.J., 1950.

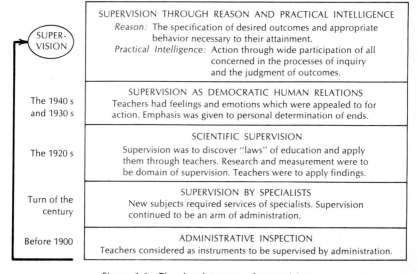

Figure 1-1   The development of supervision.

recognized problem. This view held that leadership for improvement was a shared responsibility. Teacher, supervisor, administrator, pupil, or other could serve as the leader to the extent that each was able to advance the group toward mutually accepted goals. Solution of the instruction problem and personal growth of participants were outcomes to be sought.

A pictorial review of earlier stages of supervision and the current development in this field is presented in Figure 1-1 on page 11.

DIRECTIONS OF SUPERVISORY THOUGHT

Supervision has no independent thought of its own. As indicated previously, the dynamics of supervision are in constant interrelation with the school and the social whole. However, the main task of supervision is to answer the question of who shall make decisions determining the kind of knowledge to be fostered in schools.

Supervision and Interpretations of Knowledge

The pattern of supervision has been closely associated with reinterpretations of knowledge. When knowledge was thought of as ready-made information and belief, supervisors transmitted traditional practices and disregarded personal discovery. Consequently, supervisors and teachers tended to be obedient and conservative personalities who marveled at the wisdom of the past. Somewhat later, supervisors were captivated by the precise quantitative techniques of the inductive process and concentrated their efforts on measurement and rating, deeming that knowledge was best validated by the measurement of sense perceptions. A subsequent series of social events and a counteracting psychology, focusing on the subjective qualities of the individual, led to a weakened faith in both traditional and empirical pronouncements. Rather, there was a conviction that sense perception was relative to the beholder, to time, and to the situation. Inasmuch as knowledge gained in sense perception appeared to have its source in both the physical world and the learner, supervisors sought ways of getting teachers to describe their own situations and to share their individual and partial truths. Staffs were encouraged to define their own goals, collect data on the effects of their efforts, and form their own interpersonal judgments. Validation of knowledge by consensus, in which participants established understanding within their common human association, was recommended. Subjectivity of knowledge also underlined much of the literature read by supervisors, who began to identify growth in knowledge as identical with personal becoming. They believed in an individual's maturity through a knowledge of self as true knowledge.

Nothing was really learned unless it was an expression of the whole person, one's very action and being. Current practices which are associated with this view invite active participation and personal identification with knowledge rather than objective observation, study, and reflection.

It has been noted, however, that supervisors are not always clear as to what is involved in their helping another person in accordance with the belief that knowledge is personal growth. For example, psychologists feel that supervisors need to distinguish between requests for help which have their genesis in a professional problem beyond the teacher's experiences and requests for help which stem from a teacher's personal inadequacy and unresolved dependence. If the latter are met by the supervisor, the person's lack of maturity may be reinforced.

Methods of Reason and Practical Intelligence

Two different approaches to supervision currently dominate thought and action: the method of reason and the method of practical intelligence. Reason and practical intelligence have become the latest in this series of renewed interpretations of knowledge with implications for supervision. The method of reason rests on the belief that knowledge is best obtained through a theoretical system which serves to guide perceptions and actions. The scheme itself may be discovered by logical thought which goes beyond observed phenomena of "everyday life." Supervisors, teachers, and children are assumed to behave rationally when they act in accord with a given set of theoretical or mental patterns which presumably relate to the characteristics of their own situations. These patterns include assumptions about future events, knowledge of alternatives available, consequences attached to the options, and a way of ordering consequences and options by preference.

The method of practical intelligence seeks knowledge through experimental procedures and the judgment of participants; truths must be tested for their adequacy in helping individuals learn how to judge and control their own behavior. In general, this method calls for an interest in desirable consequences as well as respect for the ways in which knowledge is acquired and improved. Supervisors using this method distrust that intellectual authoritarianism which assumes that (1) only a few have the ability to conceive of appropriate ends and (2) any "system" of thought need not be validated in concrete situations.

RATIONAL SUPERVISION   Current demands for purpose, for planning, and for the systematic knowledge believed indispensable to modern life emphasize the method of reason. Davies and Iannaccone, for instance, were among the first to propose that conceptualization was the shape of things to come in which encompassing concepts would enable supervisors to control situations as they achieve "the ability to see the enterprise as a whole."[13] Also, economists have emphasized rationalistic aspects in their studies of the planning process. Psychologists, too, have found theoretical models useful in the study of organizational communication and problem solving. These successes spur the exploration of rational dimensions in supervision. Hypotheses based upon rational models for program-innovating processes, for example, have already been formulated, and they offer suggestions for supervisors to use in effecting change. Cases in point are propositions derived from theory stating that (1) daily routine drives out planning for change, (2) change is fostered by the allocation of resources to new goals, and (3) the judicious use of deadlines is important in speeding the process of change.[14]

Modern theories of rationality assume that members of organizations are limited in their knowledge and their capacities to learn and to solve problems. Because the mind cannot immediately grasp all consequences, the supervisory staff must be able to help teachers toward the coordinated and effective behavior which reflects the broader considerations of the school. In order for teachers' own decisions to be rational, they must be related to expectations, rather than to wishes. Supervisory techniques for making teacher behavior more rational, i.e., more consistent with the school's goals, include:

1. Dividing work among teachers, limiting their attention to the immediate task
2. Making school objectives so operational and definite that it is possible to assess the extent to which they are being attained
3. Establishing standardized practices which relieve the individual teacher of minor choices
4. Making it possible for teachers to receive expert help from more than one source, yet allowing only one authority figure to resolve any conflict among them
5. Establishing systems of influence such as staff development programs, training conferences, and other arrangements for communicating those attitudes and habits which will lead to the school's objectives

13. Daniel R. Davies and Laurence Iannaccone, "Ferment in the Study of Organization," *Teachers College Record,* vol. 60, no. 2, p. 68, November 1958.
14. James G. March and Herbert A. Simon, *Organizations,* John Wiley & Sons, Inc., New York, 1958, p. 185.

6. Indicating how the school's goals contribute to the teacher's personal goals
7. Building loyalty to the school rather than to the teacher's subject field

PRACTICAL INTELLIGENCE IN SUPERVISION AND THE EXTENSION OF PERCEPTION   The use of intelligence in supervision is not altogether unexplored terrain. Most of the present concern for participation and pattern in the problem solving which accompanies the method of practical intelligence goes back to John Dewey's analysis.[15] It is recalled that he presented a certain logic of method by which conceptual frameworks were tested as tools of inquiry rather than accepted as fixed conclusions. To Dewey and those favoring practical intelligence, proposals for action are working hypotheses requiring observation of consequences, interpretation, and revision. Those favoring this method are worried about the effect of absolutistic logic upon education, "the strengthening of a reign of dogma."[16] Dewey, for instance, warned that the discussion of concepts and their logical relation to one another could substitute for inquiry. One of the most important issues in modern supervision centers at this very point: Should supervisors seek to develop their own vision as well as the vision of others through open-ended modes of thought in which inquiry is pursued and participants attempt to seek new knowledge? Or should supervisors hold a mental picture of some desired end or conclusion, personal or social, which is conceived as fixed and not to be challenged, and use this conception to control the supervising process?

Practical intelligence in supervision cannot be understood without awareness of its relation to a desire for extending vision in education. The method of practical intelligence is a method of inquiry based upon faith in the capacities of ordinary people. The teacher, in dealing with concrete situations and applying knowledge informally, is often more intelligent than the theorist who observes only a limited sphere because of the restrictions of science. Fisher[17] and Raup and associates[18] wrote extensively on this method which seeks to develop comprehensive perspective as a consequence of the use of the processes of inquiry. Briefly, it requires recognition of varying

15. John Dewey, *How We Think,* D. C. Heath and Company, Boston, 1910.
16. John Dewey, *The Public and Its Problems,* Henry Holt and Company, Inc., New York, 1927.
17. Margaret Fisher, *Leadership and Intelligence,* Bureau of Publications, Teachers College, Columbia University, New York, 1954.
18. R. Bruce Raup et al., *The Improvement of Practical Intelligence,* Harper & Row, Publishers, Incorporated, New York, 1950.

points of view and accommodation of one's own perspective to others. Recent examples of practical intelligence in action can be found in the work of Paulo Freire.[19] Under this method, supervisors encourage wide participation in policy-determining functions and seek to have participants see the significance of their emotions as well as facts. Supervisors view themselves as learners along with others in the undertaking. The intellectual expert's position in the method of practical intelligence is one of involvement in the process of judgment in working with others. Predictability of results is not ensured because the method operates within the contingency of any situation. In other words, an ultimate goal and an overall plan are not absolutes which cannot be changed. Generalizations not only are used by supervisors to guide decisions but are themselves developed along with the problem they are instrumental in solving. It is an implied assumption in the method of intelligence that in attacking particular problems, supervisors and teachers formulate intelligent insight into the interrelations of events in their given situations. If supervisory action ends in failure, then reflection and abstraction begin.

Burnham reports a trend toward practical intelligence in supervision, indicating that supervision today is not the province of a particular person or position but a rational mode of behavior for all who work and are part of the human organization of the school.[20]

Because we believe in the method of practical intelligence, later chapters of this book will deal with the techniques which are necessary if it is to be effective. Obviously, one-way communication, devastating attacks on the personal level, "busy work," urgings for togetherness, and the encouragement of teachers to arrive at decisions whether or not they possess the requisite skill and knowledge to do so will result in a half-way perception. When teachers prefer not to be involved in the method, it might indicate that they have had experiences in fraudulent planning rather than in the process of inquiry.

On the other hand, we recognize merit in the method of reason. We believe with Mannheim[21] that perspective and freedom can best be preserved when capable intellectuals are detached from special interests in society and carry out major roles in social affairs through positions in government and education. Mannheim has proposed that tribunals of experts, aiming at consistency of plans rather than satisfaction of particular interests, should determine the basic plan-

19. Paulo Freire, *Pedagogy of the Oppressed,* Herder and Herder, New York, 1970.
20. Reba M. Burnham, "Instructional Supervision: Past, Present and Future Perspectives," *Theory into Practice,* vol. 15, no. 4, pp. 301–306, October 1976.
21. Karl Mannheim, *Ideology and Utopia,* Harcourt Brace Jovanovich, Inc., New York, 1936.

ning laws and judge their validity. According to this view, intellectuals having special access to values in the culture have responsibility for mediating these values to the community. Accordingly, the services of experts and the resources of social science are incorporated into the educational planning in essential areas. Perhaps *expertise* through government is one way democracy can overcome and introduce into school operations the highest possible degree of rationality. We recommend centralization for the planning of certain basic educational policies because we believe that creative use of government and not just the inventiveness of individuals can support freedom. Our opinion is that the method of reason should be accompanied, however, by the method of practical intelligence so that the decision makers will not usurp absolute authority but rather will practice distribution of responsibility. Also, in order to keep education from becoming the tools of any one group, supervisors, as individual citizens and as members of professional organizations, must be politically active in local and national affairs, entering into the great debates about both social and educational issues, i.e., exercising their practical intelligence in areas outside the structure of the school.

Some setbacks to the use of rational methods, particularly at the national level, have recently occurred. The curriculum reform movement which began in the sixties, for example, during which scholars supported by more than 1 billion federal dollars developed and implemented courses, has ended. Restoration of curriculum development funds is in doubt, and the content of future curricula funded by the government through the National Science Foundation will be decided by members of that federal agency, not by detached intellectuals.

There are indications, however, that the rational method is viable: Mandated competency-based programs, diagnostic-prescriptive teaching methods, and goal-oriented evaluative systems are cases in point. Too, National Assessment of Educational Progress continues. This assessment, developed with the support of the United States Office of Education, the Carnegie Corporation, and the Ford Foundation, furnishes the first real measure of the nation's gross educational product, indicating what pupils know about reading, language arts, science, mathematics, social studies, fine arts, and vocational education. The assessment of the degree to which the desired results are attained provides a base line from which supervisors can check out the effectiveness of their supervision by noting subsequent improvement or regression in scores made by pupils on a wide range of categories.

The method of practical intelligence is being used in school reform. Early childhood, Head Start, and secondary school restructuring projects are cases in point. Many parents, teachers, employers, and neighborhood residents are becoming more skilled in planning for children as they work with supervisors. Neighborhood residents bring many assets to the school—they often know the ways and aspirations of the community better than the supervisor. The supervisor, using the method of practical intelligence, encourages ordinary people, many from poverty areas, both to shape the direction of their programs and to expand their perspective so that programs become more comprehensive.

CURRENT TRENDS

The approach to supervision for the twenty-first century is characterized by a continuation of both practical intelligence and rational thinking.

Unruh sees supervision at a critical moment in history.[22] She believes that supervisors must either rise to the challenge of leadership or lose their function to other individuals or agencies. Among the threats she perceives are (1) *the trend toward control over schools by government agencies*—regulations, assessments, mandates, competency tests are attempts to control by means of forms, educational audits, and allocations of funds dependent upon compliance with governmental policy; and (2) *supervisors' loss of effectiveness in working with teachers*—supervisors are sometimes perceived as lacking visibility in schools, being remote figures without realistic connections with the world of the classroom, engaging in teacher-adversary roles, and seeming unsure of how to work with faculties who are scornful of them.

Her answer is for supervisors to exercise the authority that comes from inner strengths and competencies in supervising skills. She would have them think big—not get bogged down in short-range problems. Supervisors should know how to use the complex forces at work today by working with others in setting goals and promoting action by motivating others and demonstrating purposeful behavior. Supervisors ought to have the capacity to work with adversity, to see potential in others, to anticipate future events, to make preparations that will require facing criticism.

Bishop and Firth, too, link new roles for supervisors to current challenges:[23]

22. Glenys G. Unruh, "Instructional Supervision: Issues and Trends," *Educational Leadership*, vol. 34, no. 8, pp. 563–566, May 1977.
23. Leslee J. Bishop and Gerald R. Firth, "New Conceptions of Supervision," *Educational Leadership*, vol. 34, no. 8, pp. 572–579, May 1977.

1. The struggle for governance and control by teacher organizations, legislators, and others offers supervisors the opportunity to *mediate* in the interests of students, parents, and programs.
2. Pressures for accountability and wise use of resources are opportunities for supervisors to exercise leadership in designing new outcome measures and better ways to *monitor.*
3. Changing population—increased proportion of older adults to youth and children—suggests that supervisors have opportunity to *plan* programs for a new clientele.
4. Occupational changes—new careers—offer supervisors the opportunity to *develop* programs for renewing personnel.
5. The many educational programs offered by government, business, and industries throughout the community offer the chance to *orchestrate* programs.
6. Varied life styles require improved understanding which may occur if the supervisor engages with others in learning to *value.*

In spite of widespread publicity, recent innovations in curriculum and instruction have had little impact on the schools. The implications of this situation are that supervisors are going to have to do a better job both in the education of teachers and in the introduction of courses which are more consistent with the alternative futures likely to be met by pupils. Cogan believes there are several reasons why innovative reform has done so little to improve our schools.[24] The first hypothesis is that local efforts are not supported by effective regional and national programs to help local school systems cope with the potentially useful ideas amidst the sea of innovations that overwhelm and exhaust them. Teachers and supervisors are inadequately prepared to deal with the complexities of implementing even those reforms that are promising.

Hence Cogan points to the need for clinical-classroom supervision. Clinical supervisors focus their efforts on the teacher in the classroom where new departures in curriculum and instruction are tried, tested, made, or broken. Clinical supervision means helping the teacher understand the innovation and make the changes in performance necessary to match the new requirements. To these ends, supervisors will (1) participate with teachers in selecting the innovation likely to be appropriate to each school, (2) develop a strategy designed to provide a test of the innovation within the local situation, (3) develop among the faculty a commitment to testing and experimentation, avoiding premature enthusiasm and uncritical ap-

24. Morris L. Cogan, "Rationale for Clinical Supervision," *Journal of Research and Development in Education,* vol. 9, no. 2, pp. 3–19, Winter 1976.

praisal, (4) support teachers in class and out as teachers meet the difficulties commonly associated with new patterns of behavior, (5) engage in strategy planning in order to deal with disruptive tensions and alienations, and (6) help disseminate successful new departures that will bring about change in the school.

Many of the above aspects of the current trends in supervision could be summed up as manifestations of a quest for power and the search for perspective. The concern for generalizations as guides for decisions both in the local situation and in the total social undertaking is implicit in most of the controversy over supervision. It remains to be seen whether supervision will be regarded as (1) an instrument for the manipulation of the school in the interest of society as a whole, (2) a process for the facilitation of individual learning experiences, or (3) something more inclusive than either of the preceding alternatives. If supervision is regarded as a tool of society, it will reflect the claims of society. If supervision is conceived at least in some degree as a process for teaching and molding society as well as the individual, it will be fashioned in the light of now unrealized ideals.

SUMMARY STATEMENT

What has now been said of the apparently contradictory trends in late twentieth-century supervision reflects something of the complexity of the times and the difficulty of making simple generalizations regarding the development of supervision. It does suggest some of the central issues which must be examined in greater detail. Out of the variety of principles and structures of supervision, we shall single out in succeeding chapters those issues which seem most significant for supervisors. Already, two may be indicated in these questions:

1. How can supervisors justify and make best use of processes which stem from different social philosophies and theories of knowledge, learning, and social change?
2. What should supervisors use as a basis for their decisions regarding the interests of society as a whole and the solution of problems in particular situations?

CHAPTER 2

WHO IS
A SUPERVISOR?

Bigness in education and the need to respond to the growing influence of courts and government at state and federal levels have brought many new positions into the local school system and given rise to new images of the supervisor which conflict with the traditional view of the supervisor as a personal leader. This chapter describes newer supervisory positions and the different roles associated with them. We believe that examination of these positions will reveal that they have a common requirement: a perspective of the instructional tasks, and the ability to synthesize data from many sources and to use these data in the formulation of better instructional programs. The common dimension of supervision—found in all positions of leadership—is the ability to perceive desirable objectives and to help others contribute to this vision and act in accordance with it.

SUPERVISORY POSITIONS
Reasons for Increased Number of Supervisors
The existence of a variety of titles now borne by supervisors is a consequence both of certain social necessities and of the increasing complexity of school organization. Obviously, as the tasks of the

school become more numerous and varied, supervisors increase in number and kind. Too, the growth of school organization demands more supervision. An individual or an organization can attend to only a limited number of things at a time. In school systems where various aspects of the whole complex problem associated with effective teaching and learning are being handled by different individuals and groups of individuals, it is a fundamental technique to simplify the problem into a number of nearly independent parts. Each one in a minor supervisory position, such as consultant, vice-principal, and counselor, handles one of the parts but usually omits the others from the particular definition of the situation. The subgoals held by those in the individual positions should contribute to the objectives of the school system. The greater the specialization by the individual, the greater the need for interdependence among those discharging particular tasks. Therefore, certain supervisory positions have been established to knit the different tasks together, clearing the way for intelligent actions by higher echelons. Through these supervisory positions, decisions of those in higher echelons are made clear to teachers, and those who made these decisions in turn learn how teachers feel, obtaining feedback to guide future decisions. Coordination and communication are central tasks to those occupying supervisory positions.

C. Northcote Parkinson once humorously described other reasons for the rising pyramid of official supervisory positions: (1) "An official wants to multiply subordinates, not rivals" and (2) "Officials make work for each other." School supervisors may feel overworked. Because of this feeling, they may resign, or halve the work with a colleague, or demand the assistance of two subordinates. Rather than lose pension rights or bring in a rival for promotion, Parkinson predicts they will demand the subordinates. Two are necesssary for status reasons and for keeping each in order by fear of the other's promotion. Soon several supervisors do what one did before, making so much work for each other that all are fully occupied and the original supervisor is working harder than ever.[1]

Typical Supervisory Positions and Duties in the Central Office
Supervisory positions in the central offices of urban school districts are those of assistant superintendent, director, supervisor, evaluator, coordinator, and consultant. Positions, however, are not clear-cut so far as titles are concerned; an administrator in one school system may be called a director, and a person doing the same type of work in another school system may be called a supervisor.

1. C. Northcote Parkinson, *Parkinson's Law and Other Studies in Administration*, Houghton Mifflin Company, Boston, 1957, pp. 3–4.

ASSISTANT SUPERINTENDENT An assistant superintendent usually has charge of one or more broad areas of school service in the fields of instruction, instructional materials, or other auxiliary services needed by teachers, pupils, or community. Most assistant superintendents have assignments directly or indirectly connected with instruction.

DIRECTOR A director is a professionally trained employee attached to the office of the superintendent of schools. The director's task is below that of an assistant superintendent but in charge of a major level of the school system, a comprehensive area of the curriculum, or an important general function of the superintendent's office. The work of the director is basically instructional leadership (supervision) but includes general administrative functions.

SUPERVISOR A supervisor is a professionally trained person assigned to the office of the superintendent of schools. The rank is lower than that of assistant superintendent and also below that of director. The position calls for almost exclusively instructional leadership (supervision). There are so many areas of service for which supervisors are responsible that the title is hardly descriptive. Supervisors may contribute to any area of the school program or to any service required to keep the school running.

PROGRAM SPECIALIST The specialist assists in the planning, implementation, and evaluation of training programs and workshops. The specialist coordinates staff development programs for selecting and training workshop leaders, maintaining a close liaison with district personnel.

EVALUATOR Internal evaluators are responsible for program improvement by using program evaluation as a management strategy. They design evaluations based on decision makers' need for information, including measurement of progress toward goals and objectives and data analyses. Unlike external evaluators, the internal evaluator focuses more on the quality control of program implementation on a day-to-day basis.

COORDINATOR A coordinator is an employee assigned to promote cooperation between the schools and some phase of community life or among units and individuals within the school system. In rank the coordinator is below a supervisor. Coordinators are employed for a variety of services. Consultations with teachers, supervision of the testing program, coordination of the public relations program, supervision of pupils on work experience programs, checking attendance, holding conferences with the home, coordination of the work within a subject area, and especially giving help to new teachers are among their tasks.

CONSULTANT   Consultants (resource persons) are instructional specialists assigned to promote the improvement of teaching and the curriculum by advising with teachers, principals, assistant superintendents, and others. They are especially concerned with the discovery and use of instructional aids, materials, teaching guides, methods of teaching, and resource units. They have little or no authority for decision making.

In one or more positions, the supervisor is generally responsible for six kinds of duties:

1. *Planning.* Individually and in groups; helps to develop policies and programs in a field
2. *Administration.* Makes decisions, coordinates the work of others, and issues necessary directions
3. *Supervision.* Through conferences and consultations, seeks to improve the quality of instruction
4. *Curriculum development.* Participates directly in the formulation of objectives, preparation of teaching guides, and selection of instructional aids and experiences
5. *Demonstration teaching.* Gives and arranges for classroom demonstrations of teaching methods, use of aids, and other direct help to classroom teachers
6. *Research.* Through systematic surveys, experiments, and studies, explores current conditions and recommends changes in practice

Often the central office staffs in urban districts lack uniformity. A supervisor may have charge of custodians or of mathematics. Noteworthy is the tendency for director and assistant superintendents to make decisions about goals, while those in other supervisory positions are restricted to the planning and implementing of these decisions.

The existence of top-level supervisors (assistant superintendents and directors) in the central office reflects the need for regularity and stability among the wide variety of school interests and activities. Articulation and balance of component parts must be safeguarded if the school system is to serve its purpose. These supervisors have particular responsibility to recognize and implement the ordering principles of the instructional scheme. Their specialty is the linking together of the specialities of others.

Supervisors situated between the central office and the teachers serve as representatives of the school system. They open a channel of two-way communication by which policies and decisions go down; and information, problems, and perhaps suggestions come up. Such supervisors are expected to think, feel, and act in tune with the policy decisions made at higher levels. Possibly the views of these supervisors and their fellow teachers help frame the policy decisions. The knowledge and intelligence required in a complex school system is so diversified that it exceeds what a single mind can grasp, making necessary the pooling of wisdom at the decision-making level.

We might, at this point, recall an earlier question: Should rationality, perspective, and harmony in the school's organization occur as supervisors keep each teacher well informed about the work of the entire organization so that each will know best how to serve the common cause? Or should the supervisor assign specialized jobs to each teacher in accordance with a predetermined scheme but not expect the teacher to know about the specialized jobs of others and how the supervisor's job relates to them?

Other Supervisory Positions

The superintendent, the principal, and the principal's staff—including vice-principal, counselor, department head, teaching assistant, helping and special teacher, and the like—are at times supervisors. So, too, are cooperating teachers and college staffs when they work with student teachers. University professors and personnel from professional organizations as well as state and federal departments play supervisory roles as consultants, influencing others by advisory persuasiveness.

Supervisors Identified by Staff Functions

The extended distribution of supervisory functions among administrators and teachers and the acceptance of administrative functions by supervisors have led to much of the confusion about who is a supervisor.

The functions of school supervisors have been patterned after those in industry and the military which make a distinction between staff functions and line functions. Line officers are those who have the right to make decisions, to take action in order to get things done, and to exercise necessary control over others assigned to them. Staff officers are those whose main job is helping the line officers decide what to do as well as coordinating the efforts of all and supplying necessary services. It is an administrative principle that those occupying particular positions are either line or staff. School supervisors are likely to be termed staff officers.

Influence versus Authority in the Practice of Supervision

Sometimes the category of supervisor is applied to someone who relies upon the use of influence rather than authority in effecting change, "influence" here meaning the capacity to give another the premises for action, attitudes, state of mind, and habits which will lead to the organizational goal. Communication, staff development, evaluation, and standardization practices are examples of mechanisms for influence. Many hold that it is proper for a staff member to use influence but not to exercise authority or to issue commands. Authority is a power granted by superiors to carry out responsibilities; it includes the rights necessary to the discharge of line functions. Authority is accepted when one permits one's behavior to be guided by the decisions of a supervisor without examining the merits of the decision. The more obedient one is, the less tangible are the evidences of authority.

Although effective action is not possible in an organization in which there are no recognized and accepted channels through which information and authority flow, many school supervisors indicate a desire to be rid of the onus attached to direct command and authority. They reject administrative activities and "authority as such" and prefer advising and guiding to the initiating of action and the making of policy decisions. Popularly, supervisors are seen as those who justify themselves as they are able to influence fellow executives at all levels by virtue of their factual or technical mastery, consultative skill, advisory persuasiveness—in short, by their educational effectiveness. A demand for the exercise of authority is a confession of weakness.

We question the notion that within a line-and-staff organization school leaders are administrators and not supervisors when they exercise initiative in movements for the improvement of teaching and learning, making decisions, coordinating the work of others, and issuing directions. They are supervisors when using authority as well as supervisors when exerting influence. Conditions in school situations do not always permit the operation of the logic-tight compartments of line and staff or authority and influence.

We believe it is not always desirable to distinguish the supervisor sharply from the teacher and administrator on the basis of staff classification and employment of influence. Supervisors are sometimes delegated authority and held responsible for results. Hence, they must hold others responsible for carrying out instructions. On the other hand, teachers who are without benefit of administrative title may act like supervisors as they exert influence upon others. Principals, too, may attempt to discharge the supervisory functions of staff officers as they use influence, even though their line responsibilities and authority loom large. The dilemma of one who is expected to use influence but who also is responsible for consequences is well known and is shown in Table 2-1.

TABLE 2-1   DILEMMA OF SUPERVISORS

THEY CANNOT	BUT THEY MUST
Be offensive	Be aggressive
Have all the answers	Have many creative ideas
Boss	Keep things moving
Use force	Ensure improvement
Threaten	Challenge
Accept inadequacy	Support people who need help

Source: Adapted from Kimball Wiles, "Dilemma of a Status Leader," *Educational Leadership*, vol. 16, no. 8, p. 492, May 1959.

EMERGING ROLES OF SUPERVISORY PERSONNEL

Clarification of the supervisory roles of administrators, personnel in teacher education, and consultants from outside the district is a continuous obligation. Indefiniteness and lack of understanding of these roles have led to conflict and disorder.

Role Theory and the Practice of Supervision

Conceptualization of the supervisor may be aided by role theory. Briefly, such theory postulates that a school system is a miniature society in which administrators, supervisors, teachers, and pupils represent positions or offices within the system. Certain rights and duties are associated with each position. The actions appropriate to the positions are defined as roles. It should be emphasized that a role is linked with the position, not with the person who is temporarily occupying the position. A person in a particular position learns to expect certain actions of others, and others expect a given behavior in return. The position of a supervisor can be described in terms of the action expected and the action the supervisor expects of the other. One cannot enact the supervisory role if lacking the necessary role expectations. These expectations are learned both through intentional instruction and through incidental means. The ability to learn a supervisory role is probably limited by a view of self as well as by previous experiences.

Included in the supervisor's role expectations are certain actions such as organizing abstract material, defining needs of learners, and cooperating with community groups as well as personal qualities such as good-naturedness, cooperativeness, and supportiveness. If the actions and qualities which constitute this role are congruent with the supervisor's own self-concept, then there is a high probability of performing according to the role expectations of teachers, administrators, and other members of the community. In the event that the role expectations are incongruent, the supervisor will give priority to some obligations over others. One will, for example, either heed the responsibility set by the board of education before meeting demands of the teachers or may try to placate both board and teachers by excuses. That is, one may seek others' acceptance of a failure to discharge the obligation of a role by declaring that the competing role had a hierarchical priority. Sometimes the supervisor handles role conflict by enacting subroles separately. Repudiating a subrole, "stalling," and "playing one group against the other" are examples of techniques used in resolving role conflicts.

Role Expectations for Supervisors

A series of studies shed light on the reciprocal role expectations of teachers and supervisors in the improvement of instruction. The satisfaction of teachers with the school system has been found to depend upon the extent to which they perceive that the roles of their supervisors meet their expectations. Conversely, those higher in the school's heirarchy judge teachers in terms of how well they conform to personal expectations of the teacher's role. Respective roles must complement each other if the objectives of the schools are to be accomplished. What a supervisor actually does when working with others seems to matter little. It matters more that what others think the supervisor does is what they think the supervisor should do. Members of a school system, for example, tend to evaluate a supervisor's behavior by comparing what they think a supervisor does with what they think should be done.

Among the categories of supervisors are these:

Authority-centered supervisor—one who views absolute principles, expert opinion, and common practice as the "right" answer to problems. This person works through official channels. This person's interaction tone is formal and the primary responsibility is conceived as that of achieving purposes through clarifying and carrying out the official policy adopted by the school board.

Inner-directed supervisor—one who sees desirable behavior as that which most approximates one's own values, opinions, and judgments, believing that the supervisor is more perceptive than others as to what is good and wise regarding a particular problem. Official channels and procedures are ignored, if expedient. This supervisor conceives a primary responsibility to be that of modifying, improving, and interpreting policy and procedures along lines personally thought to meet the educational needs of the community.

Work group–oriented supervisor—one who tries to help those concerned to identify their own purposes with those of the school program. This person believes that authority lies in empirical information and in the considered judgment of those who carry out and are affected by the program. This supervisor makes judgments in the context of specific situations and selects tasks as determined by the situation. Primary responsibility is conceived to be that of facilitating groups in developing standards and procedures in response to identified local needs.

Individual-centered supervisor—one who tries to approximate the judgment of those who will be performing a particular task. This person places emphasis upon fulfilling individual needs and gives priority to decisions that permit individual variation and freedom. This supervisor is sensitive to individuals and their problems, and conceives the primary responsibility to be that of enabling individuals and groups to carry out their tasks, largely self-appointed and self-defined, with as little interference as possible.

Other-directed supervisor—one who perceives ability to reflect accurately the wishes of others as the crux of leadership. This person believes that authority for goals and procedures lies in the will of the people served. Such a supervisor tries to develop friendly relations with those most influential in the school and community in order to know accurately their wishes and to see to it that expressed goals and procedures are achieved.

Supervisors and teachers prefer or rank the work group–oriented roles first, other-direct second, and individual-centered third. In contrast, school board members rank the work group–oriented roles first, authority-centered second, and inner-directed third. When working on instructional improvement, superintendents tend to fulfill the preferences of teachers to a lesser degree than the preferences of other groups such as parents or employers. Also, superintendents are seen by most respondents as employing less work group–oriented behavior than desirable; yet superintendents see themselves as employing each role category as they should. Community residents prefer a school superintendent of high autonomy—loyal to teachers—but they believe superintendents are persons of low autonomy who are chiefly loyal to the board.

With respect to the principal, most teachers expect and approve of a principal who exercises close supervision over teachers' activities. Also, the closer the supervision a principal exercises over staff members, the greater their effort to be of maximum service to their pupils. The closeness of the supervision a principal exercises over staff is positively related to pupil performance. By way of example, a recent study contrasting principals at higher-achieving schools with those at matched lower-achieving schools reveals that the former are assessed by their teachers as having more influence over decisions affecting curriculum development and the hiring of teachers and aides. Further, these high-achieving principals were rated higher in supporting new ideas, backing teachers, enhancing parent-community relations, enforcing discipline, developing instructional leadership, and distributing materials.[2]

When subordinates believe that their supervisor can exercise influence upward in the hierarchy (over the supervisor's boss), then the supervisor has an easier time fulfilling role obligations. Only a supportive style in dealing with others is likely to be more important.

Teachers whose wants and needs are in agreement with their supervising principal's expectations express significantly higher job satisfaction than teachers whose wants are in conflict with the principal's definition of the teacher's role. Maximum goal achievement should result when the principal's expectations for teacher behavior are identical with the wants and needs of the teachers. However, there is often a wide disparity between what the principal says is expected of teachers and what the teachers think the principal expects of them.

A supervisor as consultant giving help on the same problem in two different situations may be successful in one and fail in the other. Consultative service is ineffective if the administrator and consultant fail to behave according to the manner that each expects of the other.

It does not matter that consultants act as:

1. *Experts*—directing their efforts at arriving at the "right" answer for the given problem
2. *Resource persons*—directing efforts at providing information so decision makers can have a range of alternative solutions
3. *Process persons*—directing efforts toward developing others so they can solve their own problems

---

2. California State Department of Education, *California School Effectiveness Study*, Sacramento, Calif., 1977.

What does matter is that the consultant and client perceive each other's functioning in the manner they expect. Consultants who act as "process persons" are likely to fail if they agree to assist a client who is looking for an "expert." If they operate as "experts" when the client expects a "resource" or "process" person, they severely limit chances of success.

ROLE EXPECTATIONS FOR THE SUPERVISOR
AS REVEALED IN PROFESSIONAL LITERATURE

There exists a professional ideology which defines the supervisory roles of superintendents, principals, and other personnel with systemwide responsibilities for the improvement of learning experiences. This popular ideology assigns to the administrator the roles of coordinator and facilitator, which are to (1) provide inspiration, (2) encourage development of organizations for in-service education, (3) facilitate the work of groups, and (4) create a climate for growth. Basic assumptions which underlie this professional point of view are these:

1. *Change.* Individuals change as they seek to release tension related to basic needs, interests, and desires. While it is possible to induce the required tensions by external pressure, it is better to do so by helping persons see their needs or interests in a new light. External pressures of command and manipulation are not consistent with this professional view. Instead the supervisor is expected to help an individual see things in a new way either by showing how the old way of doing things no longer suffices or by helping one find new values and goals. An example would be the high school English teacher who gains a better understanding of youth, thereby developing a new aspiration to help pupils with their personal problems. With the new goal, the teacher becomes dissatisfied with present teaching methods and tension for change is induced.

2. *Group work.* Personal tensions that may arise when emphasis is on changing the teacher may be avoided when groups focus on ways to improve the instructional program. Further, a group influence can be a real asset in helping an individual change by generating new problems and forcing new adaptations. According to prevailing supervisory thought, improvement of the quality of learning experiences should be approached and conducted largely on a group basis, with the whole group participating in identifying the needs, setting the goals, planning ways of working, developing materials, putting recommendations into action, and evaluating results.

The supervising administrator is expected to provide inspiration, to be responsible for "firing up" the staff and for helping it develop a vision of what the organization might be doing. Accordingly, the administrator should make it possible for others to raise aspirations, too.

In the role of coordinator, supervisors provide opportunities for activities at systemwide and local building levels, trying also to provide a means of communication so that the curriculum-improvement activities exert a positive influence on the entire school system and not overlap or conflict. Arrangements are made for teachers with similar problems and special interests to meet, such as bringing together beginning teachers on the assumption that they have particular needs for belonging and status.

As facilitators, supervisors have sufficient faith in people, and in the ability of the group to cope with instructional problems, to accept the group's decision, even though it may be at variance with their own ideas. Of course, the supervisor has the responsibility for defining at the beginning of the group's deliberation the limitations within which its members must operate and for helping them get the facts. Although supervisors need to be skilled in the group process, they often find it difficult to play various group membership roles other than that of chairman or director because of expectations held by faculty and higher authorities. In addition to assisting the group directly in accordance with the principles of group dynamics, they make available the resources of other individuals as well as physical facilities and materials, and they release time for teacher participation in planning.

According to some humanistic perspectives, supervisors try to smooth the path of human interaction, ease communication, evoke personal devotion, and allay anxiety. Sometimes the supervisor's image depicted in professional journals is that of the humble person who recognizes that every member of the staff excels in one or more different ways. Hence, supervisors are told to consciously look for strengths in others and know that teachers are interested in doing a good job and in improving their performance. The current writings of Sergiovanni, for instance, call for "human resources supervision" by which supervisors give teachers much decision-making power with respect to curriculum materials and content.[3] Too, the supervisor's role is said to be that of creating an environment in which teachers can contribute their range of talents to the accomplishment of school goals. Note, however, that this humanistic view of supervision does

---

3. Thomas J. Sergiovanni, *Professional Supervision for Professional Teachers,* ASCD, Washington, 1975.

not foster good human relations as an end but uses a human relations approach to achieve institutional goals.

In order to understand an individual's problems, supervisors are encouraged to listen with patience and to try to put themselves in the position of the speaker, attempting to see the problem through the other person's eyes. They should be approachable and show interest by visiting others in their place of work, encouraging new ideas that are related to practical classroom situations, but helping to appraise ideas before action is instituted as well as during and after action.

THE ROLE OF THE SUPERVISOR AS A SUPERVISORY STATESMAN

There is a professional expectation that supervisors will inspire and take responsibility for crucial, purpose-setting decisions as opposed to routine housekeeping decisions.

Differentiation must be made between (1) those whose responsibilities are focused on the development of individual members of the group and their capacity to work together as a group and (2) those few who are primarily experts in the promotion and protection of the school's values. As we have seen, professional expectations have the supervisor helping members learn from their experience together by thinking clearly about their own problems and evaluating their group efforts. In such a role the supervisor's expertness has little to do with content; there is more concern for persons than for policies. In contrast, the role of the supervisory statesman differs from the human relations specialist's in that the statesman's inspiration does not derive from the processes of group interaction and the vision of a harmonious team, whatever its end may be. Instead, the supervisory statesman finds goals and commitment in the purpose and character of the school itself, not in narrow, practical aims set in haphazard fashion.

While an interest in human relations has brought a wider understanding of why and how people work, perceive, and communicate, it has left the observer with a sense of inadequacy. There is need to look beyond personal relations to the larger patterns of institutional development. This is not to say that the school's process can be understood without observing it in terms of the behavior of individuals. The problem is to link the larger view to the more limited one. The school must be institutionalized, that is, infused with values beyond the technical requirements of the task at hand. A supervisor fails when the school drifts and is exposed to vagrant pressures, readily influenced both by short-run opportunistic trends and by those who would commit the school as a whole on the basis of a partial assessment derived from a particular scientific or political perspective.

Essentially, the statesman's role consists in giving direction instead of merely ministering to organizational equilibrium; in adapting goals to the character of the organization, bearing in mind that what the organization has been will affect what it can be and do; and in going beyond bare organizational survival by seeing that specialized decisions do not weaken or confuse the distinctive identity of the institution.

This proposed role carries the assumption that supervisors have been led away from their responsibility for making critical decisions, such as defining the group aims and designing an enterprise directly adapted to these aims. Critical decisions are those which affect the ultimate development of the school. This is not to say that supervisors are free to mold the school system as they wish but that they should recognize potentialities and responsibilities as well as limitations. Nor does it imply that the school's aims are given once and for all. We know aims are conditioned by new definitions and adaptations to larger social situations. The important matter is that the process of change need not be opportunistic; it can be controlled. Accordingly, the supervisor's tasks are these:

1. *To define the school's aims.* Aims are defined in accordance with (a) the school's long-range commitments, its governing character and ability, and (b) the requirements for the school's survival after noting the findings of an assessment of the forces within and outside the school. Overgeneralization of purpose is to be avoided, for it is known that when supervisors rely upon vague cardinal principles and all-inclusive imperative needs, more realistic but uncontrolled criteria set the course. In operation, supervisory statesmen take care to consider the bearing of an existing or proposed procedure on the distinctive quality of the school.
2. *To transform neutral personnel into those with a sense of the school's mission.* This calls for utilizing the tools for analyzing the school's social structure and techniques for effecting change under a variety of conditions. Such tools and procedures for change will be described in subsequent chapters of this book; it may be mentioned here, however, that the defense of the school's distinctive values and competence may call for special measures in particular local buildings. If, for example, the supervisor in the central office has concern over the school's values but a principal is under pressure to introduce a practice without taking sufficient account of its long-range consequences, the staff member from the central office must have sufficient autonomy to lay down criteria for acceptance by the principal.

There is a real connection, of course, between the role of the supervisory statesman and the basic question of whether school supervisors are without moral choice and are mere minions, or whether they have responsibility for fashioning a distinctive way of thinking and acting and thus helping establish the foundation for achieving a particular set of goals. This, in turn, raises the question "Does the school have integrity in itself, or is it without character, merely responsive to immediate pressures?"

THE SUPERVISORY TEAM

Defining the relations among supervisors is more important than searching for a common supervisory role. We should not expect those occupying various positions to perform the same supervisory jobs. The role of the principal in supervision differs from that role discharged by coordinators and department heads. The old functions of the supervisor are no longer found in any one position, such as in the principalship, but in a team. That is to say that at one time the principal of a school was the supervisor. As a master teacher as well as the administrative authority in the school, the principal was everything to the teachers and solved their instructional problems. Subsequently, these supervisory functions diminished when new specialists arrived from the central office. Also, supervisory influence was weakened by the growth of professional organizations and the improved preparation of teachers who knew more about the instructional intents and process in a given field than the principal.

An example of the distinctive functions held by members of a supervisory team in a secondary school is seen in the combination consisting of principal–department head–supervisor from the central office. Supervisors from the central office are concerned about maintaining systemwide standards. One representing the foreign language field, for instance, will be concerned that teachers are following district policy regarding the broad goal of the foreign language program (e.g., amount of emphasis upon verbal fluency and literature). Central office supervisors are likely to be especially concerned with the problems of articulation, noting whether teachers in a given school are using the recommended materials which make it easy for newly arrived learners who come from other schools in the district to accommodate to the instruction. Also, they are protective of the continuity in instruction from elementary to secondary and higher edution. They therefore devote much of their supervision to making sure that teachers are ordering the content and learning experiences and are displaying the teaching styles that enhance such continuity.

Department heads, on the other hand, serve best as mediators between the teacher in the school and the supervisor from the central office. As subject-matter specialists themselves, they can build communication with both the teacher and supervisor, exchanging shared values of subject matter. However, unlike central office supervisors, who tend to emphasize standardization, department heads serve to encourage the teacher to depart from standardization of instruction in order to adapt objectives, materials, and teaching style in light of the particular characteristics of learners in the given school. Their role is that of helping the teacher accommodate system policy to unique characteristics of the pupils at hand.

The principal is not regarded as a specialist in the teaching of a foreign language. This itself makes the principal a valuable member of the team supervising the teachers of foreign language, bringing more objectivity to the teaching of language than would likely be found in those who are committed to the advancement of the field. The principal can maintain balance in instructional emphasis. Balance is shown in two ways. First, within the course itself there can be balance with respect to outcome, e.g., mastery of subject matter, pupil interest in the course, ability of pupils to apply the knowledge taught, and social relevance of the content apart from relevance to the language field itself. A principal can ensure more comprehensive outcomes, not being limited to thinking of objectives solely in terms of subject matter. Typically, a principal is concerned about other deficiencies of pupils and the community and how these gaps can be closed through instruction. Second, a principal must effect balance among courses and specialists in all fields. The department head and the supervisor from the central office cannot be allowed to monopolize the scarce resources of the staff for the benefit of the foreign language program if it results in destroying the effectiveness of other equally valid programs.

The principal should be clear about what teachers are attempting to achieve with pupils. Further, the principal should reach agreement with teachers (1) that appropriate instructional objectives have been selected and (2) on the kinds of evidence that will be collected to show the extent to which pupils have accomplished the desired end. Once this is done, the principal can supervise by objectives rather than by following the close supervision of process. Indicators of success in teaching will be evidence in ways such as these:

1. Improved class test scores (mean scores for class at end of course compared with mean scores at start of class)
2. Numbers and kinds of problems pupils can solve before and after instruction

3. Kinds of questions generated by pupils before and after instruction
4. Changes in quality of pupil work, e.g., "use of parallel construction in composition"
5. Numbers of pupils who continue with subsequent courses in the field
6. Record of student absenteeism and tardiness
7. Record of pupil promptness in completing assignments
8. Pupil responses to a morale inventory indicating attitude toward school, class, and teacher
9. Number and percentage of those pupils who enter the course and who finish it, i.e., success ratio
10. Number and percentage of students who engage in extra activities stimulated by the classwork
11. Number and kinds of selected books voluntarily read by students during and after the course

Especial recognition should be given by the principal when the teacher evidences success with "high-risk" learners: (1) those from low-socioeconomic homes, (2) those who lack academic and attitudinal prerequisites. Also the principal should make it clear that ordinarily the teacher who achieves a small change in pupil ability to use the subject matter taught (1) as heuristics (tools for inquiry), (2) in conversation, and (3) in retention and application should get more credit than the teacher who effects a greater change in the pupil's ability to recall subject matter. The principal as supervisor gives more credit to the teacher who gets half of the class to participate enthusiastically when the course is required than to the teacher of the elective course who gets the same percentage or more to participate enthusiastically. *In short, the principal's role in supervision centers upon the review of evidence about how well the teacher is or is not succeeding with pupils.*

The department head plays a different role, making frequent observations of the teacher at work with pupils and collecting data regarding the teacher-pupil interactions that will be helpful to the teacher. The department head must be careful, however, not to make inferences about the teacher's instruction without having specific data in the form of a descriptive record of what actually takes place during observation of the teaching episode.

The role of supervisor from the central office is to make sure that the teacher is acquainted with the instructional resources available in the district and that the teacher learns how to use these resources. There is no sense in merely acquainting the teacher with the fact that an inquiry-based instructional unit is available; the supervisor has to verify that the teachers know how to teach in accordance with such a method.

OTHER VARIATIONS IN THE SUPERVISORY ROLE

Difficulty in describing particular roles for each supervisory position arises for several reasons. First, distinctive situations make specifically different demands for supervisory behavior. Second, instead of ascribing certain roles to positions, our culture's emphasis upon achievement often makes it legitimate for anyone to play anyone else's role when the usurper has the requisite skill and can help the participants. Third, there is some uncertainty concerning the appropriate role for those in the newer supervisory positions associated with evaluation of special projects and newer emphases like mainstreaming, multiculture, and career education.

Roles of Outside Consultants

What do outside consultants do when they enter a school situation? How can representatives from federal, state, and local education offices, from colleges and universities, and from professional organizations best promote change and render on-the-job assistance to teachers? What happens to communication, lines of authority, and all the rest when an expert arrives on the scene—a supervisor whose very presence threatens the status quo?

The wide range of consultative services offered by outside consultants cuts across every aspect of instruction. There may be a need for a new developmental program in reading or a special study of anxious children. The variety of tasks means multiple roles. James and Weber, having observed sixteen consultative sessions over a period of thirty-eight days, report that 62 percent of the consultants assumed at one time or another at least half of the following roles: answer giver, listener, ex officio suggester, interpreter, reassurer, stimulator, adviser, fraternizer, and public-relations representative. Thirty-eight percent or fewer performed one of the following roles: synthesizer, evaluator, organizer, information gatherer, school sightseer, demonstrator, or criticizer.[4]

Increased use of consultants and project managers by both education and industry is providing knowledge of procedures for guiding interactions of these newer supervisors with school administrator and faculty. Pertinent dangers in the consultative role are these:

4. Edward W. James and Robert A. Weber, *School Consultants: Roles Assumed and Techniques Employed,* Southwestern Co-operative Program in Educational Administration, University of Texas, Austin, p. 15.

1. *Interference with school policy.* Schools have mores and follow informal policies which, while not spelled out in black and white, have become a tradition. Ignorance or disregard of informal practices may assume greater proportions than the violation of obscure written policy. This is particularly true of matters affecting personnel, where teachers have come to expect certain practices to be followed because the school has always done them.

2. *Undermining of authority.* There is a tendency, when consultants become deeply and closely involved in the activities of a school, for them to assume authority for certain actions on their own. A number of conditions can bring this about. The almost constant presence of consultants may lead teachers to regard them as bosses and not only obey their direct instructions but look to them for direction. If consultants detect weakness or lack of leadership, they may, almost unwittingly, move in and assume authority that is not legitimately theirs. The more technically competent they are, the more sensitive they will be to a poorly run organization. In such a situation, it takes considerable restraint to avoid interfering with established prerogatives.

   A logical extension of the process of undermining the authority of an administrator or a supervisor is a gradual (or perhaps sudden) assumption of duties and authority. This is a particular danger where the program of the consultant or project manager is extensive and is scheduled to cover a long period of time. When there is conflict between a principal and consultants, the attitude of the board or superintendent seems to be, "Since we have invested in the consultants to such an extent, we had best back them to the limit." Thus, duties that properly belong to the principal are surrendered to the consultants. There is an even greater opportunity for the assumption of authority by consultants when an occasional administrator gladly surrenders a portion of the obligations that belong to the office to anyone who will and can carry them out. This is a particular danger in a school that has been subject to difficulty of one sort or another over a long period of time; consultants who are called in to observe and correct a situation frequently find themselves filling the gap left by the careless or inefficient principal.

3. *Administrative animosity toward the consultant.* Poor handling in this volatile area can well negate the whole value of the consulting program. There are a host of possible causes of animosity toward a consultant, and one of the most prevalent is the fear of implied criticism of an administrator, a supervisor, or an entire school because an "outsider" has been called in. Many people feel that such action is a direct reflection on their efforts.

Another cause of animosity is the feeling that consultants do not fully understand the problems and difficulties of a particular situation. They are frequently considered as interlopers who enter the school, talk to a few teachers or pupils, and then, from "objective and detached" positions, make recommendations that are impossible or, at best, impractical to implement. Animosity toward the consulting personnel may also result from an administrator's fear of the danger discussed before, that is, fear that the consultant will undermine or assume authority. In cases where such usurpation has actually begun to take place, administrators are quick to recognize it and to feel that their position is being abrogated.

There is the danger of too much zeal on the part of the consultant. A "new broom" attitude that suggests "I am here to show you how things should be done" is the consultant's quickest and surest route to failure. A consultant's tasks call, above all, for diplomacy, and all suggestions must be made with tact.

4. *Dissatisfaction of similarly qualified personnel.* It is possible that there are those within the school who could do the job as effectively as the consultant—perhaps, because of their familiarity with the school, even more effectively. To avoid ill feeling, board and administrators should ascertain who the qualified school personnel are before hiring the consultant. Are there reasons why they cannot do the job as well as a consultant? Are they too close to the job? Are there policy reasons why an objective observer would be more useful or diplomatic? If, after the situation has been thoroughly investigated, it is found that for some reason outside consultants are either necessary or desirable, the reasons should be explained both to the personnel who will work with the consultant and to those with similar qualifications. People who see a highly paid consultant doing the same sort of work that they are doing, for no apparent reason, can easily lose confidence in themselves and in the leadership of the school.

There is another aspect of this problem that merits attention—the problem of recognition. When personnel of the school and consultants have worked hand-in-hand to attain a certain result, will the staff be given recognition for their efforts, or will they be ignored when credit is being assigned? This is a special problem when a new idea has come from the consultant but the drudgery of implementation has fallen to the school's personnel.

5. *Jealousy of highly paid consultants.* Consultants are often highly paid specialists, but their talents may not always be obvious to those with whom they work. When the salary of a consultant or the amount of money that the district is paying for consultant

services becomes known throughout the organization, the district must be especially careful to justify its position.

Special privileges enjoyed by consultants may also be a cause of jealousy. Consultants' obligations to their own organizations often make frequent absences from the school necessary. Hours of arrival or departure, the length of time taken for lunch, and similar apparent privileges may have an adverse effect upon staff morale, particularly among the lower echelons of supervision and among the faculty. By regularizing a consultant's privileges and allotting specific times for outside activities, administrators can often eliminate such criticism.

The Roles of Supervising Teachers

Many teachers in the United States perform major roles in the professional education of student teachers. Others have responsibility for helping fellow teachers in staff development. Known by such titles as critic, cooperating, master, resident, helping, and training teachers, they supply novices with the experience necessary for a beginning proficiency in teaching. These veteran teachers have raised questions about their responsibility, seeking clarification of the behavioral roles they must assume as supervisors. One answer is that as supervisors, teachers stress the development of the teacher-to-be as a "self-directive, creating teacher with ideas of his own." More specifically, the desired roles of supervising teachers are as follows:

1. *To help the beginning teacher find purpose in teaching.* In what ways should pupils be different after their experiences in this class? What should they know and be able to do at the end of the semester? Through such questions supervisory and student teachers together formulate a sense of direction and an overall plan. This early planning suggests tentative statements of expected outcomes for pupils and proposes the kinds of evidence which will indicate the extent to which outcomes are attained. Subsequently, pupils, too, influence the selection of purposes and methods of evaluation. Understandings of goals deepen as they are defined in practice. Purpose is revealed daily as teachers and pupils reflect upon their life in the class and consider what they must do next to attain the skills, knowledge, and satisfactions which they seek.

2. *To further the beginning teacher's sensitivity to individual students and the dynamics of the classroom.* How is the class getting along? Evaluation of the progress of pupils enables new teachers to focus upon individuals, making them aware of the different rates and different means by which pupils learn.

New teachers are encouraged to take advantage of opportunities for incidental personal conversations with individual pupils and to contribute to the success of problem-solving groups in order that they might understand and communicate with all. As they think of children and themselves as fellow learners in a common undertaking, student teachers are freed from a self-centered view of teaching.

No longer do they bluff when they do not have the answer or do they restrict the intellectual curiosity of pupils to the narrow confines of lessons, preserving their status as authority figures.

3. *To enable the beginning teacher to vitalize instruction.* What situations will cause the class to feel it necessary to engage in an important educational venture? What problem areas and sequential activities are most appropriate? How can we ensure that problems for investigation are fruitful, calling for valuable content and leading to an understanding of desirable concepts? What opportunities are there for pupils to participate in the selection of activities, identifying skills and information necessary for the success of the undertaking? How might the class generalize, apply, and determine the worth of the results? What instruction must be presented before the class can do these things? What resources and details should be considered? Presenting these and similar questions, the experienced teacher assists the new teacher in thinking through instructional approaches.

Instruction becomes effective through continuous specific attention to techniques associated with organizing materials, arranging room environment, giving instructions and demonstrations, conducting discussions, constructing evaluative measures and the like. It becomes efficient after the two teachers see and discuss profound and universal questions which are present in the daily events of the classroom. When a routine task, such as completing an attendance form, raises questions from pupils as to their obligation to provide valid information, the student teacher is awakened to the opportunity to increase pupil concern about ultimate values, e.g., the particular worth of a human being and truth as related to a person.

4. *To give the student teacher a view of teaching as learning.* One never arrives in teaching. So complex is the task of working with unique personalities in ever-changing classes that the teacher must continue to propose and test new hypotheses. The inexperienced teacher sees that experts develop original plans with each class and that these teachers regard many of their past procedures and tendencies to action as inappropriate for the present and fu-

ture. Sagacity in selecting content and relating it to the pupils' lives requires continuing scholarship and intimacy with the times.

If the student teacher is lucky and gets to work with someone who has faith in self and others, there probably will be opportunities to clarify the meaning of proposals and to try out one's own ideas, experiencing the excitement and sense of growth which accompanies intellectual adventure. Through solitary reflection and joint probing, the two teachers can extract the full meaning of experience in the belief that as they develop their processes for interpreting what has been and is taking place, they are best preparing for their futures. The security of the supervising teacher makes possible the acceptance of differences which exist between the two: The supervising teacher knows that good can come from these differences. Warm human relations grow out of the productive conflicts between them since the focus for improvement and resolution of disagreement centers upon the progress of pupils and is task-centered rather than personal.

5. *To influence the student teacher to act professionally.* The ethical patterns of supervising teachers are captured by those with whom they work. Among the desirable behaviors which new teachers may evidence are these: consulting frequently with others in a give-and-take manner, willingly sharing their best teaching practices; supporting fellow teachers even when they appear eccentric; lightening the load of custodians; using the curriculum guides of the school district, adapting them from their classes and making recommendations for their revision; showing sympathy toward parents and their problems.

Supervising teachers take care to point out ways organized teachers are becoming part of the power structure in the school and in the larger social setting, endeavoring to improve education through the establishment of higher standards and participating in educational policy making. New teachers are included in activities of the total staff and professional groups.

What do teachers of teachers do? They provide situations where new teachers can themselves discover and appropriate that learning which accustoms to action. Although inviting imitation, supervising teachers encourage originality and modification of belief and practice in terms of each student teacher's own individuality.

SUMMARY STATEMENT

To ask "Who is a supervisor?" is to invite such responses as these: (1) one who holds a supervisory position, (2) one who actually makes a difference in the operations of the school by exercising authority or influence, and (3) one who spends time on particular organizational functions. There are kernels of truth, too, in the stereotypes representing the supervisor as a personnel agent intent upon influencing others in group situations and as a central person of virtue and sovereignty in whom the teacher finds emotional support and professional guidance.

We have seen that official responsibilities and honor have been distributed among many supervisory positions. Distinctions have been made, for example, between supervisors who deal with the promotion and protection of the school's values and specialists in human relations who develop individuals and their capacity to work together as a group. Higher status is given those whose duties are to develop policies. On the other hand, the supervising teacher who helps the novice find purpose in work reminds us that in a sense every position in the school carries an obligation to promote values and make critical decisions. We believe that supervision is itself a distinctive function which holders of various positions discharge in different ways. See Figure 2-1.

At a general level there is a common dimension in the expected role behavior of those who are supervisors regardless of their positions in the school system. This common element for supervisory positions is the determination of ends to be sought, the design of procedures for effecting the ends, and the assessment of results. Supervisors in all positions are responsible for predicting what will follow from the introduction of innovations and interventions and checking the wide range of results that do occur.

Especially striking is the demand for exercise of judgment in supervision and teaching. While coordination of effort and a common body of knowledge are necessary for the individual teacher to function effectively as a part of the overall system, it is also essential that the teacher be able to make rational choices without waiting for

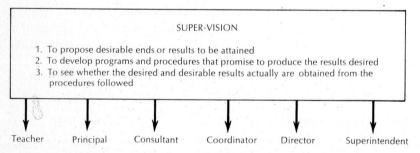

SUPER-VISION

1. To propose desirable ends or results to be attained
2. To develop programs and procedures that promise to produce the results desired
3. To see whether the desired and desirable results actually are obtained from the procedures followed

Teacher   Principal   Consultant   Coordinator   Director   Superintendent

Figure 2-1 Supervision: a dimension of behavior in many positions.

official approval. Therefore, it seems fitting to designate the supervisor as a leader who has possession of two properties: first, a clear perspective on the school's goals and an awareness of its resources and qualities, and second, the ability to help others contribute to this vision and to perceive and act in accordance with it. This description is not without issues and pressing problems:

1. Are perspectives and harmony best achieved by correlating specialized assignments in accordance with a systemwide scheme?
2. Are sense of mission and rational behavior attained when supervisors keep each teacher informed about the activities as well as the goals of the entire organization?
3. How can supervisors best resolve the conflict they face because of differences in the expections teachers, superintendent, and board hold for their role?
4. Are their supervisory positions best fitted for discharging the tasks associated with the supervisory statesman?
5. Should a school have integrity as an institution, or is it without individual character, its goals subjected to whichever pressures are strongest?
6. Why is the supervisor sometimes considered a mere minion whose human and technical skills are for hire for any purpose?

Procedures for answering these questions and for acquiring the perspective and behavior demanded of the supervisor will be developed in subsequent parts of this book. As the next step, let us see how we can best select and prepare those who are to provide vision to the schools, maintain balance in the curriculum, and offer help with the specifics for the improvement of instruction.

CHAPTER 3

THE SELECTION AND CONTINUING EDUCATION OF SUPERVISORS

Organizations with high prestige have long been concerned with selecting and developing key personnel. They have learned from experience that they cannot rely on the individual to acquire by independent effort the range of competence needed for a major leadership position. The wealth of experience essential to effective performance in a top leadership post is not acquired by one's own devices. Yet schools have only recently been concerned with systematically recruiting and developing a select supervisory group. Many schools are still appointing supervisors on the basis of their long service as teachers, their popularity with the faculty, their success in athletics, or other visible activity. It is noteworthy that a supervisor of an English department in a large high school could jest that she was nominated for the position because she lost no textbooks the previous year.

Stimulus for more effective programs and selection and preparation is also generated because of the keen competition among all professions for top-quality personnel. The disturbing acknowledgement by institutions which prepare educational leaders that education is losing in the competition for talent has led to (1) proposals for more selective admissions to graduate programs leading to degrees and supervisory credentials, (2) recruitment efforts revealing the attractions of educational leadership, and (3) higher levels of professional preparation for all certified supervisory personnel. There exists the issue of whether education is best served by encouraging large numbers to undertake the study of supervision or by restricting graduate courses in supervision to a small number of highly qualified students.

Conscious of the need for upgrading the quality of leadership, school systems and institutions offering preparation in educational supervision have begun studying means of developing more effective programs of selection and preparation. In order to understand these developments, we shall (1) survey present policies and procedures in the selection of personnel for supervisory positions, (2) evaluate certification requirements, (3) describe trends in the education of supervisors, and (4) review research on leadership, showing its implications for the selection of supervisors.

POLICIES AND PROCEDURES
IN THE SELECTION OF SUPERVISORS
Selection Procedures in School Districts

Appointment and advancement in terms of results obtained is a generally accepted method of filling jobs in higher echelons. "Didn't Jane Smith do a superior job with student teachers? . . . All right—advance her to coordinator for English. . . . Didn't pupils and faculty alike praise Ray Jones for the way he guided the student council? . . . All right—recommend him for vice-principal in charge of instruction." These after-the-fact methods are useful in that those who are good leaders in one situation tend to be good leaders in another. They are wasteful in that it is far from certain that an individual who has been good in one position will succeed in another. While both a cooperating teacher and a coordinator exercise supervision, the supervision required in the two cases is not the same kind or of the same order. Unfortunately, the Peter Principle too often dominates school advancement; people climb the ladder of promotion until they achieve a position that is beyond their capacities.

Present procedures for selecting instructional leaders are not encouraging. Extensive studies of the methods used by school boards in selecting superintendents, for example, reveal that seldom are there specific procedures or standards of selection. Interviews held with candidates are usually informal visits during which the board member sizes up the applicant by asking questions in an offhand manner. Members of school boards appear to place more emphasis on the candidate's appearance, ability to get along with others, and previous experience in a similar position than on the candidate's vision as an educational leader. Perspective and statesmanlike leadership, including possession of an educational philosophy, are sometimes not considered of consequence by school board members.

The following are common policies for selecting supervising personnel:

1. Most districts require a master's degree for anyone entering a supervisory position, and usually a minimum number of recent postgraduate courses in supervision are required.
2. Only a few systems set any limitation on age, but experience requirements vary a great deal from city to city. Nearly all school systems require several years of "successful" or "outstanding" teaching experience.
3. Persons already in the school system are given preference for promotion in the majority of school systems. Smaller school districts often, however, find it necessary to consider outsiders in order to find qualified personnel.
4. When there is a supervisory position open, most schools advertise as widely as possible. Methods include posting of announcements in all schools, mentioning the job and its requirements in the superintendent's bulletin, sending a letter to all teachers, and notifying placement bureaus and colleges.
5. Those interested in supervisory positions fill out application forms giving their education, experience, and references. These are usually checked for factual information before the applicant is allowed to go further in the procedures. Sometimes a screening committee at this point eliminates those not considered to be good material.
6. In many school districts examinations are required for those who pass the initial screen process. Often applicants have to take a written test first. If they pass this, they go on to an oral examination. The oral examination may be an informal interview or a structured interview with the discussion based on specific points on which the applicants are given numerical ratings on the basis of their replies.
7. Essay and interview sections of the examination are usually rated by committees composed chiefly of administrators appointed by the superintendent. Teachers and representatives of professional organizations serve on these committees occasionally.
8. Some districts have elaborate promotional procedures by which all qualifications of the applicant are given numerical ratings. These ratings form the basis of a list of eligible candidates. Some-

times school districts which have detailed promotional procedures still reserve the right of the superintendent or the board of education to choose anyone they feel is best qualified.

9. A number of school districts have instituted training programs for future school leaders. These programs have various names—inservice, staff development, leadership training, internship, and apprenticeship.

10. Affirmative action procedures must be followed if the school district receives federal monies. Many states, too, have affirmative action laws requiring nondiscriminatory practices in all employment.

Certification Requirements for Supervisors

Responsibility for the selection of supervisors rests not only with local school systems, but indirectly with those who set certification requirements for supervisors and with those in college departments of education who establish minimum standards for admission to programs of preparation. A recurrent point of emphasis in statements of requirements makes recency of education and experience important considerations. Verification of successful public school service of candidates for supervision often includes items such as the following: leadership in education as demonstrated by superior teaching; participation in activities such as curriculum development, individual counseling, community work, teachers' organizations, and supervision of student teachers; and selection by teachers and administrators for special responsibilities.

State certification requirements for supervisors represent the minimum standards established by law and reflect the views of official state committees, including representatives from state education department personnel, teacher-education institutions, professional organizations, as well as many persons in various official positions. In most states school supervisors must have had special preparation through college courses in (1) school organization and administration; (2) supervision: its aims, scope, and desirable outcomes, principles, and practices; (3) curriculum development and construction; (4) evaluation of instruction; and (5) courses appropriate to the type and level of responsibilities of the particular supervisory position.

Certification requirements vary from state to state. Present certification practices do not fully meet the criteria used by the National Committee on Professionalization of Supervisors in judging whether or not certification practices adequately assure qualified and competent supervisors. In the establishment of certification requirements, provision should be made to enforce professional ethics and standards. A certificate should be revoked when an individual does not meet requirements. However, agreed-upon ethics and standards do not yet exist. Too frequently, certificates are given on the basis of successful completion of courses. We lack evidence that the meeting of course requirements makes a difference in the supervisor's ability to effect indirectly or directly the improvement of instruction.

Among recommendations for improving certification is the suggestion that the number of training institutions be limited in order to bring a balance between supply and demand and to ensure a strong program. In one state, for example, in which there are eight institutions offering course work in supervision, the supply is far in excess of the state's needs, with over 7,000 licenses issued to fill 260 positions.

Life certificates are not recommended. A provisional certificate for the beginning supervisor should be renewable upon submission of evidence that the holder is effective in supervision.

PREPARATION OF SUPERVISORS

In general, recommendations for the advanced preparation of supervisors are comprehensive and suggest modifying traditional concepts of scheduling and methods of instruction. The suggested programs usually emphasize the ways teachers can be helped in the specific field to be supervised, including information on materials of instruction, their sources, availability, criteria for selection, and techniques of utilization. Preparation in the techniques of supervision gives attention to the selection, placement, and orientation of teachers, inservice programs, and evaluation of teaching success. Candidates study a variety of ways in which people work together successfully and analyze both individual and group behavior to learn how people may be helped in their professional adjustments and .interpersonal relations. Practice in the use of group processes, which includes ways of organizing groups, planning, securing participation, and problem solving, is recommended.

Experiences directed toward improvement of the skills of communication are frequently provided. These include practice in oral and written reporting, speaking to community groups, writing press releases, and preparing supervisory bulletins. With respect to curriculum development, prospective supervisors become familiar with programs in both large and small school systems and identify the performance of experienced supervisors in encouraging curriculum activity. They study the roles of professional and lay persons in the establishment of instructional goals, learn how to use the findings of research and to engage in inquiry themselves, and become familiar with a number of special answers to the problem of providing for individual differences and evaluating the total learning process.

The candidate for a supervisory position is expected to have a clear understanding of the responsibility and relationship of teachers, administrators, supervisors, and members of governing boards in the organization of school systems and in the profession.

Competency-based Programs

Recently formats that represent competency-based approaches have appeared in training programs for supervisors. Boyan and Copeland, for example, designed and tested a program for clinical supervision by which students developed a number of competencies—ability to identify criteria for successful teaching, to assemble data and make valid summary statements, to identify patterns of teacher behavior, to differentiate positive and negative teaching behavior, and to identify strategies for producing desired results.[1]

McCleary at the University of Utah employed a framework in which competencies were cast into statements indicating technical, conceptual, and human behaviors at familiarity, understanding, and application levels of mastery.[2] A series of individualized learning modules was developed treating the school-helping relationships, school climate, techniques for objective assessment of the teaching act, program evaluation, and design of educational programs. A critical incident technique was used to identify the competencies needed for effective supervision.

Other work is now underway in identifying competencies necessary for supervisors. For example, such identification is sought through content analysis of the literature in supervision, job analysis in practice, and Delphi and other panel techniques to gain consensus about the value of different competencies. Efforts are also being made to overcome criticisms of competency-based programs, namely, that they are associated with an impersonal and mechanistic approach to human development, triviality of behavioral or performance statements, and weaknesses in accountability practices.[3]

The Internship

A popular design for the program of preparation is the internship. Internship aims at relating theory and practice. The supervisory in-

1. Norman Boyan and Willis D. Copeland, "A Training Program for Supervisors: Anatomy of an Educational Development," *Journal of Educational Research,* 68, pp. 100–116, 1974.
2. Lloyd E. McCleary (ed.), *ILM Learning Module Series in Supervision,* ILM Publishers, Salt Lake City, Utah, 1975.
3. Lloyd E. McCleary, "Competencies in Clinical Supervision," *Journal of Research and Development in Education,* vol. 9, no. 2, pp. 39–35, 1976.

tern is given actual responsibility for supervising others in school settings while under the direct supervision of both (1) selected practitioners in the school and (2) university instructors.

Although variations exist in the procedures for conduct of the internship, the following illustrate common operations:

1. *Recruitment.* Candidates are sought from the school systems. School leaders are asked to nominate persons who have already demonstrated leadership and who have evidenced intellectual and emotional strengths. In some systems, nominations are made by teachers and administrators with the idea that the nominee will "come back to our own system," not necessarily work elsewhere.

2. *Preparation for supervision while teaching.* The candidate is assisted by leaders in the local school district who make available a variety of experiences. The candidate may accept leadership responsibilities in school and community committees, serve as a resource person to teachers, participate in meeting with supervisors, and help supervisors in daily work.

3. *Attendance at a summer institute for school leaders.* The candidate attends a summer program as a member of a leadership team.

    a. The team spends about two hours each day considering how the principles of supervision, basic teaching-learning processes, and human development and behavior apply on the job.

    b. For another block of time, the candidate has opportunities to work with school leaders in the study of problems of common interest. For example, an interest group dealing with initiating a systemwide testing program studies the values and limitations of tests, the selection and administration of tests, and the interpretation and use of test data. They then "spell out" the responsibilities of each school leader in this task. The program offers much opportunity for seeing how problems might be viewed by those in other leadership positions; for holding conferences, reading and preparing reports; and for considering how principles learned will apply in the particular situation in which each member expects to be working as a supervisor in the fall.

    c. Preparation for the fall assignment in a school system is also undertaken during the summer. Candidates visit the school system to secure firsthand knowledge of programs, plans, and problems and to meet many of the principals and teachers as well as parents and children. Visits to community agencies and groups are included at this time.

    d. Supervisors at the workshop become familiar with the services provided by the state department of education, meeting consultants who are available to work with them and learning ways the supervisor can assist the department with statewide activities and service.

4. *Participation in the first year of internship.* The candidate is employed as a full-time supervisor while enrolled at the university for the internship. During the internship, there are monthly meetings with the university adviser for help with personal problems, for evaluation of supervisory activities, and for planning new learning experiences. Records of supervisor's activities are regularly kept, and a copy is given to the adviser weekly. All supervisors participating in the internship meet for several three-day conferences where they share materials and study problems of common concern. Leaders for the conference are the supervisors themselves, although help is given them by resource persons from the university and personnel from the state department of education. Assessment of the intern's understandings and skills in major supervisory functions is determined at this conference, and this evaluation is used for planning work to be undertaken at the university in the summer. The second summer program at the university features development of an action-research study in connection with a problem of common concern to the supervisor and other school personnel.

5. *Participation in the second year of internship.* On-the-job study during the second year of internship is concentrated on the action-research project formulated during the spring and summer. At the end of the second year and third summer session, the candidate receives a six-year diploma and is designated as a "specialist in supervision."

    Internships offered in the several training institutions are organized on varying time bases, have no common denominator as to types or extent of experiences provided for the intern, and are characterized by few common standards of supervisory procedure. However, four criteria for evaluating them are:

1. The internship should consist largely of significant work necessary to the well-being of an ongoing educational program—not of so-called made work.
2. The internship should provide substantial opportunity for creative thought and action on the part of the intern.
3. The internship should make provision for joint planning, action,

and evaluation by the intern, the college adviser, and the supervisory administrator in the cooperating school community.
4. The internship should make provision for flexibility in the type of assignment to meet better the needs and interests of individual interns as determined by themselves and their advisers.

The internship is far from perfect. Chief among the improvements to be made are (1) more specific definition of desired learning and specification of what will constitute evidence that the learnings have been reached by the candidates, (2) more effective supervision of candidates and their work, (3) a stable method of financing the internship, and (4) research to check out the effects of internship and ways to improve it.

Internship programs offer the advantage of improving the relationships between colleges and school communities. Through these arrangements, school systems become acquainted with the philosophy of the institutions preparing supervisors, and, in turn, the institutions gain a better understanding of local problems and practices. Theory and practice go hand in hand, raising the level of the profession. It is important, however, that experiences in the program do not become disconnected, repetitive, and divorced from theory. Candidates should be helped to discriminate between desirable and undesirable practices observed in the field situation, and care should be taken that they not be subjected to repetition of routine tasks in which they have previously demonstrated competence.

Other Criteria and Programs for the Preparation of Supervisors
It is emphasized that the internship is only one method by which programs for the preparation of supervisors can be more effective. Classroom activities, seminars, surveys, and field trips can be highly significant, as indicated by these five practices:

1. Attention is given to specific needs of individual students, yet a coherent and organized program—not a collection of miscellaneous courses—is offered. Needs of individuals are based on the competence and qualities sought.
2. The institution defines the basic knowledge and competences requisite for the given specialty, and the students' work is centered on this basic content.
3. In the interest of maintaining a level of work that is truly of graduate caliber, the number of courses open to both graduate and undergraduate students is limited.
4. A special research project is required as part of the program. The

particular type of project may follow any one of a variety of directions. The project allows students to demonstrate technical skill in the field of specialization and recognize the implications of their specialty for the educational enterprise in general.

5. The institution sets a definite time limit within which the program can be completed. When too long a period of time lapses, the impact of the concentrated work required for developing a high level of specialized skill may be lost.

PROGRAMS FOR THE CONTINUING DEVELOPMENT OF SUPERVISORS

Many preparing institutions train for uncertainty and for further inquiry. Typical of the open-ended attitude of some graduate schools is the story of a dean who remarked at commencement, "One-half of what you have learned here is false; unfortunately, we don't know which half."

The answers to the problem of continuity of learning rest upon the habits of learning how to learn, which supervisors can be led to acquire. Part of this preparation entails saturating students of supervision with the teachings of social, psychological, and ethical philosophy of education as well as equipping them to be students of the subject matter with which they are to deal. The principles of these fields, however, must be incorporated in their thought processes—in the very way instructional situations are observed and courses of action are planned. It is more important for supervisors to fix controlling habits in line with theories of foundation disciplines than to imitate current practices which they perceive as succeeding in an empirical way. Without theory, methods will be picked up through blind trial and error. Any immediate supervisory skill acquired only from nonrational observation of experienced and successful supervisors will be at the cost of the power to go on learning. The supervisor who leaves the professional school with immediate proficiency in a number of techniques associated with supervision but who lacks the inquiring qualities of a student of education is not likely to grow as a director of learning. Similar conclusions have been reached regarding the preparation of teachers. "How often do candid instructors in training schools for teachers acknowledge disappointment in the later careers of even their most promising candidates! They seem to strike twelve at the start. There is an unexpected and seemingly unaccountable failure to maintain steady growth. Is this in some part due to the undue premature stress laid in early practice work upon securing immediate capability? . . . "[4]

4. John Dewey, "The Relation of Theory to Practice in Education," in Charles A.

Instead of criticizing the trainee too specifically, instructors in the university, for instance, should direct their efforts to getting novice supervisors to judge their own work critically, to find out in what ways they have succeeded or failed, and to discover the probable reasons for both success and failure.

Use of Simulation as an Instructional Method in the Preparation of Supervisors

Simulative materials have been used to relate theoretical concepts to practical problems and to encourage self-learning among those preparing for educational leadership. These materials include a variety of both printed and audiovisual aids by which selected representations of supervisory situations are presented to those in training (case studies, in-baskets, computer-based decision games, and tape-recorded and videotaped situations).[5] Participants in simulated situations actually work within the context of an elaborate case study as they assume certain supervisory positions in the study. The procedure calls for each member to act—not merely to tell what action would be desirable. Analysis of consequences of action, study of background materials, role playing, making of decisions, and discussion afforded by the simulative process are generally found to be helpful. A key advantage of this method is that the instructor can get realism into the teaching, yet control this realism so that it results in better understanding of the concepts and theory for attacking and solving educational problems. The specific problems are examined against pertinent background information designed to help one acquire the ability to see the whole picture—each problem in its broader context. In addition, because simulation provides many opportunities for learner performance, novice supervisors have the chance to assess their competencies in relation to a range of supervisory demands.

Staff Development for Supervisors

Because vastly greater numbers of working supervisors need the help of professional resources than do the smaller number of those who will be new to the job each year, cooperating programs for staff development of supervisors have been established. Professional organizations, school authorities, and colleges are working together to

---

McMurray (ed.), *The Relation of Theory to Practice in the Education of Teachers,* Third Yearbook, National Society for the Scientific Study of Education, University of Chicago, Chicago, 1904, pp. 15–16.

5. W. G. Walker (ed.), *Educational Administration on Tape,* University of Queensland Press, St. Lucia, 1974.

offer programs especially designed to meet needs over and above the traditional degree requirements. These practices include research undertakings, workshops, clinics, school study councils, informal seminars, and professional conferences—all of which are often carried on with the cooperation of school systems, state departments of education, and universities. Organizationally, however, we have seldom arrived at a program which carries the authority, standards, and conditions of work in a university and offers an equal partnership to school districts in meeting their special demands.

Our present practice, which fosters the tradition of self-responsibility for professional development among teachers and supervisors, is proving inadequate as a means of assuring up-to-date competence. As professionals, both teachers and supervisors have assumed responsibility for their own development by attending seminars, summer programs, and even classes at their own expense and on their own time. As long as changes in schools were infrequent, this tradition enabled the more motivated to avoid professional obsolescence. However, today the changes in curriculum leave the teacher and supervisor with no option other than changing. In this age of vigorous production of knowledge, a supervisor as well as a teacher can quickly lose touch with contemporary thought and action. It will become necessary to provide greater amounts of training to both teachers and supervisors and to underwrite the costs of additional education as an incentive to professional development. This support can include such items as tuition refunds, paid leaves for study purposes, and required participation in institutes and projects. Let us reiterate, however, the point that mere attendance at training sessions does not assure that the participant has gained the competence desired. We need evidence, for instance, that as a result of training, supervisors of instruction can formulate defensible goals and objectives; contrast norm- and criterion-referenced tests; state the prerequisites that learners would have to acquire or possess before they could reach particular objectives; given a teaching episode, describe what they saw in terms of a specified analytical scheme and, above all, not confuse data collections—observations—with inferences and judgments.

Most retraining programs for supervisors reflect changing values in education at large. Harris and Valverde, for example, would have supervisors retrained to serve the cause of multicultural education.[6] This training would take the form of opportunities to observe, work, play, and study in the "other worlds," similar to the training given

6. Ben M. Harris and Leonard A. Valverde, "Supervisors and Educational Change," *Theory into Practice,* vol. 15, no. 4, pp. 267–273, October 1976.

Peace Corps, Teacher Corps, and VISTA personnel. Field trips, rotating assignments within the district, anthropological field studies, and summer work assignments with those of other cultures are also suggested. These approaches should be supplemented with seminars, training exercises, and workshops to assure depth and application. The retraining of staff to permit them to function in multicultural situations is a minimum requirement.

Development through Analysis of Performance

Although a long-range objective of a school district's supervisory development program may call for the development of people, an immediate objective is to help supervisors improve performance in their present positions. In doing this, supervisors are, of course, encouraged to prepare for increasing responsibilities. Less emphasis is placed upon supervisors' personal and personality qualifications as potentials for promotion and more on the results they are able to achieve in their present work. Acceptance of the principle that "all development is self-development" has led to the supervisor's sharing in the responsibility for analyzing personal performance and setting up a development plan. One illustration is found in the situation where a superintendent of schools and a director of instruction agree at the start of the year on the objectives the director is to accomplish. They also agree on what will constitute evidence of whether or not the objectives are reached. Twelve months later the two review the accomplishments against the objectives and decide what is to be done the following year, the subordinate taking the lead in determining the developmental action necessary in light of the appraisal. This kind of developmental program promotes better understanding of the performance expected, and enables the supervisor, in this case the superintendent, to see how certain weaknesses on the part of others (the director) might be traceable to one's own weaknesses in supervision.

Development through the Training
Laboratory and Sensitivity Programs

Some supervisory development programs try to help supervisors achieve emotional maturity as a leadership variable. The criterion for such maturity is usually "how fully one says what he thinks, holding a conviction, but balancing it with a respect for others." Underlying this goal is the assumption mentioned earlier that one matures only through a knowledge of self. Leaders are held to be the ones who are sure of themselves, not threatened by the expressions of others or their feelings, and secure with their own position. However, ventures into the realm of personal help to supervisors, which have become numerous in education and industry alike, carry with them the need for distinguishing between psychological therapy and education for supervision.

The Research Center for Group Dynamics of the University of Michigan, with the Department of Adult Education, National Education Association, has been responsible for operating a national training laboratory which seeks to help leaders behave in such a way that they solve problems effectively and have individually satisfying experiences. In England, the Tavistock Institute of Human Relations has engaged in research into ways supervisors can develop the ideas, attitudes, and skills of others. Findings from these research centers in group dynamics are tried and transmitted through the various developmental programs for supervisors. Methods taught in the programs are of importance in furthering the leadership skills of supervisors and in continuing their personal growth.

Among the problems frequently considered in training programs are those of handling conflict and disagreement. Training procedures lead not only to understanding of the nature of conflict but also to recognition of the feeling which accompanies attempts to resolve it. The faith exists that warm human relations grow out of conflict actually experienced by the participants. The following assumptions and practices are often found in supervisory development programs:

Assumptions

1. Knowledge is important when it carries import for its possessor.
2. Learning is the remaking of experience which makes a difference in the behavior of the learner.
3. Learning occurs only as one can emotionally afford to learn.
4. We seek to dominate others because of our own felt inadequacies.

Practices in Sensitivity Training

1. There are numerous opportunities to diagnose the group's difficulties and feelings, and the member's perception of others.
2. The atmosphere permits expression of unpopular and disagreeable feelings relevant to the problem in order for change to occur.
3. The change sought in an individual's performance is more than an intelligent adaptation; it is a whole new pattern of personality which carries over into other situations.
4. Those seeking to improve their supervisory potential try to acquire

an increased sensitivity to social and psychological situations and to the consequences of organizational changes rather than precise answers and formalities.

The kind of sensitivity training which deals with people's feelings, tension release, and sensitive situations in which participants learn to express themselves and to understand the communications they are making is not necessarily void of reason. There is a connection between intellectual and emotional behavior, a rationality of feeling. A thought is rational when it fits accurately the object of the situation to which it refers; so, too, an emotion is rational when it fits the occasion. The new humanists rely more and more on visceral reactions to people and organizations—trusting these reactions as valid, as important data. They ask "Why do I feel this way? What about this organization makes me have this reaction? Shall I trust this signal from my gut?"

Those most concerned with intelligent behavior in organizations have long been interested in finding techniques that may be used to prevent emotions from blocking rationality. Mannheim, for example, saw the group approaches of psychoanalysis as a means not only to individual self-understanding but for dealing with the maladjustments of groups and institutions.[7] Others who favor the method of practical intelligence deliberately involve emotion in the process of judgment. Practical judgment is said to be "the process in which people are educated to see the significance of emotions and drives, so that they come to use them effectively in securing personal and social satisfaction as part of an intelligent method of creating bonds of community.[8] Generally, recognition of our feelings with regard to a problem is the beginning of intelligent behavior.

Obviously, those offering training programs for supervisors are not always successful. Sometimes supervisors grasp the course in the sense of understanding its intellectual content but are not able to achieve greater effectiveness in behavior. The personality differences of some supervisors inhibit them from making appreciable use of training. Also, the requirements of supervisory situations vary so widely that it is difficult to provide all that supervisors may want or need. A critique of the kinds of training programs offered by the National Training Laboratory's Gould Academy in Bethel, Maine, the Western Training Laboratory's Lake Arrowhead Center in California, and their rapidly increasing imitators appears in Tarcher's *Leadership*

7. Karl Mannheim, *Man and Society in an Age of Reconstruction,* Harcourt Brace Jovanovich, Inc., New York, 1941, p. 84.

8. Margaret Fisher, *Leadership and Intelligence,* Bureau of Publications, Teachers College, Columbia University, New York, 1954, p. 105.

and the Power of Ideas.[9] Among other things, Tarcher points out the limitations of sensitivity training including (1) the difficulty of applying the "new learnings" in the real world outside the retreat of the laboratory and (2) the failure of the trainees to provide the leaders with a framework of values applicable to their daily lives.

QUALITIES SOUGHT IN SUPERVISORS

Admittedly, behavior and qualities identified with successful supervision are not necessarily the same as those behaviors and qualities which facilitate ascent to supervisory positions. Nevertheless, clues to supervisory potential can be found through analysis of the leadership characteristics which enable supervisors to maintain their leadership positions.

We have already noted that one objective criterion of leadership in supervision resides in the extent to which supervisors exercise influence over others. This ability may be treated separately from the ability to change the behavior of others because of an official position with its accompanying sanctions, such as ratings and the power of recommendation. A second index of leadership is the degree to which the organization or group for which one is responsible functions as a unit. The achievement of unity is closely associated with the goal-setting and communication behavior of the supervisor. Only a limited number of other characteristics of leadership behavior have been identified; among them are technical proficiency, initiating and directing action, consideration for followers, stressing of production, and social awareness.

Let us reiterate that the research on leadership makes a distinction between the performance of a leader as a leader and the effectiveness of the performance of the group being led. The person who will emerge as a leader in a group or who will be seen as a leader independent of the effects of leadership is likely to display the following characteristics:

1. Individual personality characteristics—extrovert, assertive, socially mature
2. Education (but not age or other biographical characteristics)
3. Intelligence, general ability, and task ability
4. Training in leader techniques

However, there is no conclusive evidence that the presence of such leaders makes any difference in terms of the task performance of

9. Martin Tarcher, *Leadership and the Power of Ideas,* Harper & Row, Publishers, Incorporated, New York, 1966.

those with whom they are working. In fact, group members' estimates of performance capabilities of leaders as well as their peers do not relate very well to actual (objectively measured) performance.

As indicated previously, leadership is differently evaluated by those above and below. In a school organization those who hold positions superior to that of supervisors expect them to insist upon rather strict discipline and to follow closely standard operating procedures. Many school boards want a supervisor who has the ability to:

1. Sell, push, pressure, and persuade teachers to improvement and loyalty to the system.
2. Collect facts, weigh them, and make effective decisions.
3. Know the board's policies, objectives, and practices of the district.
4. Communicate policies and practices clearly to teachers.
5. Evaluate performance according to the board's policies and procedures.

On the other hand, subordinates expect and value a supervisor mingling with them, using consultation procedures, showing consideration for them and their needs, and being socially sensitive.

The expectations of the task and the institutionalization of the group are all factors in the situation to which the leader must adapt. In a steeply hierarchial school organization the most effective leader is one who recognizes the structure and conforms closely to its expectations.

It is generally true that teachers prefer a supervisor who "goes to bat" for them and sides with them in conflicts with higher authorities. However, if a supervisor sides with the teachers but is not capable of influencing the authorities in the teachers' behalf, it is unlikely that the teachers will want this person for their supervisor. Supportive behavior from the supervisor results in employee satisfaction only in the presence of influence upon higher echelons. It is the combination of these two conditions (supportive behavior and influence with authorities) which goes with higher satisfaction.

Teachers may not want less consideration behavior, but, recognizing the organizational context, they know they must satisfy themselves with less personal attention from the supervisor in order that the supervisor may, in turn, interact more freely with higher authorities and thus exercise greater influence upon the higher-ups.

Different people want different kinds of leaders. Authoritarians prefer status-laden leadership—strong authority and direction on the part of the supervisor. Toward weak leaders they express open hostility. Contrarily, equalitarians are able to accept strong leadership if the situation demands it, but they have no need for powerful authorities. Authoritarians care little for personal warmth in their leader but they do demand that the supervisor contribute to their movement toward group and individual goals. Equalitarians are inclined to evaluate leaders in terms of their orientation. Authoritarians are dissatisfied and uncomfortable under a nondirective leader. A group of equalitarians could be expected to go into a decline under a rigid and directive leader.

Blumberg and Amidon[10] have shown that teachers' feelings about the usefulness and productivity of a supervisory conference are affected by the manner in which they perceive a supervisor's behavior. One implication from this study is that the supervisor might find out how the teacher perceives the supervisor-teacher relationship before selecting a supervisory strategy.

There is no doubt that the confusion over supervisory functions is a major factor in the confusion over the qualities sought in the supervisor. If supervision is only to engage in routine decision making, the selection and preparation of supervisors will not be very extensive. On the other hand, if supervisors are expected to serve as supervisory statesmen with responsibility for making critical decisions affecting the school's development, selection and preparation are treated more seriously.

Trait Analysis and Personality Assessment
Early analyses of leadership and supervision included lists of the traits and other characteristics which in the opinion of the analyst were important in the performance of the job. Such lists not only suffered from the use of vague terms but appeared almost contradictory: "flexibility," "Catonian strength of conviction," "common sense," "imagination." Further, those who listed traits designated as necessary for a supervisor to possess usually did not suggest which traits were most important and which least, nor did they note how the same trait functions differently in personalities which are organized differently. Height, weight, energy, self-confidence, talkativeness, geniality, originality, and numerous other personality traits do not consistently characterize leaders. Underlying the "trait theory" of leadership is the assumption that leadership resides in an individual, that it is a possession which one can reproduce in different groups and in different situations. A more supportable contention is that a person does not become a leader because of a pattern of personality traits, but because these traits bear some relevance to the characteristics,

10. Arthur Blumberg and Edmund Amidon, *Teacher Perceptions of Supervisor-Teacher Interaction,* vol. 14, no. 1, September 1965.

activities, and goals of the group to be led. For example, the fact that personnel officials in school districts reject candidates for administrative appointments when the candidates score high in aggression and authoritarianism and approve disciplinary techniques in classroom procedures might give us more information about the districts than it does about leadership.

Earlier in this chapter the importance of intelligence was stressed in connection with education's competitive race for talent. Even this factor, however, is not the "general leadership trait" which some seek. Investigations of the relationship between leadership and general intelligence lead to the conclusion that while every increment of intelligence means wiser leadership, people prefer to be led—even ill-led—by those they can understand. Leaders are, in general, more intelligent than followers, but they must not exceed the followers by too great a margin. Presumably, wide discrepancies render improbable the unified purpose of the individuals concerned. Hollingworth, for example, many years ago noted that a leadership pattern would not form or would break up when a discrepancy of more than 30 points exists between the IQs of the leader and the led.[11]

Were it not for the hierarchial structure of the school system, a supervisor would not be expected to retain leadership in group activities. Inasmuch as personal characteristics would be more stable than the goals and interpersonal relations in the group situation, the leadership would be passed among members as they were able to contribute to group achievement.

Although the personality of the leader makes a difference in group performance, it is the evaluation of that personality by others in the situation which is important. No person can be conceived of as an informal leader without communicating with others about the problem and getting support for personal ideas. Trait analysis obscures the fact that a supervisor's behavior varies with the particular situation. A coordinator may be self-confident with a teacher but lack confidence with the superintendent. In any case we can predict member performance in group situations more consistently from knowledge of intelligence and job-related characteristics than from personal-social properties.

With respect to trying to predict which individuals will show subsequent progress in management, paper-and-pencil ability tests are more predictive of progress than personality questionnaires. The Institute for Personality Assessment and Research, University of California, Berkeley, has chosen different emphases in trying to assess

---

11. Leta S. Hollingworth, *Children above 180 IQ,* World Book Company, Yonkers, N.Y., 1942, p. 287.

individuals in making decisions. The Institute has studied persons by bringing them together with a staff of psychologists for a period of several days at an assessment center. Here, the subjects are studied in a range of situations involving, for example, real life problems, abstract problem solving, projective personality tests, objective attitude and interest inventories, and social interviews. The evidence suggests that effective persons have much in common in their cognitive flexibility, high verbal skills, and interest in as well as accuracy in communication with others.

Personality assessment includes the preparation of a psychological description and analysis of the physical, interpersonal, and group situations in which the candidate will function in the future if selected. Such an analysis requires understanding of the nature of the professional function itself, what it asks of its practitioners, and the rewards it offers. Until we know these, we do not know what aspects of a person's capacities and needs we should assess.

Motives for Becoming a Supervisor

Among the factors sometimes looked for in the selection of a supervisor is that of motivation. Granted that there must be a willingness to accept the position and the responsibilities involved, it is equally important to develop the organizational structure which will enable those of different motivations to render high-level service regardless of their individual differences.

The hypothesis that people seek supervisory positions and eminence because of economic reward has been proposed. Eighty percent of the teachers in the two southern California counties of Los Angeles and Orange wanted to go into administration at one time, primarily because of higher pay. On the other hand, the wide variability in material rewards among supervisory positions indicates that there are other incentives running through the striving for eminence and leadership. The position of supervisor often admits one into attractive associations that make possible ego-satisfying friendships and memberships. Knowing whose approval is sought by a candidate often enables one to predict future behavior.

Lauterbach declared that financial incentives are part of a complex motivation reflecting needs of self-assertion, personal security, and social status.[12] Money is important, but this incentive is likely to be unconsciously neglected when at odds with deeper needs. In Bertrand Russell's words, "What people fear when they engage in the struggle is not that they will fail to get their breakfast next morning,

12. Albert Lauterbach, *Man, Motives and Money*, Cornell University Press, Ithaca, N.Y., 1954, p. 19.

but that they will fail to outshine their neighbors."[13] "It is relative income which measures success."[14] Supervisors sometimes seek salary increases aggressively, admitting their action to be prompted chiefly by a desire to maintain a status differential.

Occasionally a supervisor will go from a well-paying position in one district to another job elsewhere which pays less but promises to allow more voice in the decision-making process or more independence of action. Satisfaction can be built into a position through responsibility and a sense of the importance of the work and the value of the enterprise.

It may be that some who seek to be supervisors want to devote themselves to service for others and to gain satisfaction from a feeling of power over them. This is one way of achieving a sense of worth. The will for power and service may be associated with pathological manipulations: "exaggerated ideas of success, combined with a drive to overwork; constant inner tension, stemming from inner passivity, regardless of the importance of the stakes; a propelling impetus toward more and more success; dissatisfaction and boredom if deprived of new excitement and resulting opportunities to show off."[15] Without realizing it, seekers of a position may be trying to prove to themselves and to others that they are worthy persons. Sensing rather than recognizing inadequacies, they seek reassurance by winning a position. Obviously, this success is only temporary, for we cannot be reassured about something we feel we do not really have. Continuous seeking of other reassurances is likely to be the pattern.

The search for self-esteem through a leadership position need not be aggressive or objectionable. Recognition of one's own desire to dominate and control can lead to freer and closer relations with others and to a diminished need to exploit others because of an unresolved tension. Further, egoistic motives for self-advancement, just as altruistic motives, can be harnessed by supervision to the benefit of all. Supervisors are able to find personal reward while helping to provide good aims, appropriate means, and satisfying outcomes for those who engage with them in the supervisory enterprise. The important question in the selection of a supervisor is not whether the person seeks leadership, service, or opportunity for research, but whether one has the ability to do the job. Effectiveness is more likely to depend on one's relations with others than on motives for taking the position. Eventually, one must prove competency.

13. Bertrand Russell, *The Conquest of Happiness,* George Allen & Unwin, Ltd., London, 1937, p. 30.
14. Lauterbach, op. cit., p. 40.
15. Ibid., p. 52.

DRAWBACKS OF BECOMING A SUPERVISOR

Where teaching is a low-status position, many will not accept supervisory positions which exist on a temporary basis because of the severe loss of status accompanying a return to a teaching assignment. Also, whether teachers are willing to vacate their status as teachers may depend on the extent to which they anticipate an estrangement from fellow teachers and an acceptance by new associates. One may be afraid of being regarded as a "climber," suitable for vilification. The effects of promotions have long been noted:

> To dissipate this awkward feeling, I have been fain to go among them once or twice since; to visit my old desk fellows—my co-brethren of the quill—that I had left below in the state militant. Not all the kindness with which they received me could quite restore to me that pleasant familiarity which I had heretofore enjoyed among them. We cracked some of our old jokes, but methought they went off but faintly.[16]

Many teachers do not particularly care to "get ahead." They have found rewards through their interest in a field of knowledge and their ability to work with children. Needing no escape from the classroom, these teachers find freedom in teaching. Many who prefer to work directly with youngsters are resentful of the salary differentials between classroom teachers and supervisors. Unquestionably, the higher salary level of supervisors weakens the attractions of teaching as a career. Professional organizations and schools of education are seriously hunting ways to give greater status to teaching in order that it will not be necessary to take advanced work in supervision and administration solely for a top salary or a professional degree. Granting a doctorate in pedagogy to those who possess unusual understanding and competence in their classroom teaching and making available opportunities for teachers to receive high salaries might keep more master teachers in continuous contact with pupils. It would also be desirable in helping to prevent teachers from experiencing the bitterness and withdrawal that often follow failure to be selected as a supervisor.

In response to a construct prepared by Presthus[17] which included "upward mobiles"—those who aspire to higher positions—and "nonmobiles"—those who have no such mobility aspirations—Powers[18] related personal characteristics to individuals identified as (1) mobile, (2) nonmobile, and (3) immobile—those who aspired but

16. Charles Lamb, "The Superannuated Man," *The Essays of Elia and the Last Essays of Elia,* The Macmillan Company, New York, 1925, p. 286.
17. Robert Presthus, *The Organizational Society,* Alfred A. Knopf, Inc., New York, 1962.
18. Thomas E. Powers, "Administrative Behavior and Upward-Mobility," *Administrator's Notebook,* vol. 15, no. 1, September 1966.

were rejected for advancement. The results suggest that the similarities of characteristics between mobiles and nonmobiles do not permit identifying an upward mobile as a unique type. Those who sought advancement and didn't get it tended to regard moving upward in the organization as a means for obtaining greater prestige, authority, and responsibility; while mobiles viewed advancement as an opportunity for improving one's income and for making greater contributions to the field of education. Those selected for advancement identified more with either the values of the organization or the needs of the people in the organization than did those who were passed over. Nonmobiles indicated that advancement was viewed by them as disruptive of established personal ties with students, teachers, and family or as too demanding or uninteresting in terms of responsibilities.

It appears that the number of conspicuous positions and the chances for attaining them will not correspond to the number of those who are hopeful of securing them. Sociologists have documented the pressure which our society places upon ambition. Carnegie's "Be a king in your dreams" and "Say to yourself, 'my place is at the top.'" and the idea that "There is no such word as fail" produce frustrations for those who do not make the supervisory or administrative lists. The loss of central goals, resignation from responsibility, cynicism, and indifference are not uncommon following such experiences. Also, one can observe the anxious and over-compliant characteristics of marionettes found among some who aspire to meet the expectations of those who have the power to promote.

FUTURE SELECTION PROCEDURES

Techniques for finding and evaluating supervisory potential are both little known and costly. Few systems would undertake a selection program at all if it were not more expensive not to do so. The supervisor who can make the right decision at the right time and stand behind it is difficult to find. It is more difficult to predict who will become an educational statesman than to assess future technicians who will play their roles—implementing whatever policies are defined. Procedures in the search for those with statesmanlike decision-making ability and emotional tolerance are likely to follow these directions:

1. *Personality assessment.* Objective instruments will be constructed for the assessment of personality which will minimize subjective aspects of the oral interview. Efforts to predict one's compatibility with others will continue.

2. *Advisory assistance.* Emphasis will be given to a professional advisory committee with wide representation from groups concerned. The committee will be expected to be guided by clear definitions of the position and the requirements necessary for the job. The training of those who sit in judgment will be undertaken. Women and members of minority groups will be employed in greater numbers.
3. *Definition of the position and its role.* Stereotyped ideas of qualities or talents required will diminish. Firsthand observations of the supervisors actually performing the duties of the position will provide a sharper understanding of the competencies presently in use and those which should be in use. Knowledge of the psychological atmosphere in which the candidate will be working will be considered necessary in making placement.
4. *Classification of prospective candidates.* Classifying a person's potential entirely on the basis of previous experience will lose favor. Initial "rotating" opportunities in which teachers and supervisors spend some time in many situations will be used to expose talent. There will be more frequent promotion of those who are not fully prepared for the immediate job but can grow into and beyond it, rather than appointment of those whose growth is already at its peak.
5. *Statistical measures.* Numerous statistical measures of the results of the candidate's efforts will be sought. Acceptance of the standards of performance for the classroom as well as identification with purpose will become more important indicators of ability. Assessment of the prospective supervisor's precise knowledge of where and why things occur as they do will be systematically tested.
6. *Present and future requirements.* Assignment of supervisors will depend upon the life history of the district. A new and expanding district will be sure to count among its supervisory staff those who daringly give direction and are able to build a common point of view among the teachers. Older established districts will want innovators to balance conservative and loyal supervisors who defend the system's traditional values. Selection will be in accordance with the long-range aspirations of the school, making possible the attainment in the future of that which is excluded in the present.

PART **TWO**

SOCIAL SYSTEMS AND SUPERVISION

The term "social system" is conceptual; it is a way of describing the interaction of persons in structured situations. A town or community may be considered a social system in which members relate to each other in a predicted fashion. Organizations within the community, i.e., home, church, school, club, can also be described in terms of predicted relationships and the patterns which maintain these relationships.

It is proposed that concepts which serve to explain the behavior of individuals in complex systems, such as a city or a nation, can be used by supervisors in understanding the miniature social systems which deserve their immediate attention: school district, individual school, and classroom. A primary reason for gaining knowledge about social systems is that it will enable one to understand the behavior of others, to predict how they will behave in given conditions, and to change the behavior of others in desirable directions. Knowledge of social systems should permit the supervisor to mediate between the institutional requirements of the school and the individual attitudes of members of the school community and staff. To understand and control the behavior of individuals within a system, one must recognize the existence of social structures, as manifested in the privileges, obligations, and powers which accompany the positions of those within the system. Further, one must be able to predict the consequences of various communication patterns and organizational arrangements.

In school supervision, an important issue today centers on the questions of whether the school as an institution shall be allowed to maintain the historical value patterns, e.g., engage in practices that are consistent with traditional images of "good education," or whether it shall be changed to an institution that must produce results and not merely carry out practices that appear desirable in themselves.

Social system theory makes possible the recognition of this issue in supervision and allows us to interpret specific aspects of the issue which would otherwise be viewed as independent and discreet problems, e.g., "How shall teachers be evaluated?" "Should school systems participate in the National Assessment of Educational Programs (NAEP) testing programs?" "Why do those in government and the Ford Foundation sometimes recommend that states contract with private corporations (RCA, Xerox, etc.) to operate educational programs rather than support the existing institutions of the schools?" Each of these problems is an indicator that there is dissatisfaction with a school system that operates more as a religious institution than as a business. Ministers are not evaluated in terms of their achievement but in terms of the extent to which their actions are consistent with the practices demanded of the faith. They are not held accountable for the changed behavior of their communicants. Managers of businesses, on the other hand, must do more than carry out the actions of a manager. They must show that these actions produce intended effects. Until recently, the social institution of the school has operated more along the lines of a religious institution, putting more emphasis on qualities (means) than on effects (ends). One consequence of this has been that there is little reliable knowledge regarding teaching practices and their effects.

It is our purpose here to review many of the important social structures which affect the relations of those in social systems and to indicate the consequences of these patterns, factors which if not understood lead to difficulty on the part of the supervisor. Underlying this discussion is the assumption that change in the behavior of the individual rests more upon manipulation of social structures than upon didactic pronouncements or emotional appeals.

CHAPTER 4

POLITICAL AND BUREAUCRATIC STRUCTURE OF SCHOOLS

OPPOSING VIEWS OF SCHOOL ORGANIZATION
The View That School Organization Is Ineffective

Social researchers, many journalists, and those who have been frustrated in influencing school practice sometimes view school organization as ineffective or weak and vulnerable. They praise the effective way in which those in technical organizations—businesses and industries—match work activities and production processes to the goal of producing desired products at a competitive price. In contrast, they criticize school managers for allowing a weak linkage between what actually goes on in classrooms and the stated goals and policies emanating from legislators, courts, and boards of education.

Consequently, those with a deficit view attempt to apply technical management techniques to the school organization. Recent efforts to prescribe specific terms to the expected outcomes from schooling—like reading-level, writing, and mathematical competencies—to demand educational audits, results, and the like are seen as ways to make the desired outcomes clear to all. Competency Based Teacher Education (CBTE), specification and observation of teaching practices, required diagnostic and prescriptive teaching techniques in the teaching of reading, detailed procedures to be followed in carrying out bilingual programs, and close monitoring to control the learner's time on task are examples of efforts to limit the teacher's discretion in determining how the prescribed objectives are to be achieved.

The View That School Organization Is Astonishingly Successful

Sociologists employing an institutional model of organizations make a very different case for school organizations than do critics of the school.[1] Institutionalists hold that school organizations have been spectacularly successful. Huge amounts of money are spent in a stable way to fund schools. School personnel have constancy, and programs show continuity. Unlike small businesses, of which nearly one-twelfth fail every year in the United States, schools almost never close. In spite of what many newspaper accounts would have one believe, parents, students, and the community at large express much satisfaction with their schools. Indeed fewer than 5 percent of the nation's population rate schools as failing.

Those using the institutional model distinguish between the technical organization of business and industry and the institutional organizations of schooling. Unlike the factory, school survival does not depend on a replicable production process that leads to a desired product. Instead, school organization survives only when it succeeds in meeting community expectations for what education is, thereby retaining high levels of legitimacy and support.

Traditionally, school managers do not try to achieve instructional ends but to attain legitimacy. Hence, school leaders must conform to public and professional expectations by seeking *accreditation,* giving more attention to the credentialing of a teacher than to the teacher's teaching effectiveness, prescribing in a very general way subjects or topics to be taught but not closely monitoring to see that this curriculum is actually taught or learned, and making sure that instruction occurs in buildings and classrooms in accordance with state laws. The longevity of schools that attempt reform is short. By way of example, two years is about as long as experimental schools in defiance of traditional definitions of schooling have lasted when they initiated procedures believed to be more effective—mixing old and young in pursuit of selected goals, making learners totally responsible for their

1. John W. Meyer and Brian Rowan, "Institutionalized Organization: Formal Structure as Myth and Ceremony," *American Journal of Sociology,* September 1977.

Karl E. Weick, "Educational Organization as Loosely Complex Systems," *Administrative Science Quarterly,* vol. 21, pp. 1–19, 1976.

Arthur E. Wise, "Why Educational Policies Often Fail: The Hyperrationalization Hypothesis," *Curriculum Studies,* vol. 9, no. 1, pp. 43–57, 1977.

decisions and actions, allowing the place of learning to depend on the interests of the group (welfare office, courtroom, or bakery). On the other hand, schools meeting accredited standards seem to go on unquestioned year after year.

The institutionalist believes that efforts by policymakers to make the schools conform to the model of technical organizations will fail for the following reasons:

1. The social system of the superintendent–principal–vice principal–supervisor is not closely coupled to the social system of the teacher–classroom–parent. The policymaking system shares few variables in common with the operating system. The different actors hold their own ideas about what education is and should be.
2. Managers of schools must keep their own members—teachers, pupils, parents—happy. To follow the technical models, mandating a single instructional procedure to be carried out in all schools creates much dissatisfaction.
3. "Top to bottom" control over both adopting and implementing innovations is costly. Adoption is relatively easy, but implementation—particularly of practices that do not seem valid to the practitioners and their clients—is very costly in terms of coordination, unpredictability, conflict, and the like. Further, such a practice is detrimental in that many desirable current innovations initiated by individual teachers and staff in particular schools are thereby lost.
4. To a far greater extent than industry, schools lack the technical capacity—knowledge—to achieve the goals set by policymakers.

RECONCILING TECHNICAL AND INSTITUTIONAL THEORIES OF ORGANIZATIONS

We believe that rational practices suggested by the technical model will best be implemented in schools by taking the institutional model into account. By way of example, Competency Based Education (CBE), whereby students must meet standards of proficiency in order to receive a high school diploma, is a growing movement. Mandating of proficiency standards with accompanying measures and curriculum is in accordance with accountability techniques of the technical organization. We believe that the operation of CBE will be implemented only when institutional criteria are met. The community and staff must regard CBE as a legitimate definition of education. Accreditation, certification, pupil classification, curriculum adoptions, and grading policies should signal the legitimacy of the effort. Only if CBE contributes to the reputation of the school and to the satisfaction of teachers, parents, and students will it become elaborated into the structure of the school.

Those voicing institutional theory are right when they say that leaders of school organizations go to the greatest length, not to accomplish instructional ends, but to maintain their schools' legitimate status as schools. Indeed the theme of this chapter is that it is essential that supervisors attend to the elements that link schools to the surrounding community in order to retain legitimacy and support.

THE FALL FROM FAVOR—A CASE STUDY

Although the following case study reveals weaknesses in supervision within the positive circumstances of growth, many supervisors are now facing unprecedented circumstances of decline. Declining enrollments, diminished resources, and public loss of confidence have brought new challenges to leadership.

Some see this kind of adversity as an opportunity. Culbertson, for example, believes that as the consequences of decline become more visible, people are more ready to make fundamental changes— a good opportunity for the supervisor to clarify directions and to articulate new values.[2] Further, it is easier to assess resources, use, and programs in times of adversity, making operations more efficient and programs more relevant. Cutbacks in programs offer opportunities to consolidate, revise, and develop new ones more in keeping with current educational capacity to recognize and accept the unpleasant—the ability to perceive and help others find potential in bleak circumstances—and not try to gloss over the situation.

William McCann is the top supervisor in a mushroomed school district. Instead of the three schools of six years ago, there are now seven. Although Mr. McCann rose in position with this growth, he now awaits dismissal. What went wrong?

The experienced school person knows what an accelerated gain in population means in supervision. Development of common outlooks, articulation of program, and orientation of staff members are problems of no mean size. Especially acute is the danger of shadow-boxing with the educational challenge, i.e., busying oneself with the administrative problems of plant construction, school finance, and business management while overlooking responsibility for decisions relative to curriculum.

Poor McCann! He and his supervising colleagues are stunned. They actually believed they had done a good job. Evidence in their behalf included new classrooms with the latest ideas in school architecture, neat schedules for the assignment of teachers and pupils to classes, and a variety of library and audiovisual materials. Faculty

2. Jack Culbertson, "Educational Leadership: The Uses of Adversity," *Theory into Practice*, vol. 15, no. 4, pp. 253–259, October 1976.

meetings, parent activities, workshops, and other usual trappings of modern schools had been initiated, too. The director of instruction had tried to see that procedures used in developing the instructional program were in accordance with what were believed to be the newer practices, practices presumed to reflect the findings of sociopsychological research and humanitarian points of view. Teachers were to be regarded as professional people, independently able to organize learning situations. The supervisory staff was available on a consultative basis. Supervisors were to offer help when asked but were not to intrude. The center for curriculum improvement was the individual school where the principal was vaguely defined as the "instructional leader," and targets for improvement were those noted by the teachers themselves.

Of course, McCann had heard of some dissatisfactions in the fast-growing system. There were always a few parents who felt that their children were not learning to read as well as they should. Principals knew, although they did not acknowledge the fact to the superintendent, that among the new teachers hired each year, there were those who were unhappy with existing conditions for teaching. Novices expressed the belief that they would like more direction from the district; others grumbled about the lack of standards and the fact that materials issued by the district and county were not articulated with approved state textbooks. Some teachers complained that it was difficult for them to "teach" because of the emphasis upon student activities. Typical official reaction to these protests was that (1) the central office staff had been too busy to develop instructional guides which would indicate anything but very general expected outcomes and suggested areas of study, and (2) teachers were free to teach as they thought best. The director of instruction was not too keen about curriculum guides anyway.

It is true that occasionally a curriculum worker or principal would voice concern that teachers and the special supervisors in art and music were not relating these fields to the regular instructional program. Too, principals eagerly commented about the way good ideas spread through their faculties. They mentioned the "creativity" shown by teachers in developing materials for the study of exotic countries. They called attention to the unusual instructional materials being introduced by teachers and praised them for their novel approaches to teaching. Diversity was in fact present. The practice of encouraging the pupils to read through self-selection of books was popular in one building, while science centers had captured the stage in nearly all rooms at another. But uniformity was present, too. In all classrooms pupils routinely filled notebooks with clippings from newspapers and magazines. They also spent more time in making the covers of these notebooks "pretty" than they did in organizing the contents in support of an important generalization. It was common practice for pupils to listen uncritically to committee reports and to ritualize their spelling.

Shortly after the stabilization of growth of the district, attacks began to center on McCann and his staff. During the conduct of a campaign for a school board election, charges of intellectual inadequacy in the school offerings were unusually vigorous. Lack of direction and continuity in the instructional program was singled out as evidence of poor supervision. Teachers were reported to be complaining about incoherent planning of the curriculum, and parents spoke of a hodgepodge of methods. Further, when the board demanded that immediate steps be taken "to improve the teaching of arithmetic and reading, to establish programs for talented youngsters, and to develop a philosophy of education for the district," the supervisors responded with platitudes about the importance of "meaningful experiences," and described some practices they thought were oustanding. Now, however, these vague generalities and the supervisors' descriptions of an isolated case were unacceptable. In fact, the supervisors were not really heard. With loss of the board's confidence, McCann and his staff are seeking other jobs.

And what went wrong? What theories can a supervisor use as a guide to action? Must the technical competence of the supervisor wait upon the teacher's request for help? Can a supervisor act upon the premises which reflect the human relations view and are supported by findings from research in group behavior, when the school board exercises its legal authority on the basis of other expectations and assumptions? Have recommended supervisory practices outdistanced the realities of power and authority? Is there no truth in principles of supervision founded on the assumption that faculty demoralization occurs when teachers are restricted in their own desire for freedom in the classroom?

Although there does not now exist the single conceptual framework for use by the supervisor in understanding all factors surrounding the "fall from favor," certain variables appear to be relevant. Political theories about power and decision making as well as sociological concepts of bureaucracy can help supervisors (1) establish boundaries within which they must work and (2) devise methods for dealing with some of their practical and immediate problems. To this end, we shall try in the remaining portions of this chapter to develop three propositions:

1. Tensions exist between *(a)* formal, legal, and political structures for the control of the school and *(b)* supervisory arrangements for

encouraging distributive and informal leadership in school affairs. Supervisors who emphasize any one of these structures in their practice to the exclusion of the others will fail.

2. There is likelihood that supervisors will be associated with low morale (dissatisfaction) if they foster false expectations regarding the nature of authority and participation in policymaking. They should therefore distinguish between *(a)* the process of deliberating policy, a policy which calls for the participation of those who have pertinent data to present (expertness), *(b)* the process of executing the policy, wherein legal responsibility for the act of decision and its implementation rests with designated officers, and *(c)* the process of judging the consequences of the decision, which requires the shared wisdom and political action of all affected.

3. The greater the accessibility of the instructional program to persons or agencies external to the school, the greater the difficulty of developing a continuous and systematic program required for the furtherance of the learners' intellectual development. Therefore, it is desirable to have a bureaucratic structure which protects the school from opportunistic influences.

A DEFINITION OF POWER

Power is the ability to propose and achieve objectives. In order to exercise power, one must be able to control the means to the ends sought. Such control may come through possession of material resources, general assent and assistance of others, the vision of a variety of future goals, as well as possession of well-tested knowledge and skills. In our society we have asserted that every individual should possess the right to seek power, although we recognize that individuals, groups, and communities differ in their opportunity and ability to attain it.

POLITICAL REALITIES AFFECTING THE SUPERVISORY POSITION

Supervisors' disregard of power outside the school not only jeopardizes their tenure but prevents them from participating in critical decisions regarding the character and program of the school. It leaves them and the school in a weakened position. Knowledge of power groups and the bias which underlies their judgment of curriculum gives supervisors the perspective with which to anticipate, assess, and influence demands which can alter the school and its tasks. In general, major policies in the local community are made by a top hierarchy. While the majority of citizens in most communities have difficulty in initiating and executing changes in the schools, those individuals who constitute the power structure use their power both

directly and indirectly on the board of education and the superintendency. Decision makers at the national level, too, are increasingly
exercising power in the schools by changing the way people perceive
education, supplying information and opinion in keeping with national policy. The increased emphasis on career education and on
multicultural and early childhood programs in schools is a consequence of positive coercive power, whether expressed through the
pronouncements of public figures or through the careful allocation
of money for particular causes.

The assignment of legal rights and responsibilities to officers at
each level of the school hierarchy illustrates the authoritative organization of the school. It is granted, of course, that the nominally supreme authority vested in officials rests ultimately on the political
expression of a popular vote.

Ignoring the position of formalized and external authority, some
supervisors have concentrated upon procedures in which authority is
assumed to reside in particular situations. In their minds, those who
work in a situation should determine appropriate outcomes as well
as means. There is merit in this belief, as evidenced by the desirable
consequences which occur when those affected by a decision
participate in its making. However, the principle is not sufficient. It
must be reconciled with political authority and adapted for dealing
with a variety of individuals. An overgeneralized acceptance of the
principle of self-determination contributed to McCann's predica-
ment. He was not able to relate the demands of traditional power to
the newer principles which minister to the individual staff member.

Three outcomes usually follow when equalitarian assumptions
and exclusive attention to internal processes of organization oversha-
dow the realities of the external and nonequalitarian structure. First,
goals set by individual faculties which are inconsistent with the goals
of the district organization and the larger community are certain to
be repudiated after much conflict and considerable cost to the persons involved, as in the case of McCann. In addition, supervisors
cannot well afford to ignore the school's hierarchial structure in
which special privileges and status differentials predominate. Certainly, supervisors should not give the impression that individual
teachers determine school policy. If each teacher acts independently,
there is no policy and disorder results. This is not to say that supervisors must not encourage wide participation in the determination of
purpose and procedure. Nor is it meant that teachers and faculties
should not be supported as they try new ideas and engage in self-
regulation. Rather it is facing the fact that no school group is autonomous in the setting of expected outcomes of instruction and that the
process of directing and overseeing the execution of public policy

with respect to the school presently rests with hierarchial and formal structures. These structures are not necessarily operating in accordance with theories of good human relations.

Second, there is often resentment when supervisors deny the existence of authoritative structure; it has become popular to play down authoritative supervision and to denounce the exercising of authority over others. Frequently, supervisors try to decrease the power visibility of their positions. This may reflect (1) a sincere interest in persons as ends in themselves, (2) a belief in the superiority of all men and women and the desire to fulfill presumed equalitarian norms, or (3) a calculated device to influence teachers by a more effective means, emotional blackmail. In these latter instances, supervisors try to obligate teachers to them by requesting cooperation even though they have the power to issue orders, tolerating prohibited practices, and showing an excessively considerate manner. The validity of these procedures has been questioned:[3]

> In their eagerness to be known as democratic administrators, some school principals deny that there is such a thing as a school hierarchy. But the denial does not alter the fact. Even though the superintendent prides himself on being a democratic administrator, even though he has decision-making groups within his school system and within his community, even though he has teacher-representation on many important committees and teacher-involvement in all phases of school administration and policy-making, notwithstanding all this democratic procedure, he is still the "head man" and is so considered by his teachers, supervisors, and custodians and by the people of the community. The hierarchy cannot be denied. Even if it were possible for such a superintendent or principal to throw off and to distribute all power and authority he would continue to be looked upon as a power figure, and, therefore, as something of a threat.
>
> Most teachers feel that it is important for school administrators to recognize the existence of the school hierarchy, to look at it, to talk about it, and to be aware of its faults and values. Surely it is helpful to teachers to be able to discuss the hierarchy with those persons at all steps in it, and to give them some thought to what it means for the work we do in in-service groups as well as in our classrooms.

Third, the effectiveness of schools and the morale of teachers are weakened when supervisors are not encouraged to examine the authority of their experience and knowledge. Some supervisors take for granted that all teachers have the ability to perceive objectives and

3. B. J. Kinnick et al., "The Teachers and the In-Service Education Program," *In-Service Education for Teachers, Supervisors, and Administrators,* Fifty-sixth Yearbook, part I, National Society for the Study of Education, The University of Chicago Press, Chicago, 1957, p. 141.

arrange appropriate learning situations independently. This is a mistake. Many teachers demand guidance when the novelty of the situation precludes their ego-involvement in particular procedures. For them, direction is not interpreted as a criticism of ability. One of the findings concerning leadership techniques is that morale is sometimes higher when supervisors are less permissive. It is necessary to admit the superior and technical wisdom of the supervisor. Recognition of varying degrees of expertness calling for the exercise of more power and authority is found in all professions.

It has been forcefully contended that educators are hypocritical when they say that all teachers are a community of equals in which the competence of the supervisor must wait upon the teacher's request for help.

Myron Lieberman believes:[4]

> The power structure of education should have an open and straightforward recognition of supervisors' technical competence where there are genuine differences in this respect; however, this does not mean that school administrators should have the power to tell teachers what and how to teach if and when the administrator has more formal training than the teachers. The school administrator with a doctor's degree may very well have had less training in mathematics and the teaching of mathematics than the mathematics teacher with only a few years of formal education. It does not make sense to give the administrator power to control content and methods even if his total training exceeds that of the teacher. The additional training must be functionally related to the behavior which is controlled. This is why the analysis has repeatedly insisted on the *inadvisability* of administrator control over instruction. Such control represents a splitting, not a fusion, of authority and technical competence. The administrator cannot know more about each and every subject and how to teach it than the teachers of the various subjects.
>
> Indeed, from a professional point of view, prevailing theories of administration and supervision should be reversed. The dominant trend is for the administrator (who tends to lack superior technical competence in instructional matters) to be vested with responsibility for the outcomes of instruction, whereas the supervisor (who presumably has superior technical competence in instruction) is being divested of power over teachers.

DECISION MAKING

Questions about the supervisor's power, authority, and responsibility center on decision making. We have already asked whether supervis-

---

4. Myron Lieberman, *Education as a Profession,* Prentice-Hall, Inc., Englewood Cliffs, N.J., 1956, p. 505.

ors, by virture of position, should make decisions regarding instructional practice without the participation of those teachers who must carry out the practice, and whether supervisors should participate in decisions regarding instructional policy.

It is impossible for one to participate in the formulation of all decisions affecting one's professional life. Whenever decisions are being made, those who have the greatest degree of expertness relative to the question at hand should be given an opportunity to contribute their knowledge. This does not mean that experts make the decision, although their data should influence it. We recognize that legal authorities or agents have responsibility for the actual decisions of policy and the execution of measures ensuring obedience. Wide participation should take place not in deciding policy but in judging the consequences of that policy. Registering of approval or disapproval of the consequences may occur through political channels. Too often supervisors and teachers have taken flight from political responsibility by conceiving their role as merely that of implementing whichever policies are defined. "The policy maker supplies the goals (ends, objectives) and we technicians, on the basis of our expert knowledge, indicate alternative means for reaching these ends." All teachers and supervisors have the obligation as citizens to influence policy through their political instruments, such as professional and political organizations. At the point of deliberating policy, however, the supervisor has special responsibility for helping authorities of the school system (1) bring policy into line with public laws and (2) make decisions on the basis of knowledge of instructional alternatives and their predicted consequences.

Supervisors should show initiative in providing relevant data to policymakers and by engaging in politics. The former is in keeping with their role of expert in predicting consequences. When an area of inquiry is opened by officials, the supervisor can exert leadership by focusing attention on certain alternative lines of action and by ascribing greater weight to certain types of evidence. A director of instruction, for example, who, in an early planning conference with a school board, points out the relative long-term cost of a remedial reading program as opposed to a developmental reading program is initiating influence over a top-level decision. When supervisors are called upon to implement a policy already formulated with respect to the teaching of reading, they are likely to act largely as technicians. When problems reach them at a late stage in the continuum of decision, they must carry out the prevailing decision even if it is ill-formed. Figure 4-1 depicts this rationale for decision making.

Admittedly, the locus of actual decision-making power is not

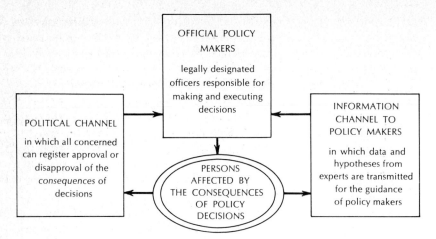

Figure 4-1   A decision-making framework.

always appropriately placed. Teachers want to accept responsibility for decision making, especially when the decisions relate to instruction and curriculum. Teachers feel that superintendents and boards of education assume more responsibility for deciding instructional matters than is desirable.[5] Too, many teachers as well as supervisors are concerned about indiscriminate decision making by both lay "advisory groups" and official status leaders who are making judgments without the requisite competence. It is necessary that our society admit the indispensability of expert judgment and that a degree of professional autonomy, a scope of independent judgment, be reserved to professional workers because of their expert skill and knowledge. If the decisions to be made require highly specialized intellectual training, the persons making the decisions should be professional experts. If the decision is primarily an ethical one which does not require expertness, then it should be a matter for a lay individual or agency to decide. Unfortunately, supervisors are not so likely to be considered experts as other specialists are. The far greater contingencies with which their problems deal make it very difficult for them to predict the consequences of the alternatives proposed. Because the school does not control all variables necessary to guide performance by pupils, school professionals find it difficult to speak with the authority of a science. Supervisors have accepted assumptions about process without really testing validity in terms of conse-

5. Chiranji Lal Sharma, "Practices in Decision-making as Related to Satisfaction in Teaching," unpublished Ph.D. dissertation, University of Chicago, Chicago, 1955.

quences, and, therefore, they are unable to defend their judgments with real evidence.

There is a reluctance of supervisors to question their own practice. Supervisors and teachers alike follow a prescientific concept of evidence, supporting practice with anecdote and analogy or appealing to a prevalent platitude, e.g., "individualized instruction," "meeting the child's needs," "moral education." Technical management with its emphasis upon accountability was partly undertaken to make practitioners assess the consequences of their teaching methods.

Further, supervisors are likely to be dealing with problems about which others are convinced they too have considerable knowledge. Usually, however, those in the top hierarchy have control over such a range of interrelated matters that the complex can be dealt with only in aggregative form. For instance, the school board may decide to emphasize reading, leaving specific programs to be developed at lower levels of the organization. Staff participation in decision making generally takes place in connection with the development of these specified programs. Numerous considerations originally not taken into account by policymakers require decisions by teachers and others when policy is translated into action in the classroom.

Under certain conditions, staff participation in decision making at the action level helps the teacher identify with the program and its purposes, ensuring that the proposal gets a fair trial and increasing the quality of the decision. A key advantage to shared decision making is that through participation with the staff and coming face-to-face with the individual problems of the teacher, supervisors may extend their own perspective. Ideally, wide participation in decision making may result in a better decision because of (1) the increased range of alternatives likely to result, (2) the inclusion of factors which contribute to the workability of the decision, and (3) the increased attractiveness of the idea to those who will be expected to carry out the decision. In reality, the conditions which make these propositions valid are difficult for the supervisor to arrange even when hierarchial factors are not considered. The topic of procedures for effective and efficient group decision making is itself so important that we shall treat it at length in Chapter 5. For the time being, our point is that decision making by a group of teachers and supervisors takes place in the context of a political system which in turn must develop its strategy with awareness of the rules and government of a larger society and in response to the demands of an unseen public. Procedures for shared decision making should be encouraged only after recognition of the limits of authority available to participants. Teachers and supervisors are governed by official leaders, and these leaders are in turn controlled by law.

THE SCHOOL'S BUREAUCRATIC STRUCTURE

The achievement of favorable long-term results requires an organizational structure which ensures consistency in operations and protects the school from both external and internal opportunism.

One way of ordering such a structure is through the development of a bureaucratic mechanism which induces an impersonal and rational orientation to the instructional task. Many teachers actually feel more powerful in their school when the school system is perceived as being more bureaucratic.[6] If the school can develop some rules of its own, it will be better able to guarantee the permanence and impartiality of thought and organization necessary for the logical progression of educational experiences leading to desired educational objectives. Pressure groups and self-oriented teachers who enthusiastically promote their favored ideas at the expense of planned educational experiences must be regulated by bureaucratic aspects in the school. A bureaucracy can also protect those teachers who are legitimately serving their function as vicars of the community by offering experiences and ideas of higher quality than are commonly available and by aiding students in the formation of concepts with which to interpret events around them critically. Without this protection, the community might lack the self-criticism necessary for survival. As a matter of fact, however, the school is never an independent social system. As indicated in the case of McCann, the crucial interrelationship is between the organization of the school and the larger external environment rather than the internal alone. Development of a strong bureaucratic organization is only a partial defense to ensure maintenance of the school's values.

Supervisors who work with teachers in extending purposes and developing a cooperating organization are part of the bureaucracy and have a responsibility for its continuance. In this connection, a supervisor has the duty to secure the teacher's compliance with tasks as defined by the system.

A Bureaucracy Protects against External Forces

The school defends itself against external forces in several ways.[7] It tries to separate itself from other government institutions. It seeks to maintain separate elections, separate budgets, and separate taxes. It isolates itself from other administrative agencies such as police and welfare. Supervisors and teachers also use the board of education as a buffer between the school and other community forces. As seen in Table 4-1, it is through bureaucratic structure and rules that protection is afforded.

6. G. Moeller, "Bureaucracy and Teachers' Sense of Power," *Administrator's Notebook,* vol. 11, pp. 1–4, 1962.
7. D. Wallace Stanley Sayre, "Additional Observations on the Study of Administration," *Teachers College Record,* no. 60, p. 73, November 1958.

TABLE 4-1   CONTRAST BETWEEN STRONG AND WEAK STRUCTURE

PROTECTIVE FEATURES OF BUREAUCRACY	STATUS OF ORGANIZATION INVITING ATTACK
1. "The regular activities required for the purposes of the bureaucratically governed structure are distributed in a fixed way as official duties."*	Supervisory staff members are unclear in their duties for instructional improvement and are not assigned on the basis of expertness. Principals who are limited in their knowledge of curriculum are designated as instructional leaders. Curriculum experts are not playing roles in keeping with their knowledge.
2. "A specified sphere of competence... has been marked off as part of a systematic division of labor. . . ."†	Responsibility for the selection and organization of curriculum is not defined in precise terms. Teachers, principals, consultants, directors of instruction, and superintendents do not check on the professional competency of participants by noting consequences of individual performances.
3. The official "is subject to strict and systematic discipline and control in the conduct of his office."	Mechanics for rendering systematic accountability of instructional practice and for directing attention are missing.
4. "The organization of offices follows the principle of hierarchy; that is, each lower office is under the control and supervision of a higher one."	The assistant superintendent of instruction has no control over principals; the supervisor is "on call" to teachers.
5. Officials are "subject to authority only with respect to their impersonal official obligations."	Some attempts at controlling personal matters of teachers are made by principals. Although these attempts are rationalized as important to the effectiveness of instruction, there is no evidence that these general variables are related to the learning of pupils.
6. "Candidates [for bureaucratic positions] are selected on the basis of technical qualifications. In the most rational case, this is tested by examinations, or guaranteed by diplomas certifying technical training, or both. They are appointed, not elected."	Personnel officers make efforts to do this, but political considerations affect the standard of the minimum level of competence a teacher should have, and ambiguous criteria are used for the selection of supervisors. High turnover in staff evidences that positions are not regarded as permanent. Criteria for achievement are not defined.

*Max Weber, *Essays in Sociology*, trans. and ed. by Hans Gerth and C. Wright Mills, Oxford University Press, New York, 1946, p. 196.

†This quotation and all others following it in this table are taken from Talcott Parsons (ed.), *Max Weber: The Theory of Social and Economic Organization*, trans. by A. M. Henderson and Talcott Parsons, Oxford University Press, New York, 1947, pp. 330–334.

Weber has specified that all operations should be governed by a consistent system of abstract rules. But teaching cannot be circumscribed by rules that do away with the need for exercising judgment. Rationality in the school program will occur by specifying results rather than techniques. We might also add that it is easier to specify outcomes than procedures when teachers have more skills and understandings relevant to the instructional task than do supervisors.

Pathologies of Bureaucracy

Thus far we have indicated that the bureaucratic structure is advantageous to the school and to the achievement of educational goals. Opposition to this kind of structure comes from those who have been frustrated by the bureaucracy in their attempt to capture the system in furtherance of their particular interests, but disadvantages of bureaucratic structures have also been found.

Excesses of bureaucratic behavior prevent schools from being responsive to need and change. Schools and staff are characterized by routinism imposed by a seedy tradition, complacency, and inertia following a long period of success. Supervisors and teachers are engaging in heel dragging after feigned acquiescence because of their desire to keep the old ways.

There are other "unanticipated" responses within the school bureaucracy, such as these:

1. Evaluation and promotion are made more often on the basis of seniority than of achievement, inasmuch as the supervisor reacts to the teacher as a representative of a position, i.e., the teacher is characterized by such classifications as first year, probationary, permanent, physical education, English, or mathematics teacher. The teacher has certain rights and duties, not as an individual or a superior teacher, but by virtue of classification.
2. Procedures originally desired to achieve educational goals assume a positive value independent of these goals. Means become ends; routine becomes a passion. A particular way of grouping pupils for instruction, for instance, is validated by habit and opinion rather than by consequences.
3. "The trouble with education is hardening of its categories." Although categorizing is a basic part of thinking, school men and women tend to restrict the categories they use to a small number rather than search for other categories that might be applied. Reliance upon the single concept of IQ as a measure of intellectual development is an illustration.
4. Interorganizational conflicts occur as departments and special service branches try to make their subgoals a part of the official doctrine for the system and to legitimize their demands. Also, special

supervisors can be so intent on their own specialty that they are oblivious to the total task. Upon occasion, a "tail" activity wags the school.

Imbalance between the concerns of the school organization and the individual has been a chief cause of pathological behavior in the school and an area of inquiry about what "teaching does to the teacher." When self-expression of the teacher or supervisor is artificially limited by the work environment, and superior effort receives no recognition, the teacher or supervisor tends to disintegrate, becoming recessive and insecure while showing aggression toward others. When there is excessive institutional concern for rules and ritual, prolonged occupancy of a teaching position results in depersonalization and rigidity.

Tongue in cheek, John Gall concludes that we do not yet understand the basic laws governing the behavior of complex organizations. His systemantics research into the causes of organizational ineptitude and systems malfunction leads to these observations:[8]

1. Things generally are not working well. In fact they never did.
2. People in a system do not do what the system says they are doing.
3. The system itself does not do what it says it is doing.
4. Even the most complex system has an unsuspected way of failing.
5. Things are what they are reported to be. If it isn't official, it hasn't happened.
6. To those within a system, the outside reality tends to pale and disappear.
7. The bigger the system, the narrower and more specialized the interface with individuals.
8. Cum and McBee cards and other records are not pupils. Professional activities often reduce teacher interaction time with pupils.
9. The system always kicks back. One cannot afford to state real personal goals in response to demands for goals and objectives. Instead one must at all costs avoid giving the impression of being an ineffective putterer or a dilettante. After committing onself in writing to goals and objectives, it is possible to spend waking and working hours achieving them most efficiently—no more puttering around chasing spontaneous impulses and temporary enthusiasms. An efficient worker will move from sub-objective A to sub-objective B in logical pursuit of K, which in turn leads toward the overall goal. One can be graded, not only on achievements for the year, but on the efficiency with which one moves toward each objective.
10. In a complex system, malfunction may not be detectable for long periods, if ever.

11. A system that performs a certain function or operates in a certain way will continue to operate that way regardless of the need or of changed conditions.

12. Any large system is going to be operating most of the time in failure mode. The key questions are: "How does it work when its components aren't working well? How does it fail? How well does it function in failure mode?" A system can fail in an infinite number of ways. When a fail-safe system fails, it fails by failing to fail-safe.

13. Some complex systems actually function. If a system is working, leave it alone.

IMPLICATIONS FOR SUPERVISION

The school is a social organization within which individuals cannot always teach what they please because of the internal restrictions imposed by bureaucratic rules and the external restrictions that come from interrelating with other social organizations in the community. Supervisors have two major problems: (1) the coordination of the instructional activities of the classroom teachers and school units to maximize sequential articulation and ensure reasonable uniformity of outcomes and (2) the maintenance of enough latitude within the public consistuency and its agent, the board of education, for the exercise of professional judgments regarding, first, what kinds of specific objectives best serve the students and the constituency and, second, what procedures are best adapted to these ends.[9]

McCann did not succeed in meeting either of the problems. The following are suggested guidelines by which supervisors can strengthen the social organization of the school in such a way that the institution can maintain itself and at the same time enhance the society and pupils it professes to serve.

Supervisors can submit their beliefs and the beliefs of the teachers to empirical tryout. The potentiality of the school has been weakened by those who have assumed that the organization for instruction can be improvised. Supervisors can take responsibility for establishing patterns for an expanding development of educational content. They should not permit individual teachers and schools to engage in activity without observing where it is leading, checking by precise methods the consequences for learners.

In order that pupils may become skilled and mature persons who are able to control their environment, attention should be given to the orderly development and organization of experiences and subject matter, enhancing a cumulative effect in learning. The significant questions to ask concerning any school system are "Who has respon-

9. Charles E. Bidwell, "A New Dilemma in Administration," *Harvard Educational Review*, vol. 26, no. 4, p. 400, Fall 1956.

sibility to identify the behavior to be acquired and the concepts to be learned?" "Who is best qualified to select particular instructional experiences, opportunities, and the like?" "How is the effectiveness of these learning experiences determined and by whom?" "Who is responsible for seeing that learners will meet a program designed to provide instructional continuities and relationships?" "Who will make the evaluations necessary for determining the next steps?" "Who will take the long look ahead?"

Supervisors should not be afraid to make suggestions. If they do not share their larger experiences and wider horizon, they are negligent. They do not have to abuse their office, but they can use their ideas as a starting point for a better plan that evolves from a reciprocal give-and-take with others. Supervisors can be aware of and use the capacities and past experiences of those with whom they work.

Closeness of supervision should vary from individual to individual, depending upon one's ability to frame purposes and arrange means to put the school's ends into operation.

The supervisor must be a realist with respect to authority. Authority is accepted whenever the behavior is guided by a decision without independent examination of its merits. When exercising authority, supervisors need not try to convince but only obtain acquiescence.[10] Authority is sometimes defined as the right to make decisions which guide the action of another. Usually it is accompanied by attempts at persuasion and suggestion. However, since persuasion and suggestion permit examination of the merits of the proposal, they are categorized as attempts at influence rather than as acts of authority. An important advantage of authority is that it permits a decision to be made and carried out when agreement cannot be reached.

Authority is useful in prescribing certain types of action and can be employed to enforce responsibility. For example, authority is present when teachers follow prescribed procedures for selecting instructional materials, resource persons, and field trips. It serves also to prevent teachers from getting conflicting commands from a principal and a curriculum coordinator.

Teachers and principals must do more than share common goals; their behavior must be coordinated. Their individual plans must be combined or at least be consistent. Authority secures the centralization necessary for the development of those plans which (1) define appropriate roles for school personnel and (2) establish premises for the selection of content and activity.

10. Chester I. Barnard, *The Functions of the Executive,* Harvard University Press, Cambridge, Mass., 1938, p. 163.

In dealing with problems which arise because teachers are unwilling to cooperate in the attainment of system goals, and problems associated with decline in staff morale, it is suggested that the supervisor offer an outlet for personal capability within the formal structure by diffusing leadership responsibility and authority. Teachers might be encouraged to share in decisions regarding operational procedures. Valuable as this supervisory technique is, it does not remove the necessity for a hierarchial authority. There are legal limitations. Decisions made by individual faculties must often be modified so that they become part of an overall general plan. Under these conditions, the supervisor cannot be an equal with teachers in all problem-solving situations. When, for instance, faculty groups present conflicting value premises, the supervisor must have the requisite authority to resolve the conflict.

Let there be no mistake about it. Shared leadership in supervision is an important tool to be used either for the furtherance of freedom or for the manipulation of others. It should, however, be used only with consideration for other aspects of the social system, especially political and legal realities.

CHAPTER 5

EFFECTIVENESS AND EFFICIENCY IN SCHOOLS

Conflict between the organization of the school and the wishes of the instructional staff has resulted in undesirable consequences, such as personal disintegration of the teacher and failures to change. This chapter discusses aspects of the social structure of the school which are related to both efficiency and effectiveness. Efficiency refers to the extent to which the school provides satisfaction to its members; effectiveness means the degree to which the school achieves its purposes.

MORALE AND SOCIAL STRUCTURE OF THE SCHOOL

Morale is regarded as the attitude and behavior which denote a willingness to be involved in the school and its work. Attempts to relate high morale to achievement have failed to reveal consistent relationships. High morale is not a sufficient condition for excellence in achievement. Nevertheless, because morale is valuable as an end in itself, supervisors try to structure for it.

Supervisors find these generalizations helpful in their structuring:[1]

1. Goodwin Watson, "Five Factors in Morale," in Goodwin Watson (ed.), *Civilian*

1. *A sense of positive goal.* Without a sense of purpose, activity seems unclear, and teachers do not become involved. There must be a magnetic pole for drawing the aspirations of teachers. Definition of goals is a task to which all should contribute.
2. *Mutual support.* If several teachers are engaged in a purposeful and common task, they probably will feel a greater sense of support than if they work on unrelated activities.
3. *A sense of commitment.* Complacency about the schools and the values schools represent is a liability. Teachers should be helped to feel a personal commitment to theoretical ideals about the purpose of schooling, who should be educated, methods of instruction, and the like, and be ready to defend them at any cost.
4. *A sense of contribution.* The supervisor has to find ways to help individuals contribute to group tasks and reward them for their efforts. Eventual achievement of a task which is not a sure thing brings the greatest reward.
5. *A sense of progress.* Supervisors should emphasize the amount of progress, thus providing an awareness of results. Progress is measured by determining how much distance has been covered and must yet be covered to reach the goals. Supervisors are usually the ones to evaluate progress because of their perspective and knowledge of assessment procedures. It is not enough to have a goal and know that there are techniques for reaching it; one must feel a sense of achievement toward the goal. Too, morale is much stronger when teachers see that they have the competence to improve existing conditions.

EMPHASIS UPON PARTICIPATION IN DECISION MAKING

The success of industrial experimentation which provided for group members to participate in decisions quickly led to similar practice in school supervision. It is recalled that one of the most talked-about experimental examples of action by participation supported the hypothesis that participation in the decision to effect change would overcome group resistance to the change and lead to higher productivity.[2] Perhaps the findings from studies of small group behavior were applied too readily to school situations. We have already mentioned the difficulties involved when a school system disregards the authority-possessing power which lies outside the enterprise. At the systemwide level, at least, supervisors should heed the traditional hierarchial forms necessary for economic and political reasons. Also,

---

Morale, Second Yearbook, Society for the Psychological Study of Social Issues, Holt, Rinehart and Winston, Inc., New York, 1942, pp. 30–47.

2. Lester Coch and John R. P. French, "Overcoming Resistance to Change," *Human Relations,* vol. 1, no., 4, pp. 512–532, 1948.

at the school level, the principal who attempts to act as a spontaneous group leader and to encourage equal participation faces the fact that equality does not exist within the framework of the school hierarchy.

Nevertheless, there is much evidence that participation in decision making is a powerful force for modifying the behavior of a group. It is far from clear why participation is so effective. The motivation and the change brought about by participation are explained in these general ways: teachers see themselves and their teaching in a new light; participating groups themselves improve communication within the school organization; and teachers get a more realistic picture of the importance of problems and practices within the system.

Explanation of the basic factors which underlie the relation between participation procedure and goal acceptance is only a beginning. Although participation increases the likelihood that a goal will be set which is congruent with individual goals, sometimes individual preferences are set as one engages in group participation. There is the possibility that discussion leads to more adequate knowledge of the goal and its value to participants as well as a more realistic view of its attainability.[3] Perhaps, too, a positive evaluation of the goal is derived from hearing that other members value it.

Logically, we might expect that when supervisors directly communicate decisions without prior consultation, there would be more consistent behavior, fewer alternative ends and means, than when free and equal discussion is stimulated. The fact that this does not occur and that participation does not lead to any departure from a system's goals and means has been explained in two ways.[4] First, there is often a cultural attitude which makes at least token participation in decisions a condition for their acceptance. The less the visibility of power differences, the less the resistance. Second, where there is participation, the setting permits the organizational hierarchy to control in part what is proposed. There is a kind of human relations which is manipulative rather than affective. Inasmuch as teachers will plan anyway, better to have a supervisor present to influence this planning.

Acceptance of goals is heightened by a goal-setting procedure involving participation or at least the feeling that one has the opportunity to participate if one desired. It may be that the possibility of

3. Harold H. Kelley and John W. Thibault, "Experimental Studies of Group Problem Solving and Process," in Gardner Lindzey (ed.), *Handbook of Social Psychology,* vol. II, Addison-Wesley Publishing Company, Inc., Reading, Mass., 1954, p. 757.
4. James G. March and Herbert A. Simon, *Organizations,* John Wiley & Sons, Inc., New York, 1958, p. 54.

participation is more important than the actual participation.[5] Actual influence over a decision being made is often of less importance to individuals than acknowledgment of their influential positions.

INFORMAL STRUCTURE IN THE SCHOOL

Informal structure is represented by those interpersonal relations in the school that affect both its effectiveness and its efficiency. It includes the personal relations that develop among teachers and supervisors, such as cliques and friendship groups. Informal groups are the source of much social control. They are able to exercise power or set expectations which may or may not be at variance with the formal organization of the school.

The "bungalow boys," a group of teachers located in temporary buildings at an expanding school plant, were able to develop their own pattern of behavior, resisting the goals and processes being furthered by official leaders of the school. These rebelling teachers expressed their indifference by ignoring topics of general school interest and instead focused on subjects which were irrelevant to the organization. Even little requests, like asking for the prompt return of audio-visual equipment, were met with grumblings by those in this informal group.

On the other hand, a group of primary teachers who lunched together and shared ideas and instructional materials set expectations that called for each member to work in school after 3:30 P.M. to participate in school-community activities, and to perform other tasks peripheral to the instructional task but held as desirable by the school hierarchy.

Sometimes these influential informal groups are formed along subject-matter lines, e.g., cliques of teachers of English or teachers of physical education. Again, the individual school or teachers' club within a district comprises the informal structure. The traditions, status system, routines, and communication patterns of informal groups are seldom spelled out like those which appear in the handbooks issued by the district and school. But the unofficial leaders within these groups frequently exercise more power than supervisors in summoning teachers to action, either negatively or positively. Facetious comments by informal leaders belittling a suggested curriculum change can destroy official plans; support by these leaders can create a climate of acceptance. An important implication for supervisors is

5. D. G. Marquis, H. Guetzkow, and R. W. Heyns, "A Social Psychological Study of the Decision-making Conference," in H. Guetzkow (ed.), *Groups, Leadership, and Men*, Carnegie Press, Carnegie Institute of Technology, Pittsburgh, 1951, pp. 55–67.

that they should learn as much as possible about the informal structure of their own situations.

Conflict between Individual and Organizational Demands

Perhaps the most helpful way of interpreting informal groups, suggesting appropriate ways of working with them, is to regard them as reaction to a conflict between the individual's personal desires and the demands of the school organization. Whenever teachers join a system, they give up some individual freedom concerning the values and objectives that guide their individual decisions. The teacher must acquire an organizational personality which ensures that personal actions will be consistent with the decisions of the system. Efforts of different persons must be coordinated if instructional consequences are to be maximized. Organizational restrictions upon individual teachers are entirely proper when the consequences of teaching extend beyond the immediate classroom situation. Those entering teaching must abide by a set of ground rules regulating their behavior as teachers. For example, the individual teacher may believe that only those who can profit from an education should receive it; but in that teacher's institutional role the teacher must carry out the practices which show the most promise for making education profitable to all. But whenever the school system attempts to impose pressures for action which are seen as exceeding those necessary for the institutional task, teachers should not be expected to behave as organization creatures.

Conflict between individuals and the framework of the school may be most productive. If there were no protest by teachers against the organizational pattern, the institution would lose one of its strongest safeguards—self-correction.

We assume that human beings are always striving for "self-actualization," a tendency to maintain themselves and to guarantee the constancy of personality. Hence there is likely to be incongruence between the needs of a mature personality and the requirements of formal organization.[6] Healthy teachers will experience frustration, conflict, and failure when they (1) have minimized control over instruction, (2) are expected to be passive and subordinate, (3) deal predominately with decisional situations of short-time perspective, and (4) are induced to perfect and use a few shallow abilities. Informal structures serve as a partial remedy for these conditions, mitigating feelings of dependence. Informal relationships mark the attempt on the part of the individual teachers to salvage their own directions,

6. Chris Argyris, *Personality and Organization,* Harper & Row, Publishers, Incorporated, New York, 1957.

a means by which one can take an active role in influencing the formal organization. Without informal organization, the teachers may become indifferent to the quality of their teaching. "Given no responsibility, he showed none; treated as an automaton, he behaved as such."[7]

Supervisory Reaction to Resistance by Informal Groups

There is always danger that in rejecting what appears to be antagonistic behavior of informal groups, supervisors will develop programs negatively rather than positively. When this happens, of course, supervisors are being guided by that which is rejected instead of constructively developing a sound program. How should a supervisor react to informal groups who resist improvement by showing apathy, disloyalty, lack of enthusiasm, or who give their attention to ways of bettering personal status instead of giving time to the welfare of students? Three common responses and their predicted consequences are these:

1. *Restrictive reaction.* This reaction is a crackdown. There is a reduction in personalized relationships and an increase in the use of trappings of authority. Rule making is more common, and supervision is closer. Supervisors communicate the system's policies and practices clearly to teachers and make it known that evaluation of teachers will be strictly and honestly in accordance with these policies and practices.

   The impact of the crackdown upon teachers does not always bring the results desired. While teachers tend to become more passive and centered upon the organizational goal, they are also likely to be anxious about the future and rigid in their behavior.[8] Rules, for example, provide cues for teachers beyond those intended by the supervisor. By defining unacceptable behavior, supervisors may also increase knowledge about minimum acceptable behavior. It is hypothesized that the disparity between the ideal goals of the school and the minimum acceptable effort being made by teachers is about as disconcerting as the original condition, leading to even closer supervision and a higher tension level in the informal group. That is, in setting a minimum performance level, supervisors do not really want teachers to conform only to the specified level; they want each teacher to achieve maximum potential. The able teacher who does just what is required and no

7. Ibid., p. 34.
8. Clyde M. Campbell, *Practical Applications of Democratic Administration,* Harper & Row, Publishers, Incorporated, New York, 1952, pp. 107–108.

more is still seen as resisting, a behavior which often invites further negative restriction on the part of the supervisor.

There are some grounds, however, for the belief that imposed structure and direction aid the faculty in solving problems of complex patterns which require decisions in early phases, inasmuch as the supervisor is able to induce all teachers to proceed from a single initial conception.

2. *Persuasive reaction.* Persuasion is that approach to informal group adaptation which tries to sell teachers on the value of official leadership and its goals through "human relations" by *(a)* giving teachers confidence in themselves and a feeling of belonging, *(b)* giving teachers a proper understanding of their task and accentuating positive aspects of the work, and *(c)* keeping teachers informed of progress being made in improving their working conditions.

Under this approach, programs which stress "communication" and "participation" are exemplified in workshops, conferences, social activities, and joint projects such as beautification of the school grounds. Channels for keeping teachers informed of the supervisor's action on teachers' problems are maintained because "it pays good dividends in building a feeling that someone is concerned about how staff members feel and is spending effort to help them." Teachers are told that they are important and that the supervisors are truly interested in them. Participation by teachers is encouraged in noncritical meetings. This participation usually lacks give-and-take expression and offers no rejection of the district's plans. Teachers do not openly challenge official leadership.

Group spirit is "built" by increasing the number of social occasions in which the staff gets together and by keeping the faculty informed about special contributions that individuals are making. The worth and importance of each individual is stressed, but derogatory remarks and hostile feelings are not vocalized. In bulletins or talks to teachers, supervisors make sure the content of their communication deals with the school's interests and specifies the response they seek.

An interesting variation in the process by which formal authorities react to a hiatus between consent and control is "cooptation."[9] Cooptation occurs when those teachers who reflect the sentiments of the informal group or have the confidence of relevant dissenters are brought into a leadership position within the

---

9. Philip Selznick, "Strengthening Leadership in Cooptation," in Robert Dubin (ed.), *Human Relations in Administration,* Prentice-Hall, Inc., Englewood Cliffs, N.J., 1951, pp. 23–340.

formal organization as a means of winning consent. Respect for those in control and the establishment of stability are, of course, expected to follow. The practice of appointing key figures in teacher groups to school administrative committees is a case in point. Individuals coopted share in the responsibility for power but ordinarily do not hold power themselves.

There are three criticisms of this persuasive approach. First, a faulty assumption underlies each procedure, namely, that teachers are at fault, not the formal organization or leadership. The fact that the school bureaucratic structure might need changing rather than the teachers' attitudes is not considered. Second, the procedure assumes that it is good to reward those who do as the district wants and that teachers should feel dependent, passive, and grateful to official leaders. Third, the approach has many unanticipated consequences. Teachers do not express their true feelings because they might not be "pretty" or "nice." This makes it difficult for supervisors to know about concerns which are vital to the success of the school system. Critical discontent, which could serve to strengthen the school organization if overtly recognized and valued, often comes out in covert expressions of disloyal and destructive attack upon the schools and their operations. Fourth, appeals to one's "professional attitude" in connection with projects which are not seen by the teacher as important lead to a corruption of the term "professionalization," and it becomes "exploitation." As one teacher said, "When the principal prefaces a request with the comment, 'You are a professional person,' I know I'd better watch out." Telling teachers they are important when they see that they have little responsibility may only increase their dissatisfaction and the antagonistic behavior within the informal group.

3. *Nondirective reaction.* Supervisors who react to teachers' withdrawal or other forms of protest by advocating equal participation in decision making are likely to hold the belief that individuals are more important than the institution and that the development of teachers is the chief end of supervision. From this viewpoint they develop principles stressing nondirective and group-centered approaches which call for *(a)* listening, helping others clarify thoughts and arrive at their own decisions; *(b)* understanding individuals rather than conquering them; *(c)* noting the growth and self-insight achieved by individuals, instead of trying to achieve predetermined goals quickly; *(d)* encouraging individuals to determine their own goals and the means they intend to use to achieve these goals; and *(e)* recognizing conflict and tensions, knowing that when feelings are expressed and discussed better understanding can result.

Acting upon these principles, the supervisor believes that responsibility for change and development rests with the individual teacher. The supervisor is concerned with developing the potentialities of teachers so that they may become more capable of constructive self-direction, freeing them from overdependence on the skills and insight of the supervisor. Therefore, supervisors are careful not to usurp initiative, self-confidence, and interest in a particular solution to the group task because they know that teachers will then show less of this behavior than they otherwise would. In casting aside an official role, the supervisor tries to be free from teachers' need for dependence and to reduce their anxiety about the outcomes of the action.

In meeting with the faculty group, the supervisor accepts the group at its existing developmental stage and places responsibility upon the members for planning its future life. By suspending one's own ideas, the supervisor has no need to get them across and is free to "be the other person." Meanings are made clear as the supervisor reflects contributions and relates them to previous ones. This supervisory process brings a reduced threat of devaluation; teachers achieve a clearer expression of ideas and open their minds to new understandings, thinking more flexibly. In listening, the supervisor neither agrees nor disagrees, avoiding expressions that convey intent to influence, such as "You might try this" or "That is a good idea." The supervisor recognizes that approving statements may threaten and embarrass, as well as further the teacher's dependency. In answering factual questions, the supervisor responds in a manner that demonstrates an interest in helping teachers reach good solutions rather than in protecting his or her own prestige.

As noted in Chapter 4, it is unrealistic to give exclusive attention to the point of view that supervisors should focus upon the development of teachers through informal leadership. The principles for working with individual teachers in informal group settings are different from those to be used in working within the formal organization. The pattern of action centering on individuals and the informal group constitutes only a part of the school's social system. Group-centered leadership must be weighed against the political structure of the school. But perhaps the chief objection to the nondirective approach is that the school is not primarily a psyche organization in which the interaction of teachers is itself the object of membership. When groups are permitted to focus on purely personal goals rather than on the common task, there is less satisfaction with each other, with the leader, and with the decisions reached.[10] For some groups, designated leaders' con-

10. N. T. Fouriezos, M. L. Hutt, and H. Guetzkow, "Measurement of Self-oriented

trol over procedures and the extent to which they alone perform leadership functions is directly related to satisfaction of members.[11] When there is an opportunity to become more autonomous, many become confused and anxious perhaps because of the increased responsibility. The consequences of any style of supervision are affected by the expectations of members and outsiders concerning how the supervisor's role should be performed.

4. *The inclusive reaction.* Supervisors who view their tasks as inclusive make every effort to link individual, small group, and bureaucratic structure. They combine the authority of their office with persuasion and personal influence. The principle of operation is best represented by an adaptation of "the law of marginal antisepsis":[12] Whatever is undertaken in order to attain the objectives of the school must at least be harmless to the individual teacher; whatever is done for the good of the individual or the informal group is at least harmless to the school and its tasks. Since school life is multidimensional, supervisors vary behavior. They offer warm acceptance to the individual but make it known that the teacher is accountable for achievement of the system's goals. Emphasis upon maintaining a friendly atmosphere is not pushed beyond the point where it reduces effectiveness. Innovation is encouraged along with the demands for attainment of prescribed ends. Supervisors do not hesitate to use "buddy-buddy" groups, coffee-drinking groups, faculty cliques, and standing committees in furthering tasks, nor are they indifferent to weakness in the bureaucratic structure which shows itself in faculty indifference, buck-passing, laziness, and other forms of resistance.

Inclusive supervisors recognize that the school by its very nature will have conflicts, but they hope to reduce these conflicts by understanding what they are. Supervisors come to an understanding with teachers about the areas of authority which they retain for themselves and the limits of decision making delegated to teachers. Within the latter limits, teachers must accept consequences of their actions.

Obviously, inclusive behavior requires that a supervisor be highly adaptable, keenly sensitive to varied situations. Ability to diagnose the dynamics of the organization, groups, and individuals is necessary for combining the imposed structure for supervi-

Needs in Discussion Groups," *Journal of Abnormal and Social Psychology,* vol. 45, no. 4, pp. 682–690, 1950.

11. L. Berkowitz, "Sharing Leadership in Small Decision-making Groups," *Journal of Abnormal and Social Psychology,* vol. 48, pp. 231–238, 1953.

12. George V. Sheviakov and Fritz Redl, *Discipline for Today's Children and Youth,* Association for Supervision and Curriculum Development, Washington, 1956, p. 25.

sion and the voluntary motivation of the teacher. Assessment of the school situation is enhanced by understanding of specific factors which affect effectiveness and efficiency.

SPECIFIC FACTORS DETERMINING EFFECTIVE AND EFFICIENT OPERATIONS

A variety of factors may determine the degree to which a staff working together fulfills its purpose and at the same time provides individual satisfaction. In the paragraphs which follow we shall indicate the manner in which such factors as clarity of goals, types of task, size of group, and friendship relations affect the quality of the work accomplished. Throughout the discussion, however, one should remember the distinctions already made between the two kinds of groups: (1) the informal group, in which any person may be the leader and be able to direct and control others in the pursuit of a cause and in which there is also a shared feeling of concern and (2) the formal group, in which the position of leadership is maintained by the organization and in which the objectives of the group are arbitrarily set rather than internally determined by the teachers themselves.

A supervisor must also keep in mind the dangers of generalizing findings from research on small-group behavior to problem-solving groups in school settings. The tasks performed by groups which exist for experimental purposes of the researcher are often less complex than those presented to teachers. Word puzzles, for instance, need not require the same attack as inquiry upon the nature of intellectual development of children. Just because research in small groups leads to the conclusion that effectiveness and efficiency are maximized when members take an active part in choosing the goals and devising their own solutions to problems, supervisors should not encourage such participation in sponsored workshops and formal study groups. The findings of studies made of small groups in isolation from formal organization are suggestive but not directly applicable to school situations. Too, a small group of teachers may effectively and efficiently attain their goal and still not contribute to the effectiveness of the school system.

Clarify of Objectives and Paths to Goals Necessary

Studies of the effect of unclear objectives on both individual and group adjustment and organizational strength have particular implications for schools where there is often a gap between institutional functions and classroom practice.

In a carefully designed investigation of the consequences of varied clarity of group goals and paths to these goals, Raven and Rietsema demonstrated that it is not enough for individuals to know "exactly what to do."[13] One also needs to be told how an immediate assignment contributes to a long-range goal and how one's part links with that of others in the attainment of the ultimate aim. Where the latter conditions prevail, it has been shown that participants are more interested in their personal task and less hostile. Those who have a clear picture of the group's goal and paths to this goal experience greater feeling of commitment and sympathy with emotions expressed in the group. They also are more willing to accept influence from the group than are those who are unclear about the goals and paths.

The influence is that supervisors should keep teachers completely informed of the objectives and procedures of the organization. It is not enough that teachers believe the system has a general goal, namely, the education of children and youth. They must know what to do and how their actions fit into an overall plan. An unstructured group situation has adverse implications both for teachers' individual adjustments and for relationships with others.

Necessity for Linking Three Kinds of Goals

In one sense an objective or goal is that which directs and maintains individual and group behavior. Supervisors have a major responsibility for arranging those conditions which will link system goals, individual goals, and group goals. The public goal of the school may be to further intellectual development or to develop citizenship. It is the job of supervisors to clarify for the teacher these abstract public objectives. They also hope the objectives will gradually become "internalized" to the point that teachers will acquire an attachment to them and the procedures that will lead to their attainment. Supervisors must in addition concern themselves with action designed to make particular goals found in individual classrooms and schools consistent with the broad objectives of the system as a whole.

Teachers may be more or less aware of the meaning of goals that are publicly formulated by the system. However, they are certain to have personal goals, such as the desire to be recognized as intelligent persons and to be secure. They are also likely to hold group goals in common with other teachers where the progress of one constitutes progress for all. Effectiveness and efficiency are dependent upon the degree to which these three kinds of goals are integrated.

13. Bertram H. Raven and Jan Rietsema, "The Effect of Varied Clarity of Group Goal and Group Path upon the Individual and His Relation to His Group," *Human Relations,* vol. 10, no. 1, pp. 29–45, 1957.

Ineffectiveness of Abstract Goals

The supervisor experiences serious difficulty in linking system goals when the statements of objectives are vague. Overabstracted goals, such as "citizenship," "academic excellence," "critical thinking," are not sufficiently concrete to provide direction to activity. It has been fashionable in school organizations to state objectives or goals which mean all things to all people and which serve as a compromise to the various interests which sustain the institutions. This tendency, of course, is not reserved to schools. The lack of accountability which accompanies general goals is well illustrated by an incident at a meeting of a political party's platform committee. An opponent of a certain plank drew much laughter over his remarks: "You can put into it what you want—in generalities—but don't be so specific." Although general statements may be necessary to influence public opinion or protect an organization, they must be made specific in order that individual teachers and their respective groups can be willing and effective partners in the task. This is not to say that the absence of clearly formulated goals precludes a teacher or group from becoming identified with the organization and its procedures. It is all too easy for a staff to become enamored with the process of their daily operations and in a ritualistic manner place values upon certain activities without knowing whether the consequences are relevant to the unique functions of the school. Regularized faculty meetings, workshops, or a tradition of orientation days can become important to supervisors, just as the selection of classroom officers or the writing of a set number of compositions can become the ineffective stock-in-trade of a teacher.

Supervision by Objectives

The primary need in school systems is the operationality of organizational objectives. There must be a way to observe and tell how well objectives are being achieved. There is some indication that improved measures of educational progress will support a movement toward supervision by objectives. If the objectives of the enterprise can be made clear to individuals, they may find that their own ambitions coincide with the institutional goals.[14] Often one can have more responsibility and latitude in working out appropriate means to the ends inasmuch as the goal of the program is jointly agreed upon. It would be a mistake, however, to assume that having common goals means that individual participants in a school will automatically select for themselves the most effective roles for achieving these goals.

14. Marshall E. Dimock, *Administrative Vitality,* Harper & Row, Publishers, Incorporated, New York, 1959, p. 189.

We have already shown that in a cooperative system the selection of an appropriate means also involves a knowledge of the actions of others.

There are at least two ideas in supervision by objectives which hold much promise: First, the school is forced to analyze and operationally state the aims from which all teachers receive their mandate. In formulating objectives, teachers have, of course, a chance to offer facts and points of view, but they will also be held responsible for the adequate attainment of the objectives finally agreed upon. Once it is clear that teachers and others are to be held accountable for pupil acquisition of certain ideas, skills, or attitudes, there is less evaluation of teacher effectiveness on the basis of process and more attention to pupil performance. Already supervisors and teachers are beginning to focus upon operational ends of instruction, specifying both the concepts and the skills the learner should acquire and the area of life in which these are expected to be used. For example, school objectives are increasingly regarded as "enabling," and their connection to the likely future demands of college entrance, civic, and career requirements is shown. Also, instead of condemning the practice of "teaching to the test," which often obscures the results desired, there is more concentrated effort to make clear the performance expected and to provide opportunities to practice it throughout the instructional period. Both instruction and tests are being geared to intended instructional objectives.

Second, school districts are allocating a larger share of their budget to evaluation of instruction in terms of pupil gain. This procedure places in demand those supervisors who can help teachers improve their instruction. Furthermore, in accordance with supervision by objectives, the task, instead of the arbitrary wish of a taskmaster, dominates. This is in contrast to teachers acquiescing out of fear to institutional demands from an authority figure because they are reduced to compliance by the emotional appeal of a consultant. A principal, for example, often carries a sanction or threat in the form of a rating. The limitations of a sanction are (1) that it causes teachers to "cover up" their earnest desires for assistance with a weakness or difficulty and (2) that unless the wielder of the sanction continues surveillance, the teacher selects another pattern. On the other hand, supervision is also unsatisfactory when supervisors feel that they must lose the taint of authority and exercise influence by waiting in the faculty lounge or library until they can meet the teacher in an "unthreatening" situation, hoping for an opportunity to win the teacher's confidence before "selling" their advice. The plan for supervision by objectives promises to change this. Once teachers know that their evaluation does not rest upon the opinion of an administrator but upon the extent to which they achieve the instructional objectives which they themselves agree upon, they voluntarily make more fundamental improvements in instruction. Further, the consultative service of supervisors is no longer regarded as something which can be ignored without cost. Supervisory help is sought and used when directly related to the attainment of the goals upon which the teacher's own success depends.

Experimental Evidence regarding the Consequences of Supervising by Objectives

It is recalled that supervision by objectives shifts the evaluation of teachers from how they teach (as if we know what constitutes the optimum in method) and from their particular personal characteristics to the results they obtain with learners. Unlike merit rating, which assumes that all teachers are teaching pupils who are equal in their teachability and that there is a common level of attainment to be reached by teachers working with the same subject matter and grade level, supervision by objectives regards results as satisfactory or unsatisfactory in terms of a particular class or particular learners within that class. It is important, however, that teachers be able to justify to the supervisor in advance the objectives they have selected and what they will offer as evidence that learners have or have not obtained the desired gain. An agreement is drawn by the teacher and supervisor in advance of the teaching sequence (the sequence can relate to a day's lesson, several weeks of instruction, or a year's program). The agreement is tentative inasmuch as the two parties can renegotiate at any time. Substitute criterion measures for revised objectives must, however, be acceptable to both parties, and justification should be presented on the basis of observation of pupils' performance that indicates the desirability of other, higher-priority objectives.

The effects of this supervisory practice are: (1) Supervisors tend to see teachers are more successful in the teaching act when there is agreement in advance on what will constitute evidence of success. (2) Pupils achieve more when the criterion for teaching success is pupil gain rather than ability to follow recommended teaching procedures. (3) Teachers prefer to be evaluated in terms of the progress of their pupils (equating for their initial ability to learn) rather than in terms of ability to carry out recommended procedures, in terms of their character (i.e., the extent to which they are models for their pupils), in terms of their ability to plan, or in terms of their ability to work well with the faculty. Supervision by objectives does not appear to produce undue pressures upon teachers, nor does the practice restrict pupil advancement in a range of desirable directions.

Identification with the Objectives of the School

Most of us will work for a common objective if we feel a direct personal gain will follow or an indirect reward will be derived from its completion. It has also been noted that in addition to personal interest in a task, one develops an organization personality,[15] in which behavior is determined not by personal motives but by the demands of the institutional objectives. One identifies with an objective when making decisions in terms of a focus upon consequences. We have previously mentioned the fact that many persons also identify with the organization itself rather than with the functions it is to fulfill. It often happens that administrators and teachers alike give their allegiance to a particular school, grade level, field of knowledge, or department instead of to the overall objectives of the system. The problem of narrow organizational identification with its resultant rivalries, jealousies, and limited perspective is a special responsibility of supervisors. It is up to the supervisor to weaken those narrow identifications which may prevent, say teachers from pointing out something in their own school situation which is against the interest of the objectives of the system. To counteract a teacher's fear of prejudicing personal and local popularity, the supervisor must develop loyalty to a larger system. Some suggestions from the theories of Simon[16] and Thelen[17] are:

1. The teacher's salary, prestige, friendship, and other personal incentives can be tied to the success of the total school district instead of associated solely with the achievements of a given school or an informal group.

2. Teachers' perspectives can be extended to see more than the particular values, knowledge, and options available in their own schools.

    a. Instead of being "procedure-oriented"—that is, instead of being expected to accept common practices and ideologies, resent unorthodox views, and rely on existing roles or customs—the faculty can become "purpose-oriented." Purpose orientation requires that all ideas be tested against the larger purposes of the system and that any conflict be resolved by appeal to the best evidence.

    b. Those teachers who are members of opposing groups can

---

15. C. L. Barnard, *The Functions of the Executive,* Harvard University Press, Cambridge, Mass., 1938, p. 188.
16. Herbert A. Simon, *Administrative Behavior: A Study of Decision-making Processes in Administrative Organization,* The Macmillan Company, New York, 1958.
17. Herbert A. Thelen, *Dynamics of Groups at Work,* The University of Chicago Press, Chicago, 1954.

be brought together to develop new agreements, ways of working, and expectations. District committees which cut across levels and areas are cases in point.

Supervisory practices affect the degree to which individuals identify with the organization. The more the supervisor facilitates the satisfaction of personal goals by individual members of the organization, the stronger is their identification with the organization. The more general the supervision, and the more the supervisor is oriented toward individuals rather than just the work of individuals, the stronger the tendency to identify with the system.[18] However, if teachers ordinarily face tasks which are highly complex in relation to their capacities, they will want close supervision.

While the most serious misdirection results when objectives are vague or means to the objectives are unclear, the sharing of goals also tends to be a function of the interaction patterns within district and school. Individuals are more likely to identify with a district and its goals when they interact or have close contact with others in the district. To some extent, a district can hasten agreement of goals by the careful screening of applicants for positions, hiring those with homogeneous expectations. Once teachers and supervisors have been recruited, continual unity depends upon making clear the specific criteria which will indicate attainment of the goal and arranging for interaction of school personnel. By interaction we mean contact between two or more persons which causes each member or member activity to act as a stimulus to another. It includes the channels of communication between members and the way activities necessary to accomplish purposes are divided among participants.

The Supervisor's Role and Interaction

Increased interaction, friendliness, and similarity of activity tend to go together. The liking of one person for another depends upon the amount of interaction and the importance of the other's activities. Those who hold favorable opinions of supervisors are likely to interact frequently with them, and this frequent contact itself leads to favorable opinions. Where a job has little intrinsic interest and there is a feeling of pressure and impersonality, it is important that supervisors maintain friendly, informal relationships which are not directly related to the instructional task. The building up between supervisor and teacher of a feeling of identification with and an understanding of each other's personal problems often augments the supervisor's

18. James G. March and Herbert A. Simon, *Organizations,* John Wiley and Sons, Inc., New York, 1958, p. 74.

influence upon a teacher's professional performance. Both those who are highly competent and those who have particularly extensive informal relations have more contact and exercise greater social control. The factor which predisposes others to associate with an individual also induces them to follow the recommendations that person gives. Blau[19] found that the one who is sought by others becomes differentiated in status with the power and prestige bestowed. Frequency of contact not only indicates but determines status.

Scientific explanation of the connection between teachers' liking for a supervisor and their interactions with that supervisor corresponds to our commonsense notions. First, persons generally express a liking for another person to the degree that the person's activities measure up to their ideas of what behavior ought to be in the circumstances. In other words, a popular supervisor or an informal-group leader is likely to meet group norms or standards of behavior. Not only the supervisor but the objectives and activities of the school system are apt to be rejected when a supervisor does not live up to teacher expectations. Second, most of us think that the actions of the one we like are better than the activities which those we dislike are doing. Third, people have ambivalent feelings about interacting with a supervisor: they admire status and thus they want to associate with the supervisor. In most schools teachers hold two different kinds of norms. They believe that a supervisor should be a "good guy" but also that the supervisor should make decisions. It is difficult to be a "good guy" yet avoid negative expressions like "Jones doesn't supervise at all—always praises our work and is satisfied with everything."

Group Interaction

The practical problem of conducting faculty meetings, conferences, and workshops as well as the necessity for dealing with informal groups has caused supervisors to notice patterns of communication and problem solving which are crucial factors in interaction. Channels of communication available to members are directly related to the effectiveness of groups. Studies of small groups have shown that when the leader directs the activities of the members without either consulting their wishes or informing them of future plans, groups spend a great deal more time in giving attention to the group task.[20] Also it has been found that persons are more effective in terms of

19. Peter M. Blau, *The Dynamics of Bureaucracy,* The University of Chicago Press, Chicago, 1955, p. 130.
20. Kurt Lewin, Ronald Lipitt, and R. K. White, "Patterns of Aggressive Behavior in Experimentally Created 'Social Climates,'" *Journal of Social Psychology,* vol. 10, pp. 271–299, 1939.

speed and accuracy in solving problems when communication is channeled through a central figure (Y wheel design in which the superior is the hub) than when there is a "wide open" pattern (circle) design.[21] Supervisors do not generally act upon these findings, partly because of the equalitarian bias of teachers and also because the findings are only half-truths. The other half of the story is that members are more dissatisfied under restricted communication patterns. In other words, effectiveness may occur without efficiency. Those who are relegated to a peripheral position can be productive, but they are likely to be less satisfied. The more central one's position, the greater the gratification received from the activity. Circular arrangements result in more congeniality; networks which do not permit two-way communication leave teachers with the feeling that they are left out and unsure of themselves.

The correlation between satisfaction and performance is not clear. While it appears that in many instances the two are negatively related, the observation might be based on too short a time interval. Over a long period of time one might find that satisfaction contributes to effectiveness. Certainly if supervisors must depend upon teacher motivation as well as effective organization, they should see that teachers are rewarded for group success. In the long run both individual and group reward are likely to be less when a group or organization permits individuals to express personal needs instead of directing participants to the group goal or to the solution of the group's problems.[22] There will be much dissatisfaction with the decisions reached, with the procedures used, and with the supervisor's handling of the situation when a group's discussion is characterized by self-oriented comments. Self-oriented comments are those by which someone attempts to enhance personal status, dominate the situation, make others dependent, and relieve personal tensions through aggression or catharsis.

Need for Control of the Group

Certain self-expressions must be curtailed if the individual teacher is to receive the rewards which accrue in the form of prestige brought by identification with a school noted for its academic achievements and carefully developed programs. The bigger payoff in personal reward which rests upon group goal attainment is sometimes lost to short-term satisfaction which comes to one who goes off on tangents

21. Harold J. Leavitt, "Some Effects of Certain Communication Patterns on Group Performance," *The Journal of Abnormal and Social Psychology*, vol. 46, no. 1, pp. 38–50, January 1956.
22. Henry W. Riecken and George C. Homans, "Psychological Aspects of Social Structure," in Lindzey, op. cit., pp. 786–832.

of personal interest, reducing group effectiveness. Not only the supervisor but the group itself must be alert to those who "talk all the time" and wander afield. When troublesome behavior occurs it should be regarded as an indication of a needed structure within the group. Perhaps the task or purpose has not been clarified. While there is no particular set of procedures which can be used for controlling the quality of work in groups, there are understandings which can aid the staff in looking at itself.

In a classic book treating group dynamics, Thelen described in specific detail a number of useful principles which seem to result in effective group operation.[23] His description of these principles and control devices is a fruitful study which bridges the theory of interaction and its application. Included in these principles are the following ideas:

1. Make each individual statement the property of the group, not the possession of the one who makes the suggestion. The group should determine for itself whether or not the suggestion is a useful one.
2. Emotional expressions by individuals reflect the need of the group itself. If scraps are going on, the chances are that others are getting gratification out of the fight.
3. "In all but extreme cases, problem people are to be considered group problems." If someone bothers everyone, the question should be "Why does his sort of behavior bother us; why can't we deal with it?"
4. Since individual contributions arise when the group tries to do something, and everyone contributes to the solution, all are entitled to consider how serious a problem is for the group and whether members need to do something about it.
5. "A problem is whatever everyone feels to be a problem."
6. "The group moves by consensus and agreement, not by taking sides in disputes."
7. "Steam-roller tactics and persuasion are of no avail because they block the objective evaluation of consequences and possibilities of correction. . . ." Data and exploration of the obstacles individuals see should replace ambiguity, vagueness, and inability to assess the costs of alternatives.
8. "Whenever the group does not know what it is doing, it ought to stop and find out." One way to do this is for the group to describe what it is doing. Members will know how to participate only when they know what the group is doing.

23. Thelen, op. cit., pp. 285–289.

9. All seriously intended contributions should be responded to. "If the contribution seems of no value, it is better to admit an inability to see its implications for the group than to ignore it." Again, a purpose-oriented group can permit rejection of an idea without rejection of the individual.
10. "No individual can speak for the group. . . ." One can report one's own thoughts and feelings and also give impressions of the group. "But no man really knows how others think and feel. . . ."
11. "The aim of the group should not be to get participation equally distributed among members." The aim should be to deal with the group's problems—although all should be allowed to contribute if they wish and there should be no barriers that prevent needed contributions. Opportunity for more people to achieve prestige is found when there is frequent change of activity.

Cooperative versus Competitive Groups

Both effectiveness and efficiency are maximized when personal and group goals are congruent. Integration of individual motives and group goals is achieved through cooperatively organized groups. A cooperatively organized group is one in which no single member can move toward individual goals without also forwarding the progress of others toward their goals.

Cooperatively organized workshops and study groups, for example, invite teachers to attack common problems, plan together, and share the results of their efforts. Most important, evaluation of their group undertakings is a joint affair in which members are told that their "grade" or appraisal depends upon the merit of their performance as a group. This procedure for evaluation is in contrast to the one followed in competitive situations; there members are ranked individually on the basis of how much each contributes qualitatively and quantitatively to the solution.

Cooperative groups show more productivity per unit of time, greater mutual comprehension of communication, greater attention to fellow members, greater coordination of effort, more pressure to achieve, greater friendliness during discussion, and more favorable evaluation of the group and its products by the members.[24]

Members of cooperative groups are more likely to maintain strength and regulate the group themselves. Competitive groups engage in self-expression which, as we have seen, often leads to both less productivity and more member dissatisfaction.

A successful supervisor believes that teachers work hardest to

24. M. Deutsch, "An Experimental Study of the Effects of Cooperation and Competition upon Group Process," *Human Relations,* vol. 2, no. 3, pp. 199–231, 1949.

meet their own needs and that it is the supervisor's business to arrange conditions so that teachers find it to their advantage to work
cooperatively. The reward to the individual teacher through group
effort will be greater only when the sequential steps necessary to
attainment of the group goals are so simple that each one can perform them and at the same time learn whether the step has been
satisfactorily completed. This knowledge of results can be a powerful
reward. Constructive accomplishment in a group such as a curriculum committee, a class, or a community task organization usually
follows these considerations:

1. What do we actually hope to accomplish both immediately and in
   the future? Are these outcomes stated in terms of particular behaviors rather than as high-level abstractions?
2. How do these efforts fit into the larger context of the school's
   role? What is the group's defined responsibility? To whom is the
   group responsibile?
3. What will we do differently as a result of this effort?
4. Is the task divided into small steps and is there a plan for evaluating and reporting outcomes from these simple steps?
5. What participants are required?
6. What will each person do?
7. What knowledge, resources, and other assistance are necessary?
8. What information will we need? What consequences must be
   continuously reported if we are to alter our planning on the basis
   of knowledge of results? How can this best be undertaken?

Individual versus Group Problem Solving

The overwhelming emphasis upon group work as a means of facilitating individual change and improvement in professional practices
of teachers is generally well placed. But the superiority of group solutions in the decision-making process over individual solutions is not
always demonstrated. The practice of decentralizing responsibility
through the establishment of teacher councils and other structures
for decision making opens up the matter of individual and group
problem solving as well as the factors affecting the quality of decisions.

Accuracy of perception and judgment is not necessarily better
because a group pools its intelligence. A minimum basis for making a
valid judgment must exist. True, a group solution can be more than a
statistical pooling of ideas. The experience of working in the group
has an effect which can facilitate individual learning as individuals
reject incorrect ideas that would escape their notice if they were
working alone.

One reason for the popularity of group activity as a supervisory process is that it is a convenient way to make public many opinions. But why is it important to share these differences of opinion? Because one will be better able to reach a correct judgment if aware of the great variety of judgments possible in any given situation.

The effectiveness of group effort as compared with individual effort depends upon the degree of identification members have with the group, the responsibility they assume for the outcomes, and the kinds of rewards for successfully completing steps in the problem-solving process.

Superiority of group effort has been attributed to the resistance that vague ideas meet in the demands of group communication. The very act of formulating an opinion for communication to the group may lead to a sharpening of an idea. Reduction in errors is also found to be associated with the practice of members' responding to the contribution and not to the status, friendliness, or other personal characteristics of the contributor.

Conversely, the social stimuli of group work may interfere with the task when intellectual processes or concentration is involved. An individual may be more effective alone than with others.

The intellectual responses of thought are hampered as group work continues.[25] While group work heightens motivation to perform the common task, it also presents distractions which make the task more difficult, reducing the quantity and quality of work.

Attraction to a group is related to production, anxiety, and attitude toward place of work.[26] Members of closely knit or cohesive groups are less anxious and under less pressure to achieve. However, when cohesive groups perceive their supervisors as supportive, they achieve higher production than those groups that are less united. Hence, the attraction of a group for its members can be either a force for positive benefit or a negative influence in an organization, depending upon the supervisor's success in establishing a feeling of confidence and security.

Statements like the following indicate that groups are not always effective or efficient decision-making instruments:

"Let's stamp out committees."

"I'm always glad when the meeting is over—I hate the bickering."

"We lost this time, but we'll lay for that guy until we can put him in his place."

25. F. H. Allport, *Social Psychology*, Houghton Mifflin Company, Boston, 1924, p. 274.
26. Stanley E. Seashore, *Group Cohesiveness in the Industrial Work Group*, Institute for Social Research, University of Michigan, Ann Arbor, 1955.

"I don't think we can solve this problem by voting. We must get at the real issue of educational standards."

Such comments occur when:

1. *The supervisor is adhering too closely to procedural rules and lacks sensitivity to the interest of individual members, blocking participation and creating apathy.* A formal procedure threatens and leads to a reduction in the number of ideas produced. New ideas and new members need protection. The group should be helped to create jobs and to be aware of talent within its members who are potential sources of help in the matters being discussed.
2. *There is conflict between private and public interests,* i.e., there are underlying animosities and "hidden agenda." Conflicting motives of individuals, subgroups, or the group as a whole cannot be fitted into the task. Action is almost impossible while the members work on private purposes, moving illogically on the surface task. Some members are afraid of examining long-held beliefs or practices; others fear they will lose power. In back of some members are invisible social organizations or forceful personalities that control their behavior. One's resistance to progress is often due to the fact that the group is approaching a decision which one knows will be difficult to explain to friends in another group.
3. *The supervisor may neglect to make clear that each person might see things somewhat differently.* It is important to lessen feelings of guilt and increase the tendency to put more concerns in the open. In this connection, it is recommended that the supervisor issue statements such as this: "Perhaps we haven't said all we feel about the issue. Maybe we should go around the table so that any further ideas can be brought up."
4. *The members are not willing to assume mature responsibility for the way the group acts.* The group has not looked at its own procedures nor devised a method of evaluating so that it can improve its process. Remember, members do not know how to participate until they know what the group is doing. Too much bickering reflects lack of clarity of the group's problems and the behaviors necessary to solve these problems.
5. *The staff is unrealistic in expecting frequent unanimous decisions.* Members should not expect unanimity to follow discussion. It is better to seek tentative agreement or consensus upon the simple steps which might lead to the goal and to encourage dissenters to participate in the evaluating of the effects of these steps.

Before surface acceptance of a decision as opposed to deep level of commitment can be achieved, the group must provide positive satisfaction to the individual rather than constrain membership or threaten to withhold the sanctions of tenure and promotion. Also, let's not sell voting short. The superiority of groups may rest upon the process of voting. Those persons with high confidence and valid information are more likely to respond and carry more weight in a group vote.[27]

6. *The group is too large for decision making.* In addition to the obvious difficulty of reaching a consensus when the group is large, other changes in structure occur with increased size. Subgroup coalitions representing minority views offer more effective resistance, and members feel their impulse to participate is inhibited.

In large groups only the more forceful ones show their abilities and share ideas. After a group exceeds about seven persons, there is much less participation.[28] Concern for motivation has led to the Principle of Least Group Size, which recommends the structuring of groups into the smallest number in which it is possible to have represented at a functional level all the social and achievement skills required for the particular activity.[29] The use of subgroups may contribute to effectiveness of the large group by helping the individual share responsibility and receive the rewards of recognition. Again, however, factional conflict must be expected when the subgroup works out the limits of its power.

The chief question in deciding upon individual or group problem solving is "Does the problem require group action?" If the problem is one that calls for change in the behavior of others, it is advantageous to effect group decision rather than to rely upon individual choice. Motivation and thought processes are modified by (1) other members, (2) the social situation, (3) anticipated social reactions, and (4) the responsibility for communicating and implementing the decision. If the problem or decision can be more effectively communicated in a face-to-face situation rather than in writing, a group meeting is likely to be the answer because such a meeting can help clarify responsibilities. If the supervisor does not feel sufficiently knowledgeable regarding a particular problem, it may be wise to consider the organization of a committee composed of those who can best supply the necessary information.

27. Herbert Gurnee, "A Comparison of Collective and Individual Judgments of Fact," *Journal of Experimental Psychology,* vol. 21, no. 1, p. 110, July 1937.
28. Kelley and Thibault, op. cit., p. 762.
29. Herbert A. Thelen, "Group Dynamics in Instruction: The Principle of Least Group Size," *School Review,* pp. 139–148, March 1949.

RECAPITULATION AND PROCEDURES

In this chapter we have tried to indicate those aspects of the school's social structure which must be taken into account if the school's objectives are to be attained and if teachers are to be satisfied. We have seen that supervisory actions which disregard motivation and the personal goals of teachers are responsible for such malfunctions as complacency, inertia, resistance, and withdrawal from teaching. The value of informal groups, participation, interaction, and clarity of objectives has been stressed. Informal groups help to compensate for those supervisory practices or conditions which tend to make teachers feel they are being used or are unimportant. Friendship, leadership, feeling of worth, and a release of tension are among the outcomes from membership in informal work groups. The power of the group in guiding individual teachers is great both because teachers value association with others for its own sake and because such association enables them to get rewards that they cannot get alone.

Supervisors have attempted to strengthen the official organization by capturing the power which lies in informal associations. Sometimes efforts are made to make formal activities, e.g., workshops, faculty meetings, etc., assume the characteristics of informal groups. At other times, informal leaders are brought into the official family or assignments of teachers are systematically manipulated so that pressures from informal groups are consistent with the system's demands.

Theoretically, if the formal organization can reduce feelings of dependence, provide opportunities for leadership, and release tensions, there will be less likelihood that informal groups will form. If they do, these groups will supplement rather than resist the official norms of the system. The difficulty in such an approach is that it often conflicts with present political and legal structures as well as with the system's need for authority. Then, too, the motivations of teachers are often more complicated than usually contemplated. Some individuals enter groups with attitudes that bias interaction with them. Without common background and outlook, it is difficult to establish free and spontaneous interaction. Teachers who are predisposed to mature self-realization will welcome responsibility and shared leadership; those who have been rewarded for dependent behavior will expect close surveillance and direction. Unless teachers are task-oriented and possessed of the skills and understanding for leadership and membership roles necessary for the functioning of face-to-face groups, there is little likelihood that individual efficiency and instructional effectiveness will occur.

The potential capacities of the teacher will be fully used only when the teacher is a member of a well-knit staff that has high skills of interaction and high performance goals. Where these conditions exist, supervisors should deliberately endeavor to foster cooperative interaction among the total staff, not just among a few friends.

Small groups such as those representing a grade level, department, or school should be linked into an overall organization by means of which participants hold membership within and between various segments of the school and system: teams of teachers working with special youngsters, teachers of children in the primary grades, study groups for developmental reading, district administrative councils, and faculty advisory committees. Through their own membership and teacher representation in these groups, teachers should have opportunity to exert influence in the school's hierarchy commensurate with their experience and knowledge. To feel that one can exercise no influence, especially over one's own class, department, or school, is detrimental to the school and the system. A reciprocal influence process is likely to weld the system into a more effective organization. All decisions must, of course, conform with broad policies made at higher levels; but decisions affecting only a class or a school should be made without reference to others since the relevant information is present and the responsibility given increases the individual's sense of importance and personal worth.

Ideally, any member of the staff can propose problems for group consideration, but each problem is treated from a systemwide point of view. In the presence of a group composed of interlocking memberships, it is less likely that the problem will be resolved to the advantage of a particular person or interest and to the disadvantage of others. With the group form of organization, teachers soon learn to seek only those decisions which are in the best interest of the system as well as themselves. In addition, group action is usually accompanied by high motivation on the part of each member to do his best to implement the decision.

Basic to efficiency and effectiveness is a common identification with professional values which make the process of attaining school objectives a source of satisfaction. Such identification rests upon recruitment standards, lengthened periods of service, and evaluation on the basis of results achieved. Unfortunately, these conditions are not always found in school situations. Provisional credentials, high turnover in staff, and periodic ratings by principals using extraneous criteria are more customary.

Both the public and the school organization are better served when supervisors and teachers are held accountable for the consequences of their operations. Such accountability means taking a good look at what one wanted to accomplish, what was done, the results, and the costs. The teacher and supervisor are not solely accountable for the results, but they are accountable for knowing these results and, if they are not satisfactory, should have a valid explanation and suggestion for subsequent improvement. Most teachers want to evaluate the success of their actions because evaluation furthers both learning and satisfaction. Where there is nothing definite about the outcomes expected from the performance of teachers, there is no common acceptance of either performance standards or objectives. In other words, effectiveness and efficiency have been hindered by a lack of specific objectives and criteria indicating their attainment.

Inasmuch as the trends for the future will be toward greater effectiveness of schools, we can predict that supervision will take these directions:

1. Supervision by objectives will continue. Every supervisor and teacher will be expected to be concerned with the rational accomplishment of school objectives in which harmony of system, school, and individual goals will be achieved by specifying results rather than techniques.
2. Particular schools, teams of teachers, and individuals will be encouraged to make necessary adjustments in order to attain objectives. Information as to the pathways followed by others to common objectives will be shared.
3. Personnel policies will place greater emphasis upon the adequacy of the teacher's preparation and competency. Those without the necessary academic and professional training will serve as assistants, not as teachers. The professional teacher will share status with others in the school's hierarchy, leading to a diffusion of rationality and identification with the objectives of the system.
4. Supervisors will begin to recognize the importance of informal groups and to regard them as assets, seeking ways to extend the development and contribution of these groups.
5. There will be a sharpening of the distinction between the authority necessary for *(a)* coordination and stability and *(b)* bureaucratic restraints that reduce efficiency by engendering apathy and resistance. Legitimate authority will be made manifest and used along with influence by supervisors.

CHAPTER **6**

STRATEGIES AND TACTICS FOR PROGRAM IMPROVEMENT

"Strategy" and "tactics" are terms representing the act of employing certain procedures adroitly for the accomplishment of ends. Strategy involves the development of objectives and a plan of action for a large-scale operation; tactics call for skillful direction of specific tasks and arrangement of particular conditions which contribute to the fulfillment of the plan.

There are various levels of strategic planning. At the classroom and individual school level there are strategic estimates of educational requirements and tactics necessary to implement decisions made in the strategic planning of local systems and state bodies. State and local systems in turn are influenced in their planning by the policies of national strategists, who view the school as an additional instrument for tactical use in the attainment of the American objective of preservation of society against disintegration from within and against assault from without.

Throughout the nation changes in schools occur when, for example, (1) congressional committees are advised that America is linguistically unprepared either to defend itself in the case of war or to exercise the full force of its leadership in building a peaceful world;

and (2) work force studies indicate that x number of persons will be needed for specified posts before a given year. Monies are made available for the development of new media which will make possible the extension and alteration of vocational education, and organized groups are encouraged to plan the nationwide reform of the curricula bearing upon national interests. But local supervision must provide leadership in interpreting these new proposals, appraising them in light of desired goals, and selecting from among the recommendations those that seem most appropriate for the school system. Supervisors also have responsibility for initiating the systematically planned programs for educating the teachers who will carry out the proposals. Although the government has entered the field of teacher preparation through such enterprises as summer institutes sponsored by the National Science Foundation, there is no assurance that teachers specially trained in programs apart from the school itself will either be given the opportunity for carrying out the new procedures in their own teaching or be able to change the local program. Valuable as the newer, more encompassing developments may be, the school supervisor must articulate them with the local situation. In the last analysis, there is need for a local strategy for program improvement.

It is not our purpose to imply that curriculum change is dependent upon a national strategy. As a matter of fact, there is much argument about whether there is or should be a national strategy for curriculum change. Some hold that we are entering a period in which our survival requires that the federal government influence the direction and policies of schools. Others believe that the ends of teaching are sufficient unto themselves, that schools must not become instruments for national policy. Most officials at the national level express a desire for increased individual citizen participation in the formulation of school policy. They advocate broader local control by increasing the number of school boards in densely populated areas as one step in this direction. Obviously, national projects are altering the course of schooling in the United States, but these changes are more the result of partial adaptation to immediate pressures than responses made in accordance with a comprehensive federal strategy for education.

Change without strategy is common. Schools have often drifted, responding to the strongest pressure from state and federal agencies, private foundations, accreditation agencies, and citizen groups. Locally, the increasing weight of conflicting ideas from these forces is encouraging schools to assume institutional responsibility, to establish controlling functions to guide their decisions, and to resist many immediate pressures.

To a large extent there is a trend in the schools toward long-range planning and clear statement of objectives. This trend reflects the universal demand for direction and the effort to fit democratic government for prolonged competition with totalitarianism. At all levels, there is a shift from the overgeneralization of purpose and the practice of working out compromises among conflicting groups. Instead we are witnessing the establishment of sharply defined choices of policy to guide decision making.

Reservations about the establishment of national educational goals have been expressed. Such reservations are also voiced wherever there is discussion of procedures for planning and innovation in school settings: In a free nation should we attempt to confine individuals with plans made by others? How can there be planning when there are so many imponderables in life? Isn't it better to let many enterprising minds plan in their own way, inventing and adapting? Doesn't the inbuilding of purpose challenge creativity? Is it possible to translate the goal values of American life into institutional terms? These questions must be kept in mind as we assess the strategic factors involved in the process of directed change.

ELEMENTS OF STRATEGY FOR CURRICULUM CHANGE

Strategy is a convenient way of talking about the objectives of the school and the basic factors to consider in effecting curriculum change. Before giving special attention to the procedures available to supervisors in their work for instructional improvement, it is necessary to consider two requirements of a sound strategy: valid objectives and a basis for course of action.

Valid Objectives of Strategy

Objectives must be operational and consistent with the functions of the school. There can be no strategy without objectives. Schools have frequently been charged with failure to determine, proclaim, and pursue consistently basic objectives. The habit of sanctimoniously protecting classroom practice by appeal to abstract goals such as "worthy home membership," "citizenship," and "understanding of the environment" has led to misconception and misdirection. There are signs that we have passed the time when schools can get by with pious hopes and high-sounding shibboleths. Supervisors are beginning (1) to state what schools should strive for, (2) to determine the capabilities needed for attaining these objectives, and (3) to lay concrete plans for their implementation.

The school must devote its major energies to what it can do best. Therapeutic and custodial functions are not automatically the responsibility of the school. The fundamental purpose of education is to see that children do not grow up "naturally." It is rather to see that they are systematically conducted through carefully planned series of experiences which will develop their desirable potentials. The major purpose of schooling should be kept clear. In the hierarchy of values fostered in schools, distinguished intellectual attainment should occupy a leading position.

Such statements of purpose as that above are still not adequate to develop strategy at lower levels but must be refined in the district, school, and classroom until there are agreed-upon criteria for determining the extent to which the objectives are being reached. The objective "developing critical thinking," for example, might be considered appropriate in accordance with the previous statement of purpose. However, this objective is nonoperational in its present form, i.e., it has not been made clear how it will be possible to observe and test how well pupils are thinking critically. In order to determine what steps to take in achieving this end, it would be necessary to specify the subject matter or areas of life in which one is to think critically and the skill, method, or other action which is indicative of critical behavior. As a general goal, a system might decide that critical thinking in science will be shown by ability of pupils (1) to identify scientific problems; (2) to isolate a problem from a mass of given scientific material; (3) to suggest hypotheses; (4) to design experiments; (5) to draw generalizations from scientific data known or given; or (6) to reason quantitatively and significantly. This general type of goal is operational enough for undertaking a concrete problem of action, for it permits measurement of the contribution of particular instructional programs; but it is inadequate for individual classroom planning. At this level, the teacher has to ask "What must pupils know and be able to do if they are to identify a scientific problem?" The answer will suggest specific operational objectives— concepts and behavior stated as expectations for the learner—which will become new subgoals for the teacher in planning and guiding the arrangement of the teaching-learning situations. Note that these definitions of purpose are open-ended enough to avoid placing ceilings on human endeavors, yet sharply focused enough to establish areas of institutional responsibility.

Simple and related objectives must substitute for complex objectives. In the present context we are stressing the importance of stating objectives which permit teachers and supervisors to handle programs of limited complexity. The teacher is not expected to set broad educational goals which depend upon study of the enterprise as a whole, including (1) its inner impulses (the many informal groups and personal interactions which affect the system) and (2) external demands from the larger society. Nor is the superintendent as the top-level supervisor responsible for analyzing the complexities of instruction in a particular classroom. The superintendent need not select the tactics necessary for working with pupils whose behavior cannot be predicted in advance. The teacher and the superintendent each has a primary responsibility for a restricted range of situations and a restricted range of consequences.

Staff development must be related to objectives. In order that overall and individual classroom goals may be consistent, in-service programs should focus upon (1) securing agreement on the objectives and principles that will be used as the basis for action and (2) acquainting participants with relevant activities of others in the system. Problems encountered at the classroom and district levels must be communicated if objectives are to be realistic. Teachers must be aware of the pressures upon supervisors, just as the latter must appreciate the difficulties of classroom instruction.

Unless staff development is related to the school's educational objectives appropriately defined at all levels, the selection of activities by participants will be inconsistent and will preclude intelligent action and the development of organized educational experiences. Once these objectives are made explicit, freedom of action is increased. When objectives are operational and accepted, a staff can center on a variety of problems of special concern to the immediate members: study of children, preparation of materials of instruction, promotion policies, and the implications of community changes. These activities must follow the statement of objectives, for they are not ends but means. A group program-improvement activity dealing with the problem of classroom control, for example, is relevant only as control is necessary to the attainment of behavior changes in pupils specified in the objective. Concomitant results from the group's program, of course, should be considered in subsequent planning.

Parenthetically, those who plan self-development are responsible for a knowledge of the participants and the subject matter which will enable the activities to lend themselves to school objectives. Participants should be able to state precisely how the supervisory activity will improve instruction, indicating the evidence of effectiveness in terms of pupil behavior. Requisite advanced planning should be firm in its direction, but flexible enough to permit free play of individuality; it should invite those contributions and expressions of interest which are related to the common outcomes sought. An overlapping group form of organization is particularly useful in performing the processes necessary to develop an integrated set of system objectives and corresponding objectives for subunits and individuals in the school organization.

The point of view expressed so far is a departure from current practice. In our opinion, the popular notion that the primary objective of programs for instructional improvement is that of "teacher stimulation and growth" is misplaced. The logic of present practice goes as follows: The teacher makes the actual curriculum through the learning activities of pupils. Hence any improvement in instruction must come through the improvement of the teacher. This popular view also assumes that stimulation and growth are best furthered when teacher activity is emphasized, and that nearly any study undertaken by teachers will contribute to instructional improvement. We regard this position to be a half-truth. Instead of extolling the importance of the teachers' growth and activity, supervisors must give priority to the objectives of instruction. Participants have often merely become more facile in discussing child growth and development without altering their classroom practice in accordance with the new knowledge.[1] Without focus upon classroom objectives and accompanying indicators of pupil progress, there is no assurance that the in-service program is relevant to instruction. Nor is there a valid way teachers can appraise their growth as instructors. Once teachers are able to evaluate the results they are obtaining with present procedures, they are in a position to offer innovations for improvement, bringing contrariety to uniformity and status quo.

In advocating instructional improvement through supervision by objectives, it should be clear that neither the objectives of the school nor the goals of individual teachers are stable and unchanging. Both must change in response to evaluation of subsequent effects of the objectives and to altering conditions. There is, consequently, at all levels of the school hierarchy, a continuous process of examining and modifying (1) objectives, (2) methods for achieving them, and (3) indicators of attainment and other consequences.

Objectives in school are more limited than are educational goals. Education consists of three processes: (1) instruction necessary to satisfy physical wants; (2) instruction in the customs, rules, manners, and morals necessary for harmonious living; and (3) instruction in the theories necessary for the explanation and prediction of natural events, i.e., theories or ceremonies by which humankind tries to control present or future life. Many agencies other than the school have responsibility for these instructional tasks. The church provides theory and practice for propitiating the mortal being and the spirit.

1. Ronald C. Doll, "Teachers' Attitudes toward the Initial Steps in a Curriculum Improvement Program," unpublished doctoral study, Teachers College, Columbia University, New York, 1951.

Stanley Dropkin, "Attitudes of West Orange Teachers by Types of Participation," unpublished doctoral study, Teachers College, Columbia University, New York, 1954.

The home furthers manners and morals. Vocational institutions offer training in the specialized skills and understandings necessary to holding particular jobs. Political parties as well as primary groups equip members with the rights, duties, and "know-how" of political competence in society.

Failure to distinguish between education and schooling places an impossible burden upon the school, an institution deliberately charged with the specialized task of simplifying the environment. A school must be a place where pupils can pursue intensively a restricted number of studies without the distraction of competing demands, and where they can abstract the key ideas or theories of nature with which to interpret the complex events of life. One criterion of a valid objective is that it grants access to facts and ideas upon the basis of which rational judgments can be made. Supervisors can also use this criterion before accepting those tasks which call for teaching children to brush their teeth, serving as custodial agents for working parents, writing essays of indoctrination, acting as the date bureau for the teenage set, and selling physics, welding, or some other going interest of the government.

Objectives are related to contemporary life. The immediate demands of contemporary life can be helpful in the selection of objectives. Crucial problems of society call for interpretation of the basic principles, concepts, and meanings taught in the school, and offer opportunity for validating them. But to say that the school should be closely associated with life does not imply that it shall duplicate thought and practice of a particular community. Occupying a central position in the social structure, the school can serve as a mirror to society by indicating conflicting pressures, ideals, and practices. It is obligatory that supervisors make known the consequences upon classroom learning which arise from changing social structures and conditions. They should be in a position to make clear what the school can accomplish in light of these changes and the means at its disposal. While cooperating through community councils and the like in the planning of action programs for improving community relations and education in general, supervisors must not permit the school to assume the total responsibility merely because it is the only institution which reaches all youth. The school alone cannot undertake the solution of major social problems for at least two reasons:

1. It does not control the variables necessary for resolving cultural difficulties. It has not the authority, organization, or staff to alter economic, political, and other social forces which underlie the situation.
2. Preoccupation with social problems and the constraint of immedi-

ate practicality would get in the way of the school's responsibility for systematically arranging central ideas which are not obvious nor necessarily present in problems of the moment.

A realistic perspective of objectives demands that curriculum planners be continuously aware of cultural change. This is shown in the following illustration, which features the lag in curriculum planning and the likelihood of acting upon assumptions about conditions which no longer exist.

Early in this century educational prophets protested the gap between an academic curriculum for an intellectual elite and the dynamic content of American life. At that time the school was seen by persons of vision as the only organized agency competent to educate young Americans in all aspects of life.[2]

> Neither the home, the church, nor the press can be expected to do it. Certainly, the home, which in an ideal democracy would serve as the most potent educational agency, is not now equipped to attack the problem. . . . American home life gives little promise of being able to lift itself above the dead level of humdrum monotony which now characterizes it. It is the product itself of an eighth grade education; it is still too often supported physically by an income insufficient to maintain even a minimal comfort standard of living; hence its attention is still centered on the struggle for physical existence.

By mid-century, schools had responded to the conditions of 1900. Most schools were launching programs of education for family living, health, and vocational training, and were trying to attack the social problems resulting from industrialization and organization. However, between mid-century and 1967, schools reversed themselves in response to suburban living. Appropriate schooling for the 1960s was more like the narrow intellectualistic and academic programs of 1890. Facetiously, one could say, "Resist all changes for fifty years, and you will find yourself on the forefront of progress."

By the spring of 1967, however, schools were responding once more to conditions of urban social disorganization more akin to those seen by the early prophets of the twentieth century. There were numerous programs for disadvantaged children and their parents, i.e., Head Start, vocational training. Many more encompassing functional courses revealed the concerns of the day, i.e., sex education, alcohol, and narcotics. Administrative innovations also reflected the social pressures. For example, we began to see plans for educa-

2. Harold Rugg, "The School Curriculum and the Drama of American Life," in *Curriculum-making: Past and Present,* Twenty-sixth Yearbook, part I, National Society for the Study of Education, The University of Chicago Press, Chicago, 1926, p. 5.

tional parks which were intended to bring together a larger community than the conventional school-served area.[3] The concept of the park addressed itself to the problems of racial, social, and economic integration by breaking down both the boundaries of small neighborhoods and the social systems of institutions such as school, housing, recreation, business, and health.

Now there are articulate demands from regional publics in different types of communities that the school give its major attention to teaching the three R's. At the end of twelve years of schooling, the knowledge of reading, writing, arithmetic, and science is seen as of immediate importance, and other facets of the school's program are to proceed from it.

The problem for supervisors will be how to relate (1) social concerns and (2) the central ideas which are so difficult to acquire without systematic instruction. Schools must identify the intellectual tools (reading, mathematics) which they are responsible for transmitting and must also identify the kinds of problems to which these intellectual tools should apply. What current situations in the everyday life of the child can we use to effect linkage with the disciplines and present social concerns? This is not to say that social problems of the present must dominate those of the future but that teaching well the abstract tools and ways to apply them to present conditions is the best way to ensure that learners can meet well the unknown future.

Subject-matter specialists aid in validating objectives. We have seen that valid objectives show clearly the kind of behavior expected as well as the specific content to which the behavior applies, such as pupils' use of principles of molecular motion in predicting and controlling problems of evaporation and condensation. Content specialists help validate these objectives by indicating the basic concepts, generalizations, principles, and techniques of particular disciplines which can uniquely serve to explain and control the world about us. We look to the subject-matter specialist to indicate the set of processes and standards of performance which enable people to analyze certain kinds of situations and to test solutions. Those who have a special competence for tackling completely strange problems in a specific field should share the intellectual techniques and systematic view which constitute their competence.

Studies of the learner are sources for valid objectives. As Dewey indicated, "There is no such thing as educational value in the abstract."[4] The capacities and current level of performance of the par-

---

3. S. P. Marland, Jr., "The Education Park Concept in Pittsburgh," *Phi Delta Kappan*, vol. 48, no. 7, pp. 329–332, March 1967.

ticular set of individuals with whom the school is dealing certainly should be a guide in the selection of objectives. Objectives should include ideas which the pupil does not now hold but should hold. To be valid, an objective must also be within the pupil's range of capacity. "That the immature cannot study facts and principles in the way in which the mature experts study them goes without saying. But this fact, instead of exempting the educator from responsibility for using present experiences so that learners may gradually be led, through extraction of acts and laws, to experience of a scientific order, sets one of his main problems."[5]

Objectives are consistent with ideology. Finally, the objectives should be consistent with the image of the fundamental values of the society the school serves. Where concrete plans for action are formulated, there is opportunity for continual debate regarding the interpretation of these values.

While the ideal of educational opportunity has been implemented in the practice of granting to all the right to schooling at public expense, interpretation of the concepts of equality and individual freedom in school has only begun. American ideology which emphasizes respect for the worth and dignity of each person and asserts that "all men are created equal" will be interpreted anew in these kinds of decisions:

1. To what extent should we differentiate between pupils with respect to both educational outcomes and experiences? Can we avoid giving to those who have and taking away from those who have not as we plan, for instance, programs for the talented and the culturally different? More specifically, which pupils will be assigned the best-prepared teachers?
2. Will objectives based upon pupil preferences and individual potential in a variety of areas endure in light of the occupational needs of the nation? How can the school best further individuality by which one rises above self and thinks in terms of the good of all?

In all our talk of the good of society it is agreed that the individual shall not be sacrificed for that good. Indeed, it is believed that real social progress will come only when opportunity is given to individuals to develop, provided they are not selected because they represent a particular group or level of intelligence.

4. John Dewey, *Experience and Education,* The Macmillan Company, New York, 1938, p. 46.
5. Ibid., pp. 98–99.

The Process of Change as Basis for Courses of Action

Thus far we have emphasized the importance of developing a strategy for curriculum improvement based upon objectives sought for pupils. This focus is essential if curriculum planners are to undertake the intensive study of teaching and learning in what are peculiarly school problems. This means that the first priority is not assigned to the search for more fields of knowledge which are becoming more intimately related to strategic decisions. That can be left to the researchers. Nor is it assigned to the strengthening of the process skills and attitudes of town-hall democracy, the pursuing of the "search of self," or the "releasing of creativity," although all these may be by-products of curriculum improvement. The formulation of objectives is a prerequisite to the supervisor's immediate concern: the intelligent, imaginative, and comprehensive application of the knowledge we have about curriculum and instruction. A second requirement for a sound strategy is the selection of a plan of action to attain the objectives. Pursuant to the latter task, it is necessary to consider the factors involved in the development of an organizational plan of change.

There is as yet no single set of principles for effecting curriculum change. It is true that many of the behavioral sciences have studied one or another aspect of change. By setting out in broad outline some of the systematic knowledge about the process of change now available and suggesting its application, supervisors may select courses of action which are preferable to that based solely on intuition, experience, or certain currently exalted slogans.

The Psychological Approach to Organizational Change

Studies of the psychology of change within an institution have shown that the concepts of the psychology of learning can be relevant to programs of curriculum improvement. Farson,[6] Coffey and Golden,[7] and Ginzberg and Reilley[8] have garnered psychological generalizations useful in controlling the process of change in large organizations. Using these sources as well as the pertinent psychological principles for effectiveness, we present the following factors as important in effecting change:

6. Richard E. Farson, "Paradoxes in Consulting with Community Organizations," paper presented at American Psychological Association annual meeting, New York, Sept. 4, 1966.
7. Hubert S. Coffey and William P. Golden, Jr., "Psychology of Change within an Institution," *In-Service Education of Teachers, Supervisors, and Administrators,* Fifty-sixth Yearbook, part I, National Society for the Study of Education, The University of Chicago Press, Chicago, 1957.
8. Eli Ginzberg and Ewing W. Reilley, *Effecting Change in Large Organizations,* Columbia University Press, New York, 1957.

1. *There ought to be clear evidence that the leadership is strongly supporting the new proposals for change.* People are responsive to what their leaders want. No one should remain in doubt about how the principal feels about a change in the case of an individual school or about the attitude of the superintendent in decisions of a system-wide nature. By way of example, a curriculum worker in a large secondary school was successful in getting initial approval for a series of curriculum-planning conferences. The fact that the principal did not participate in the sessions nor inquire about them when they were over led the teachers to believe that the proposed changes were unimportant or not desired. Consequently, changes were not effected and the curriculum worker was discouraged by loss of influence with the teachers. It is also recalled that if the supervisor is recognized as influential with authorities in the system the better satisfied subordinates will be. Attempts to help others when one is perceived as noninfluential do not increase anyone's satisfaction.

2. *Individuals realize that their own future is intimately linked with the fortune of the schools and the proposed change.* The more the system strengthens its position, the greater the advantage (prestige, security, etc.) there will be for those who serve it well. Pervasive identification is of great help to supervisors seeking wholehearted acceptance of a plan. Through consultation, both status leaders and teachers will have a better perception of the need for change. When supervisors and teachers share each other's demands and pressures as part of a problem-solving situation, their different perspectives can become channels for facilitating change rather than barriers.

3. *There is institutional resistance to forces which endeavor to change the character of the school.* Supervisors and teachers have a loyalty to the way they see the school and their role in it. This resistance is itself desirable, for without it there would be no stability or integrity. Resistance may mean that the change is taken seriously enough to endure once it is accepted. When new conditions put present practices to strain and modification is necessary, the process should save as much of the old as is relevant. The prospect of the new is likely to arouse anxiety in some teachers. The more confidence teachers have in the integrity of supervisors, the more such feelings will be under control. Consultation and factual announcement during initial stages of the change, so that rumors of impending change do not have free run, lessen disturbance.

4. *The behavior of individuals is affected by the actions of the group to which they belong.* Teachers are likely to be more positively

oriented to a plan for change when it is approved by an informal group to which they are attracted. The influence of the group stems from the desire to be identified with the group which serves as a frame of reference against which opinions, attitudes, and behavior can be evaluated. If persons are members of small supportive groups in which they can express feelings of doubt, hostility, and excitement, they can better strike out into the unknown.

5. *The success of any plan for change requires that individuals have opportunity to master new skills.* Once objectives at which changes are aimed are illuminated, the learning of new skills becomes paramount before teachers can alter their behavior patterns. The fostering of aspirations without providing means produces behavior which is withdrawn, aggressive, or ritualistc.

   Teachers should have the chance to practice with the kind of behavior and content necessary to the attainment of the new objective. If, for instance, a proposed curriculum change calls for pupils in the elementary school to recognize the difference between numbers and the symbolism of numbers, it might be necessary to ask teachers to illustrate ways in which the same number can be represented by different number systems and to suggest how these ideas can be used in their own classrooms. Incidentally, the setting of the informal group is an excellent place for a teacher to practice a new performance, making observations and getting reactions for improvement. Teachers, like children, must know whether their new responses are correct if they are to acquire the new skills.

6. Briefly, the following conditions make possible the teacher's ability to change: *(a)* The teacher wants to learn and is propelled by a personal standard of accomplishment. Prestige and approval can be gained to the extent that the teacher can further the learning of pupils in the direction of the objectives for the classroom. *(b)* The teacher has been given the necessary cues which indicate those elements in the situation which lead to the correct response; i.e., the supervisor has spelled out the response which the change requires. *(c)* The teacher has been given time and support for sufficient practice of the new response. Work loads have been relocated when necessary. *(d)* Rewards for the new response occur through indicators of improved instructional effectiveness and the reinforcements which are related to progress toward the objective.

7. *The process of change is expedited if effective measuring devices are developed.* As indicated above, teachers gain a clearer understanding of the objectives and principles which should guide their actions when appropriate measuring instruments are designed and perfected. Feedback of the results of the change being introduced

as well as a periodic audit facilitates the plan of action by informing supervisors where further action or revision of objectives is
indicated.
8. *Big changes are sometimes relatively easier to make than small
   ones.* People, individually and in the school organization, are re-
   markably able to resist change, for as Farson says, "Most of the
   changes they confront are relatively small and easily resisted."[9] But
   people do not have much experience in resisting big changes—
   perhaps they cannot mobilize resistance because the change is
   too big. "Moving someone's desk ten feet can stir up a storm of
   resistance, but a sweeping realignment of the organization can be
   accomplished without much difficulty because people are seldom
   confronted with large-scale change and do not know where to
   start resisting."[10] The phenomenon is similar to a school board's
   inability to discuss a million-dollar item on its budget, though they
   argue in great detail about a hundred-dollar item.

QUESTIONABLE STATEMENTS ON
HOW TO BRING ABOUT CHANGE

Rules or slogans regarding curriculum change have appeared so frequently in professional journals during the last thirty-year period that
it is sometimes supposed that the sayings are eternally true despite
the most unbelievable changes in everything else. This is not to say
that these admonishments are wrong or useless, but that our respect
for them should not be so extreme that we enshrine them as dogmas
or that they become a bias which prevents a view of the obvious.

1. *Discussion leads to change and action.* Coch and French studied
   the effectiveness of different methods of introducing changes.[11]
   They found that informal group resistance to change could best be
   overcome and efficiency and effectiveness obtained by involving
   all group members in planning the change, arranging for them to
   learn the required new operation and to give suggestions. They
   also found that a method by which a few representatives chosen
   by their group participated in the planning and then trained their
   associates was superior to the customary method where the supervisor did the planning for the subordinates and told them about it
   at a meeting. The method of partial participation was somewhat
   less effective than where all participated.

   A number of similar studies followed the work of Coch and
   French, leading to the conclusion that new standards are more

9. Farson, op. cit., p. 3.
10. Ibid.
11. Lester Coch and John R. P. French, "Overcoming Resistance to Change," *Human
Relations,* vol. 1, no. 4, pp. 512–532, 1948.

readily accepted when the individual participates in setting them than when they are introduced by fiat or with exhortations and assurances. We have already discussed the necessity for considering the conditions which must accompany participation before such a conclusion is warranted. It will be recalled that there is danger in asking faculty members to discuss problems with which they have had very little experience and do not have the background out of which to formulate recommendations for desirable change. We have also previously established that participation of the faculty in decision making results in higher morale, and greater willingness to change, but does not guarantee that changes will be more intelligent or will improve the program. The point which is now to be made is that many supervisors base their plan of action upon the assumption that discussion itself is the critical factor influencing change and action. Many programs for curriculum improvement have used the idea that group discussion, as an influence technique, is a more effective inducement to action than a lecture method or no persuasive attempt at all. This is not necessarily true. More recent studies have discounted it. While decision is essential in effecting change, discussion is not.

In her studies, Bennett found that desired behavior occurs more frequently *(a)* when members are asked to make a decision and *(b)* when they perceive near unanimity.[12] Whether a lecture or group discussion precedes the decisions and whether individual decisions are made public or not has no effect on the outcome. Increasingly, the implication is drawn that in effecting change it is most important both to work for decisions and to arrange conditions where the wisest decisions can be made. Discussion alone is not enough. If a wise decision requires the drawing of conclusions by one whose superior knowledge or ability is in the area under consideration, it should be part of the plan of action. The informational influence of an authority who points out the reason for change to the teacher without discussion may lead to more stable change than that which stems from the social influence of a group discussion. As suggested by Dill, many are quite willing to let supervisors make decisions for them.[13] Some dissent in participation can be traced to basic personality factors. Some can be traced to the perceived constraints on the individual autonomy on the job.

2. *One cannot use force in effecting change.* It might be correct to

12. Edith B. Bennett, "Discussion, Decision, Commitment, and Consensus in 'Group Decision,'" *Human Relations,* vol. 8, no. 3, pp. 251–273, 1955.
13. William R. Dill, "Decision-making," in *Behavioral Sciences and Educational Administration,* NYSSE Yearbook, 1964, pp. 199–233.

say that one should not use force. Professional literature seldom recognizes that change can be produced by force. The position of the supervisor against the use of force may seem unrealistic when viewed against a world setting which at times appears to reverse the moral order and proclaim "might makes right." Realistically, force is a dominant method in schools, too. To the extent that supervisors control values important to teachers, force can be applied. Coercive influence comes from the ability to reward and punish through the threat of poor ratings, nonpromotion, transfer, or other forms of personal approval or disapproval. The use of force is usually unintentional. At times, supervisors think they are gaining acceptance of a plan because of its merits, but teachers are thinking of the retaliatory power which can be applied (real or imaginary) if they do not go along with the change. In fact, force is probably most effective when it is not necessary to use it actively. We believe that force should be acknowledged as an instrument for the attainment of strategic objectives but that its use can be minimized. Supervisors should be alerted to its presence if they are to avoid its harmful effects. In the long run, its values are often transient. Social psychologists have found that coercive power becomes less effective as soon as the subjects' behavior no longer is observable.[14] Full support of the group and no threatening behavior by the supervisor versus a situation in which the supervisor has, without clear justification, threatened subjects will show that both groups display conformity in their public behavior but that the noncoercive supervisor will exert more influence in private attitudes. Coercion also results in greater hostility and tension.

The use of force often closes the normal lines of communication and leads to the introduction of synthetic formalities. Its direction is negative. While it might sometimes be necessary to use force in order to arrive at the place where reason can take over, force itself contributes nothing to reasonableness.

DeCharms has provided evidence in support of his proposal that one's primary motivation is to be effective in producing changes in his or her environment—to be the locus of causation. Because of the desire to be "origins" of their behavior, people are constantly struggling against the constraint of external forces—against being moved about like "pawns." It is DeCharms' hypothesis that when persons perceive their behavior as stemming from their own choices (i.e., see themselves as origins), they cherish that behavior and its results. Conversely, when persons perceive

14. Bertram H. Raven, "The Dynamics of Groups," *Review of Educational Research,* vol. 29, no. 4, pp. 332–339, October 1959.

their behavior as stemming from external forces (i.e., see themselves as pawns), that behavior and its results, though identical in other respects to behavior of one's own choosing, is devaluated.[15]

3. *The dynamics of the learner coming to know is a movement out of self into externality multidimensionally.* Such vague but emotionally satisfying expressions as this have been used to explain the change process of children and frequently appear as guidelines for supervisors in such forms as "Supervisors do not attempt to develop programs for change; they create a climate for growth." or "Experience is the best teacher." These emotional phrases usually represent a point of view which holds that change requires primarily a climate or "garden" for growth and removal of restrictions hampering the evolution of the individual. They represent an invalid application of a biological analogy and belong to the doctrines of "naturalism" and "developmentalism" which appeared in the eighteenth and nineteenth centuries. These prevalent expressions agree with Froebel's assumption that all that one can become lies within and that the purpose of an agent of change is to bring more out of humanity, not put more into it.[16] There have been many desirable supervisory practices in accordance with this belief: Supervisors have attempted to build programs of improvement by giving words of encouragement to discouraged teachers, recognizing minor contributions as a spur to greater achievement, considering individual differences in the staff, respecting the right of people to be different, taking the time to find out how a proposed change looks to teachers, being willing to listen, working on problems of concern to the individual, and performing other actions to provide the security necessary for teacher growth.

Our criticism of the "climate of growth" approach to change is that it assists those changes of behavior which would arise as a consequence of maturation or chance factors in the larger society rather than those which are tied to classroom learning. Just as children are not likely to acquire through random experiences the concepts required for reading in mathematics, so teachers require a limited range of alternatives if they are to concentrate upon their instructional task. The supervisor, therefore, must consider in developing programs for curriculum improvement only those aspects in the life of "the whole teacher" which are known to be related to classroom performance. The environment for the in-service program must be arranged to result in changes consistent with the

15. R. DeCharms, *Enhancing Motivation: Change in Classrooms,* Irvinston Co., New York, 1976.
16. Friedrich Froebel, *The Education of Man,* D. Appleton and Company, New York, 1887.

objectives of the school. When supervisors try to consider all variables in the life of a teacher, they are likely to treat those which
are insignificant to curriculum and instruction and, because of the
complexity of this inappropriate undertaking, to overlook items
central to the primary changes sought. Further, in order to help
teachers recognize essential factors in the classroom which are not
obvious to them, certain meanings must be brought especially to
their attention. Rather than let the teacher "learn by experience"
in the natural way, staff development should deliberately structure
artificial situations in which teachers can be rewarded for making
appropriate responses to specific problems. The use of mini-les-
sons and simulation devices and materials in which teachers face
standardized situations demanding action and find reward in
newly acquired responses is one way this can be achieved.

THE SEARCH FOR NEW PROGRAMS

The big difference between schools that are just sort of getting along
and those that are out in front lies chiefly in the promptness with
which the latter detect relevant challenges in the environment and
new opportunities for innovation in response to these challenges.
Instead of being "pinned down" by urgent problems which are
handed to them, these schools give attention to problems which are
not immediate. As indicated in Chapter 4, successful school systems
are quick to formally adopt fashionable innovations as well as quick
to incorporate them and to let them disappear. The supervisor who
wants to improve a school on this score develops the habit of asking
"What new things or events are happening in the world right now
that this school ought to look at?" More than this, this supervisor
develops a number of prods and rewards that set others looking for
problems. The staff is alerted to developments in other fields which
throw light upon (1) the new ways of teaching by which intellect
becomes a product rather than a prerequisite and (2) techniques for
unlearning inappropriate conceptions. Implications for the school
from the spreading of a political doctrine and the latest technical
achievement are topics for speculation by all.

In helping teachers shift to new programs of action, the supervisor tries to alter levels of aspiration and satisfaction. This occurs as
the outcomes of instruction are periodically reviewed and when exchange visits, demonstrations, and other activities make the staff
aware that there are courses of action that yield substantially better
results than the present program. Evaluation on the basis of results
rather than techniques fosters an orientation to search and a sensitivity to the environment.

The practice of changing a condition so that older methods are
no longer appropriate is another way of increasing innovation. A

"textbook-bound teacher" sometimes becomes "creative" when trying to fulfill the new responsibility of student adviser. Such private adaptations are to be encouraged when the teacher is clear about objectives and the effect of the innovation upon others. We have already pointed out that the path to new adjustments is paved with the security found in the social support of peer group and supervisor. One of the real contributions a supervisor can make is to aid teachers in their search for innovations by indicating likely sources of information. Teachers who are dissatisfied with their present approach will welcome knowledge as to what they can get from others, for without it they must find an answer in a more painful fashion.

Organizational theory suggests that most innovations in a school are borrowed rather than invented. Borrowing takes the form of either direct imitation or the importing of new personnel.[17] The former is exemplified by supervisors who visit a reading clinic in another district and subsequently start a similar one in their own system, avoiding many of the errors and costs associated with the initial development. The importing occurs when "avoidance of inbreeding" is a factor in the selection of personnel and when a group of new persons from a subculture not previously represented become members of the staff. Perhaps it is unrealistic to expect that schools or individuals will engage in vigorous search for innovations while they have responsibilities in existing programs and are caught in daily routine. But most are willing to go out to meet new events when they have a clear sense of objectives, secure conditions, a favorable work load, and the knowledge that the system expects innovation.

PATTERNS OF DIRECTED PROGRAMS
FOR CURRICULUM IMPROVEMENT

Many proposals have been offered for modification of the curriculum. Some of these require surface changes, such as the listing of additional offerings or the introduction of the latest instructional materials. Other proposals entail a fundamental redefinition of the school's purpose and require a shifting of values. It is expected that teachers and the public in general will bring countervailing pressures for continuance of the established and familiar and that there will be resistance to what appears to be another educational epidemic. In the past, this opposition to change has been quite successful. Ross, for instance, in 1957 reported that fifty years was required from the first introduction of an adaptation in the first school of a state until 100 percent of the schools were using the adaptation.[18]

17. James G. March and Herbert A. Simon, *Organizations,* John Wiley & Sons, Inc., New York, 1958, p. 188.
18. Donald Ross, *Administration for Adaptability,* rev. ed., Columbia University,

Kimball Wiles believed that an important dividing line in strategies for curriculum change was 1957.[19] Before that date change occurred by the strategy of *pragmatic evolution.* Emphasis was given to local school districts preparing their own course of study and teachers in individual buildings developing their own curriculum.

Commencing in 1957, curriculum change occurred through *directed change,* whereby change was not equated with chance but with plan. Innovation was linked to long-term goals set by out-of-school persons in government, foundations, and universities. The curriculum materials associated with these goals were produced by other than local school personnel.

However, the directed change strategy was less than successful. Even though innovations were introduced into school systems, teachers did not always use them as the planners intended. John Goodlad and associates completed a six-year study documenting the effect of the change strategy in the schools.[20] They learned that most of what goes on outside in the name of schools has little to do with the schools' functioning and never comes to roost there; a great deal that does come to roost there is so inappropriate that it does more to impede than to aid school functioning.

Currently, there are other strategies suggested that promise to compensate for the directed change model. Goodlad proposes an "inner-outer" approach with the single school as the organic unit of change. He recommends help and guidance from an informed, caring outside resource that will stimulate school staffs so that they will be aware of what is required for improvement and be discriminately selective in what they reach out for and bring into the school. His responsive strategy for change involves staff dialogue (total and subgroup) in making decisions, taking action, and evaluating both the process and its outcomes. It also calls for a supporting infrastructure consisting of peer schools to exchange perspectives on the same problems and to assuage the loneliness of effecting change. The existence of a stable, prestigious institution or agency ready to assist the schools is also important to the strategy. Sustained external support from an aware but sympathetic alternative drummer is an essential element in the response strategy.[21]

Teachers College, Metropolitan School Study Council, New York, 1957.
19. Kimball Wiles, "Contrasts in Strategies of Change," in R. L. Leeper (ed.), *Strategies for Curriculum Change,* Association for Supervision and Curriculum Development, Washington, 1965, pp. 1–10.
20. John I. Goodlad, "What Goes On in Our Schools?" *Educational Researcher,* vol. 6, no. 3, pp. 3–6, March 1977.
21. John I. Goodlad, *The Uses of Alternative Theories of Educational Change,* Phi Delta Kappa International, Bloomington, Ind., 1975.

One central point should be made regarding innovations in the schools. An innovation is not an end; it is a means. The introduction of peer teaching, new materials for the teaching of the disadvantaged, learning-resource centers, and the like is not enough. The supervisor must know what these innovations point to. In what way will learners be different as the result of these innovations? Unless there is a logical connection between the innovation and the outcome sought from the innovation, regard the change with suspicion. More than that, evidence ought to be collected to show whether or not the predicted results occur. When helping a school board decide which of several instructional systems to adopt, the supervisor should emphasize the results to follow from the innovation rather than the innovation itself. For example, consider the adoption of a "modular curriculum." Usually this means scheduling learning activities in accordance with a flexible arrangement rather than the traditional forty-five-minute class period, five days a week. The promoters of this idea believe that modifying the structure of the schools' scheduling will open doors to consideration of new ends, e.g., the mastery of new content, the development of new attitudes and skills on the part of learners. This assumption may be useful, but it must be checked out. Furthermore, in scheduling hours of independent study for learners or large blocks of time for laboratory experiments, supervisors should habitually ask themselves what do I expect learners will gain from this arrangement that they cannot gain from the present practices? How will this difference show itself?

A fundamental thesis of this book is that change in schools will occur more rapidly when more attention (e.g., measurement of product or outcomes from the school experiences) is given to the results of practice. Mathew Miles has advanced a similar belief that goal ambiguity encourages the institutionalization and ossification of teaching procedures.[22] Progress toward the goals of schools is not unmeasurable although we have preferred to say it is. The failures to state goals operationally and to collect evidence regarding the extent to which our practices are successful in leading learners to these goals have led to acceptance of existing practice, not to the search for better (more effective and economical) practice.

"If it cannot really be determined whether one course of action leads to more output than another, then why stop lecturing?" In explaining why so many adoptions are unstable, Lippitt points out

---

22. Mathew B. Miles, "Planned Change and Organizational Health: Figure and Ground," in Richard O. Carlson et al. (eds.), *Change Processes in the Public Schools,* University of Oregon, Center for the Advanced Study of Educational Administration, Eugene, 1965, p. 22.

that there is a lack of clear feedback to reinforce the change efforts which tell educators whether their tryouts are being successful in the direction that they had hoped.[23] In those fields where innovations come more rapidly, there is also knowledge of results—not just the innovation itself. The farmer notes whether or not the new seed or fertilizer brings better crops; the doctor notes whether or not the new drug gets the temperature down or the patient up. Teachers must be taught to note whether the innovation they are trying has a payoff for the pupils and to collect indicators that show the extent to which the payoff is occurring for all children. Knowledge of results in terms of what happens to learners is replacing the need for teachers to seek encouragement and reassurance from supportive colleagues and supervisors that they are doing a good job. Many good ideas in teaching are lost and more poor ones retained because they are not objectively evaluated. The systematic means of checking results of innovations is a pressing need.

Innovation and Improvement

The basic fallacy of much criticism of the school is "the tendency in contemporary criticism to equate innovation with excellence." As a result of this, school supervisors live under a veritable reign of terror. On the one hand, they are constantly accused of perversely ignoring new trends; on the other, they are just as often charged with "wasting public funds" on expensive frills that may within a few years be of no interest or educational value.[24]

Adoption of a new mathematics or humanities curriculum or the introduction of new administrative features such as magnet schools is not made in fully reasoned fashion. Some proponents of the change are satisfied to rest their claims on the superiority of the content (that the new math is most representative of the field). Others, especially administrators, are likely to press for or resist the innovation in the belief (1) that it will be more or less trouble, viz., that it will upset the staff or require more meetings for explaining the change to the public, (2) that it will threaten the survival of traditional and comfortable practices, and (3) that there is no evidence that the change will result in sufficient benefits beyond the present practice to justify the additional cost in money and time necessary to introduce the innovation.

23. Ronald Lippitt, "Roles and Processes in Curriculum Development and Change," in R. L. Leeper (ed.), *Strategy for Curriculum Change,* Association for Supervision and Curriculum Development, Washington, 1965, pp. 11–28.
24. The statement is paraphrased from one voiced by Edourd Roditi in connection with a similar condition faced by museum curators who must make wise or foolish decisions regarding selections of modern art. "Ex-Titan of the Tate," *Saturday Review,* May 27, 1967.

There are signs that education may at some time have its *Consumers Guide* for reporting important information about specifications, critical characteristics, and actual school performance of instructional materials, equipment, and systems for preschool through junior college. A case in point is Educational Products Information Exchange (EPIE),[25] which was established in 1966 with the intent of providing the information regarding school products which will be most helpful in making decisions about the suitability of a product in the light of local educational purposes.

Confusion regarding ends and means is a chief stumbling block to instructional improvement. At the classroom level teachers sometimes tend to value a procedure such as a grouping practice, a certain way of asking questions, a traffic pattern, a manner of conducting discussions. The failure to ask "What are the intended consequences from these procedures?" is serious. The failure to collect evidence regarding whether both the intended consequences and the unforeseen ones occur is, in a way, unethical. At the administrative level the confusion of practices (arrangements) with results is perhaps even greater. Principals, for example, may recognize that something specific should follow from a kindergarten teacher's activity involving block play—knowing that this activity is not an end in itself. Yet these same principals are likely to be blinded by their own activities. Ask them what differences in pupil gain they expect as a result of a new staffing pattern or a new scheduling arrangement and they will have difficulty in specifying amounts and kinds of differences that logically follow.

Increasingly, however, teachers and administrators are collecting evidence on whether or not predicted results occur and are asking If results are obtained as intended, are there any undesirable side effects? Are the results of any value in helping meet new demands of the world; that is, how does the innovation help meet the demands of citizenship, vocation, and sane living?

Examples of the kinds of evidence collected in order to more fully assess the effects of innovation are as follows:[26]

1. How long is it taking for learners to master the principles taught (relative economy of instructional time)?
2. How often are the principles used in new situations (relative value in terms of application)?
3. How long is the knowledge retained (relative retention value)?

25. A division of the Institute for Educational Development, 52 Vanderbilt Ave., New York, N.Y. 10017, P. Kenneth Konoski, director.
26. Harry J. Broudy, "Innovations and Curriculum Decision," *CTA Journal*, January 1967, pp. 14–16.

4. How quickly is the knowledge relearned (relative savings value)?
5. How easily can a learner acquire additional or new knowledge in the field (relative degree of learning to learn)?
6. How much desire do learners have for continuing their learning in the subject (relative attitudes toward the subject)?

Organized programs in response to curriculum demands are likely to increase in importance. Understanding of the patterns for directed programs which have been followed may be helpful to the supervisor in devising better ways of developing programs for curriculum improvement.

Programs for curriculum improvement have tended to follow four patterns: (1) bargaining, (2) persuasion, (3) politics, and (4) problem solving.[27] Where bargaining has been used, disagreement over the objectives is seen as fixed. *Bargaining,* therefore, acknowledges and legitimizes heterogeneity of practice, permitting modification on a picemeal basis. *Persuasion* assumes that everyone is in favor of certain broad objectives and that if there is disagreement over the way individual schools are moving, these differences can be mediated by reference to the common goal. *Politics* also assumes a conflict of interests but uses the basic strategy of including potential allies (community groups and teachers) in getting support for the plan. In *problem solving,* it is assumed that objectives are shared and that all must identify a solution that satisfies the shared criteria. Action-research, where the staff assembles information and seeks new solutions, is consistent with this problem-solving pattern. Trends and points of emphasis in these patterns are shown in the descriptions which follow.

Bargaining Has Long Been the Pattern

Benjamin Franklin in 1749 presented revolutionary ideas for the curriculum. His *Proposals Relating to the Education of the Youth of Pennsylvania* could well be used, with minor changes, as a prospectus for schools today. Advocating, for example, student experimentation in science and a functional approach to the teaching of English, Franklin recognized important demands for living successfully in a current world. It was his desire to make a clean break with the traditional program and methods of the Latin Grammar School, but in order to obtain the wealth and influence necessary for the institution which could carry out the change, he resorted to bargaining, deferring to those with different educational values. The Latin classics

27. This differentiation of patterns follows March and Simon's analysis of organizational reaction to conflict: James G. March and Herbert A. Simon, *Organizations,* John Wiley & Sons, Inc., New York, 1958, p. 129.

were included as an essential part of the curriculum even though Franklin himself wanted the priority placed on other studies. Instead of education leaping ahead one hundred years, there was a compromise with tradition and Franklin's program failed to exemplify itself completely.

In his famous Sachs Foundation Lecures, Professor Briggs commented upon the story of Franklin's failure, which has been repeated time after time in the later development of the curriculum:[28]

> The first cause of failure was the necessity of compromise with tradition. Both an influential part of the public and the available teachers respected the conventional program so strongly that they forced an organization of three departments—a Latin, an English and a Mathematical—each with its own master. Before his death Franklin felt called on to protest the treatment of the English school, the master of which, he said, had been reduced by discrimination in favor of the classical studies to a position subservient to the Latin master.
>
> A second cause of failure . . . to achieve the ideals that Franklin had proposed was that the teachers, however much they might have sympathized with the proposed program, had only a general plan, with no textbooks, detailed syllabi, or knowledge of suitable methods. They had vested interests in what they themselves had been taught and, being humanly selfish, were doubtless reluctant to give up the impartation of the acquired knowledge that had given them prestige. Even if they had wholeheartedly accepted Franklin's program, they would have been supermen had they been able in their full schedules to invent or organize the details of courses that would have made their novel instruction successful. Likewise, they knew in a way how to teach what they had been taught, but the new subjects did not lend themselves to memoriter work, and the masters could not devise suitable new methods that were convincingly effective with those who were accustomed to assigned lessons that would be recited verbatim the next day.

Curriculum Change by National Committees Using Persuasion

At the end of the nineteenth century, planned programs for curriculum change came largely to be the prerogative of national committees and commissions. Prior to that time, governing boards, administrators, and textbook writers were responsible for additions to the curriculum, and curriculum change was characterized by the piecemeal addition of new courses. National groups, including the Commitees of Ten and Fifteen[29] and the Commissions on the Reorganiza-

28. Thomas H. Briggs, "The Secondary School Curriculum: Yesterday, Today, and Tomorrow," *Teachers College Record,* vol. 52, no. 7, p. 403, April 1951.
29. U.S. Bureau of Education, *Report of the Committee on Secondary School Studies Appointed at the Meeting of the National Educational Association,* July 9, 1892 (hereinafter cited as *Committee of Ten Report*), Washington, 1893.

tion of Secondary Education and Life Adjustment Education for Youth[30] have issued pronouncements utilizing a persuasive approach. That is, an appeal is made by the committee for broad general goals to which all adhere, i.e., "preparing for life," "unifying the people," and "achieving self-realization."

Specific recommendations from these national bodies have reflected, however, the perspective and interest of the academicians and school administrators comprising the particular committees. Usually, the recommendations have been formulated by a priori methods without scientific investigation. National strategists have frequently shaped the curriculum by their opinionative recommendations through appeal to high-level goals, to the prestige of the organization, and to the status of the specialists designing the recommended program.

Even more important in effecting the recommendation, perhaps, have been other pressures evoked by those implementing the strategy. Instructional materials, including textbooks and courses of study, have been prepared in accordance with the committees' reports. Policies regarding college entrance examinations have altered from time to time in order to conform to the recommended changes. Testing services have been asked to develop instruments for evaluating proposed outcomes which resulted from deliberations by national groups. Also, the policy statements themselves are made available as a framework for discussion and as an outline for the various action programs conducted in state and local systems. These action programs include provision for the training and assistance of those who must carry out the program.

National campaigns for change are advanced by pinpointing responsibility to designated individuals for translating the program into effective action. In this connection, leaders in education effect a close liaison with school administrative organizations and leaders in teacher-education centers. Procedures at the level of action rely upon political strategy, an approach which differs from both (1) the persuasive appeal to common ideals and (2) the acknowledgement under bargaining that disagreements about curriculum are permanent and that those who differ must be outbid rather than converted.

Report of the Committee of Fifteen on Elementary Education, published for the National Education Association by the American Book Company, 1895.
30. U.S. Bureau of Education, *Cardinal Principles of Secondary Education: A Report of the Commission on the Reorganization of Secondary Education Appointed by the National Education Association,* Washington, 1918.
U.S. Office of Education, *A Look Ahead in Secondary Education—Education for Life Adjustment,* Bulletin no. 4, Washington, 1954.

Politics as an Approach to Organized Programs for Change
Curriculum planners employing a political strategy try to manipulate factors crucial to change. Their procedures follow some such pattern as this:

1. *Selection of a leadership team.* A professional steering group is chosen in which each member has a particular role to play in the proposed change and because the superintendent respects their judgment and objectivity. In the typical school system, the basic composition of the group would be the superintendent, curriculum director, principal, and two teachers. The team may have more members, but generally it is better to have the smallest number that will embrace the requirements for initiating the program. In large districts there may be a central office team with representatives from all the schools in the district. This central coordinating team is formed in conjunction with leadership teams in each school who are responsible for the program in their own buildings. A leadership team is composed only of professional persons; there are no advisory or lay members, for this elite alone must make policy decisions to guide the course of events.

　　The key person in developing an effective program is the superintendent, who must recognize the importance of the change and be willing to devote time and effort to planning the change with the team. The superintendent usually takes responsibility for seeing that the school board, staff, and community understand the change. The principal is also needed for supporting teachers as they endeavor to change in accordance with the plan. The principal's enthusiasm or opposition can determine the success or failure of the program. Further, the principal has special responsibility *(a)* for interpreting the program to faculty, student body, and patrons and *(b)* for scheduling and coordinating events in the building. The curriculum director is essential because holders of this position usually have *(a)* comprehensive understanding of the total curriculum, *(b)* ability to select and organize content, *(c)* familiarity with resource materials, and *(d)* competence in evaluation. The classroom teachers are expected to reflect the perspective of their fellows in the planning phase. Later they will demonstrate and interpret the program. For this reason, they should be known to supervisors and fellow teachers as influence figures of ability. It is important that all team members have enthusiasm for the ideas underlying the program.
2. *Considerations and tactics of the leadership team.* How much time should be allowed for change? Should the change occur on a broken front, in which those most ready are approached first, or

on a uniform front, in which the plan is put into operation at one time throughout the system? When should the proposed change be announced? How can the results of the change be noted and accountability be maintained? Such questions are faced by the leadership team once it has been decided to effect the plan.

Through interviews and informal discussion with a representative sample of those in the system, team members seek cooperation, alternative proposals, and relevant information about the readiness of the staff for change. The development of the plan of action takes time, for it cannot be borrowed from other systems. It must be forged by the team in light of the district's unique history as well as its present and likely future conditions. The plan will flounder unless the team is sensitive to such factors as memories of former plans which were introduced and failed, forces of tradition, outside pressures, as well as the anticipated effect upon the position and power of those to be involved. But calculated risks must be taken if the plan is to get off the ground.

In some situations it may be better to move on a broken front and to effect initially only part of the program. This is not only because schools and teachers differ in their readiness for change but also because the strategists do not control enough of the forces for change and must gain support by small successes. On the other hand, evidence from other institutions which are bureaucratically organized as opposed to the open society indicates that a total change on a uniform front can be more effective. The elimination of segregation of the Armed Forces is given as an illustration of how a bureaucratic organization can effect rapid change by clarifying through specific directions what is expected and moving with such authority, certainty, and speed that those who would otherwise organize for resistance never have the chance. It is customary in schools, however, to take the course of gradual diffusion of practice in effecting change.

The strategy of "starting small and spreading" has been used in attempts at mass curriculum change in the nation's schools.[31] Usually, in these instances, change is introduced among a few teachers who feel that the new proposal is an answer to a problem. Some teachers will adopt it and try to make it work in spite of those who say it is a poor idea. When the change is to begin on a small scale, it is generally believed best to include only those teachers who want to participate and who are among the most skilled and respected leaders on the teaching staff. Caution must be taken that the program

31. William S. Vincent et al., *Building Better Programs in Citizenship,* Citizenship Education Project, Teachers College, Columbia University, New York, 1958.

does not become tagged as belonging to a particular school or teacher. If it becomes "the Valley School's program," adoption is delayed. This need not occur if it can be made clear that the initial teachers are serving as representatives of all, and steps are taken to involve others in the progress of the plan. After pioneers demonstrate the effectiveness of the innovation and show that no one need fear it, others will try it. It is at this point that change can be introduced to all schools and teachers who should make use of it.

It is important that everyone understand the immediate change as well as the model toward which the system is moving. Uneasiness created by rumors resulting from initial inquiries during the preplanning phase can be lessened at special meetings where final decisions are announced and the main outline of the plan is clearly delineated. The formal announcement includes (1) the reasons for the plan and the care taken in developing it, (2) a realistic assessment of the difficulties expected in implementation, and (3) positive emphasis upon the long-range advantages. The announcement cannot include all details, but it should make explicit the responsibilities that are attached to supervisors and teachers. The staff should know the extent to which authority and responsibility for detailed planning have been delegated to them. Before too long, it might be advisable for the author to prepare a personal responsibility chart in which the author notes personal understanding of the proposal and conception of the specific role it demands. Opportunity for acquiring the understanding of new principles and the proficiency required by the change must, of course, be provided.

Appropriate measurement and control devices are necessary if the leadership team is to judge whether schools and teachers are making sound progress and to adapt the plan as experience dictates. A few basic performance yardsticks and scheduled reports are included in the original plan, but others are fashioned after the plan is implemented. Supervisors and teachers develop new measures and refine existing ones in light of particular conditions. Indicators of change must be related, however, to the objectives of the plan. Active participation in the development of these devices aids individuals in understanding more fully the directions in which change is desired. In those instances where individual schools and teachers have been given major responsibility for deciding upon the appropriate manner of reaching the objective, it is necessary that there be an increased number of adequate measures of performance. Only in this way can supervisors and teachers be held accountable and improvement be assured. Results help the professional staff to test the significance of their judgment in the classroom and suggest further action by the leadership team. Ordinarily, the results call attention to other requisites of the planned change and to the inadequacy of in-service education.

Politics in a New Way

In their impatience with school resistance to change, those outside the establishment are devising new strategies. Fantini and Weinstein, for example, use sociologists as change agents directly working upon both administrators and teachers.[32] The sociologists deliberately seek to direct communication from the very top levels of the system to the bottom levels with no intervening mediators, e.g., subject-matter supervisors who usually influence decisions concerning instructional policy. Subject-matter supervisors are intentionally bypassed. "We went over their heads on all the major issues. We thus brought about their alienation from the program and criticism for whatever was done without their involvement." One change agent tries initially to become a confidant of the teachers, at times asking them "What materials would you like that you have never been able to get before?" Suggested materials are acquired for teachers with lightning speed. This kind of prompt action generates an atmosphere of motion.

Similar actions are taken with principals to break down their resistance to change. Principals indicate the services they have always wanted but never received. These additional services (e.g., extra secretary) are promptly filled, but each additive carries with it the requirement that the added personnel must interact with the change agent. Principals are also invited to "status meetings" with top district officials and prominent community leaders. They thus have the feeling of movement in top circles of policymaking, and thereby offer less resistance to the change proposals coming from the outside change agent.

Parallel to the action with teachers and principals, another outside change agent meets with the board of education and the superintendent. This meeting projects purpose and direction. The presentation by the change agent is given before a crowded meeting designed to generate public enthusiasm for the proposed changes. The superintendent is invited to "lean" on the change agent for counsel. "Make use of my outside perspective" is the theme.

The change agents continue to work with the teachers and principals. The agents demonstrate new approaches and techniques, in-

32. Mario Fantini and Gerald Weinstein, "Strategies for Initiating Educational Change in Large Bureaucratic School Systems," paper presented to Columbia University, Teachers College, Public Policy Institute, New York, April 1967.

troduce new materials, and at times arrange for resource people to fill gaps as indicated by the teachers and principals.

Problem Solving as a Pattern in Curriculum Improvement

Problem solving represents an attempt to secure private as well as public agreement to a change. It is used as a means of getting teachers, for instance, to accept objectives not because of the promise of a paycheck, but because of a belief in the worthwhileness of the objective itself. When curriculum does not change because individual teachers do not change, there are efforts by curriculum planners to involve the faculty in the search for additional information on the alternatives available to them and the consequences attached to these alternatives.

The involvement of teachers in problem-solving activity as an approach to curriculum improvement was introduced through organized group program-improvement activities which generally followed the prevailing educational interest by studying "the development needs of pupils" and reflected social conditions by undertaking surveys on "the current needs in our community." Workshops and conferences in which participants attacked problems of concern to themselves were frequent.

From a vantage point of the present, there is a tendency to criticize these early problem-solving efforts to improve the curriculum. The implications for the classroom of the studies undertaken were seldom drawn or acted upon. Individual effort did not lead to overall curriculum plans which had consistency in the experiences offered pupils. There were almost no investigations of the effect of these problem-solving activities on pupil accomplishment. To be fair, one has to consider the needs and purposes which existed at the time these activities were initiated.

School-based staff development today is based upon the concept that it is desirable for teachers to be involved in the identification and articulation of their own training needs. Each school is regarded as a renewal center seeking to improve the school's program through staff development. In his study of school-based programs, Lawrence found that when teachers participate in programs as helpers to each other and as planners of the in-service activities, they tend to have greater success in accomplishing their objectives than they do when in programs conducted without teacher assistance.[33] Further, Lawrence found desirable consequences from these prac-

33. Gordon Lawrence, "Patterns of Effective Inservice Education," unpublished paper, State Department of Education, Tallahassee, Fla., 1974.

tices, such as teachers choosing goals and activities for themselves, constructing or generating materials and ideas, sharing and helping each other, differentiating training experiences for different teachers, and linking the training to a general effort of the school rather than a "single shot" program unrelated to a development plan.

Teacher participation in child-study programs does not seem to affect pupils' reading and arithmetic achievement, but may result in more positive ways of working with children and more "democratic" classroom organization.[34] Typical topics of staff development today might include Individualized Instruction and the Slow Learner, Motivation through Language Arts, Improvement of Pupil-Teacher Relations, and Reading in the Content Fields. We need more precise evidence that workshop experience produces significant change in the behavior of teachers. The participation of teachers in cooperative programs of curriculum planning does not seem to result in greater student achievement than that which occurs when the curriculum is planned either by supervisors alone or by teachers working individually.[35]

One should not assume from this that the problem-solving approach to curriculum improvement is ineffective. On the contrary, it can produce more of an effect than any other pattern, provided steps are taken to see that (1) the problems selected by teachers are related directly to the objectives of classroom instruction, (2) the activity is not dispersed without a guiding plan for the school curriculum as a whole, and (3) attention is given to factors associated with efficiency and effectiveness in the problem-solving process.

In summarizing the research and conclusions from case studies of in-service education, Howey concludes that strategies which integrate training with daily teaching are one means to strengthen teacher commitment to continuing growth.[36]

One example of the problem-solving approach features the efforts of a third-grade teacher in a group program-improvement activity who sought to further the progress of "slow" readers.[37] This teacher was clear about the behavior being sought from pupils but had evidence of failing to help them attain it. Together supervisor

34. Richard M. Brandt and Hugh V. Perkins, Jr., "Teachers Change as They Study Children," *Childhood Education,* vol. 34, no. 5, pp. 218–222, January 1958.
35. George K. McGuire, "The Effect on Student Achievement of Teacher Participation in Curriculum Planning," unpublished Ph.D. dissertation, University of Chicago, Chicago, 1959.
36. Kenneth R. Howey, "The Future Emergent Definition and Social Issues," *Cultural Pluralism as Social Change,* Inservice Teacher Education Concepts Project, Stanford Center for Research and Development in Teaching, Stanford University, Stanford, California, 1976.
37. Hilda Taba and Elizabeth Noel, *Action Research: A Case Study,* Association for Supervision and Curriculum Development, Washington, 1957, pp. 27–58.

and teacher searched for those factors which are known to be associated with nonreading and which were present in the particular classroom. Further diagnosis revealed that pupils were missing many basic sight words, and were not able to attack unknown words. The teacher was helped to devise procedures by which the pupils could develop the use of context clues and have concrete experiences in making the words meaningful. The teacher was guided through additional steps of problem solving to find out what words the pupils did not know in the material to be used. Diagnosis was followed by experiment in which there were sequential presentation of the material, careful formulation of questions which would call for use of the desired vocabulary, and other events, all of which were planned as simple increments of instruction. Events offered immediate reward to the pupils and were cumulative in the direction of the reading skills sought. There was continual measurement of changed behavior, and five months after the experiment started results on an alternate form of the reading achievement test revealed gains ranging from one month to one year and three months. The significance of this account for our purposes is that it points up the importance of helping a teacher (1) think about the problem in a more fundamental way, considering factual evidence and causal factors, and (2) relate problem-solving activity directly to those objectives of the individual classroom which are consistent with the functions of the school.

AN ISSUE IN THE DEVELOPMENT OF
STRATEGY FOR CURRICULUM IMPROVEMENT

The main effort of this chapter has been to provide a picture of existing strategy and tactics for curriculum improvement and to indicate factors which are associated with sound strategy. Further comment on one of the salient issues raised in the discussion is warranted.

There exists the concern that an intellectual elite will select the strategy for curriculum development and that the rights and welfare of an unwary public will be violated. This concern is part of a larger social issue: Is society best served by the method of practical intelligence, whereby all learn how to participate in the processes of planning—a method which seeks to develop common purposes for life? Or is it best served by the method of reason, whereby persons of expertness and democratic intent are given the authority for planning strategy so that social affairs are conducted in the fairest, most efficient manner—a method which aims at consistency of plans rather than satisfaction of particular interests?

Supervisory acceptance of the first alternative carries with it the obligation to generate leadership among all citizens and to improve methods and conditions for discussion and problem solving. Cases in point are those situations where supervisors endeavor to make the school a center for social reconstruction by involving adults and pupils alike in the attack upon local problems and engage in goal-setting discussion, posing such questions as "What do we want our community to be like in 19—?" and "How can the school best cooperate?"

We must avoid, however, a simple "grass roots" approach. If not, an older criticism will once more be made: "One of the most pathetic signs on the educational horizon—myriads of local school committees, whose members have had little or no scientific training, trying to produce a modern science curriculum."[38]

Instead of holding meetings and presenting questionnaires to determine what the schools should teach, supervisors should adopt a sounder approach of spending time in the "study of conditions and trends in contemporary society and . . . requirements for living in the second half of this century. Their findings may reveal definite implications for changes in educational objectives, curriculum, and instructional methods of the schools."[39] Also there is need for the leadership and participation of persons who possess certain professional competencies, i.e., those who can claim (1) specialized knowledge of the academic disciplines and (2) the knowledge of instruction, curriculum designing, and organizing.

We sympathize with those who want to see lay participation in curriculum planning. The school has been one of the few institutions where a scattered public could recognize itself and express its interest. Inasmuch as citizens feel even more remote from civic, national, and international affairs, it is desirable to preserve those neighborly vehicles by which individuals are able to feel the effect of their voices in crucial public matters. Further, such participation makes possible the innovations and new creations which are essential in the execution of an adequate plan. Is there not a way in which the school can enlist the community in the process of curriculum change without jeopardizing its primary responsibility for helping pupils acquire and use those thought processes associated with the systematic organized subject matter? There are several propositions which lead to an affirmative answer:

38. Alexander Calandra, "Some Observations of the Work of the PSCC," *Harvard Educational Review,* vol. 29, no. 1, p. 22, Winter 1957.
39. E. T. McSwain, "Who Should Guide the Public Schools?" *Educational Leadership,* vol. 14, no., 7, pp. 424–425 , April, 1957.

1. No one person or group arrogates the last word on objectives of the curriculum—and gets away with it. Professional authority is granted to individuals demonstrating superior knowledge, but the privilege is revocable by decisions of the people through their elected representatives.
2. The public relies on supervisors who possess certain professional competencies to present to the elected representative body definite recommendations for improving the curriculum for children and youth. Supervisors are not primarily arbitrators or facilitators and must not keep silent on recommendations for the public and teachers.
3. The public may have opportunity to react to the recommendations before the elected body makes its decision. The development of practical intelligence among adults in the community could occur at this time as they engage in the process of judgment.
4. Groups and individuals in the community can aid in devising supplementary learning situations and in attacking those conditions which are shown to be detrimental to the instructional program. But in their collaboration with the community, supervisors must guard against making incidental functions dominant and responding to pressures which attenuate the systematic organization of learning. It is proper for the professional staff to cooperate in community undertakings for the purposes of gaining information related to the conditions of formal learning, i.e., (1) relevant aspects of pupils' out-of-school experiences and (2) situations for the application of the intellectual techniques being taught. The school's contribution to the community, however, must be within its own field of action. It must not put the immediate concern of the community before the pursuit of intellectual truth.
5. The adaptation of the fact-finding and fact-interpreting described in a later chapter will provide the knowledge of consequences by which both citizen and expert can judge the effectiveness of the curriculum and can effect improvement. Until there is systematic evaluation, communities will either do "what has always been done, or adopt and discard innovations with each spin of fashion."

PART **THREE**

HUMAN FACTORS IN SUPERVISION

The materials in Parts One and Two dealt with the nature of supervision, social systems, and related supervisory functions. Propositions were offered concerning the nature of the forces which shape positions of authority and determine the direction of planning and action. A review of the functions of schools and tasks to be accomplished indicated that with knowledge supervisory statesmanship can be developed to lead, alter, or reverse trends in teaching and learning. In our discussion thus far consideration has been given to the overall supervisory function in organizations.

In Part Three our purpose is to examine a number of interrelated factors which affect the quality of group life in schools. One important ingredient in our inquiry is the proposition that wisdom for understanding the behavior of others, in order to accomplish the most good and the least harm, comes both from self-examination of one's own motives and behavior and from reflecting on the forces affecting what others do and the how and why of what they do. Supervisors, in relationships with individuals and groups, assess continually their own strengths, lacks, and successes, using feedback on their behavior to determine new ways of proceeding or to effect change.

Acquiring new skills and eliminating ineffective ones, along with understanding one's own behavior, are steps toward the kinds of self-development which enable mature persons to influence others in like manner.

In the chapters to follow attention will be given to (1) knowledge requisite to understanding the communication process and developing skills useful in person-to-person communication, (2) some of the conditions germane to change and innovation in schools, (3) the dimensions of creative behavior in adults and children and values of recognizing and encouraging creative expression, and (4) factors in learning of particular concern to supervisors in working with adults.

CHAPTER 7

SUPERVISORS' AND TEACHERS' PERCEPTIONS OF EACH OTHER

Currently, in this country, nearly 1,500 institutions provide academic and professional education for teachers. The majority of teachers in our schools are products of these institutions. The institutions vary in size, resources, degrees of commitment to teacher education, standards of selection, curriculum objectives, quality of instruction, and, perhaps of most importance to the success of beginning teachers, they vary in the quality and quantity of teaching experiences provided their graduates.

Although there are common elements in the programs of study and instructional methodologies in teacher-education institutions, the graduates, themselves, will bring to teaching differences in values, motives, career expectations, and socioeconomic backgrounds. Supervisors should understand that the values of college and university graduates, important indexes of modes of social behavior, vary in degree with an individual's (1) institutional affiliation, (2) field of study, and (3) length of time in the field of study or type of institution.[1] Although values held by graduates are not uniform, ranging, as

1. Robert Eugene Dougherty, *An Analysis of Graduate Students' Value Patterns,* doctoral dissertation, University of California, Los Angeles, 1975.

they do, from traditional to emergent, such diversity can be a latent force to effect educational innovation and change in a cosmopolitan direction.

In building and maintaining competent staffs, supervisiors must take into account some important factors, such as (1) values held by the community and the cultural resources of the region, (2) resources provided by the school district, (3) quality of the work environment, and (4) incentives for the professional growth of the staff. And in planning appropriate in-service programs for staff development, supervisors will profit from understanding:

1. The kind and degree of individual talent among the staff
2. The values held by individuals and ways in which these values influence preferred goals and modes of social and teaching behavior
3. The extent of each teacher's present and applicable knowledge about teaching and repertoire of instructional skills
4. The motives which presently appear to sustain individuals or groups in attaining career goals, and means by which motives may be changed or redirected
5. Directions which in-service professional improvement must take[2]

MOTIVES FOR BECOMING A TEACHER

The motives which cause individuals to become teachers range from a generalized liking for children, or religious beliefs, or a desire to impart knowledge or serve humankind, to a need to acquire power

2. N. L. Gage (ed.), *Handbook of Research on Teaching,* Rand McNally and Company, Chicago, 1963. (See, for example: W. W. Charters, Jr., "The Social Background of Teaching," pp. 715–813; J. W. Getzels and P. W. Jackson, "The Teacher's Personality and Characteristics," pp. 506–582.)

Gloria Buchanan Houston, *Relationships between Rokeach Value Survey Measures and Educational Purposes: Advisory Councils and Principals,* doctoral dissertation, University of California, Los Angeles, 1974.

Fred N. Kerlinger, "Attitudes toward Education and Perception of Teacher Characteristics: A Q Study," *American Educational Research Journal,* vol. 3, no. 3, pp. 159–168, May 1966.

Tamao Matsui et al., "Relations between Supervisory Motivation and the Consideration and Structure Aspects of Supervisory Behavior," *Journal of Applied Psychology,* vol. 60, no. 4, pp. 451–454, August 1975.

National Society for the Study of Education, *Teacher Education,* the Seventy-fourth Yearbook of the National Society for the Study of Education, part II, The University of Chicago Press, Chicago, 1975.

Curtis Richard Smith, *The Values of School District Personnel and Their Rankings of Selected Personnel Practices,* doctoral dissertation, University of California, Los Angeles, 1976.

Robert M. W. Travers (ed.), *The Second Handbook of Research on Teaching,* Rand McNally, Chicago, 1973.

Harmon Zeigler, *The Political World of the High School Teacher,* Center for the Advanced Study of Educational Administration, Eugene, Ore., 1966.

and manipulate others. The limitations of applicability of some academic specialtiies can serve as motives also. For example, a student majoring in music, art, or physical education often turns to teaching since other avenues for using an education in these fields may be relatively limited and teaching offers one an opportunity to earn a living. Some persons may have entered teaching primarily (1) to earn sufficient money to enable them to prepare for another, preferred vocation, (2) to buy time because their goals are still amorphous (this is especially true of liberal arts graduates), (3) to obtain an insurance policy in the form of a teaching certificate, or (4) to support another person who is establishing a vocation or is out of work.

The initial motives which lead individuals to enter any vocation are subject to change. Motives may become transformed by on-the-job experiences. Persons who entered medical school motivated by a desire to serve humanity, perhaps as general practitioners in a small town or low-income area, may decide that the economic rewards of a specialized or exclusive practice provide the life-style and financial security that are more appealing as they grow older. Newly trained teachers who enter the classroom with the idea that they want only to acquire enough experience to gain the requisite skills to become a school administrator may develop insights which influence them to continue teaching in the classroom. However, it is just as likely that teachers will want to change to other avenues, such as college teacher, researcher, supervisor, or curriculum specialist.

The various motives that attract persons to teaching, their persistence in time, and the relationships of these motives one to another and to a number of external teacher characteristics have been reported in a study by Masling and Stern.[3] The authors first identified a number of unconscious teacher motives, and they then constructed a set of Teacher Preference Schedules which were administered to undergraduate education majors and to in-service teachers. Comparisons between the responses of the two populations were made. The authors noted (1) that "the choice of a career may be based, in part, on rational cognitive factors such as the results of interest and aptitude tests, job opportunities and chances for promotion, and on awareness of one's strengths and limitations," and (2) that the influence of noncognitive, nonrational forces (unconscious motives) were important factors in vocational choices.[4]

In summarizing the findings of their study the authors reported the following conclusions:[5]

3. Joseph Masling and George Stern, "Changes in Motives as a Result of Teaching," *Theory into Practice,* vol. 11, no. 2, pp. 95–104, April 1963.
4. Ibid., p. 95.
5. Ibid., p. 104.

(1) . . . Motives change as a result of experience; (2) motives differ between male and female teachers; and (3) the subspecialties within education have a different appeal for different teachers. The motivational differences between the sexes and between the elementary and secondary teachers serve to emphasize that there is no single stereotype of "the teacher." Recruitment of teachers need not be based exclusively on the appeal of working with children; other motives appear to be equally meaningful to potentially excellent teachers. There is a variety of possible careers in education, each of which may serve a different set of underlying motives.

Masling and Stern identified a series of ten patterns of motives and indicated the gratifications received from each and the attitudes which sustain and justify them.[6] This series is presented in Figure 7-1. Awareness of the wide range of career motives noted in these findings should sharpen supervisors' perceptions of teachers as they are

6. Ibid., pp. 98–100.

MOTIVES	GRATIFICATION (Sample Illustrative Items)	ATTITUDE
1. *Practical* Persons in whom this motive is dominant utilize teaching as a means of achieving pragmatic, utilitarian, tangible goals. Involvement in teaching is limited to the instrumental value of the occupation in terms of hours, salary, vacations, and similar sources of gratification. Since the primary emphases are on non-academic activities, the supporting attitudes necessarily justify detachment.	*Instrumental Rewards* *Item:* Finishing all my work during the school day, so that when I go home my time will be my own.	*Detachment* *Item:* It wastes a lot of the teacher's valuable time when he has to deal with problem children himself, instead of being able to refer them immediately to the principal, guidance officer, or school psychologist.
2. *Dominant* Individuals with this orientation need reassurances regarding their own superiority and value. The subordinate status of the pupil is a significant source of gratification for them, and they derive considerable pleasure from activities that keep the child in that position to the enhancement of their own. These behaviors are justified in terms of the need to maintain discipline.	*Children's obedience* *Item:* Running my class with a firm hand.	*Maintaining discipline* *Item:* There are fewer disciplinary problems when pupils are somewhat fearful of the teacher.

Figure 7-1   Motives for teaching and their gratification and attitude components.

MOTIVES	GRATIFICATION (Sample Illustrative Items)	ATTITUDE
3. *Orderly* The motive here is to codify and regulate behavior, minimizing the uncertainties inherent in personal interactions. Teachers guided by it are characterized by a compulsive preoccupation with rules and procedures, and are most gratified by demonstrations of bureaucratic timing and organization in the classroom and school. They justify this in terms of the need for developing good pupil habits.	*Obsessive compulsions* *Item:* Having pupils do over papers that are not neat.	*Developing good pupil habits* *Item:* Every assignment must specify exactly what the pupils are to do and how they are to do it.
4. *Dependent* The major gratification for teaching comes from close supervision and guidance. Teachers express their personal insecurities by reliance on support from authority figures. Supporting attitudes justify compliance and co-operation with authority on the ground that superiors know best.	*Support from superiors* *Item:* Having a principal who takes a close interest in the things I do.	*Co-operation with authority* *Item:* A teacher can seldom go wrong in following his principal's or supervisor's advice.
5. *Nurturant* Teachers with this orientation are characterized by a pervasive feeling of affection for children and a desire to assist and support them. They are warm and loving in their relationships with children, devote themselves freely to their pupils' problems, and derive their greatest satisfactions from the reciprocal affection and gratitude of the children. They justify these activities on the ground that a child's greatest need is love.	*Children's affection* *Item:* Having a pupil confide in one as a parent.	*Providing love* *Item:* A pupil's first need is for warmth and tenderness.
6. *Exhibitionistic* Teachers in whom this motive is dominant are oriented toward personal display and attention-seeking. They achieve satisfaction from opportunities to entertain and captivate their pupils. They have a pervasive need to be admired, and rationalize their exhibitionistic activities in the classroom on the ground that clowning, personality, and showmanship are essential qualities for effective instruction.	*Children's admiration* *Item:* Being appreciated by the children for my sense of humor.	*Showmanship* *Item:* A little clowning is a good way to hold the student's attention and make the learning process more pleasant.

MOTIVES	GRATIFICATION (Sample Illustrative Items)	ATTITUDE
7. *Nondirective* The motive here is to minimize the pupils' expression of dependency on the teacher. Teachers feel rewarded to the extent that their pupils demonstrate capacity for self-direction, and they identify with an ideology which stresses respect for the integrity of the child and justifies the use of pupil-centered classroom techniques in the name of self-actualization.	*Children's autonomy* *Item:* Inviting pupils to question my decisions and express their own opinions.	*Encouraging self-actualization* *Item:* Children should never be embarrassed or made to feel inferior by a teacher.
8. *Preadult-fixated* Persons having this orientation prefer the society of children to that of their peers; they feel essentially inadequate in the role of an adult. Their greatest pleasures in teaching come from sanctioned opportunities to participate vicariously, and sometimes directly, in the activities of their pupils. Their attitudes reflect an idealization of childhood and a justification for identifying with pupils.	*Vicarious participation* *Item:* Being invited by the pupils to join in their games or parties.	*Identification with children* *Item:* Communication between the teacher and his pupils is facilitated if he can get them to accept him as a "pal," as one of them.
9. *Status-striving* The ascribed status of the teacher is more important than the teaching function. Whether for socioeconomic reasons, family ambitions, or personal identifications, teachers find considerable gratification from the prestige that teaching confers on them. The significant attitudes in this case reflect a preoccupation with professional dignity and propriety	*Prestige* *Item:* Being selected to represent the teaching profession on a civic committee.	*Professional dignity* *Item:* Teachers are among the cultural and educational elite of the community.
10. *Critical* The central drive is a dedication to reform and improvement. These teachers are the organizers and critics of the profession, and they find gratification in the opportunities that exist for championing the cause of the underdog. Relevant attitudes involve criticism of contemporary practices in educational administration and a generally negative view concerning the qualifications and motives of authority figures.	*Promoting teacher's rights* *Item:* Fighting for better pay, sickness and accident prevention, retirement provisions, etc., for teachers.	*Reforming schools* *Item:* Many of the most important decisions affecting the schools are made by people who know nothing about education.

in the real world. The effective supervisor focuses on the actions of teachers in particular situations rather than on divining their motives.

Although the motives of teachers and the makeup of their personalities, like those of other adults in society, are a complex of traits embedded in the nature and nurture of past experiences, motives are conditioned also by the kind and quality of experiences in a teacher's professional life. Some persons value the feeling of professional worth, satisfactory peer relationships, or the security which teaching can offer above the greater financial rewards of other professions. Unfortunately, beginning teachers sometimes find themselves in a school system or a community which restricts their behavior or requires adherence to a pattern of behavior quite different from that which they experienced previously in associations with other adults. As a result, they may consider themselves to be members of a second-class society and begin to think of finding different ways of earning a living. By way of illustration is the remark of a teacher who resigned from teaching in a school system noted for its rigorous restrictions on the professional development of its teachers and its high turnover rate: "I rejoined the human race after I resigned from teaching and went to work for the XYZ Corporation."

Our concern is with the motivating forces of the professional environment, which can be influential in changing behavior and determining the degree to which teachers are to be effective, mature, functioning members, not only of the school staff but of society. For example, the mature university graduate who has demonstrated skill in beginning teaching, who has met certain standards of scholarship, and who has had emotional and intellectual experiences of a cultural nature should be encouraged to expand these patterns of behavior and helped to obtain satisfactions consistent with personality structure and individuality.

Supervisors must recognize how important it is for teachers to have as many opportunities as any other professional group for participating in decisions related to their own welfare, for determining policies affecting their responsibilities, for engaging in the kinds of research which will help them in their teaching, and for assessing their own professional achievement. Those responsible for the supervisory operation must provide constant reinforcement for mature behavior and view teachers as colleagues who are (1) engaged in a mutually vital and challenging task, (2) concerned with their own destiny, (3) equipped with various degrees of expertness, and (4) responsible and accountable for achieving results. In like manner teachers must perceive supervisors as experts using training, experience, and technical resources for the achievement of these same worthwhile ends. Both supervisors and teachers need to develop sensitivity to the personalities of others, and strive to understand others' expressions of feelings and beliefs. To gain insight into the ways each perceives reality is to approach maturity.

SENSITIVITY TO PERSONALITY

Although the dimensions of personality are varied and complicated, the supervisor can strive to be objective in matters such as (1) developing an understanding of the manysidedness of personality; (2) acting in regard to others in terms of observable behavior and resisting simplistic, unitary, or categorical perceptions or explanations of the behavior of others; and (3) understanding that, no matter what the behavior of others may be, as long as all such behaviors are accepted as expressions of individual personalities, no hurt or threat need be cause for retaliation or kept buried. The objective acceptance of others is the key concept implied here.

One of the most critical, and at the same time most difficult, skills a supervisor can develop is the ability to recognize the complexities of personality, both of oneself and of others. Sometimes personalities are perceived from what appears on the surface, yet many aspects of personality are hidden or not consciously recognized or have never been cultivated. The supervisor invariably can improve awareness of the different manifestations of personality and the significance of behavior in varying situations.

Each of us has an individual personality which is unique and can be viewed from different directions. According to Guilford, ". . . an *individual's personality, then, is his unique pattern of traits.*"[7] These aspects or traits of personality are defined as:[8]

> . . . any distinguishable, relatively enduring way in which one individual differs from others. . . . "Trait" is thus a very broad general term. A trait of personality may be as inclusive as a general attitude of self-confidence or as narrow as a specific habit, such as a conditioned muscular contraction in response to a sound. A trait may be a characteristic indicated by behavior, as in the two examples just given, or of physical make-up. The former is a behavior trait, the latter a somatic trait.

The modalities of traits which make up the aspects of human personality are presented in Figure 7-2. Adapted from Guilford's work, these traits can be defined briefly as follows:

1. *Somatic traits.* These are of two kinds—morphological and physiological. Traits of morphology are those relating to bodily structure

---

7. J. P. Guilford, *Personality*, McGraw-Hill Book Company, New York, 1959, p. 6.
8. Ibid., p. 6.

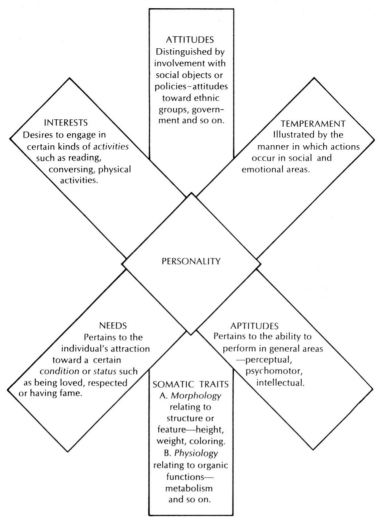

Figure 7-2 Modalities of traits representing different aspects of personality. (From J. P. Guilford, *Personality*, McGraw-Hill Book Company, New York, 1959, p. 7.)

or features, such as height, weight, and skin coloring. Traits of physiology relate to organic functions, such as heart rate, basal metabolic rate, and body temperature.

2. *Needs, interests, attitudes.* These are motivational traits which pertain to what a person does—to things one strives to do or to obtain—rather than to how one feels. Needs are continuing desires for certain conditions, such as being comfortable, receiving recognition, or being respected. Interests are long-standing desires to indulge in certain kinds of activities, such as handwork, sports, thinking, or conversing. Attitudes are distinguished by the fact that some social objects or policies are involved as seen in attitudes toward birth control, income tax, or certain ethnic groups.

3. *Aptitudes.* These traits pertain to the ability to perform and to how well a person performs. Although there are as many aptitudes as there are actions to be performed, they can be described in a limited system covering three general areas: perceptual, psychomotor, and intellectual.

4. *Temperament.* Traits of temperament relate to the manner in which actions occur. They can be defined broadly as one's disposition—being confident, cheerful, impulsive, or other similar emotional or social behavior.[9]

Attempting to understand the factors controlling the needs, interests, and attitudes of others (rather than random judging or categorizing) will enable the supervisor to place the right or relative value on these behaviors. To know how a particular individual's temperament is constituted is a real step in understanding whether hostility or receptivity to certain ideas is likely to occur. There is no reason for the supervisor to probe the "why" of such behavior or to type persons as those who resist and those who accept ideas. Rather, it is important to be sensitive to the *kind* of behavior which is being manifested—to the situations which elicited it—and to meet this behavior with requisite and reasonable responses of a questioning or additive nature. The acceptance of an individual's behavior provides supervisors with a basis for maintaining the lines of communication, so that they can continue to work effectively with individuals. It does no good to label the behavior of others, no matter how much it may relieve the supervisor's own feelings. When certain behaviors are displayed frankly and openly in group or person-to-person communication, it is of little value for supervisors to tell other persons that they are showing such-and-such behavior (or to categorize them unconsciously). The behavior itself tells the supervisors what they need to know. Labeling behavior helps neither to control nor to change it.

To welcome or at least accept from other individuals every kind and form of behavior called forth by the tensions which occur in problem situations is to have a basis for better understanding and communicating. If unwanted behaviors are screened out or rejected by either direct or subtle means, the other person's defenses may be mobilized, resentments precipitated, and channels of communication closed. A hard lesson to learn in working with others is the

9. Ibid., pp. 7–8.

desirability of accepting statements of position, concepts, and expressions of temperament. If, for example, certain individuals hold the view that pupils of a certain ethnic group cannot learn certain concepts, they should have complete freedom to state their views. They must discover for themselves the reasons for clinging to their belief. Aggressive action to change this particular behavior will be fruitless, and rejecting or categorizing responses with terms such as prejudice or stereotype will not help. Argumentation and confrontation are to be avoided, even if these approaches appear on the surface to break down some individuals' barriers to ideas other than their own. Instead of achievement an eruption of emotions may result. Overt behavior, whatever its nature, should be recognized as providing opportunities to bring the views of other persons to a conscious level so that their ideas can be tested against facts and knowledge in due course. Where discussions take place in a climate as unemotional as possible, individuals may eventually arrive at changed configurations of behavior as a result of their own insights.

Reflection and acceptance are, therefore, important behaviors on the part of supervisors. To develop insight about one's feelings toward other persons and to understand one's real conception of others helps one to relate what one says and does to the other's behavior in specific situations. And this is a skill of singular importance. Supervisors who have this skill invite a climate in which other persons are taught something about themselves, about supervisors, and about getting along with others.

MANIPULATION AND THERAPY: NO-NO'S IN SUPERVISION

Supervisors who believe that changes in group behavior can be effected by procedural manipulations may find that such mechanical approaches lead to dissatisfactions and group tension and produce ineffective results. Prescriptive procedures for manipulating groups might include How to Set the Stage for Controlling a Meeting, How to Warm Up the Group, How to Avoid Negative Feedback, How to Handle the Maverick, or How to Whip Up Enthusiasm. Procedures which are not directly related to tasks, or do not involve individuals in purposes, tend to subvert the essential reasons for bringing groups together and rarely are effective in attaining desired results. The emphasis, instead, should be on implementing indigenous concerns of the group, for example:

1. For what purpose have we come together?
2. What problems need to be defined?
3. What hypotheses should be developed?

4. What plans need to be formulated to attack the problem?
5. How will the results be assessed?

There are times when most individuals may be faced with psychological or personal problems, and the question sometimes arises whether supervisors should behave as therapists; that is, should they engage in the act of counseling others on personal problems? It seems fundamental that one should not engage in clinical counseling on personal problems unless one is professionally qualified to follow through with the counselee. The personal and psychological problems of individuals are outside the purview of the supervisor's professional responsibility. Supervision, like teaching, is not therapy. And the supervisor should differentiate between professional counseling about matters directly pertaining to teaching and personal counseling or clinical therapy. Listening to a teacher's personal problems may be opening a Pandora's box of trouble. Even in such a seemingly innocent gesture of concern as listening, the supervisor *is* initiating a counseling relationship and setting expectations which he or she is not qualified to fulfill. Amateur therapists can produce miscounseled and misled individuals. There is quite a difference between the case of the teacher whose classroom problems reflect technical difficulties and the teacher whose teaching problems reflect anxieties caused by personal or interpersonal problems outside the work environment. In the latter case a supervisor's understandable concern to remedy the situation may be expressed best by encouraging all such troubled colleagues to seek expert professional assistance germane to the particular problem outside the school if possible. Many school districts, recognizing that personnel in any organization may require professional or psychological services, provide lists of referral agencies or practitioners for the benefit of the staff.

MODES OF SMALL-GROUP BEHAVIOR
The study of small-group behavior by a number of investigators has led to better understanding of what goes on among individuals in group situations.[10] Interrelations among various individual, group,

10. Robert T. Golembiewski, "Small Group and Large Organizations," in James G. March (ed.), *Handbook of Organizations,* Rand McNally & Company, Chicago, 1965, pp. 87–141.
    Robert L. Kahn, Donald M. Wolfe, Robert P. Quinn, J. Diedrick Snoek, in collaboration with Robert A. Rosenthal, *Organizational Stress: Studies in Role Conflict and Ambiguity,* John Wiley & Sons, Inc., New York, 1964.
    Joseph E. McGrath and Irwin Altman, *Small Group Research,* Holt, Rinehart and Winston, Inc., New York, 1966.
    Edgar H. Schein, *Organizational Psychology,* 2d ed., Prentice-Hall, Inc., Englewood Cliffs, N.J., 1972.

and organizational variables have been studied by Kahn and others in their investigation of the nature, causes, and consequences of organizational stress. The authors noted that "organizations are reducible to individual human acts; yet they are lawful and in part understandable only at the level of collective behavior."[11]

In an extensive study about small-group behavior, McGrath and Altman first developed a classification system to describe and interpret small-group research which was then applied to a sample of 250 studies selected from a corpus of some 2,699 investigations.[12] A data pool of approximately 12,000 empirical relationships was generated. Only a few broad generalizations from the McGrath and Altman study are abstracted here, providing, it is hoped, clues and hypotheses for examining transactions in small groups and suggesting avenues of inquiry for supervisors in their own particular situations.[13]

1. Member performance in group situations can be predicted with more consistency from knowledge of *objective* measures of intelligence, general abilities, and task aptitude than from subjective self-estimates or subjective peer estimates of individuals' abilities. While individuals may not be able to judge or predict one another's capabilities, they do appear to be able to judge the leadership potential and performance of others, whether objective or subjective measures are used as predictors.

2. Individual capabilities, in themselves, whether objectively or subjectively measured, are not adequate predictors of overall group performance. Exactly in what ways individual abilities become transmuted into effective group performance is not yet clear; the translation of individual abilities into group achievement in varied work situations warrants continued study.

3. Favorable individual attitudes toward a group task (attitudes resulting from an individual's level of status in a group, work conditions, task success) appear to reflect an individual's personal success, but seemingly do not necessarily increase his performance level or relate to the character of interpersonal relations existing in a group.

4. Authoritarian attitudes in small groups (experimental studies excepted) show "very little relationship to most interaction behaviors and inconsistent relationships with performance on tasks of various types." Authoritarian or permissive attitudes may be related to member expectations (among other variables); when group members hold expectations of authoritarian behavior they are as well

11. Kahn, et al., op. cit., p. 398.
12. McGrath and Altman, op. cit.
13. A summary of chap. 6, "Generalizations from Small Group Research Data," from *Small Group Research* by Joseph E. McGrath and Irwin Altman, used by permission of the publishers, Holt, Rinehart and Winston, Inc., Copyright © 1966 by Holt, Rinehart and Winston, Inc., New York.

satisfied with persons having that kind of attitude as with persons who are permissive.[14]

5. Group members who possess high social or task status in a group tend also to possess and use power and to have favorable reactions to the group. Members with such high status are perceived by others as possessing appropriate skills, work habits, influence, and qualities of leadership.

6. The more opportunity groups and individuals have to engage in task training and to work together effectively, the better their individual and group performance.

7. Though the general view that smaller groups tend to be more effective has some face validity, the evidence on minumum or optimum group size for most effective performance is not clear. However, several concomitants of small group size would include: . . . 1. Less perceived need for guidance and for a definite leader but less perceived competence and ability of the group as a whole, 2. Fewer expressed ideas and less change in attitudes or other responses by members, 3. Less-frequent perceptions of the leader as exhibiting coordinating behavior, clarifying rules, or wisely delegating authority, 4. Greater perception of group task success.[15]

8. Interpersonal attraction (liking other group members) appears to be related to individual's perceptions of the social status and task accomplishment abilities of other members. Groups with high interpersonal attractiveness tend to have increased perceptions of group task success and a higher rate of interpersonal communication.

9. Individual performance in groups is enhanced by freedom from restraints from the environment, the opportunity to participate in decision making (though final decisions may be made at other levels), and by knowledge of performance and rewards.

10. A number of conditions are characteristic of effective leadership:
    a. Combinations of individual personality traits—assertiveness, social maturity, and extroversion—but not others which seem similar
    b. Quality of education and training in leader techniques (age and other biographical characteristics were not factors)
    c. Intelligence and superior abilities in performing general and specific tasks
    d. High frequency rate in proposing problems, and persistence in seeking the information needed to solve problems
    e. High ego involvement and group status

11. Groups with effective leaders are characterized by "good work rela-

14. U. G. Foa, "Relation of Workers' Expectations to Satisfaction with Supervisor," *Personnel Psychology,* vol. 10, pp. 161–168, 1957.
   Raymond A. Katzell, "Contrasting Systems of Work Organization," *American Psychologist,* vol. 17, pp. 102–108, February 1962.
15. McGrath and Altman, op. cit., p. 59.

tions with other groups, care for equipment, orderliness, and a range of indexes of morale."[16]

Without overplaying the group-versus-individual issue, it would seem as unreasonable to reject the significance of the individual as to reject the importance of the group. Individual diversity and mutual cooperation essentially are not in conflict. Most persons, having been raised in groups, have worked effectively in them at one time or another. Group processes, depending upon purpose, are important in any society or organization. To hold the view that individuals should work in their own intellectual or psychological tent is as unwise as to hold that only groups can engage in effective action. Both individuals and groups have a contribution to make in setting and solving problems. The relative emphasis to be placed on the individual or group relates to (1) the purposes and dimensions of any particular task, (2) the expertness and motivation of the individuals who are involved, (3) the kinds of situations in which individuals produce creative expressions most effectively, and (4) the differentiation of responsibility. In any organization, overlooking the possibility of a continuum of individual and group processes leads to emphasis on one or the other and sets up false dichotomies.

In studies which involve problem solving, planning may be a group act, research an individual task, production the result of both individual and group effort, and collating data a product of either individuals or groups. The final agreements represent both individual expertness and the wisdom of the group. For example, the production of a large lens for an observatory telescope involves both the specialized talents of individuals and continuous group cooperation in the planning stages and during production. The tasks involved in the firing of a space rocket require that individuals in such an operation plan and flow in and out of groups, assume individual responsibility, cooperate on tasks where complete unity or understanding is vital to success, and evaluate results both as individuals and in groups. It is the talent of the individual which makes an emergent group viable, not the reverse.

We know that where there is effective communication, access to necessary information, and opportunity for participation, groups can be used to develop cooperation among individuals. The individual is unique and the use of talent is of critical importance. Groups come into existence to accomplish what cannot be done by individuals alone. The formation of groups can result in the diversification of responsibility and tasks and the multiplication of human talent, and

16. Ibid., p. 62.

it can provide a structure for testing the ideas and hypotheses of individuals. Groups are more apt to be successful when they have a common purpose and are made up of persons whose technical competence relates to the group task. But the quality of groups rests on the quality of individuals. It is the individual who should be central in all cooperative staff endeavors. It is said that Hitler once noted, "The group is everything and the individual is nothing." A man in the street wisely asked, "How can the group be everything if I am nothing?"

MODES OF INDIVIDUAL BEHAVIOR

In working with individuals supervisors should make a conscious effort to be aware of individual reactions. And in the course of improving the process of working together the supervisor can assess the dimensions of hindrances to learning (1) by careful observation of how individuals react to various situations, (2) by obtaining feedback on proposals for action, and (3) by informal inventories of how others view particular problems or tasks. The establishment of the kind of atmosphere which makes it acceptable for teachers to think objectively about their accountability to the job will help immeasurably to increase understanding between supervisor and teacher. The skillful use of communication techniques (discussed in some detail in another section) is important here.

By constant feedback from individuals on how they view problems, conflicts, or tasks, the supervisor establishes the climate of freedom for individuals to express needs and to suggest openly better ways of working together. In developing insight into the behavior of others, by consciously seeking to have others communicate their reactions to situations without fear of reprisal, and by accepting all proposals or personal reactions as hypotheses or generalizations to be tested, the supervisor improves his or her own behavior.

The varied forms of overt behavior which individuals display are, in general, modes of adaptive behavior for handling situations. Thus traits of personality represent characteristic reactions to problems and situations. Modes of behavior which seem negative in social situations should not be judged necessarily as forms of malingering; rather, they may be ways to get persons out of a dilemma. For example, suppression of overt expressions of hostility because of the likelihood of domination, coercion, or threat by the supervisor as leader of a group may well cause the hostility to be suppressed, reduce effectiveness, and even do harm to an individual.

Most specific modes of behavior, like overall social behavior, are characterized by compromises. Individuals rarely achieve complete satisfactions, and their modes of behavior represent their compromises. Fortunately, these compromises are usually at a conscious level, and if the constituents which make up the compromise are known, behavior will be better understood. Negative modes of behavior occur when the achievement, recognition, security, sensory gratification, or response are thwarted. The need for satisfactions develops early in life, and the individual consciously becomes aware that getting many of these satisfactions is fraught with painful experiences or guilt. Thus some modes of behavior become disguised outlets for painful conflict. Sometimes the ways of meeting situations result in habitual patterns of behavior, and although the original stimuli which brought forth the behavior disappear, the habit of responses remains.

Knowing the nature and the components of conflict which create and sustain certain modes of behavior is important in trying to understand others. Persons react to situations in various ways in terms of their personality makeup. Some avoid problems because they do not know how to meet contingencies or have rarely had success in such endeavors; others must be supported and given help; and still others attack problems vigorously on their own. The supervisor who anticipates the various modes of behavior which may occur is in a better position to arrange an environment conducive to effective responses and to take into account the kinds of situations which stimulate individual performance best. Many modes of behavior are inevitable even though they may seem inappropriate. The recognition that there are wide differences in behavior will help supervisors differentiate tasks among those who appear aggressive or self-assertive and others who are shy or reserved or who express feelings of inadequacy. In working with individuals the concern should be less with the symptoms of behavior and more with encouraging others to express their views freely. The varieties of personality characteristics should be viewed realistically as strengths and not as shortcomings.

Supervisors, aware that all persons, including themselves, have conflicts and varied modes of responses to particular situations, realize the value of bringing conflicts to a conscious level and talking about problems in an atmosphere of acceptance. However, at certain times individual behavior can block effective understanding and hinder appropriate group action if not recognized and redirected. A directive approach on the part of the supervisor may be necessary, particularly in those situations in which individual behavior may jeopardize important outcomes for the majority. No modes of behavior are to be considered permanent. New goals and tasks, and changes in group membership may often help individuals to cope more effectively.

PROBLEMS IN WORK ENVIRONMENTS: TEACHERS' REFLECTIONS

When teachers are worried about their teaching effectiveness they usually show their concern in one form or another. Informal reactions of teachers concerning some of the obstacles to satisfaction in their teaching often can provide information which may be useful in reducing such hindrances. By way of illustration, some typical reflections of teachers regarding obstacles confronting them (organized under several broad categories) are presented in the list which follows:

1. *Dependence upon definite instructions.* Persons who feel highly uncertain and hesitant, who balk or worry excessively when they do not know exactly what they should do and how they should do it or what is expected of them or what to expect of others, may worry or get mixed up and be unable to perform as efficiently as they would ordinarily. Reactions which reveal this difficulty are:

    If supervisors would only be more definite and stress the main points in their discussion so that I would have some idea of their explicit points—instead, everything they suggest is vague and open-ended.

    Why don't they tell us what they would like us to do in the workshop instead of suggesting we develop *any* problem?

    I was asked to do a series of demonstrations for the visitors from India, but was not told the purposes of the demonstrations or what the visitors would have liked to observe. I'd get up in front of the class and wonder what the expectations were; then I would get confused and fumble the ball. I did not find out until later from some of the foreign visitors that they had been told that I was going to emphasize the use of materials.

2. *Dependence upon a solid foundation or systematic steps.* Such persons need to have complete certainty about one step in the process of learning before proceeding to the next.

    I always have a psychological block to overcome. I have to practice and rehearse one thing at a time before I feel free to go on to the next.

    If the principal would only suggest one thing at a time—let me get real proficient on that, and then go on to the next thing—I would do a better job.

    I never feel I develop competency in anything. One week the supervisor stresses writing anecdotal records like mad, the next week, pupil observation, and the next week something else. There is no continuity or central purpose to the suggestions.

I don't have time to read the research on one problem before the supervisor is off on another tack.

3. *Difficulty in building confidence.* Such persons can establish a stable confidence, but they require considerable reinforcement or concrete experience before they can so achieve.

Confidence is of the utmost importance to me. I can develop confidence and maintain it, but first I have to prove definitely that I can do a job; until I do, I feel confused and tense.

I was asked to make several reports for the teachers' seminar and I was afraid of making mistakes, but the supervisor had me rehearse what I was going to do. When I did make some good reports after that it was OK, and I did not have any trouble with succeeding reports.

4. *Anxiety about progress.* Persons expressing this behavior need to see ahead clearly before proceeding. They want to know the target at which they are aiming.

I felt ill at ease when I first started the workshop. But once I saw that some progress was being made and could anticipate what to do next with the group, I was all right.

If only the supervisors would let me know how I stood in the mathematics program they helped me to initiate. I never was sure whether or not I was making progress. If they had merely asked me how I was doing, I would have felt better about the whole program.

5. *Confidence easily disrupted.* Such persons have the ability to conduct worthwhile teaching activities, but require intelligent support and satisfactory reinforcements for their efforts. Lack of such support may result in worry, withdrawal, and loss of motivation.

I spent nearly two years developing a special reading program with my high school classes, and the test results showed progress beyond expectations. The supervisor's only comment was: "Apparently your program has resulted in good achievement, but you push your pupils too hard; you should give more emphasis to making them like school—that is one of our major purposes."

Every teacher at my demonstration complimented me on the overhead chart showing relations among the celestial bodies. My supervisor noted that all displays should be at eye level and in not more than two colors. No comment about the content, which I felt was of more importance than the physical arrangement.

6. *Oversensitivity to change.* Some individuals react strongly to any change, whether it be a change in person-to-person relationships, such as a change in supervisors, or changes in methods of teaching. They react by losing efficiency in their teaching.

If only they hadn't changed supervisors on me. I was doing fine and could really communicate with my first supervisor. Then I got a different one, and now I am all mixed up.

I don't care what the superintendent says about everyone's having similar objectives in this system. Supervisors all have their own ways of doing things. You cannot do it several ways at once—so you get confused.

If the general and special supervisors would only unify—that is, get explicit ideas of what we are all trying to do—so that I wouldn't have to react differently every time I work with a different supervisor, I could do a better job.

7. *Sensitivity to criticism or to suggestions interpreted as criticism.* Certain individuals become tense or annoyed at suggestions which they interpret as criticisms, or conversely, the absence of suggestions.

When the supervisor raises questions about my work, I get tense and overanxious.

My supervisor is always quick to comment before hearing my side, and it makes me ill at ease.

Some supervisors have a "goody-goody" approach to everything. When I give a reaction to something their immediate response is "Good thinking!" or "That's good!" They have no values—can't tell the real good from the "goody-goody." How do they know it is good? I wasn't sure of my proposal and wanted to ask some questions, but I was shut off. Such judgments leave me hanging.

8. *Desire for independence.* Some individuals find it difficult to tolerate being in the position of student or learner, and their inner rebellion is shown by unwillingness and resistance to learning.

Every time I work with these supervisors, I feel like a passenger in my own automobile. I may have the wheel in my hands, but they are doing the driving. I don't feel independent. I am given no opportunity to show what I can do nor am I allowed to test my ideas.

I guess there are some of us who just have to do things by ourselves and can't take directions from others. All of us have to test our own hypotheses once in a while.

I am sort of a rugged individualist. I want to have a few things my own way—want to do things myself. I don't want anybody telling me what to do. My supervisor has never recognized this trait in me.

9. *Tendency toward self-analysis and self-consciousness.* Some persons appear to be overly self-conscious and self-analytical. The attention to self may impair one's efficiency in professional activities. Self-conscious persons are hesitant to secure information or ask for help. They are tense and worry about failure.

I am self-conscious at times. I don't like to ask too many questions. If it is something I don't know anything about, I would rather wait to figure it out myself.

I would be willing to discuss things more with our supervisors, but they never try to draw me out. They don't seem to recognize that I am a withdrawing person. They ignore me in any group and always talk to their cronies. I would be willing to participate more in their projects if they would only recognize me once in a while.

I tried too hard—got too tense—worried about the stigma of failing. As a result, I didn't do well at all in the job of leading the discussion group. If the supervisor had helped me a little, it might have come out differently.

10. *Oversensitivity to leader direction.* Some persons tend to be more attentive to the presence, opinions, expectations, and reactions of supervisors than to learning the task at hand. This may produce a general emotional tension involving overanxiousness to please or fear of displeasing and hypersensitivity to criticism and opinion.

I am more afraid of the principal's reaction than of how I might perform.

The supervisor talked too much. One meeting day I took the bit in my teeth and asked if I could talk, and I improved a lot in self-confidence as a result.

I can never concentrate on a task when supervisors are listening to what I have to say. I feel I am not expressing my true feelings, but only talking to please them. I find myself trying to confirm their beliefs rather than trying to express my own.

11. *Overdependence upon the leader.* This factor is related to the previous item, with the addition of a strong desire for individ-

ualized attention from the leader and a consequent sense of frustration and tension when this desire is unsatisfied.

Anyone could be a better teacher if supervisors and principals had an interest in your teaching. Just makes me wonder if it is all worthwhile. Supervisors ought to fit themselves to what teachers want to do, not the opposite.

It seems to me that the supervisor is not interested in whether or not we are good teachers. Maybe I am too new at teaching, but I feel every beginning teacher should have someone to look up to. I don't seem to have anyone.

I did much better the first year I was teaching because I felt my supervisors tried to help me and I learned. This year the new supervisors seem indifferent to me. If I had them always supporting me and showing confidence in me, and I could place confidence in them, I would do 100 percent better.

I have to get my support from my husband. My supervisor has no interest in me whatsoever.

These statements by teachers (not unusual in contemporary organizations), while focusing on supervisory roles and functions, reveal much about their own self perceptions. As such they provide valuable clues for supervisors to consider in interpreting individual behavior. Certainly, the statements reflect a desire as expressed by teachers for well-defined and regularized work environments, with some tolerating more unknown elements than others. Work situations require continuous study, and the following questions may help supervisors in their observations:

1. Do individuals prefer their work assignments to be outlined definitely for them, or do they prefer less structured ways of accomplishing tasks?
2. Do individuals learn or perform best by immediate involvement in a particular activity, or do they benefit from a period of orientation or study?
3. In a problem-solving situation do persons work best in groups or on their own?

Answers to these questions can provide information to help supervisors and teachers devise work situations in which they both will feel comfortable.

SUMMARY STATEMENT
The effects on staff relations in schools are generally salutary when opportunities are open for all staff members to discuss issues, adjust

roles freely, and select those tasks which they believe they have a reasonable chance of completing either on their own or with assistance.

In general, reactions of teachers relating to unsatisfied personal, social, and professional needs reflect various kinds of tensions which may cause a consequent reduction of an individual's ability to function adequately. In some cases, of course, individuals may actually perform better than their self-assessment would indicate. In many instances, the reactions resulting from tension and conflict are inevitable in some degree, and supervisors should not be dismayed when they occur. Many responses are beyond one's power to change, control, or direct, since they arise from remote causes. However, supervisors reduce the impetus for such behavior by recognizing the diversity of individual behavior, by being flexible in adjusting their own behavior, and by placing themselves and others in a work environment where mutual success can be attained.

Effective supervisors face up to their limitations. They do not pretend to know all the answers, or suggest propositions and give advice beyond their knowledge or ability. They make every effort to define areas of influence and to acquire the requisite skills for attaining purposes. By readiness to admit difficulties, to concede failure at certain times, and to try to solve problems cooperatively, supervisors and teachers help each other face facts, take the consequences of actions, and persevere at tasks.

CHAPTER **8**

COMMUNICATION

The importance to be attached to the study of communication was anticipated by Elton Mayo several decades ago:[1]

> Social study should begin with careful observation of what may be described as communication: that is, the capacity of an individual to communicate his feelings and ideas to another, the capacity of groups to communicate effectively and intimately with each other. This problem is, beyond all reasonable doubt, the most oustanding defect that civilization is facing today.

Underlying much of the study of communication is the recognition that (1) communication makes social life possible, (2) social organizations cannot exist without effective communication, and (3) when communication among individuals fails, their capacity for effective cooperation and productive effort also fails. Communication inquiry has ranged over a number of fields, as, for example: (1) psychological and sociological studies of the theory and application of

---

1. Elton Mayo, *The Social Problems of an Industrial Civilization,* Harvard University, Graduate School of Business, Division of Research, Cambridge, Mass., 1945, p. 22.

the process between persons and among groups in formal and informal settings, (2) investigations in linguistics concerned with the relationships of language to cognitive and affective behavior, and (3) research in symbolic logic dealing with the development and application of mathematical formulations to problems of communication.[2]

COMMUNICATION PROCESSES

Communication processes have been viewed as a moving of ideas translated into signs (sometimes called symbols) from a communicator who formulates a message to an interpreter who, in turn, interprets the message. Communication is considered most effective when the *intent* of the communicator and the *effect* received by the interpreter are the same, that is, when the signs (symbols) closely represent the same things in the experience of the communicator that they represent in that of the interpreter and, of course, the reverse—interpreter to communicator. Since communication occurs among human beings in formal and informal social settings, the process is inevitably conditioned by individual differences in human temperament, degrees of knowledge, kinds of expectations, and roles. For communication to be effective, both communicator and interpreter must recognize that a constant selective process is going on in the mind of the other, and that assumptions, points of view, feelings, and degrees of "message acceptance" are coloring and influencing responses.

Communication processes are central to the life and effective functioning of schools. Some of the important components of a generalized communication system, helpful to a supervisor's working

2. Colin Cherry, *On Human Communication: A Review, a Survey, and a Criticism,* New York: The Technology Press of the Massachusetts Institute of Technology, Cambridge, Mass., and John Wiley & Sons, New York, 1957.

Harold Guetzkow, "Communications in Organizations," in James G. March (ed.), *Handbook of Organizations,* Rand McNally & Company, Chicago, 1965, pp. 534–573.

Willard R. Lane, Ronald G. Corwin, and William G. Monahan, *Foundations of Educational Administration: A Behavioral Analysis,* The Macmillan Company, New York, 1966–1967, chaps. 3 and 4.

Rensis Likert, *New Patterns of Management,* McGraw-Hill Book Company, New York, 1961.

George A. Miller, *Language and Communication,* McGraw-Hill Book Company, New York, 1951.

Charles Morris, *Signs, Language, and Behavior,* Prentice-Hall, Inc., Englewood Cliffs, N.J., 1946.

National Society for the Study of Education, *Media and Symbols: The Forms of Expression, Communication, and Education,* The Seventy-third Yearbook, part I, Chicago, 1974.

knowledge of all aspects of communication processes, have been set forth clearly by Miller:[3]

Communication means that information is passed from one place to another. Whenever communication occurs . . . the component parts involved in the transfer of information comprise a communication system. Although the specific character of these parts changes from one system to another, there are general functions that the components must perform if the communication is to succeed. By abstracting these necessary functions that every communication system must perform it is possible to describe a sort of idealized communication system in very general terms.

Every communication must have a *source* and a *destination* for the information that is transferred, and these must be distinct in space or time. Between the source and the destination there must be some link that spans the intervening space or time, and this link is called a communication *channel*. In order that the information can pass over the channel, it is necessary to operate on it in such a way that it is suitable for transmission, and the component that performs this operation is a *transmitter*. At the destination there must be a *receiver* that converts the transmitted information into its original form. These five components—source, transmitter, channel, receiver, and destination—comprise the idealized communication system. In one form or another these five components are present in every kind of communication.

In most communication systems the source of the information is a human being. From his past experience and present needs and perceptions this source has information to pass along to others. The transmitter . . . is the human speech machinery. This machinery operates upon the information and changes it into a pattern of sound waves that is carried through the air. The channel of principal interest to us will be the air medium that connects the talker's speech machinery with the listener's ears. The ear is a receiver that operates upon the acoustic waves to convert them into nervous activity at their destination, the nervous system of the listener. This particular system is called the vocal communication system.

Many other examples of communication systems can be described. When a person writes himself a note on his memorandum pad, the writer at one time is the source, the process of writing is the transmitter, the permanence of the pad is the channel that spans intervening time, the reader's eyes are the receiver, and the same person at a later time is the destination. A telegraph system is a simple example: the source supplies a sequence of letters that is converted by the transmitter into dots, dashes, and spaces, the receiver reconverts the signal into letters, and the message is passed along to its destination.

The operation of the transmitter is often referred to as *encoding*. The code is the pattern of energies that can travel over the connecting

3. Miller, op. cit., pp. 6–8.

link. The receiver reverses the operation of the transmitter and reconverts the coded message into a more usable form. Thus the operation of the receiver is referred to as *decoding*. . . . Any system of symbols that, by prior agreement between the source and destination, is used to represent and convey information will be called a code. Thus, in the sense we use the word here, the French language is one code and the German language another. Spoken English is the code that will interest us primarily, but similar considerations apply for all codes.

One additional factor must be considered before the idealized communication system is complete. This factor concerns the possibility of error. Mistakes may occur in encoding or decoding the messages or may be introduced while the signal is in transit over the channel. If the people communicating are unfamiliar with the code, or if they are unable to distinguish the differences among the symbols, errors become likely. If there is a disturbance in the channel that changes the individual symbols or permutes their order, errors in communication result. It is sometimes convenient to lump all these sources of error together under a single name, *noise*. When we say that a communication system is noisy, we mean that there is a good chance for error to occur. If the chance of error is very great, we say that the noise level is high. If errors are very unlikely, we say the noise level is low.

The higher the noise level in a communication system, the more difficult it is to get reliable information over that system. In most communication systems, therefore, some provisions are made to combat the deleterious effects of noise. Just what the countermeasures are depends upon what kinds of errors are most likely.

Even when communication processes are skillfully employed so that individuals and groups are relating to the flow and content of cognitive and affective data in a meaningful way, variables of varying complexity affect the process. Whether in formal or informal social settings, communication is conditioned inevitably by individual differences in human temperament, degrees of knowledge, kinds of expectations, and roles.

ONE-WAY VERSUS TRANSACTIONAL COMMUNICATION

One-way communication is directive and requires no feedback. In this system person *A* simply transmits a message to person *B*. The influence is all one way, providing the communicator with control and power and assigning the recipient a passive or nonparticipative role. Traditional hierarchial notions of establishing a fixed place for the source, direction, and use of information serve to illustrate how communication may be perceived in its narrowest sense.

In transactional communication a bargain is involved, and an equal exchange of values between the communicating agents is expected. The transactional process has been described as "an exchange of values between two or more parties, each gives in order to get."[4] The social model of humans is one of participation and sharing and not that of a robot or laboratory subject whose behavior is directed by one-way communication aimed at control, influence, or manipulation. Bauer has provided an excellent description of the relationship between one-way and transactional models.[5]

I shall here discuss the relationship of these two models in the area of social communication. I shall set up two stereotypes. First, the social model of communication: The model held by the general public, and by social scientists when they talk about advertising, and somebody else's propaganda, is one of the exploitation of man by man. It is a model of one-way influence: The communicator *does* something to the audience, while to the communicator is generally attributed considerable latitude and power to do what he pleases to the audience. This model is reflected—at its worst—in such popular phrases as "brainwashing," "hidden persuasion," and "subliminal advertising."

The second stereotype—the model which *ought* to be inferred from the data of research—is of communication as a transactional process in which two parties each expect to give and take from the deal approximately equitable values. This, although it *ought* to be the scientific model, is far from generally accepted as such, a stage of affairs on which W. Philips Davison (1959) makes the comment:

. . . the communicator's audience is not a passive recipient—it cannot be regarded as a lump of clay to be molded by the master propagandist. Rather, the audience is made up of individuals who demand something from the communications to which they are exposed, and who select those that are likely to be useful to them. In other words, they must get something from the manipulator if he is to get something from them. A bargain is involved. Sometimes, it is true, the manipulator is able to lead his audience into a bad bargain by emphasizing one need at the expense of another or by representing a change in the significant environment as greater than it actually has been. But audiences, too, can drive a hard bargain. Many communicators who have been widely disregarded or misunderstood know that to their cost.

Davison does not contend that all the exchanges are equitable, but that the inequities may be on either side. He only implies that neither the audience nor the communicator would enter into this exchange unless each party expected to "get his money's worth," at least most of the time.

4. Raymond A. Bauer, "The Obstinate Audience: The Influence Process from the Point of View of Social Communication," *American Psychologist*, vol. 19, no. 5, May 1964, pp. 319–328. Copyright © 1964 by the American Psychological Association, and reproduced by permission.

5. Bauer op. cit., pp. 319–320. The internal quotation is from W. Philips Davison, "On the Effects of Communication," *Public Opinion Quarterly*, vol. 23, p. 360, 1959.

OPEN VERSUS RESTRICTED COMMUNICATION

A number of studies have produced evidence as to the positive effects of open communication systems on the behavior and achievement of individuals and groups. In one of the several investigations conducted by Roby and Lanzetta a study was made of the performance of three-member groups, each group performing tasks under conditions in which the amount of essential information needed to carry out the task varied from none to three-fourths of the total.[6] The results of the study indicated that groups with direct access to the greatest amount of readily available and relevant information achieved the highest levels of accuracy in performance. The need for group members to communicate with one another in search of information to perform tasks was held to a minimum.

When placed in direct control of communication content, individuals and groups have more opportunity to initiate and implement organizational goals and effect performances that are mutually satisfactory. Once established, open systems and flexible arrangements of persons and tasks provide impetus for solving problems.[7]

Among the promising techniques developed to utilize the potential talents of persons in problem-solving situations, and in so doing to reduce semantic and psychological contamination in communication which arises in face-to-face groups, is that of the Delphi method developed at the RAND Corporation, Santa Monica, California.[8] The Delphi method is designed to extract opinions, judgments, relevant data, or hypotheses on particular problems or questions from a group of experts. Each person works independently, but receives pertinent communications through a central source from all others working on the same problem; in turn each expert feeds back

6. T. B. Roby and J. T. Lanzetta, *A Replication Study of Work-Group Structure and Task Performance,* Randolph Air Force Base, Operator Laboratory, San Antonio, Tex., June 1957 (Research Report No. AFPTRC-TN-57-85).

See also by the same authors: *An Investigation of Task Performance as a Function of Certain Aspects of Work-Group Structure,* Lackland Air Force Base, Air Force Personnel and Training Research Center, San Antonio, Tex., June 1956 (Research Report No. AFPTRC-TN-56-74); and "Conflicting Principles in Man-Machine System Design," *Journal of Applied Psychology,* vol. 41, pp. 170–178, 1957.

7. Robert K. Merton, "Bureaucratic Structure and Personality," in Hendrik M. Ruitenbeek (ed.), *Dilemma of Organizational Society,* E. P. Dutton & Co., Inc., New York, 1963, pp. 119–131.

8. Norman Dalkey and Olaf Helmer, "An Experimental Application of the Delphi Method to the Use of Experts," *Management Science,* vol. 9, pp. 458–467, 1963. For a description and evaluation of the Delphi technique see Harold Sackman, *Delphi Critique: Expert Opinion, Forecasting, and Group Process,* Lexington Books, D. C. Heath & Company, Lexington, Mass., 1975. See also: Richard J. Tersine and Walter E. Riggs, "The Delphi Technique: A Long Range Planning Tool," *Business Horizons,* vol. 19, no. 2, pp. 51–56, April 1976.

any reactions to a central source, and this cycle of interaction continues until a consensus appropriate to the solution of the problem is reached. The Delphi method has been described by Helmer[9] as a technique

> . . . which has the virtue of not requiring face-to-face confrontation, and the method of substituting a computed consensus for an agreed-on majority position. . . . The Delphi technique eliminates the need of committee activity altogether, thus further reducing the influence of certain psychological factors, such as specious persuasion, the unwillingness to abandon publicly expressed opinions, and the bandwagon effect of majority opinion. This technique replaces direct debate by a carefully designed program of sequential individual interrogations (best conducted by questionnaires) interspersed with information and opinion feedback derived by computed consensus from the earlier parts of the program. Some of the questions directed to the respondents may, for instance, inquire into the "reasons" for previously expressed opinions, and a collection of such reasons may then be presented to each respondent in the group, together with an invitation to reconsider and possibly revise his earlier estimates. Both the inquiry into the reasons and subsequent feedback of the reasons adduced by others may serve to stimulate the experts into taking into due account considerations they might through inadvertence have neglected, and to give due weight to factors they were inclined to dismiss as unimportant on first thought.
>
> A convenient consensus formula, applicable whenever the solicited judgments can be cast in numerical form (or even if they can merely be linearly ordered), is to use the median. Aside from being independent of a particular metric, it has the intuitively appealing quality that it can be viewed as the outcome of a democratic voting procedure, in the sense that half the panel considers the correct answer to be less than or equal to the median, while the other half considers it to be greater than or equal to the median. An obvious variant of the simple median is a weighted median, giving more than one vote to the opinions of experts whose judgment objectively deserves preferential treatment. For example, even self-assigned competence scores may justify such differential weights. . . . If, in addition to a consensus, it is desirable to have an indication of the spread of opinions among the experts, that is, of the amount of their "dissensus," it may be expedient to state the interquartile range of their responses (which is the interval containing the middle 50 per cent of them).

In contrast to open systems of communication restricted systems are apt to operate under the following conditions:

---

9. Olaf Helmer, *Social Technology*, Basic Books, Inc., Publishers, New York, 1966, pp. 16–17.

1. Information flows only in and among selective echelons. For example, information is restricted to persons in an inner advisory council or to members of the top management staff who in turn pass on or withhold information as they desire.
2. Communication is downward, and the channels are limited in provision for upward feedback. For example, persons in lower echelons may receive information relative to organizational goals as these are perceived by the top hierarchy but in turn have little opportunity to react or furnish feedback. This restriction can lead to limited interest in or sabotage of new proposals.
3. Communication is strongly status-centered, and inviolate meanings are attached to pronouncements from a central office or to statements of particular individuals. For example, the validity of information depends upon who gives it, and the tendency of communicators in this instance is to discuss or report only those matters which support status and to avoid communications which may threaten maintenance of status.

Restricted communication systems which are characterized by these examples, or where similar factors are involved, tend to lead to mistrust, misunderstanding, and conflict between teachers and administrators as well as among peer groups.

Situations, in good part, determine the types of communication which are most appropriate. Where there are uniform expectations on the part of staff members, or where problems are structured or deal with previously determined content and no feedback is necessary, one-way communication, either written or oral, seems preferable (e.g., a supervisor's report summarizing research findings or an oral summary of committee findings). A problem of change, analysis of conflict issues, or the determination of objectives would seem to require more than one type of communication, including any or all of the following: (1) person-to-person discussion to explore or structure the ideas and feelings of a person or group about a topic; (2) written proposals or summaries presented as a basis for discussion; (3) analysis or examination of an observation; and (4) the use of audiovisual media (e.g., displaying a chart to provide information about a problem, or showing a motion picture to elicit responses and obtain emotional commitment to an idea).

PERSON-TO-PERSON COMMUNICATION

Person-to-person communication may be employed by supervisors to effect changes in an individual staff member's behavior, to discuss problems of varying nature, to discover vis-à-vis the ideas and feelings of others, or to transmit the supervisor's own ideas. The description of person-to-person communication which follows primarily relates to the role of communicator and interpreter in oral discourse. However, many of the factors which operate in this process operate in other forms of communication as well. In any communication process—when persons are communicating—a kind of transmission belt is operating. Ideas themselves are not communicated by means of this transmission system, but ideas which have been translated into symbolic forms, such as words or signs. Symbolic representation is used with the hope that it will generate in the minds of others the same ideas as the communicator holds.

To highlight essential elements in person-to-person communication, a model showing the flow of ideas, or symbols which stand for ideas, in the message channel and the factors affecting communication is presented in Figure 8-1.

Two persons are represented: the *communicator* and the *interpreter*. They are faced with the problem of communicating with one another and with providing meaningful content, ideally representing

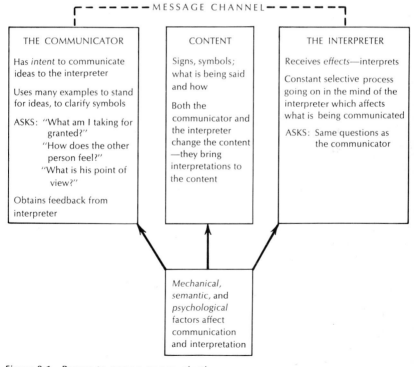

┌ ─ ─ ─ ─ ─ ─ MESSAGE CHANNEL ─ ─ ─ ─ ─ ┐

THE COMMUNICATOR	CONTENT	THE INTERPRETER
Has *intent* to communicate ideas to the interpreter	Signs, symbols; what is being said and how	Receives *effects*—interprets
Uses many examples to stand for ideas, to clarify symbols	Both the communicator and the interpreter change the content	Constant selective process going on in the mind of the interpreter which affects what is being communicated
ASKS: "What am I taking for granted?" "How does the other person feel?" "What is his point of view?"	—they bring interpretations to the content	ASKS: Same questions as the communicator
Obtains feedback from interpreter		

Mechanical, semantic, and *psychological* factors affect communication and interpretation

Figure 8-1 Person-to-person communication.

the same things to both persons, in the message channel. The communicator starts with an idea to be communicated (if the idea generated is not clearly formulated, effectiveness is reduced from the very beginning of the process), and then the idea must be translated into message form, by means of symbols, generally either spoken or written, for representing the idea. After the communicator has translated the idea into a message, the message is transmitted to the interpreter. Various factors may hinder or help movement of the message through the message channel and affect its interpretation. These factors may be classified as mechanical, semantic, or psychological. Mechanical factors include the kind of situation in which communication takes place, how the voice is used in oral communication, and such hindrances as mannerisms and external noises. Semantic factors have to do with linguistic skills, vocabulary, nomenclature, and the interpretation of symbols. Psychological factors include needs, beliefs, attitudes, and expectations, as well as feelings of security or lack of security, and the status system.

The message becomes a stimulus to which the interpreter responds with a discriminatory response. The message is translated into an idea by a selective process. In effective communication the idea from the communicator's mind (intent) ends up in the interpreter's mind (effect), equivalent in meaning to the original idea of the communicator. However, in the actual communication process this sequence does not occur regularly or systematically because of distortions resulting from negative factors operating in the communications network. Obviously, when distortion is reduced, communication is improved.

PROBLEMS FACED BY COMMUNICATORS

When recognized, factors which lead to distortion can be reduced.

1. Communicators may face difficulties relating to feelings about themselves. For example, they may feel that seldom are they able to make themselves understood; typically they have difficulty communicating ideas to others. Because of this concept they find it necessary to formulate messages several times over and in several different ways. They may send a message phrased in one way, but not being satisfied that it is clear they rephrase it, and so on through a number of changes. Thus, interpreters are confronted with a number of formulations of an idea, each of which may be different from the others, and have difficulty in knowing what is being said. Communicators, striving to be understood, display lack of skill in formulating their statement of ideas, and more often than not are misunderstood.

2. The assumptions held by communicators and the feelings they have about interpreters may have the effect of distorting ideas as they become translated into messages. For example, a communicator may dislike the interpreter, yet does not wish to or is not able to express directly this hostility, because it is a relatively submerged feeling. Nevertheless, this hostility may be reflected in the message which is transmitted. To the causal observer a statement such as "Do you know what procedures our former supervisor used to study this problem?" may sound like a reasonable question, but what comes through to the interpreter of the message is a feeling of comparison, a criticism of a particular way of working. The person who asked the question may not have been aware of its impact, but because of buried hostility an impression of hostility was imparted.

3. As communicators, we may or may not be aware of the kinds of persons with whom we are communicating. To communicate effectively, we must learn to take into account other persons' points of view and personality makeup so that we can frame messages which will more accurately reach their targets. We have to take into account such factors as the kind and degree of knowledge interpreters possess regarding a particular topic. We have to know with what nomenclature they are likely to be most familiar. If communicators use technical terms unfamiliar to others, messages will appear in symbols unfamiliar to them. For example, if a person is talking about learning theory to a group of experts in the field, messages would contain symbols of one order; if talking to a group of lay persons on the same topic, messages would have different content. The communicator has to know as much as possible about the interpreter's frame of reference because it is in this personal framework that messages will be decoded or interpreted.

4. Communicators need to know how other persons perceive them. If interpreters respect persons to whom they are giving attention or generally have good feelings toward them, the messages received more likely will be viewed favorably. If feelings are negative toward the communicator, it may be difficult for the communicator to get any messages through, even though they are, in an objective sense, basically good ideas. Most persons have experienced this kind of frustration.

5. Another factor affecting the communication process relates to the assumptions or expectations about the organizational system in which persons are operating. All of us need to be aware of the ways in which individuals behave in an organization. On what aspects of an organization are values placed—security, prestige, or reward system? What kinds of behaviors are expected or not ac-

cepted on the part of individuals—docile, conforming, creative, or instrumental? If an organization is one wherein operations require open and widespread communication and high levels of skill in discourse, individuals will reflect this atmosphere in their behavior. If the organization is restrictive and only limited kinds of communication are encouraged, this atmosphere certainly will be reflected. The implications for the supervisor seem clear. If teachers behave passively or are resistive, the expectations and atmosphere of the organization may need examination.

6. An individual's facility with words and the precision with which meanings are attached to words are particular determinants in effective communication. Since words stand for ideas, their choice and patterning are critical. The wording of bulletins or memos requires careful attention to clarity and precision. Individuals read only that which they bring to read with. Whether in spoken or written form, skillful use of examples which illustrate or stand for an idea will increase the prospect of having ideas understood. Feedback techniques also help the communicator to discover how much has been understood and to adjust messages accordingly.

PROBLEMS FACED BY INTERPRETERS
Factors comparable to those described for communicators also exist for interpreters as, for example:

1. The conscious feelings one has about oneself. Supervisors may have excellent technical skills, but feel that teachers really do not care for them as persons. While responding to technical behavior, teachers may show little interest in particular supervisors as human beings. At least this is the way some supervisors may view themselves. Because of this self view, supervisors, whenever certain persons communicate with them, assume that they are personally disliked. And so they misinterpret the messages received, thus contaminating others with what they *think* others feel about them, even though others may not have these feelings at all. The feelings we have about ourselves affect the way in which we interpret the messages of others.

2. Unconscious processes are operating within interpreters. They may have self-doubts about their own competence, including shortcomings that they can never examine too closely or accept. They may deal with shortcomings by diffuse activity, by driving others, or by avoidance mechanisms. When someone offers a suggestion or raises a question to help improve a particular situation, it may be interpreted as a criticism of technical competence or an attack on some imagined area of sensitivity. The reaction may be

to reject the suggestion outright or to say "This does not concern you; it is my problem." Responses such as this are a defense against one's own feelings of inadequacy and are unrelated to the content of the communication messages being received.

3. Interpreters also make assumptions about the communicator as they listen to a message. The other person's personality traits, knowledge, or attitudes are assessed while a message is being received, or even before the message is formulated. The quality of assumptions in relation to messages can affect strongly modes of interpretation, leading either to wrong conclusions, or, hopefully, to more effective understanding.

4. Assumptions which are made about organizational and social situations affect interpretation. If supervisors feel that teachers' suggestions or decisions are of critical importance to successful operations, they will respond differently to communication messages than they would if they consider themselves the supreme decision makers, and treat teachers' ideas in accordance with this self-centered view.

5. Many communication skills are of equal importance to both the interpreter and the communicator. Most important is the skill of really listening—the ability to hear what is being said from the other person's point of view, and to draw only those conclusions which are validated by mutual understanding and agreement.

USEFUL SKILLS IN IMPROVING COMMUNICATION

The skills to be described in this section have been found to be useful in interpersonal communication. They are neither new nor unique, and persons long have used them with varying degrees of success. However, it is how certain skills are used that determines the degree to which the communication process is successful. Inappropriately used skills may not only obstruct communication but also arouse unexpected antagonisms. One should remember that understanding another person is influenced by one's perception of the other's feelings and meanings. By evaluating carefully the results of the skills we employ, each of us has the opportunity to understand better the beliefs, feelings, and perceptions of others, and in so doing not only are others helped to understand us, but we gain insight into our own selves. Simple as the following skills appear to be, their successful use is dependent upon insightful practice and constant evaluation.

Paraphrasing

Paraphrasing is a way of checking with other persons to be sure you understand their ideas or suggestions as they intended them. Any means of revealing your understanding of other persons' comments constitutes a paraphrase. The objective is to provide information to other persons so that they can determine whether you understand their message as they intend it.

Persons newly introduced to the idea of paraphrasing frequently take it too literally and incorrectly assume that their task is merely to translate the other person's statement into different words. This can lead to "word-swapping," which does little to improve understanding. People attempting to understand the skill of paraphrasing also frequently ask if an effective paraphrase should be more specific or more general than the original comment. The answer is that either may be an appropriate way to convey your understanding.

Paraphrasing has potential for increasing the accuracy of communication because it allows speakers to assess a listener's understanding. If speakers think they have been misunderstood, they can provide additional information to clarify their meaning. In addition, paraphrasing allows listeners to convey their interest in other persons. Thus the paraphrase serves to enhance interpersonal relations as well as the clarity of communication.

Perception Checking

A second basic skill for understanding other persons is checking with them to make sure that you understand their feelings. This skill complements paraphrasing in that it focuses on the affective aspects of a message rather than ideas. To check your perception of others' feelings, you describe what you perceive to be their feelings. This description should tentatively identify others' feelings without expressing approval of the feelings and without attempting to interpret or explain the causes of the feelings. Checking the feelings of another conveys this message: "This is how I understand your feelings. Am I accurate?"

Understanding the feelings of others is a difficult task. Emotional states express themselves simultaneously in words and in nonverbal behaviors such as body movements and physiological changes. Quite often the nonverbal cues are the only accurate source of information available for understanding others' feelings. Instead of resting on your first inference about the meaning of these ambiguous cues, perception-checking allows you to verify your assumptions about the emotions the other person is experiencing. An additional benefit of perception-checking is that it conveys the idea that you *want* to understand the other as a person. Thus it has potential for improving interpersonal relations as well as increasing clarity of communication.

Describing Your Own Feelings

Describing your own feelings helps others to understand how you feel so that they can respond to you with greater efficacy. Although feelings get *expressed* in many different ways, usually people make no attempt to *describe* or identify directly the feelings themselves. When you merely express your feelings, the other person must try to infer your emotional state from a variety of cues. Since these cues are often ambiguous or even contradictory, the likelihood of misperception is great. When you directly describe your own feelings, however, the chances of misinterpretation and resultant action based on false assumptions are decreased.

Dissatisfaction and hostile feelings often indicate that faulty communication and misunderstanding have occurred. When these feelings arise, you and the other person should discuss how each sees the situation or the relationship. In this way, you may discover that your feelings come from misperceptions of the situation or misunderstandings of the motives of the other person. More accurate communication should cause the hostile feelings to abate. On the other hand, if your feelings of rejection are a response to the actions of other persons, they may want to change their own behavior. This desire for change is particularly likely if others become aware that their actions are arousing feelings in you or others that they do not intend. In this case, you have helped them to reduce their "blind area" by providing them with a description of your own feelings.

There are strong norms in our culture against expressing emotions openly and also against acknowledging that you perceive the other to be experiencing emotion. Perhaps this provides a partial explanation of the fact that trainees find the description of feelings the most difficult of the skills presented here. They often ask for guidelines regarding the appropriate times to describe their feelings. One of the best criteria, with regard to negative feelings at least, is to ask yourself whether you are going to harbor anxious or resentful feelings against the other. You should share your feelings when you feel that you will be uncomfortable if you do not.

The aim in describing your own feelings is to provide the other with accurate information about your emotional state. It should not be an effort to coerce the other into changing any annoying actions so that you will not feel as you do. Do not threaten the other with your feelings. By reporting your inner state, you are providing information that is necessary if the two of you are to understand each other and improve your relationship.

Describing Behavior

In a behavior description you should report specific observable behaviors of the other without evaluating them and without making inferences about the other person's motives, attitudes, or personality. As you develop skill in describing behavior you will become a better observer of the behaviors of others. You may find that there is sometimes little observable evidence to support your conclusions about others.

The objective in describing behavior is to provide other persons with a clear picture of the specific behavior to which you are responding. In addition, you will usually need to communicate additional information concerning the nature of your response. Behavior description is often used in conjunction with one of the other communication skills. When you describe those specific behaviors that have prompted a perception check or description of your own feelings, you will usually increase other person's understanding of you and also help them to become aware of the effect of their own actions. A behavior description is often useful in accompanying a perception check; for example: "You have brought up the issue of gum-chewing three times this afternoon. Does that mean you feel strongly about it?"

If you and another person want to communicate clearly and improve your relationship, the behavior description can be a valuable skill. Each of you will become more aware of your impact on the other, and you will both achieve a clearer picture of your own actions.

Giving and Receiving Feedback

Feedback—whether it is given or received—can be carried out most effectively by using the four communication skills described above. Here are some examples. *Paraphrasing:* "Did I understand you to say that you do not agree with the current plan?" *Behavior description:* "This is the third time you've asked that. Can you say more about your question?" *Describing own feelings:* "I felt antagonistic toward your laughing." *Perception-checking:* "You seem to feel very strongly about the point you were making."

Some rules for effective feedback are useful. It should be given with the following guidelines in mind:

1. *Noncoercive.* Feedback should be given so that it does not demand that recipients change their behavior.
2. *Consideration.* Feedback should be given after a careful assessment has been made of the feelings of recipients. This does *not* mean you should avoid showing anger (for example) to others. It means others should be ready to deal productively with it. Sometimes givers of feedback will have to wait for a time when they are able to present their feelings clearly and others are ready to listen.

3. *Descriptive.* Feedback should involve a clear report of the facts rather than the reasons why things happened as they did.
4. *Recency.* Feedback should be given close to the time of the events causing reaction.
5. *Changeability.* Feedback should be given about behavior that can be changed. For example, it is not very helpful to tell persons that the color of their eyes bothers you.

Taking a Survey
In taking a survey, conveners pose the decision; one or two people clarify it by paraphrasing. Then all in turn state their reactions to the proposal. Individuals should be as brief as they can, but they need not restrict themselves to "yes" or "no." They can say that they are uncertain, that they are confused and want to hear more, that they are experiencing some pain one way or the other, or that they do not want to talk about it. A group taking a survey, however, cannot allow individuals merely to remain silent. If they want to say nothing, they must say explicitly that they want to say nothing.[10]

SUMMARY STATEMENT
Because of the complex nature of communication it is doubtful whether any one theory or set of prescriptions will provide the one best way to make use of communication processes. Supervisors will find that improvement in their communication skills may be facilitated by (1) testing many communication strategies, (2) examining the consequences of the intended purposes of communication in various situations, and (3) evaluating continuously the kind and quality of predicted responses.

Some systematic ways for supervisors to organize communication procedures include:

1. *Knowing the precise purposes for preparing the communication.* Limit memos to essential items in order to avoid confusing or diverting the interpereter by an unprogrammed miscellany. Give attention to the major needs or information required to carry forward a particular operation in preparing other forms of communication.
2. *Developing a systematic set of communication techniques.* Be sure that all persons know that certain classes of bulletins deal with particular areas of thought, that memos deal with other specific areas, and that working papers primarily are used for the pre-

10. From Richard A. Schmuck et al., *Handbook of Organization Development in Schools,* National Press Books, Palo Alto, Calif., 1972, pp. 39–42.

sentation of content materials. Classifying, labeling, or giving a series listing for bulletins, reports, and other materials in terms of their purposes and targets provide focal points of attention. The interpreter is helped to attend to the message if its label defines its intent.

3. *Using several media for the same target if necessary.* Among the possibilities are written information, audiovisual techniques such as schematic materials and diagrams, person-to-person discussions, and group meetings.

4. *Obtaining feedback whenever possible.* Obtain written or verbal responses to determine understanding, and constantly encourage suggestions and criticisms.

5. *Writing or speaking only to the essentials.* Be parsimonious in using communication media. Overloading a staff with an excess of verbal and written information, ideas, or proposals, especially without any chance for feedback or follow-up, results in extinction of discriminating responses. Avoid repeating information available in prior communications.

CHAPTER 9

CREATIVITY AND CHANGE

CREATIVITY

In a nation that values creativity, individual expression, and vision in its citizens, and where schools attempt to develop human talent to its fullest, the fostering of creativity is an important educational objective. Such an objective requires that supervisors and teachers have a broad knowledge of the dimensions of creative behavior in adults and children, insight and skill in recognizing creative expression, and the ability to establish working climates conducive to creative expression.

Considerable information has been accumulated about the general nature of creativity—its identification, its characteristics, and the kinds and degrees of creative expression observable in many fields of human endeavor.[1] In place of reviewing and analyzing the numerous

1. Silvano Arieti, *Creativity: The Magic Synthesis,* Basic Books, Inc. Publishers, New York, 1977.

F. Barron, *Creativity and Psychological Health,* D. Van Nostrand Company, Inc., New York, 1963.

F. Barron, *Creative Person and Creative Process,* Holt, Rinehart and Winston, Inc., New York, 1969.

studies and reports on creativity, we have chosen to present what we consider to be some important elements in the creative process, to be followed by a comprehensive report on a series of investigations concerned with the creative process and the development and functioning of creative persons.

1. Creative abilities may be found in different degrees in all individuals; the potential for creative expression in any population, given appropriate conditions for such expression, is widespread. However, only a relatively small number of persons are distinguished for their creative productions. In the majority of persons creativity never reaches complete expression due, perhaps, to the effects of constraining environmental forces and/or an individual's temperamental functioning.

2. Creativity is a convenient label for a complex set of cognitive and motivational processes in individuals—a collection of abilities and traits. The creative process is not a mysterious force. Creative solutions to problems are not the result of a sudden flash of insight from the "unconscious mind" or magical powers of insight but rather are analyzable as resulting from the brain's mode of operating in thought processes, shaped by both heredity and environment.

3. The creative process does not seem to be programmed in a time sequence, nor does it appear that any particular gestation periods preceding creative production can be set or predicted. However, there appears to be a preparatory period during which persons saturate themselves with ideas and information before arriving at a synthesis of ideas. For example, a mathematician's creative solution to a problem in mathematics may result from ten minutes of thought at breakfast or from twenty preceding years of teaching

M. Dellas and E. L. Gaier, "Identification of Creativity: The Individual," *Psychological Bulletin,* vol. 73, no. 1, pp. 55–78, 1970.

Jerome Kagan (ed.), *Creativity and Learning,* Houghton Mifflin Company, Boston, 1967.

Donald W. MacKinnon, "Selecting Students with Creative Potential," in P. Heist (ed.), *The Creative College Student: An Unmet Challenge,* Jossey-Bass, San Francisco, 1968.

Morris I. Stein, *Survey of the Psychological Literature in the Area of Creativity with a View toward Needed Research,* U.S. Department of Health, Education, and Welfare, Cooperative Research Program of the Office of Education, Cooperative Research Project No. E-3, Research Center for Human Relations, New York University, New York, 1962.

C. W. Taylor and F. Barron (eds.), *Scientific Creativity: Its Recognition and Development,* John Wiley & Sons, Inc., New York, 1963.

Ellis Paul Torrance, *Guiding Creative Talent,* Prentice-Hall, Inc., Englewood Cliffs, N.J., 1962.

mathematics, discussing mathematical theorems with others, and personal thinking or hypothesizing.

4. Creative persons tend to engage actively in problem-solving tasks, and achieve desired goals more effectively in supportive environments.

5. True creative behavior, while characteristically novel or unique, also is likely to be reality centered; that is, creative responses occur in the real world and relate to real problems.

6. True creative behavior is characterized not only by production of ideas but by a kind of intellectual accountability demonstrated by persistence in exploring, developing, applying, and evaluating promising ideas.

Characteristics of Creativity

Deriving conclusions from a series of longitudinal studies, MacKinnon has provided a definitive report summarizing the salient characteristics of creativity and the modes of teaching which contribute to the development of creative talent:[2]

> In any attempt to discover the distinguishing characteristics of the creative person one must first decide what creativity is, since creativeness has been so variously defined and described. As I see it, true creativity fulfills at least three conditions. It involves a response that is novel or at least statistically infrequent. But novelty or originality of thought and action, while a necessary aspect of creativity, is not sufficient. If a response is to lay claim to being a part of the creative process, it must to some extent be adaptive to, or of, reality. It must serve to solve a problem, fit a situation, or in some sense correlate with reality. And thirdly, true creativity involves an evaluation and elaboration of the original insight, a sustaining and developing of it to the full.
>
> What I am suggesting is that creativity is a process which has a time dimension, and which involves originality, adaptiveness, and realization. It may be brief as in the jam session of a jazz band of it may involve a considerable span of years as was required for Darwin's creation of the theory of evolution.
>
> Whatever light I shall be able to throw upon the personality of the creative person comes in the main from findings of researches carried on over the last several years in the Institute of Personality Assessment and Research on the Berkeley campus of the University of California.
>
> In these current investigations of creative work and creative workers in the arts, sciences, and professions, which are aided by a grant

2. Donald W. MacKinnon, "Investigation of Creativity in Teachers and Students," paper presented to the special seminar on "Identification of Creativity in Teachers and Students: The Creative Personality" at the ninth Annual Creative Problem Solving Institute, State University of New York at Buffalo, June 24–26, 1963. Used with the author's permission.

from the Carnegie Corporation of New York, we have been seeking to discover those characteristics which differentiate highly creative individuals from less original and creative persons, and which distinguish creative people in one field from those in others; investigating the processes whereby fresh insights arise, inventive solutions are achieved, and new media for artistic expression are discovered; and searching those aspects of the life situation or social and cultural milieu of individuals which facilitate or inhibit the appearance of creative thought and action.

In these investigations we employ what has come to be known as the assessment method, that distinctive method of psychological research which was developed in the Office of Strategic Services during World War II for the purpose of studying the functioning of highly effective individuals. Its essential feature is that the persons to be studied are brought together for several days at an assessment center, where they meet with each other and with staff members, and participate in a series of experiments, psychological tests, and interviews covering the life history and professional career. In order to understand the development and functioning of highly effective and creative persons, we believe it is necessary to observe, and if possible to measure, as many aspects of personality as one can, and it is for this purpose that the highly varied, multidimensional observational and testing procedures of personality assessment have been developed and are being used in the Institute's study of creative persons.

As representatives of artistic creativity we have studied poets, novelists, essayists; as representatives of scientific creativity, engineers, research scientists and inventors; and as representatives of creativity which is both scientific and artistic, we have chosen to work with mathematicians and architects. Thus we are in a position to say something about what characterizes the creative worker and his mode of work in each of the areas studied. But what is more important for our concerns today is that many of our creative subjects were teachers in their field as well as creative practitioners of it. From them we have learned something about the characteristics of creative teachers. And from what our creative subjects have told us about themselves as students and about those teachers who most influenced them and especially about those who most fully nurtured their creative potential, we have learned something about those modes of teaching which are most conducive to the fullest development of creative talents.

It is from this background of experiences that I make bold to describe the creative teacher and teaching as a creative art.

1. You will not be surprised to hear me say first that creative teachers, like all creative persons, are intelligent. But this is not the most important thing to say about them. It is not surprising that no feeble-minded subjects turned up in any of our samples, the individual members of which had been nominated for study because of their outstanding creativeness, but it is worthy of note that in our various

groups intelligence (as measured by the Terman *Concept Mastery Test*) is not significantly correlated with creativity. Among creative architects the correlation of the two variables is −.08, among research scientists −.07, values not significantly different from zero.

Obviously this does not mean that over the whole range of creative endeavor there is no relation between intelligence and creativity. It signifies rather that a certain amount of intelligence is required for creativity, but beyond that point being more or less intelligent does not determine the level of a person's creativeness, and the level of intelligence required for creativity is sometimes surprisingly low.

What is more important than the level of intelligence as measured by an intelligence test is the effectiveness with which one uses whatever intelligence he has. In a study of leisure-time inventors I discovered that the inventor who held more patents than anyone else in the group earned a score of 6.0 on the Terman *Concept Mastery Test*! (By way of comparison, average scores on this test are for creative writers 156, research scientists 118, architects 113, Air Force captains 60.) Let me hasten to add, though, that these are not IQs, and, obviously, the inventor in question is not so dumb as his score of 6 would suggest.

The Terman *Concept Mastery Test*, which consists of Synonyms-Antonyms (essentially a vocabulary test of intelligence) and Analogies (a test of word knowledge, general information and reasoning ability) is scored number right answers minus number wrong answers. One who guesses on such a test when he is not certain of his answer is apt to be penalized, and will, of course, be penalized if his guess is wrong. If, for example, we count only the correct responses which our inventive inventor gave, he scores 87 rather than 6! He clearly has a fair amount of correct knowledge which he can record, but also a good deal of wrong information which he does not hesitate to give. He thus reveals in taking an intelligence test a willingness to take a chance, to try anything that might work, and this attitude also characterizes him in his inventive activity. He is typical of many who make up for what they lack in verbal intellectual giftedness with a high level of energy, a kind of cognitive flexibility which enables them to keep coming at a problem with a variety of techniques from a variety of angles; and being confident of their ultimate success, they persevere until they arrive at a creative solution.

This kind of person should remind us that creative giftedness is not to be equated to high verbal intelligence, and while the creativity of such persons may not be of the highest order, it is nevertheless worthy of respect and encouragement. It is easy for a supervisor or principal to be impatient with this kind of student, but patient waiting for their solutions and sympathetic understanding of their persistence in arriving at them may well result in the appearance of creative behavior in the most unlikely teachers as well as in the most unlikely students.

For those, on the other hand, who are truly intellectually gifted, whether student or teacher, I believe there is nothing which will so much contribute to their creativeness as holding for them the highest standards of performance and repeatedly setting tasks for them or better still encouraging them to set problems for themselves that are on the borderline of the limits of their performance. To work just this side of frustration, when every bit of one's ability is required, is the best way I know to maximize the creativeness of behavior which will be evoked.

2. Creative persons, whether they be teachers or students, are original. This statement will strike you as a tautology if, like many, you conceive creativity to be essentially a matter of novelty or originality of response. With such a notion I would strongly disagree, for, as I see it, originality is only a part of true creativeness.

Originality of response, if we focus upon that for the moment, has two aspects which must be distinguished: the quantity or number of original responses which one can give vs. the quality or goodness of the response. In our investigations we find that, in general, those who are most fluent in suggesting new solutions tend also to come up with the better ones. The quantity and quality of original responses correlate $+.53$ in one test (Consequences) and $+.78$ in another (Unusual Uses).

These correlations are low enough, however, to suggest, and indeed this is our finding, that some persons tend to make many original responses which are not very good, while others make fewer but generally better or more fitting ones.

These findings point to individual differences in creativity, some persons being strong in just those aspects of the creative process in which others are weak. The implications are obvious: there is no single method for nurturing creativity; procedures and programs must be tailor-made, if not for individual persons, at least for different types of persons.

To nurture the fullest creativity in those most fertile with new ideas, greater emphasis must be placed upon seeking the implications and deeper meanings and possibilities inherent in every idea. This is a matter of pursuing ideas in depth and with scope, not criticizing and rejecting, which is so easy to do and which is so crippling to creativity. Insights, however fresh and clever they may seem, do not enter the stream of creative solutions to urgent problems unless their consequences are tested in application and revised and extended to meet the requirements of the situation for which they were first devised. What I am suggesting is that mere fluency in unusual ideas will not alone make for fresh and creative solutions to problems, but in some persons rather to "freshness" in its worst sense.

Getzels and Jackson[3] cite the story given by one of their student

---

3. The internal quotation is from J. W. Getzels and P. W. Jackson, *Creativity and Intelligence,* John Wiley & Sons, Inc., New York, 1962.

subjects in response to a projective test picture as evidence of creativity (albeit creativity which they concede might drive a teacher dotty). The story reads as follows: "This man is flying back from Reno where he has just won a divorce from his wife. He couldn't stand to live with her anymore because she wore so much cold cream on her face at night that her head would slide across the pillow and hit him in the head. He is now contemplating a new skid-proof face cream."

Unlike Getzels and Jackson I would not interpret this story as indicative of a "mind that solves problems by striking out in new directions." Such fresh ideas as one finds in this story are not likely to lead to creative solutions, for they reveal too much freshness for freshness's own sake, too much striving for shock-effect, and insufficient concern for reality problems. Persons with this kind of originality, which I refuse to call creativity, need to be taught to pay more attention to the demands of reality and to sacrifice some of their fluency for greater attention to the quality and appropriateness of their ideas.

On the other hand, those who have few original ideas, but usually of a high order of excellence, may well be encouraged to increase their output. These tend to be the rather shy, withdrawn, more introverted persons. They more than the fluent type are in need of understanding and encouragement, if their original ideas are to be made known to others. Indeed, there is some evidence to suggest that persons who produce few original ideas but of uniformly high quality, actually experience many more ideas than they are willing to make public.

3. Creative persons are independent in thought and action, and these traits are so characteristic of them it is difficult to believe that they were acquired after the school years. According to their own reports this independence of spirit was already theirs in high school though tending to increase in college and thereafter.

One can well believe that creative teachers as well as students with creative potential will often chafe under the discipline and requirements of group coordinated activity. It is not that they are lazy, or that their level of aspiration is low, or that in their rebellious attitudes they are "rebels without a cause." The problem (if one permits it to become a problem) derives from their high level of energy which they seek to channel into independent, non-group-coordinated striving for extremely high goals of achievement which they set for themselves and which may well conflict with those goals which are set for the group.

Since it is a fundamental characteristic of creative persons that they are strongly motivated to achieve in situations in which independence of thought and action are called for and have much less interest in or motivation to achieve in situations which demand conforming behavior, I can only conclude that those who are genuinely interested in nurturing creativity must be prepared to grant more autonomy to those with creative potential and even reward them for behaviors which may at times be disturbing of group harmony.

For the most part, though, persons with creative potential will not so much actively disrupt group activities as they will passively and at times stubbornly resist efforts to integrate them into the group. Not infrequently persons of creative potential, whether students or teachers, concerned with their own experiences of both inner life and outer world, more introvert than extravert, and more isolate than social, may wish to pursue projects of their own making, and often enough will do so.

If such persons seem one-sided because of their lack of interest in group activities, I can only answer that many of the highly creative persons we have seen are not especially well-rounded. They have one-sided interests, and sharp edges to their personalities, and marked peaks and dips on their personality-test profiles. We will not create our able students or our teachers in the image of the highly creative if we always insist upon their being well-rounded.

Here we come face to face with a sharp conflict of values in our society today: the emphasis, on the one hand, upon togetherness, the integration of the individual into the group and its activities, good group dynamics, and smooth inter-personal relations; and on the other hand, the nurturing of creative talent.

All our evidence points to the incompatability of these opposed values and goals. On one test of interpersonal behavior the subjects of a nationwide sample of creative architects revealed even less desire to be included in group activities than that expressed by the naval and civilian personnel who volunteered to man the Ellsworth Station outpost in Antarctica during the International Geophysical Year.

It is conceivable, of course, that outstandingly creative persons develop their desire for aloneness and time apart for contemplative thinking as a result of the strong distaste for group participation which they acquire in being forced earlier into group activities. If this were indeed the case, we might be depriving them of much of their motivation for creative activity if we were to free them from participation in group activities and grant them more time for their individual pursuits. This, I must say, seems unlikely to me and so I continue to believe that one of the best methods for nurturing creativity is to de-emphasize group participation with its demands for conformity and to provide maximum opportunity for the able person to work out his own interests.

It is not easy for one who has always to deal with groups of persons, whether they be students or teachers, to welcome non-conforming behavior. It is not non-conformity as such that is deserving of respect or even of acceptance, and certainly not non-conformity for non-conformity's sake which ends by being conformity in reverse, but rather that kind of non-conforming, independent behavior which is an expression of the wholehearted commitment of the individual to truly creative goals.

4. Creative persons are open to experience both of the inner self and of

the outer world. As between perceiving (becoming aware of something) and judging (coming to a conclusion about something) creative persons are on the side of perception, open to and receptive of experience and seeking to know as much as possible about life.

The perceptive attitude expresses itself in curiosity, and is the hallmark of the inquiring mind. The open mind can, of course, become cluttered, and may, until it goes to work ordering the multiplicity of experience which it has admitted, reveal a good deal of disorder. And having to deal with confusion and disorder in one's own mind may be sufficient cause for anxiety, and especially so until one has found or evolved some higher order integrating and reconciling principles.

At such times a perceptive and understanding teacher, supervisor, or principal may be of the greatest help in communicating an emphatic understanding of the turmoil going on in the disquieted person and in conveying to him a quiet, even unspoken confidence that the anxiety which he is experiencing will pass.

The other way, the non-creative way, is the rigid control of experience, repressing impulse and imagery, blinding oneself to great areas of experience, and never coming to know oneself.

To grow creatively is not the easiest way to develop, and for some it would be too risky and dangerous an undertaking. Those who succeed reveal a richness and actualization of the self which the judgmental person, who in the extreme case prejudges experience and thus becomes the prejudiced person, can never achieve. More than most, creative persons are able to recognize and give expression to most aspects of inner experience and character, including the feminine in the case of the man and the masculine in the case of the woman, admitting into consciousness and behavior much which others would repress, integrating reason and passion, and reconciling the rational and irrational.

Young persons of creative potential often will not show these traits which are so characteristic of the mature creative person. Moreover, it can be safely assumed that many who will eventually show these traits are, during their earlier years, troubled and disturbed, experiencing conflicts of role, crisis in religious belief, uncertainty with respect to a multiplicity of possible life goals, and so on.

It is in respect to this aspect of creativity—the openness to experience and the necessity of finding integrating and reconciling symbols—that the subtlest and wisest skills of the teacher as counselor are needed. My own thought is that when such counsel can be given inconspicuously or casually in the directing of the young person to more and more sources of knowledge out of which he can find the answers which he needs it will be most conducive to the development of his creativity. Such non-directive counseling is not suited to all, but it is, I believe, the type of guidance indicated for the person with creative potential.

5. Creative persons are intuitive. Having stressed the perceptiveness of the creative person, I would now emphasize the intuitive nature of his perceptions. In perceiving one can focus upon what is yielded by the senses, the sense-perception of things as they are, the facts; and in the extreme case one can remain stuck there, bound to the stimulus, the presented material, or the situation. This I shall call sense-perception. Or one may in any perception be more alert and responsive to the deeper meanings, the implications, and the possibilities for use or action of that which is experienced by way of the senses. This immediate grasping of the real as well as the symbolic bridges between what is and what can be, I shall call intuitive-perception.

One would expect creative persons not to be stimulus- and object-bound, but alert to the as-yet-not-realized, in other words, characterized by intuitive-perception. And that is exactly what we find them to be in all our studies.

Whether the disposition to sense-perception or to intuitive-perception is constitutionally or temperamentally determined I cannot say with certainty. It is my impression that the preference in perception is at least in part so determined, but I also believe that the style of one's perceptions and cognitions can also, at least in part, be learned and trained.

Rote learning, learning of facts for their own sake, repeated drill of material, too much emphasis upon facts unrelated to other facts, and excessive concern with memorizing, can all strengthen and reinforce sense-perception. On the other hand, emphasis upon the transfer of training from one subject to another, the searching for common principles in terms of which facts from quite different domains of knowledge can be related, the stressing of analogies, and similes, and metaphors, a seeking for symbolic equivalents of experience in the widest possible number of sensory and imaginal modalities, exercises in imaginative play, training in retreating from the facts in order to see them in larger perspective and in relation to more aspects of the larger context thus achieved; these and still other emphases in learning would, I believe, strengthen the disposition to intuitive-perception and intuitive thinking.[4]

If the widest possible relationships among facts are to be established, if what I would call the structure of knowledge is to be grasped, it is necessary that the student in whatever field have a large body of facts which he has learned as well as a large array of reasoning skills which he has mastered. You will see, then, that what I am proposing is not that the student in learning or the teacher in teaching neglect acute and accurate sense-perception, but that both should use that to build upon, moving always to an intuitive understanding of that which is experienced.

6. The creative person has strong theoretical and aesthetic interests. On a test of values, the Allport-Vernon-Lindzey *Study of Values,* which

4.   See Donald W. MacKinnnon, *"The Nature and Nurture of Creative Talent,"* American Psychologist, vol. 17, no. 7, pp. 484–495, July 1962.

measures in the individual the relative strength of the six values of men as these have been described by the German psychologist and educator, Eduard Spranger,[5] namely, the theoretical, the economic, the aesthetic, the social, the political, and the religious values, all of our creative subjects hold most dear the theoretical and the aesthetic.

A prizing of theoretical values is congruent with a preference for intuitive-perception, for both orient the person to seek some deeper or more meaningful reality which lies beneath or beyond that which is actually present to the senses. Both set one to seek truth which resides not so much in things in themselves as in the relating to them one to another in terms of identities and differences and in terms of over-riding principles of structural and functional relationships.

Theoretical interests are carried largely in abstract and symbolic terms. In science, for example, they change the world of phenomenal appearances into a world of scientific constructs.

One is not on such firm ground in dealing with theoretical concepts and issues as one is in dealing with concrete objects. Accordingly, to be forced to deal with ideas rather than things can be an anxiety-provoking experience and especially for the young. Here the role of the teacher or supervisor in helping his charges to gain self-confidence in dealing with "theory" rather than with "fact" can be of the greatest importance. A concern with theoretical ideas will appear as "unrealistic" to less gifted and tougher-minded persons (and, of course, there is a sense in which they are right). Those who are developing such interests may experience another source of insecurity: at times the hostile and rejecting attitudes of their less gifted peers. At such times they may find themselves more extreme "isolates" than even they wish to be. The guide and mentor who in his or her own mature and effective person shows a high evaluation of the theoretical, provides the younger person with a model with which he can identify and thus helps him more confidently to permit within himself the development of his own theoretical interests.

Although there may appear to be some conflict between the theoretical value with its cognitive and rational concern with truth and the aesthetic value with its concern with form and beauty, these two values, as I have already indicated, are the two strongest values in our creative subjects. That they are both emphasized suggests that for the truly creative person the solution of a problem is not sufficient; there is the further demand that it be elegant. The aesthetic viewpoint permeates all of the work of a creative person, and it should find expression in the teaching of all subjects if creativity is to be nurtured in the school. Aesthetic values are stressed in art and

5. The internal reference is to Eduard Spranger, *Types of Men: The Psychology and Ethics of Personality* (authorized trans. of the 5th German ed. by Paul J. W. Pigors, Ph.D.), Max Niemeyer Verlag, Halle Salle, Germany, 1928.

music and perhaps to a lesser degree in the language arts; it is no less important that they be recognized and emphasized in mathematics, in physics and chemistry, in history, in shop-work—indeed, in all subjects.

7. The creative teacher like all creative persons has a strong sense of destiny which includes a degree of resoluteness and almost inevitably a measure of egotism. But over and above these traits there is a belief in the foregone certainty of the worth and validity of his creative efforts. This is not to say that creative persons are spared periods of frustration and depression when blocked in their creative striving, but only that over-riding these moods is an unquestioning commitment to their creative endeavor.

Another, probably related, characteristic of the creative person is that he knows who he is, where he wants to go, and what he wants to achieve. In Erikson's[6] phrase, the creative person has solved the problem of his own identity.

In Erikson's theory of ego development, however, the major problem of adolescence and early adulthood is to find one's own identity instead of losing oneself in a diffusion of conflicting roles.

Ego-identity and sense of destiny, though characteristic of the mature creative person, are not likely to characterize even the most able students whom on other grounds one may believe to have great creative potential. One of our creative architects had already at the age of four decided that he would become an architect; but he was the exception. It was much more common to find our creative subjects struggling with the identity problem during the high school years, in conflict about themselves and their life goals, and even troubled by the fact that they possessed so many skills and interests. As a consequence they were pulled in many directions, and tempted by the possibility of several quite different careers. What a young person needs in the face of such conflicts is a tolerance for ambiguity, and support in remaining tentative with respect to his life career and in resisting the dangers of premature closure which may cut off forever certain avenues of future development. Some of our creative subjects found their identity in high school, others not until well after college.

Our several investigations suggest that there is no domain of interaction between student and teacher in which the teacher can so effectively nurture the creative potential of the student as in supporting him in his tentativeness and openness to career possibilities and protecting him from pressures to solve prematurely his identity problem.

Parents often enough play an important role in shaping the identities which their children achieve, but with respect to the career aspect of the identity and whether it is followed creatively or in a

6. The internal reference is to E. H. Erikson, *Childhood and Society*, W. W. Norton and Company, Inc., New York, 1950.

banal fashion, the life histories of our subjects testify repeatedly to the signal importance of some one teacher during the high school or college years.

This teacher by his or her devotion to a field of study or work, exhibiting the excitement and satisfaction which comes from a deep absorption in its problems and its challenges, stirring the imagination of the student by a clear exposition of the structure of knowledge in the field of study, and seeking to respond creatively to its still unresolved problems offers the student a model with which he can identify. Most often it is not the profession of teaching with which the identification is made but the field of study which is taught with so much skill, devotion, and excitement, or the professional fields to which it may later lead, e.g., medicine or law, and a host of others.

From observation of this kind of teacher—a true exemplar—the student learns something of the delight and joy and fresh insights which come from confidence in one's competence and in the exercising of one's skill, and is motivated to acquire through study and hard work the knowledge, skills, and competence which alone provide grounds for a confident setting for oneself of ever more difficult problems in the field of one's interest.

The teacher who does not try to force interest but rather encourages the student to explore many different paths until he has found the right one for himself will have contributed far more than he or she will ever know to that sense of destiny which was only a potentiality within him when he was seeking to find his identity during his high school years.

You will have noticed that I have used essentially the same terms in describing the creative teacher and the student with creative potential. This may seem strange to some of you, to others irritating, but I have done so out of the profound conviction that the person who has the capacity to grow creatively, regardless of his age, is constantly creating of himself that personage which most fully actualizes his potentialities. The truly creative person remains ever a student. His education does not cease with schooling, for learning remains with him a lifelong pursuit. The art of creative teaching is to nurture in students the aspiration to a life of learning and a striving for the fullest realization of their potentialities, by revealing to them one's own enduring commitment to the same high goals.

Providing a Creative Climate

Creative behavior is a function of the transactional relationship between an individual and his or her social and work environment. What teachers do for students is, in part, a reflection of their school's environment. When teachers work in settings designed to liberate creative talent, their individual classrooms inevitably will tend to reflect a comparable atmosphere. However, the formal social organization of the school cannot provide automatically for the degrees of freedom necessary for creative expression—the kind of freedom which artists or writers have when they work on their own. In order to nurture creative expression or provide better opportunities for its development, supervisors may need to intervene to arrange differentiated work environments tailored to individuals or at least to a specific type of individual. For example:

1. For some individuals (and even small work groups) a high degree of autonomy and independence in the work climate may be required, with freedom to explore frontier areas of thought or work on complex problems. De-emphasizing group participation, and providing maximum opportunity for individual pursuits, while not always easy to accomplish, may yield creative expression beneficial to all.
2. Individuals who may have less need for autonomy because of the nature of their interests or the problems they are studying will usually work best in situations where they have wide access to selected resources, or data, or to the ideas of other persons. Since all persons have the potential ability to improve creative output, it is possible to maximize creative output among persons whose creativity is not of the highest by setting tasks that require the utmost of each person's ability.
3. Since esthetic values (form and beauty) and theoretical values (abstract and symbolic) are so important to creative persons, every effort should be made to provide an environment which reflects the first value and to stress those aspects of instruction which nurture the second.

Because of the independence of creative persons, they may be least motivated to achieve in situations demanding conforming behavior. By practicing a little forbearance in judging or criticizing others, supervisors may do much to help other individuals realize their creative potentialities and gain the satisfaction of achievement. Supervisors, in their relationships with teachers, may well follow the simple procedure of asking other adults to determine their own preferred work situations, and, then, make certain that an acceptable work environment is provided.

We believe that the work climate in a creative school is at its best when:

1. Opportunities for individual creativity are enhanced by design.
2. Emphasis is on results rather than on means—teachers, like, say, architects or artists, are accountable primarily for the results they achieve and not for the means they employ.

3. Cosmopolitan views of problem solving and instruction are highly valued.
4. There is no one best way for all persons to achieve maximum results—the focus of teaching is on discovering what works best for each individual.
5. Such factors as status, position, or role as determinants of who does what in schools are minimized, and the values of individual and group creativity are maximized.

CHANGE
On Innovation and Resistance to Change

We live in a society of organizations to which a majority of social tasks have been entrusted, and all organizations are faced with effecting change in order to meet current and predicted future demands of the society which supports them. Change, resulting from innovation, may occur in a variety of ways—from creative expressions which produce some new element or significant innovative idea, from trial and error, serendipity, or practical resourcefulness. However change occurs, it has been recognized as an important process in the structure and/or function and survival of cultures, institutions, and organizations.[7] Innovations or innovative ideas, conceived by an individual or group, are ideational concepts to be examined or employed in providing answers to existing or predicted problems rather than instruments of change in themselves. Change results when an innovation is adopted and disseminated.[8]

The kinds of changes which have taken place in schools over a period of many decades have resulted from various internal and external influences including, at one time or another, some or all of the following: (1) legal mandates, (2) policies or practices adopted or adapted from other schools or organizations, (3) administrative edicts, (4) principles derived (or inferred) from educational thought and/or demands of persons or groups, and (5) a range of societal crises, responses to which have varied from technological to affective, and from expected to unpredicted or foreseen.[9]

In general, criticism of schools has focused on the belief that (1)

7. Gilbert Kushner et al., *What Accounts for Socio-cultural Change?* University of North Carolina at Chapel Hill, Institute for Research on Social Science, Chapel Hill, 1962.
8. William H. Lucio, "The Philippines–University of California Language Program: A Model for Innovation," *School Year* (Philippine Normal College), vol. 1, no. 4, pp. 13–17, June 1965.
9. For a comprehensive analysis of the structure and incentive systems of public schools as they relate to the adoption and implementation of educational innovations see John Pincus, "Incentives for Innovation in the Public Schools," *Review of Educational Research*, vol. 44, no. 1, pp. 113–144, Winter 1974.

schools have been slow (if not resistive) to accept and disseminate innovations, (2) schools must be prodded into directing their efforts in rational and productive ways, (3) the change process in schools tends to be concerned more with means than with objectives, and (4) more emphasis has been given to the rhetoric than to the substance of change.[10] Like other large bureaucracies, schools, by their very nature, tend to avoid those kinds of innovations which may disturb their normal routines. Individuals or groups have been known to display considerable ingenuity in circumventing plans which require change, regardless of the possible benefits which predictably should result.[11]

Efforts to introduce innovations and make changes in an organization sometimes are seen as threatening to an individual's self-image, or tending to derogate prior training and experience, or requiring significant changes in attitudes and/or the development of new, if not different, work habits. All persons in organizations, of course, have learned that unwanted changes can be resisted effectively by means of the power of informal subsystems existing in most organizations. Because persons in subsystems usually can agree upon or rally around some common purposes for action, they may act as a group, or as individuals, to screen out innovative ideas and resist or sabotage efforts at unwanted change. Supervisors must consider that resistance to change on the part of groups or individuals may occur for a number of reasons:

1. Because persons have had little or no part in decisions about contemplated changes, but believe that they should have had at least an opportunity for participation
2. Because persons may have proposed a worthy innovation only to find it assigned to others for implementation, thus losing ownership in their creative idea (of critical importance to some individuals)
3. Because persons, even though thoroughly committed to a particular change, have not been provided with the resources or time to

10. J. Victor Baldridge, "Organizational Change: The Human Relations Perspective Versus the Political Systems Perspective," *Educational Researcher*, vol. 1, no. 2, pp. 4–10; p. 15, February 1972.
    Andrew W. Halpin, "Change: The Mythology," in William G. Monahan, *Theoretical Dimensions of Educational Administration,* The Macmillan Company, New York, 1975, pp. 459–472.
11. J. Victor Baldridge and Terrence E. Deal, *Managing Change in Educational Organizations: Sociological Perspectives, Strategies, and Case Studies,* McCutchan Publishing Corporation, Berkeley, Calif., 1975.
    Ernest R. House, *The Politics of Educational Innovation,* McCutchan Publishing Corporation, Berkeley, Calif., 1974.

develop the knowledge or practice the skills requisite to implementing a particular operation

Schools have gained a reputation for *reacting* to change-inducing forces rather than for *acting* to create such forces themselves. We believe that the validity claimed for educational innovations (designed to improve school operations, learner achievement, or teacher effectiveness) has been based more on judgmental than on empirical criteria, more on evidence of face validity than on significant correlates. It has been noted, also, that the validation process for educational innovations has been measured primarily against criteria of bureaucratic and social acceptability—"Criteria that are far more tenuous than those of a competitive market, but no less important for the actors in the bureaucratic marketplace."[12]

Work Climates and Guidelines for Change

A number of investigators have supported the concept that the importance attached to the work climate of an organization determines the kind and amount of acceptance and involvement in change that is most apt to occur.[13] Supervisors, responsible for effecting change, have found that conflict, tension, and resistance to change among individuals may be alleviated by improved working environments. A feeling of security coupled with a desire to make changes for the benefit of all can lead to productive behavior.

Findings about innovations in organizations, derived from a report of a seminar conducted by the Graduate School of Business, University of Chicago, provide a number of provocative ideas concerning the kinds of work climates which support innovative behavior. These ideas, applicable to supervisory planning and effective staff operations, are related reciprocally to strategies (described previously) for providing creative work climates in schools.[14]

1. Innovations are more likely to occur in the kinds of climates in which:
   a. Recognition is given to beliefs that important problems exist and that no obvious solutions are in sight.

12. Pincus, op. cit., p. 119
13. Donald D. Peltz, "Creative Tensions in the Research and Development Climate," *Science,* vol. 157, no. 3785, pp. 160–165, July 14, 1967.
    Francis A. J. Ianni (ed.), *Conflict and Change in Education,* Scott, Foresman and Company, Glenview, Ill., 1975.
    William G. Monahan, *Theoretical Dimensions of Educational Administration,* The Macmillan Company, New York, 1975. See, particulary, chaps. 10–12.
14. Reprinted from *Trans-Action Magazine,* "Special Supplement: The Innovating Organization," vol. 2, no. 2, pp. 29–40 (summaries from reports on pp. 29–34), January–February 1965.

 b. An active search for solutions is conducted rather than a dependence upon chance to discover new ideas.

 c. Potential innovators believe that their solutions, once proposed, will be accepted by others and tried out, when the idea is one which will fit the general goals, strategies, and preferences of the organization.

 d. Freedom from restricting time pressures and excessive evaluation processes is assured.

 e. Energy-sapping justifications with regression toward routine data-gathering to support prior conclusions do not occur inevitably.

 f. Involvement includes persons in the organization with as wide as possible a spread of knowledge and training in formal and informal modes of problem solving, in order to provide a cosmopolitan range of alternatives and counterbalances for the biases and provincial interests of individuals.

2. Optimal conditions for creative innovations, according to some cumulative bits of evidence, seem to occur when persons, while having control over the direction and scope of their work, are exposed to the ideas and criticisms of other persons whose competences are not necessarily in the same area. Effective mechanisms to develop cosmopolitan interests and efforts might include: (1) the involvement of an immediate supervisor, (2) a potential user of the innovation, or (3) the consultative ideas of several colleagues with at least comparable skills. For instance, scientific organizations have discovered that innovative processes can be enhanced by:

 a. Providing diversity in the individual's working tasks so that time is spent on task dimensions ranging from basic and applied research to product invention and improvement, and technical activities.

 b. Remembering that groups developing narrow specialties tend to lose vitality.

 c. Being aware that groups which stay together too long without change in composition tend to become less productive, communicate less with others, and lose their feeling of active competition (in a sense they become captives of their own programs).

 d. Helping maintain the rate of the problem-solving cycle (proposing questions, gathering appropriate data, and generating new questions) with the realization that the momentum of the cycle may lessen with the aging of groups or individuals.

 e. Keeping the search for solutions moving by setting general but not rigidly held-to deadlines for task accomplishment.

 f. Encouraging the conclusion of a project by suggesting seductive new problems, or new groups with which persons may engage, even before their previous problems are completely solved.

Arranging an Environment for Innovation

The brief description of staff participation in a curriculum study which follows is intended to illustrate some of the elements involved when an environment is deliberately arranged for innovation and change. "Arranging the environment" means providing content for thought and responsible action. It means providing ideas, source materials, a creative work climate, and technical assistance whenever and wherever needed. Above all, it capitalizes on the fact that, as learning organisms and task-oriented professionals, teachers will respond to competent instrumental leadership.

The central curriculum council of a school system approved a project designed to revise the program of teaching geography in its secondary schools. Two years were allotted by the council to complete the study. A supervisor-teacher study team of five members was assigned responsibility for initiating the study with the involvement (at a later time) of the teaching staff. The intent of the study was to investigate contemporary thinking about the scope of the field of geography, to be followed by a determination of teaching content related to factors pertaining to the human habitat, and the development of new instructional sequences. An expert in the field was employed to serve for the entire period of the study.

As a first step the study team carefully prepared a working paper to serve as a basis for the initial discussions of the teaching staff. Incorporating theories, principles, and methodologies for the study of geography, the working paper included (1) outlines of content areas: the orderly treatment of physical elements of the human habitat, ways in which human beings utilize their physical environment, distribution of physical and cultural elements composing the human habitat, and interpretation of variety in the human habitat; (2) a list of a full range of possible goals and instructional objectives that might be involved in an assessment of needs (construction of the list being primarily the responsibility of the expert); (3) a suggested plan of the ways in which community, students, and teachers could participate in the selection of goals to be derived from the projected needs assessment; (4) suggested standards against which to evaluate results; and (5) illustrations of possible instructional sequences which could be developed within a central theoretical framework.

Activities subsequent to the initiation of the project included (1) preparation by the teaching staff of a calendar of operations with target dates for completion of tasks; (2) self-selection and/or assignment of tasks to be undertaken; (3) plans and assignments for continued research based on study of the original working paper; and (4) a tryout of various instructional sequences in classrooms with systematic observations, testing, data collection, and periodic feedback of results to other staff members.

Reactions of the teaching staff to the study procedure indicated that they were favorably impressed with the substance of the proposal as detailed in the initial study paper and motivated to work on a task which they perceived as "yielding dividends" in their teaching. The attention and scholarly effort which teachers perceived to have been given to their teaching interests contributed in no small way to their willingness to commit themselves to the project. Teachers were challenged to discover new ideas and to realize how much there was to be learned, not only about the field but about teaching.

This indigenous approach to curriculum development certainly differs from what might be called the "adoptive" approach, whereby a curriculum or instructional program developed and used in one school system is adopted by another system with few, if any, modifications or analyses of its appropriateness. Adoptive procedures for curriculum development provide little or no opportunity for teachers to study all aspects of a particular curriculum problem, develop instructional objectives, devise instructional sequences, or determine how a program will be implemented and evaluated. Such reactions by teachers to adoptive curriculum development practices as the following are not unfamiliar: "Get out scissors and paste, a curriculum revision is coming." "Here we go again on one of those wild-eyed innovations." "Better clear the closet shelf for another illegitimate adoption." "I see that Supervisor Z has dug up another bone."

By contrast, in the procedure we just described, a study team, with the help of experts, carefully prepared data on the basic understandings underlying the field and accomplished the initial steps by gathering materials, outlining objectives, and suggesting instructional sequences. Motivation was effected by this technique, since the materials prepared by the study team automatically eliminated the necessity for time-consuming search for information on the part of busy teachers. Provided with key ideas, hypotheses, and data by the study team, they were able to devote their energies directly to the central task of studying the problem.[15]

Degrees of Freedom

There are some myths about change which have functioned to rationalize rejection of and resistance to change in schools: "Supervisors are mere minions executing the bureaucratic blueprint." "Supervisors supervise and teachers teach what has been laid out in their contracts." "There's no such thing as creativity in a bureaucracy." However, programs in innovative schools (operating within the same bureaucratic structures as all others) demonstrate that there are few constraints on freedom to introduce change.

15. Carol H. Weiss, *Evaluating Action Problems,* Allyn and Bacon, Inc., Boston, 1972.

Supervisors, at any level, have wide latitude in introducing new purposes and influencing the directions of change. The degrees of freedom in generating and supporting the kinds of innovations which can make a noticeable difference in programs, instructional methods and materials, the physical environment, and development of staff knowledge and skills are widespread. Supervisors should analyze their own particular situations to determine the extent of the constraints (real or imagined) on their ability to generate innovative ideas and programs. We suggest several areas in which innovative thought and action may be applicable:

HUMAN VALUES   Decisions relating to educational policy and practices rarely have been developed on the basis of rigorous, scientific models or procedures to produce uncontrovertable solutions to problems of change. Effective supervisory decisions, therefore, generally involve a somewhat pragmatic approach which does take some account of the inherent ambiguity, paradox, and disarray surrounding most educational issues but which, in the final analysis, is based on and controlled by human value priorities.[16]

PERSONNEL SELECTION   There are few existing state laws or rules of boards of education in which the kinds of persons to be employed in schools (other than base line standards of health and specified certification) are specified. Though formal criteria regarding traits, attitudes, values, beliefs, and experiences are not operative in personnel selection, we recognize that latent criteria do exist in certain instances, but their power is minimal and is rapidly being reduced by the actions of courts and legislatures. Because the ranges of available human talent, temperament, education, and experience are infinite—the possibilities for building truly cosmopolitan subcultures of teachers in schools are also infinite.

DEVELOPMENT OF RESOURCES AND PROGRAMS   Supervisors are free to determine and/or give special emphasis and support to a variety of practices or operations: (1) particular programs (early childhood, career counseling) or practices (reading centers, tutorial instruction), (2) staff development programs (special training for para-

16. R. W. Sperry, "Bridging Science and Values: A Unifying View of Mind and Brain," *American Psychologist,* vol. 32, no. 4, pp. 237–245, April 1977.
   See also a discussion of the Quality of Life (QOL) studies concerning the place of values in satisfying an individual's (or society's) perceived psychophysiological needs, in Norman C. Dalkey with Daniel L. Rourke, Ralph Lewis, and David Snyder, *Studies in the Quality of Life,* Lexington Books, D. C. Heath and Company, Lexington, Mass. Copyright © by the RAND Corporation, 1972.

professionals, teachers' study centers), (3) special consultant resources (parent councils, teacher/parent task forces, outside experts), (4) use and abuse of resources, (5) methods, resources, persons to be used in problem solving (citizen committees, consultant teams, grass roots methodologies).

INCENTIVES   The human costs of change (i.e., overexpenditure of psychophysiological energy, lack of status in the organization, feelings of teachers that they lack the skills to accomplish changes) can be minimized, and threats to individual performance reduced, by emphasizing results teachers obtain and not particular means employed. A variety of incentives may be used, ranging from the remunerative (mini-grants, summer stipends, tuition grants) to the global and more affectively appealing rewards (academic recognition, released time, or flexibility in work loads).[17]

ANTICIPATING AND GRASPING THE FUTURE   Supervisors are in a key position to explore the latent will of the people of a community and to postulate possible future states, to encourage teachers and members of the community to envision problems not yet on the horizon and to develop tentative solutions. To illustrate: (1) "If the board and staff need to dismiss the chief administrator two years from now, what plans should be made now and how much money should be set aside in the existing budget to seek a replacement?" (2) "There is a movement in this state to eliminate present tenure laws for teachers. What plans should we be making in this school district to meet the change, assuming it will occur in five years?" (3) "What needs of paramount interest to the parents and children of this district should be brought to the attention of the state legislative analysts before the legislature is even aware that they exist?"

OPERATIONAL FLEXIBILITY   Supervisors are in an advantageous position to initiate innovative strategies designed to achieve more flexible operations and improve staff effectiveness. Among the promising practices applicable to improving staff performance are (1) *Gleitende Arbeitzeit,* or "gliding time," and (2) ergonomy. Gliding time, a concept developed by Christel Kammerer, a West German management consultant,[18] is a system of self-arranged, individualized work patterns, based on the idea that individuals appear to run on

17. Willis D. Hawley, "Horses before Carts: Developing Adaptive Schools and the Limits of Innovation," *Policy Studies Journal,* vol. 4, no. 4, pp. 335–347, Summer 1976.
18. Betty Ann Stead, "Women's Contributions to Management Thought," *Business Horizons,* vol. 17, no. 1, pp. 32–36, February 1974.

different psychophysiological "time clocks" and that they are most successful when they can plan their working times for periods when they are most productive. Gliding time has been employed successfully in industry, in hospitals, and to some extent in schools. Reports indicate that individuals maintain high morale and the amount of work they perform increases in gliding time systems.

Gliding time can be applied effectively in realigning work patterns in schools to meet individual psychophysiological requirements of children and teachers. For example, in urban communities, where the occupations of parents require their leaving early and returning late, or vice versa, schools have adapted the school day to match the time needs of pupils from such households. Pupils arrive and leave at different times during the school day, and their rest and play periods, in-school meals, and on-site afterschool activities are scheduled to fit varying time modules. Teachers and paraprofessional staff adjust their work times accordingly.

Ergonomy can be described as "the science of matching machines to persons, not persons to machines." The concept was developed in industry and the armed services in order to match machines (tools, aircraft, spacecraft, instrument controls, etc.), as well as perceptual and psychomotor tasks, with individual capacities. In essence, tasks or equipment are adjusted to or matched with an individual's knowledge or skill rather than the reverse of fitting persons to a task. The concept has been applied with some success in schools by matching teaching assignments and tasks with particular skills or styles of teachers. For example, teachers, themselves, select methods they find most effective, in terms of their own abilities rather than those selected by others. In consultation with one another they match their specialized skills to fit needs, aptitudes, or even values of particular students, a reversal of fitting pupils to teachers.

Supervisors must be realistic in considering the applicability of concepts such as gliding time and ergonomy to their own situations. In general, strategies will be more successful when staff members are involved in their selection and implementation, discover what works best for them, and perceive that they "own" the ideas.

Caution: You May Need a Local Guide

Supervisors must recognize that there are sensitive areas of change which schools, at times, must bypass because they may have neither the social and/or legal mandates nor the technical resources to engage with certain problems. Schools cannot expect to solve major social problems that other institutions or agencies continue to foster or condone. Various aspects of racial understanding, some, of a complex and diffuse sort, may be beyond the purview of schools. An example should suffice to illustrate the issue: An in-school innovation (utilizing behavior modification techniques), designed to socialize a particular group of "X Ethnic-Americans" in the community, was suggested to a school community with some enthusiasm by a supervisor. The school staff (and some parent council members) believed that the innovation had a modicum of face validity. After all, teachers in most public schools believe that they are responsible for teaching pupils how to deal with persons different from themselves. Teachers do that very thing within the micro social community of the classroom every day, using low-risk Rogerian approaches to improving human relations which do not violate the values of pupils (or the terminal values of parents).[19] Within the context of the school, apparently these efforts had been acceptable to the particular community in question. "So," thought the supervisor, "why not improve on these efforts of individual teachers by developing a socialization program to include teachers, pupils, and interested parents?" Apparently the supervisor should have given the whole package more thought and less action (technical), because the innovation was shot down, albeit with simple grace and power, to wit—the "X Ethnic-American" head of the parent council spoke thus: "X Ethnic-Americans do not give their children to the school for special programs of socialization—the families take care of this." The idea was completely unacceptable! The idea may have had face validity, but no value validity.

Lest what has been said about this episode be misinterpreted, it must be noted that carefully designed projects can be accomplished successfully when responsible action is taken to meet social problems in such areas. However, they require, among other things, (1) a deep knowledge of the values held by the community, (2) extensive preparation with many publics, and (3) often an extensive retraining of teachers. Innovative proposals in sensitive areas will have more chance to be successful when they are wanted by a group to be "changed" and above all when they bear a close relationship to what individuals value most.

How Much Does That Innovation in the Window Cost?
Effective in-school innovations are not necessarily dependent upon the amount of funding provided. Rather, the human and technical

19. Milton Rokeach, *Beliefs, Attitudes, and Values: A Theory of Organization and Change,* San Francisco, Jossey-Bass Inc., 1968.
    Milton Rokeach, "The Measurement of Values and Value System," in Gilbert Abcarian and John W. Soule (eds.), *Social Psychology and Political Behavior: Problems and Prospects,* Charles E. Merrill Books, Inc., Columbus, Ohio, 1971.

talents of the total school community are the major resources for innovation. Effective innovation and change take place in schools where the instrumental values and perceptions of parents, teachers, and students support program change and development as a routine way of action.[20] All of these parties, generating ideas, developing materials, experimenting with varied practices whether of a micro or macro order, and using the power of a bureaucracy, are the most important instruments for change. The kinds of innovation "packages" either "bought" by schools or "sold" to them by various agencies external to the school (often supported by federal or state funds) usually contain preset goals, preplanned procedures, and operational sequences. That they constitute the best way to introduce innovations or are useful instruments of change is open to question. The countryside is littered with the wreckage of "one-shot" well-funded innovations, the long-term effects of which disappeared with the drying up of funds—unloved, unwanted, unnecessary!

There is little evidence to support the idea that unless an innovation is well funded it will not succeed. On the contrary, it would seem that a Spartan approach—a "do-it-yourself with whatever you can lay hands to in the way of resources"—yields more innovative/ change dividends and may have more lasting effects on schools. Furthermore, the oft heard plaint that "educational innovations cannot be mounted without money" will be valid no longer. It may be that schools are going to be called upon to utilize less and less and achieve more and more! That is, reduced expenditures for change programs and increased use of the productive talents of school personnel in generating innovations will be the accepted practice. There is evidence that staff development programs, the development of school-site decision models, and similar procedures employed by schools throughout the country are capitalizing on the talents of teachers in this effort. Individual schools and their staffs thus are becoming central resources for inquiry/innovation/change.[21]

Teachers and supervisors across the country and abroad (particularly in England) are finding that a good portion of instructional materials, artifacts, or physical equipment required for new or experimental programs in individual schools and classrooms can be "bought free." Schools noted for their innovative practices are reported to be relying on materials and equipment that are either scrap, surplus, or "scrounged."[22] In the long run, the most valuable

20. Ernest R. House, "The Micropolitics of Innovation: Nine Propositions," *Phi Delta Kappan,* vol. 57, no. 5, pp. 337–340, January 1976.
21. Larry L. Zenke, "Staff Development in Florida," *Educational Leadership,* vol. 34, no. 3, pp. 177–181, December 1976.

resource for survival may be our "fund" of available human intelligence and talent (the costs of which are no more than the use of the human cortex). There is growing evidence that creative resources are widespread and available to schools on a voluntary basis. *Voluntarism,* more and more, may become a way of action in American communities as schools, faced with new demands upon their resources, along with declining revenues and enrollments, seek to maximize the use of all available resources to develop innovative programs. To cite an example: A group of management analysts, resident in a large western county, voluntarily formed a research team and offered their services without reimbursement, to help school districts conduct organizational studies and develop plans to maximize the use of their present and projected resources.[23] Having the services of such a group of community experts available would be salutary for any school district!

Maximizing the use of human resources while minimizing financial costs of change are important elements in achieving worthwhile educational results. In a time of declining or shifting material resources school districts, seeking to develop imaginative and innovative programs, may discover voluntarism to be one of the most powerful of democratic instruments for change.

STRATEGY AND CHANGE

Most strategies for change have been based on a research/development/dissemination model on the assumption that change flows primarily from a knowledge base.[24] This model is similar to linear models employed in agricultural or medical research, where a treatment is developed in a laboratory, tryouts are conducted, and the researcher takes the results of treatment to the practitioner, who then puts them into practice.[25] The model has not been effective in solving problems of educational change for several reasons: (1) the idiosyncratic preferences of practitioners and their perceptions of what

22. Far West Laboratory for Educational Research and Development, *Educational Programs That Work,* Far West Laboratory (1855 Folsom Street, San Francisco, CA 94103), 1975.

Lil Thompson, "Priorities in Conflict," Section Address, the Forty-fourth Annual Claremont Reading Conference, Feb. 4 and 5, 1977 (proceedings of the Conference published in the 1977 Claremont Reading Conference Yearbook, Claremont Graduate School, Claremont, Calif.).

23. Jack Birkinshaw, "Special Analyst Treats Schools' Ills: Efficiency Expert on Call for Any County District," *Los Angeles Times,* Sunday, July 17, 1977—W—p. 6.

24. Egon G. Guba, "Development, Diffusion and Evaluation," in William G. Monahan (ed.), *Theoretical Dimensions of Educational Administration,* The Macmillan Company, 1975, pp. 371–396.

25. See a related discussion in Chapter 12, pp. 279–281.

is worthy of application, (2) inertia and/or resistance of the school bureaucracy (which has its own strategies for change), (3) the range of differences in technical skills and knowledge among school personnel, and (4) the increased involvement of school personnel in the decision-making process and, concomitantly, the power to screen innovations.

Not only have the imperfections in the model itself lessened its legitimacy, but in the last decade different views of what constitutes educational change held by society at large, on the one hand, and, by schools on the other, have tended to place schools in a survival mode vis-à-vis change. The demands for improved schooling from a concerned public, the interest of legislatures and school districts in maintaining quality schooling while faced with finite economic resources, have resulted in more or less conservative views of the ways to effect change in public institutions. Consequently, schools may turn to using simpler survival or "grass roots" methods of change, less costly, less elaborate, easier to implement and fitting better with the functions of a school bureaucracy. One can predict that under these conditions there will be (1) more emphasis on the wisdom of "good practice" (as in England, where the thought and action of practitioners are central to change efforts), (2) less dependence on ideas of "researchers" outside the school, from scholars whose views of areas of educational change are derived from the perspectives of their own disciplines and thus may be considered too reductionist by practitioners, (3) increased emphasis on in-school inquiry and analysis, with results being shared among schools through channels other than the scholarly or academic, and (4) more indigenous development of innovations in schools and less interest in innovative implants from outside the school.

Whether such measures will meet what appears to be an inevitable demand for educational change of a different order than heretofore is open to question. However, when the transient rhetoric and oversell which seem to accompany any new proposals for change cool, the practical intelligence of the American people leads one to believe that there will always be support for educational changes which display originality and vitality, and can be shown to have validity for improving the quality of education.

CHAPTER 10

LEARNING AND SUPERVISORY BEHAVIOR

Learning has been defined as changed behavior resulting from or accompanying practice or experience. Behavior appears to be shaped by complex cognitive processes in which actions vary among learning tasks and within tasks and from one aspect to another. Although no agreed-upon, universal laws of learning have been established, theorists have formulated a number of learning principles which they believe underlie and help to explain behavior.[1] Certainly, teachers employ learning principles of one kind of another, intentionally or not, in their classroom teaching. There are few teaching acts for which learning principles cannot be inferred whether from what teachers do or from their descriptions of their intent.

Two approaches to the study of learning, *reinforcement* and *cognitive* learning theory, have provided testable hypotheses and explanations of how human behavior is shaped and learning takes place. Selected aspects of these two perspectives, and some general principles of learning, will be discussed in this chapter. Readers are

---

1. Wilbert J. McKeachie, "Psychology in America's Bicentennial Year," *American Psychologist,* vol. 31, no. 12, pp. 819–833, December 1976.

invited to examine the materials from an adaptive rather than an adoptive point of view, and to determine which among the ideas are useful for their own understanding and application.

APPROACHES TO UNDERSTANDING LEARNING
General Principles of Learning
Illustrative of general principles to be derived from studies about learning are those described by Miller and Dollard,[2] in which factors in learning were divided into four steps—drive, cue, response, and reward—and a series of questions were posited. In adapted form they are:

Drive (motivation). Do they motivate? The learner must *want* something.

Cue (stimulus). Are the cues relevant? The learner must *notice* something.

Response (participation). Do they call for participation? The learner must *do* something.

Reward (reinforcement). Do they provide some form of reward for performance? The learner must *get* something[3]

From a behavioral point of view, these four factors, or steps in learning, have been helpful in explaining certain learning and instructional processes. The idea that drives (motivation) and rewards (reinforcement) are closely related—that persons must want what they get in order for it to act as a reward—has face validity for understanding adult behavior. When adults desire to learn and are supported in the conviction that they *can* learn, they *do* learn.

The following observations provide some general propositions applicable to studying and understanding learning processes:[4]

---

2. Neal E. Miller and John Dollard, *Social Learning and Imitation,* published for the Institute of Human Relations by Yale University Press, New Haven, Conn., 1941.

3. Neal E. Miller and Collaborators, "Graphic Communications and the crises in Education," *Audio-visual Communication Review,* National Education Association, Department of Audio-visual Instruction, Washington, vol. 5, pp. 63, 95, 1957.

4. Ernest R. Hilgard, *Theories of Learning,* Appleton-Century-Crofts, Inc., New York, 1956, pp. 486–487.

See also Benjamin S. Bloom, *Human Characteristics and School Learning,* McGraw-Hill Book Company, New York, 1976.

Robert M. Gagne, *The Conditions of Learning,* Holt, Rinehart and Winston, Inc., New York, 1965.

Ernest R. Hilgard and Gordon H. Bower, *Theories of Learning,* 4th ed., Prentice-Hall, Englewood Cliffs, N.J., 1975.

National Society for the Study of Education, *Theories of Learning and Instruction,* The Sixty-third Yearbook, part I, Chicago, 1964.

1. In deciding who should learn what, the capacities of the learner are very important. Brighter people can learn things less bright ones cannot learn; in general, older children can learn more readily than younger ones; the decline of ability with age, in the adult years, depends upon what it is that is being learned.
2. Motivated learners acquire what they learn more readily than those who are not motivated. The relevant motives include both general and specific ones, for example, desire to learn, need for achievement (general), desire for a certain reward or to avoid a threatened punishment (specific).
3. Motivation that is too intense (especially pain, fear, anxiety) may be accompanied by distracting emotional states, so that excessive motivation may be less effective than moderate motivation for learning some kinds of tasks, especially those involving difficult discriminations.
4. Learning under the control of reward is usually preferable to learning under the control of punishment. Correspondingly, learning motivated by success is preferable to learning motivated by failure. Even though the theoretical issue is still unresolved, the practical outcome must take into account the social by-products, which tend to be more favorable under reward than under punishment.
5. Learning under intrinsic motivation is preferable to learning under extrinsic motivation.
6. Tolerance for failure is best taught through providing a backlog of success that compensates for experienced failure.
7. Individuals need practice in setting realistic goals for themselves, goals neither so low as to elicit little effort nor so high as to foreordain to failure. Realistic goal-setting leads to more satisfactory improvement than unrealistic goal-setting.
8. The personal history of the individual, for example, his reaction to authority, may hamper or enhance his ability to learn from a given teacher.
9. Active participation by a learner is preferable to passive reception when learning, for example, from a lecture or a motion picture.
10. Meaningful materials and meaningful tasks are learned more readily than nonsense materials and more readily than tasks not understood by the learner.
11. There is no substitute for repetitive practice in the overlearning of skills (for instance, the performance of a concert pianist), or in the memorization of unrelated facts that have to be automatized.
12. Information about the nature of a good performance, knowledge of one's own mistakes, and knowledge of successful results, aid learning.
13. Transfer to new tasks will be better if, in learning, learners can discover relationships for themselves, and if they have experience during learning in applying the principles among a variety of tasks.
14. Spaced or distributed recalls are advantageous in fixing material that is to be long retained.

As we have noted, there are no universal laws or principles of learning which provide ready-made prescriptions for studying and solving learning problems. The suggestions and cautions which follow should be viewed in this light:

1. Determine the critical elements of the knowledge, skill, or attitude to be learned in order to apply learning procedures that are most appropriate and effective.
2. Untested acceptance of "what learning theory says" can lead to rationalizing or freezing a particular educational practice.
3. Supervisors and teachers must determine the usefulness of hypotheses and practices suggested by educational psychologists or learning theorists in the light of their own expertise and experience.
4. Regardless of how adequately learning principles have been tested in laboratory situations, and how useful theories are in suggesting directions in which answers can be sought, learning practices are best tested under actual conditions of use in the classroom.
5. In-school inquiry and analysis, which involves teachers actively in studying, interpreting and applying learning theories in their classrooms, provide the best laboratories in which to examine a wide range of variables (e.g., student characteristics, subject matter, instructional methods, etc.).
6. Theoretical principles should be *adapted* to practical learning problems or situations, not *adopted;* the appropriateness of any learning principles should be assessed in terms of both purpose and desired outcomes.[5]

Reinforcement and Learning

Reinforcement theory is a behavioral point-of-view in which learning defined as changed behavior resulting from or accompanying practice or experience is analyzed in terms of observable events. To be certain that learning has occurred, some measurement or evaluation of behavior before and after a learning experience must take place. Thus teaching would be the act of presenting stimuli which result in a change of behavior in a predetermined manner.[6]

5. McKeachie, op. cit.
See also Wilbert J. McKeachie, "The Decline and Fall of the Laws of Learning," *Educational Researcher,* vol. 3, no. 3, pp. 7–11, March 1974.
M. C. Wittrock and Arthur A. Lumsdaine, "Instructional Psychology," *Annual Review of Psychology,* vol. 28, pp. 417–459, 1977.
6. B. F. Skinner, *Science and Human Behavior,* The Macmillan Company, New York, 1953.

Supervisors can give thought to ensuring that stimuli to change the environment do indeed result in predetermined, intended, and explicit changes in learner behavior. Both supervisors and teachers need to keep clearly in mind the desirability of stating objectives in measurable terms in order to effect systematically the desired changes in learners. As long as objectives are stated vaguely—"the objective of this in-service program is to develop a deep under-standing of ethnic differences," "our objective is to develop perspective among the staff in teaching mathematics"—teachers may have difficulty in determining what they are aiming toward, or whether or not they have achieved their objectives. Unmeasurable objectives lead to a dilemma, because teachers, as well as supervisors, cannot discover how successful they have been. Success in staff training may well depend on (1) whether the desired changes in behavior have been clearly specified (that is, not only brought to a conscious level in the supervisor's own mind but also communicated to the learners) and (2) whether clearly defined ways of assessing behavioral changes, with objectives agreed upon by both teachers and supervisors, have been determined. We believe, of course, that desired and desirable professional behavior(s) can be defined best by teachers themselves or in consultation with other teachers and/or supervisors.

RESPONDENT AND OPERANT LEARNING   Respondent learning may be described in terms of elicited behavior—behavior that is controlled by a stimulus, such as a knee reflex, a visceral autonomic response. The learning of fears, likes, and dislikes is an example, and can be illustrated by the type of advertising in which one stimulus is paired with another with the intent of molding the opinions or emotions of a particular audience. This kind of learning is indeed a powerful one. Something happens *to* learners; they are not trying to solve problems or to learn a task; they are passive organisms, being shaped or molded. Respondent conditioning might best be thought of as emotional learning (the learning of attitudes or reactions to the subject, a problem, or an issue) operating on an association basis. For example, if supervisors are visibly interested in problems of teaching science (science is considered to be stimulating and exciting), the chances are good that teachers with whom these supervisors work will also acquire these same types of emotional responses toward

---

B. F. Skinner, "The Science of Learning and the Art of Teaching," *Harvard Educational Review*, vol. 24, pp. 86–97, 1954.

B. F. Skinner, *The Technology of Teaching*, Appleton-Century-Crofts, New York, 1968.

science. On the other hand, if supervisors are not particularly interested in a particular field, teachers may acquire a less than enthusiastic attitude toward it.

Planning to ensure that staff members become emotionally involved or committed to certain tasks is well worth supervisors' efforts. A vivid emotional experience is not easily forgotten. It is important to select those kinds of experiences which have desirable emotional concomitants of persistent value. Activities which can generate favorable attitudes and responses include viewing and discussing worthwhile films or dramatic presentations, observing particularly talented teachers, and face-to-face discussions with a spectrum of authors and researchers.

Operant learning deals with responses that are under the control of the central nervous system, including motor skills. In operant learning the key to whether persons learn a certain motor response is what happens *after* they make that motor response—the *consequences* of it. In teaching operant motor skills particular attention is given to what happens following the motor response, a consequence referred to as *reinforcement,* because it strengthens, or reinforces, the response that preceded it. It should be noted that reinforcement, by definition, is in terms of *effect upon the response.* If the reinforcement strengthens the response—makes the response more probable—it *is* the reinforcement. Reinforcement in one situation well may be depended upon in others.[7]

Reinforcements are most effective when they are immediate, or if there is minimum delay between a response and the occurrence of reinforcement. Studies with human subjects have shown that the closer reinforcement occurs to the actual response, the sooner that response is learned. Supervisors and teachers sometimes experience delay between the completion of a task (response) and its evaluation (reinforcement). For example, it may take teachers a week to discover whether the materials they prepared or the demonstrations they presented were acceptable. Or a staff team may prepare a revision of

---

7. See H. M. Parsons, "What Happened at Hawthorne?" *Science,* vol. 183, no. 4128, pp. 922–932, Mar. 8, 1974. In a detailed analysis of data from the oft-cited Hawthorne studies, Parsons presents new evidence to demonstrate the effects of operant conditioning in shaping the behavior of the workers involved in the Hawthorne studies. He finds that the consequence of responding is the important extraneous variable which has not been considered hitherto in any interpretations of the studies. The variable consists of information feedback coupled with financial reward. Not only had the Hawthorne workers been informed of their output rates on a daily or even more frequent basis, but they also had received financial rewards—the higher their output, the more money they received. This, along with other evidence, leads Parsons to conclude that the Hawthorne effect resulted from operant reinforcement contingencies.

a report card only to wait for six months before receiving an evaluation of their work from a curriculum council. Some individuals find that goal achievement or task accomplishment is sufficient to reinforce their performance without any feedback, controlling the direction of their behavior by consequences. However, for most individuals working at complex tasks, performance is more effective or efficient, and more quickly changed in new directions, when feedback (whether evaluative or nonevaluative) is provided. Generally, behavior which is not reinforced is likely to be weakened or extinguished.

SUCCESSIVE APPROXIMATION   Among the various ways to elicit desired responses is the technique of successive approximation, by which step-by-step practice in performing a task yields successful approximations of more complex behavior to be required later. The probability of correct responses in such cases depends upon the direction given in leading from one task to another. Care to ensure that movement from simple to complex tasks is properly paced prevents wasted time and lowered morale on the part of busy teachers or staff. Sensitivity in noting when staff members are ready to move ahead may help secure optimum results even while changing tasks as rapidly as possible. Supervisors should avoid initiating the study of a task by a detailed description of its total complexity or by an involved analysis of how the problem finally may be resolved if by so doing staff members become lost and cannot make the appropriate responses. It is a rare individual who can visualize and place in order all the dimensions of a complicated task when a proposal is first described. Teachers are as capable of understanding purposes as any other group of professional persons, but the complexity of "hardware" can be discouraging if learning situations are not well structured.

TRANSFER THROUGH SIMULATION   Supervisors, in common with training personnel in other organizations, are responsible for devising training situations which contain elements transferable to real life tasks.[8] Simulation processes have been used widely in training exercises, e.g., space flight–training missions, pilot training in flight simulators, business games, laboratory training in medicine with models, and law students' practice in moot courts. Transfer can be effected by devising training tasks which are similar operationally

8. Dale L. Bolton (ed.), *The Use of Simulation in Educational Administration,* Charles E. Merrill Company, Columbus, Ohio, 1971. (See chap. 1, "A Powerful but Underdeveloped Educational Tool" by Luvern L. Cunningham.)

to the final tasks for which they are a preparation. By isolating the critical factors of a task for systematic study, making certain that tasks resemble as realistically as possible the actual ones to be performed later, controlled, low-risk learning experiences in which mistakes can be rectified easily can be provided.

Simulated learning activities, properly organized, often can provide better learning experiences than their real life counterparts, because learners receive the right reinforcement for appropriate responses. Useful simulation activities for supervisors include: micro-teaching, sociodrama, videotapes of conferences or demonstrations, and a range of simulation in-basket exercises. Transfer is most likely to be effective (1) when the simulation problem or task is proximate to its point of application, (2) when problems are realistically related to the situation in which they are expected to be applied and not just "talked about," and (3) the simulation tasks are not so complex that nonobvious but important details will be overlooked.

INTERFERENCE   In almost every learning endeavor interference may be operating to impede learning. For example, the presentation of too much material at one time, or the injection of items or ideas related to but remote from the central topic, can induce interference in learning. Developing one idea or concept at a time to make each stand out is an effective learning technique. Interference can be reduced by separating potentially confusing materials, such as similar concepts, in time and space. When a person presents two similar ideas, saying, "let us not mix up this idea with this other idea," listeners may do just that. Distinctive learning materials—diagrams, schematic presentations and iconic models (which look like what they represent), or the use of several modalities (sound, touch, color, sight) because they differ in more than one dimension—also are effective tools in clarifying ideas, reducing interference, and increasing retention.

MOTIVATION   Teachers' existing behaviors are largely functions of prior motivation, reflecting their personal and professional learning experiences. Why are teachers motivated to achieve in the classroom, or, on the other hand, why have they become apathetic toward professional learning tasks? There can be numerous reasons for the presence or absence of motivation, one, that so-called reinforcements were not so in reality; past behaviors were not rewarding. Some teachers, for instance, are not at all affected by praise of their classroom teaching performance, letters of commendation, or public recognition of their special contributions. They just do not care about these kinds of reinforcements. In fact, the use of such rewards may have unintended consequences.[9] Supervisors need to find out what individual teachers *do* care about—exactly what does motivate them—and try to reduce nonmotivating elements. We should seek to discover the kinds of reinforcements that teachers, in general, respond to favorably, and those they dislike and respond to unfavorably. It might be that teachers do not value rewards such as social approval because this consequence has not occurred in the past when they exhibited what they believed to be appropriate behavior. Suppose that after what was considered to be a superior job of demonstration teaching, a teacher never learned what kind of evaluation resulted. Was there acknowledgement or recognition of excellence, or did anyone care? To illustrate: After giving a series of carefully prepared lessons in which it was clearly demonstrated that slower-learning pupils could be taught to grasp the meaning of certain mathematical concepts, one teacher reported that the new supervisor's only comment was "The blinds in your room were not straight during your demonstration."

We should be aware that lack of motivation, apathy, or negative attitudes may be caused by ideas or tasks which teachers perceive as being too difficult. Sometimes proper environmental stimuli have not been provided to bring out behaviors of which teachers are capable, or the tasks teachers are performing are not important to them. Perhaps the consequences of a particular pattern of behavior came entirely too late—there was too large a gap between the behavior and its recognition. Negative attitudes on the part of fellow teachers toward a topic or subject of interest to a particular teacher, or even a negative attitude toward the whole teaching job, affect motivation. These are emotional responses which individuals may be in the pro-

---

9. The effects of extrinsic rewards, such as praise, upon the intrinsic motivation of either adults or children are not at all clear. There is evidence to believe that praise, as feedback to strengthen performance, is not always rewarding, but may have negative effects, especially if it does not meet the recipient's desire for congruity. Supervisors should weigh carefully the consequences of using praise as a method of reinforcing teachers' performances. Simple informational, nonevaluative feedback on performance may be more effective than praise in helping teachers become self-dependent in evaluating their own performances.

Frank P. Bordonaro, "The Dilemma Created by Praise," *Business Horizons,* vol. 19, no. 5, pp. 76–81, October 1976.

Evan R. Keislar, "The Teacher as Informal Evaluator of Student Performance," *UCLA Educator,* vol. 19, no. 2, pp. 57–62, Winter 1977.

D. L. Martin, "Your Praise Can Smother Learning," *Learning,* vol. 5, no. 6, pp. 42–51, 1977.

William W. Notz, "Work Motivation and the Negative Effects of Extrinsic Rewards: A Review with Implications for Theory and Practice," *American Psychologist,* vol. 30, no. 9, pp. 844–891, September 1975.

cess of developing for themselves or acquiring from other teachers or even from supervisors with whom they come in contact.

Supervisors and teachers should bring to a conscious level those impediments to good performance (task interference, inadequate feedback, unwitting punishment, or lack of reinforcement) which can be resolved by rational discussion in most instances. Those impediments, such as, say, lack of specific skills or level of skills expected, which result from inadequate preparation or training will require the remedial action of retraining (see Chapter 11). Certainly, professionally accountable persons can and should agree on ways to "sabotage" peripheral and nonsensical impediments to their learning which occur in bureaucratic systems and tend to limit rational behavior and inhibit motivation.[10] Supervisory action at all times should be predicated on a desire to help teachers to be self-dependent and self-motivated.

Cognitive Approaches to Learning

In reinforcement theory learning is viewed as a change in a learner's behavior due primarily to reinforced practice (occurring in an environment designed to control and reward learning). Cognitive approaches to learning, on the other hand, emphasize that persons learn by utilizing their abilities to construct their own meanings and interpretations of events, information, and situations. Persons develop their own information processing strategies, learn to teach themselves to discriminate among ideas and events, and thus become self-motivated learners.[11] Cognitive views of learning emphasize that persons learn:

1. By being asked questions which require thought and some form of overt and/or covert response or action
2. By attempting to make changes in their own or others' ideas or in their social and/or physical environment
3. By observing and reflecting on other persons' behavior or performance in new or recurrent situations

10. J. Victor Baldridge and Terrence E. Deal, *Managing Change in Educational Organizations: Sociological Perspectives, Strategies, and Case Studies,* McCutchan Publishing Corporation, Berkeley, Calif., 1975. (See chap. 2, "Organizational Change," by Daniel Katz and Robert Kahn, pp. 35–74; and chap. 19, "Rules for a Machiavellian Change Agent: Transforming the Entrenched Professional Organization," by J. Victor Baldridge, pp. 378–388.)

11. Albert Bandura, "Behavior Theory and the Models of Man," *American Psychologist,* vol. 29, no. 12, pp. 859–869, December 1974. Wittrock and Lumsdaine, op. cit., pp. 417–459.

4. By attempting to analyze the discrepancies between what they believe and what they practice
5. By individual systematic study, listening to lectures, studying and analyzing, participating in discussions, developing verbal constructs, and by working in groups

In brief, cognitive views of learning emphasize that persons can learn without need for practice or reinforcement of overt behavior. They learn by actively changing perceptions of experience, by constructing new meanings, and by interpreting events.

Supervisors in using cognitive approaches to staff learning envision their task as that of helping teachers (1) to provide their own stimuli for self-learning as they study materials, prepare reports, conduct research studies, and select references and resources pertinent to their purposes, (2) to pose problems which they are motivated to solve, with realistic expectations of solving them successfully, and (3) to provide their own cognitive and affective reinforcements for learning.[12]

PROMOTING STAFF LEARNING
Defining Objectives

One needs a goal in order to learn, if only to provide affirmation of achievement and success. Knowledge of the purposes of a learning task, and some form of external or internal reinforcement for achievement, are valued by most adults. In promoting staff learning, supervisors should be able to formulate the same precise definitions of objectives or concepts that teachers need to learn and that teachers should be able to formulate in helping pupils to learn. In addition to defining concepts, the learning sequences necessary to develop concepts and the required learner responses (child or adult), must be made explicit. As examples: (1) teachers of elementary school mathematics should know the precise ways in which the dividend-divisor-quotient relationship can be defined and presented to pupils, and when application of the concept should be approved, or given immediate correction, and (2) teachers should clearly understand the many functions of zero (that zero can be a placeholder, or that zero is not any one thing, or that zero is a number and one of the ten primary digits) in order to be able to reinforce pupils' responses. When teachers can use ideas and materials meaningfully, because they are not working with mechanical prescriptions or half-truths

---

12. Moshe F. Rubinstein, *Patterns of Problem Solving,* Prentice-Hall, Inc., Englewood Cliffs, N.J., 1975.

about a concept, they are better able to "set pupils' pencils to paper."

In brief, basic understandings provide a foundation for reliable generalizations in teaching-learning situations. Often teachers' instructional uncertainties may be due to having never learned particular concepts to be taught and how to develop them. A continuing instructional responsibility of supervisors and teachers will be (1) to define precisely what is to be taught, (2) to determine logical instructional sequences, and (3) to provide appropriate practice and assess the results thereof.

John Dewey once spoke of the need for "dramatic rehearsal" as a prelude to teaching, a rehearsal in which the teacher actually goes through a program planned for children. It is this dramatic rehearsal of concepts, principles, and responses that supervisors and teachers should engage in mutually, so that teachers have embedded in their nervous systems the basic ideas to be taught with appropriate language and proper reinforcement. Supervisors and teachers need to test one another in model teaching tasks, experimenting with different kinds of practice and follow-up activities, with evaluation pegged to the purposes of teaching. This approach helps avoid teaching in a mechanical way (e.g., "Always invert the divisor when you multiply") and focuses on the process of grasping the essential concept, sharply defining it, and teaching to elicit only the specific responses called for.

Varied Approaches to Implement Objectives

There are numerous ways for supervisors to set up a system of checking on their own teaching while working with a staff member. This is where process enters the picture. A seminar-summary approach which brings together results to date may be used, either by the supervisor alone, a small staff team, or other individuals. However the seminar is conducted, its purpose is to assess progress toward goals. Feedback from participants is achieved by such questions as: "To what extent are we achieving the objective as defined?" "Is this what we originally decided to try to accomplish?" "What further tasks must we plan?" The supervisor carefully thinks out in advance the possible contingent steps to be taken in directing actions of group members. Although large planning groups may suggest topics for study or raise questions, usually small teams of two or three, or even individuals, can best execute the project. Small work teams, of course, are accountable to the larger group, and their findings are open to examination. The results of teamwork can be fed back to the larger group for questions, further assignments, and the involvement of others in the tryout of certain proposals. It should be kept in mind that "only those directly involved need execute"; others act as analysts, evaluators, and consumers. The law of parsimony applies here; otherwise, the supervisor who has as many projects as there are staff members would seem to have mounted a horse and galloped off in all directions. The leadership of supervisors bulks large in determining through consultive effort only those tasks which are important and which must be done instead of initiating as many studies as there are ideas. For example, supervisor X attends a meeting and hears what school system Y has done, returns to his or her own school system and initiates the same project without regard to determining its specific goals. Or the local board of education member hears that a neighboring school system has eliminated its developmental reading program and has hired only remedial reading teachers—then the heat is on to adopt the same program in the local district.

Supervisors, faced with such pressure, should gather as much evidence as possible to support valid educational positions. The strategy of emphasizing educational objectives and obtaining hard evidence in the form of evaluative data as to their attainment can be an effective weapon to counter many of the mindless proposals bombarding supervisors.

Appropriate Pacing of Work to Facilitate Learning

Differentiating the segments of a project or study so that staff members can choose or accept those most suitable to their abilities helps achievement of purposes. Supervisors seek consensus on reasonable goals and welcome self-selection on the part of the staff for assignments and determination of target dates for the completion of responsibilities. In consultation with study groups a calendar of events is determined and the "contract" adhered to firmly. The emergency meeting, or a statement such as "We will just have to put in extra time on this," is avoided. A staff well committed to the mission of the school will usually determine the time and place for extra effort voluntarily. Supervisors may spend much time in small-group or individual consultation in order to pace work at a reasonable level. After a group has selected a problem and planned a work program, individual members begin to move at varying rates. Supervisors assume a consultative role to assist teachers with their particular responsibilities, having assessed the differential abilities among staff members and determined "who does what best and who likes to do what best."

In order to keep things moving (and at the same time reduce interference or forgetting) there are several safeguards supervisors might consider, such as (1) making the various aspects of proposals so distinctive that everyone involved can see relationships, (2) defining tasks and separating them from other tasks by use of meaningful associations, (3) making certain that they, themselves, understand what they are about, (4) seeing to it that proposed studies are geared to the overall program of the school, (5) assuring transfer by using actual situations to try out ideas or proposals looking toward application, and (6) using case studies and classroom demonstrations and relating them to principles of learning and teaching.

In helping teachers learn how to learn, supervisors assist staff members to supply their own frame of reference, set reasonable expectations for the accomplishment of tasks, and receive rapid reinforcement. Supervisors emphasize the need for verifying principles or setting up a rationale for self-study so that efforts of individuals can be placed in an overall framework. Techniques can be emphasized after staff members have conceptualized the approaches they are to use. After a procedure is selected in accordance with reasonable levels of attainment, supervisors take responsibility for seeing that the work is logically distributed over a period of time and that self-teaching and retention occur. There is a sharp difference between knowledge and understanding.[13] Supervisors who recognize this difference in working with teachers realize that they do not transfer facts to learners but help learners to translate data, make use of facts, and find meaning for themselves. It requires insight on the part of supervisors to set the stage, provide content, and pose hypotheses so that the learning which occurs is a remaking of experience which guarantees a genuine difference in the behavior of teachers. Teachers are led to define problems, to integrate past experiences, to obtain new data, and to test their ideas in practice.[14]

Association between Effective Learning and Commitment to Tasks

Supervisors recognize that effective learning is associated with commitment to specific and essential tasks and problem-solving activities. Learning may be initiated when one does not know the answers to a problem. The learner who has a problem usually will seek an answer. Learning often is accompanied by personal disturbance. Problems, however, do not always arise spontaneously, and the supervisor's responsibility is to help set problems in terms of mission and purposes. Problems are more likely to become visible in a cli-

13. Nathaniel Cantor, *The Learning Process for Managers,* Harper & Row, Publishers, Incorporated, New York, 1958, p. 143.
14. Gary M. Ingersoll, "Assessing Inservice Training Needs through Teacher Responses," *Journal of Teacher Education,* vol. 27, no. 2, pp. 169–173, Summer 1976.

mate where hypotheses are constantly being proposed. This atmosphere is a two-way street, and the feedback which is provided encourages staff members to engage in problem-solving activities. However, it should be observed that profitable types of feedback revolve around the testing of ideas and task orientation and not ego-orientation of supervisors. Blame fixing and recrimination as means of improving staff participation are not profitable techniques. Resorting to negative measures when teachers do not resolve problems may be showing them "how wrong they were" but doing nothing to help them to see "what is the right thing to do." Supervisors who are leaders in bringing learning out of confusion ask such questions as "What is the problem we are trying to solve?" "How effective are we in solving a problem?" "What steps do we need to take next?"

Recognizing Resistance to Change

Sometimes persons resist new learnings which conflict with established ways of behavior.[15] There are few human beings who welcome confusion or unsolved problems. New ways of behavior are often difficult, especially when individuals are faced with the discomforts of myth destroying or changes in the status quo. It is often easier and certainly more comfortable to justify things as they are, to deny the need for change, to use ready-made prescriptions, or to fall back on anecdotes or personal testimony to defend positions. "The X school system does not do it this way." "What is wrong with what we have been doing in reading?" "I tried that in my classes several years ago, and it was not successful." "In a college class last summer I learned that Y method is already out of fashion." Supervisors, therefore, must be aware of mechanisms developed by individuals to maintain established ways of behavior and to defend themselves or organizations against unwanted change. Among these mechanisms are rationalization, lying, projecting, and compulsive processes, such as talking about and around a topic.[16] Some persons are adept at talking themselves and others out of uncomfortable situations.[17] Supervisors who are aware of the effect these mechanisms have on the communication process may not always be able to meet the resistance to change, but they can recognize the symptoms of poor communication, of the need to work around the biases of individuals. They can learn to focus effort on tasks and to avoid blame or the fixing of guilt. Unquantified emotional language, such as "Our read-

---

15. Cantor, op. cit., p. 144.
16. Ibid., p. 145.
17. Ibid.

ing program is miserable and you have got to change it or we are in trouble with the board," is an example.

Most individuals experience feelings of guilt, shame, or lack of self-esteem when they have not met responsibility, or have avoided a decision, or have not faced up to solving critical problems. Supervisors who bring problems into the open and are prepared to face facts and take the consequences rather than disguise, conceal, or distort wrong decisions are more likely to obtain positive learning behavior among staff members. Just as the teacher-model affects the behavior of children, supervisors who are consistent, objective, task-oriented, and technically competent are more likely to find the same behaviors reflected by others. This implies that supervisors will provide the kinds of ideas for learning, for designing studies, for testing results, that will obviate the avoidance mechanisms, the feelings of insecurity that result from highly personalized approaches to problems.

Accepting Differences among Learners

Recognition of differences among learners is not new to classroom teaching. However, supervisors may stress this principle in working with children but negate its application in their own work with adults. The supervisor is charged with setting a consistent climate where staff members can afford and dare to be individuals and can express opinions and ideas, even if these views conflict with those of the supervisor or others. Recognition of differences among learners encourages creative thinking. There should be "no fear of disapproval, no threat to self-esteem, no ugly competitiveness, no badgering sarcasm, no wisecracking but a deeply felt sense of mutual respect and common seeking for growth and development."[18] When supervisors recognize the differential abilities existing both in themselves and in others, as well as the difficulties and confusion experienced in learning situations, the resistance to change, the need to defend positions, and the desire to be right, they are in a better position to establish themselves as mature coworkers and leaders.

18. Ibid., p. 150.

PART **FOUR**

TECHNICAL FACTORS IN SUPERVISION

Technical factors in supervision, the subject of this section, and human factors, to which we gave attention in previous chapters, are interrelated. Technical skills, derived from technologies and practice, are necessary tools in planning, directing, and managing complex operations. Human skills are based on knowledge and understanding of societal values and practices, the dimensions of human behavior, and the unique pattern of traits which makes up individual personality. Though specific technical skills are required in such activities as in-school research, program development, and qualitative or quantitative assessment, the maintenance of a balance between human and technical factors is necessary to safeguard human values, goals, and purposes. When human institutions are taken over by narrow technicians, they lose their raison d'être.

In the three chapters of Part Four we discuss supervisory thought and action concerning (1) ways of appraising and improving teaching performance based on a strategy of supervision by objectives, (2) dimensions of research in schools and technical skills requisite to conducting educational inquiry and analysis, and (3) principles underlying curriculum improvement and development.

CHAPTER 11

APPRAISING AND IMPROVING PERFORMANCE

Appraising teacher performance long has been a matter of concern to educators at all levels of schooling. Numerous investigators have (1) described the difficulties in formulating definitive criteria for the appraisal of teaching, (2) attempted to isolate factors of relevance to teaching for analysis, and (3) devised qualitative and quantitative measures in their efforts to discover valid indices of teacher performance.[1]

1. Bruce J. Biddel and William J. Ellena (eds.), *Contemporary Research on Teacher Effectiveness,* Holt, Rinehart and Winston, Inc., New York, 1965.

Gary D. Borich, *The Appraisal of Teaching: Concepts and Process,* Addison-Wesley Publishing Company, Inc., Reading, Mass., 1977.

Ned A. Flanders and Anita Simon, "Teacher Effectiveness," in Robert L. Ebel (ed.), *Encyclopedia of Educational Research,* 4th ed., Collier-Macmillan Ltd., London, 1969, pp. 1423–1437.

N. L. Gage (ed.), *Second Handbook of Research on Teaching,* Rand McNally & Company, Chicago, 1973. See chaps. 5 to 7 dealing with observation and assessment procedures.

N. L. Gage, *Teacher Effectiveness and Teacher Education: The Search for a Scientific Basis,* Pacific Books, Palo Alto, Calif., 1972.

Gladys S. Kleinman, "Assessing Teacher Effectiveness: The State of the Art," *Science Education,* vol. 50, no. 3, pp. 234–238, April 1966.

The materials in this chapter will (1) survey and assess some of the criteria which have been used as bases for appraising teacher effectiveness and (2) describe and illustrate a strategy, based on a concept of supervision by objectives, for improving and/or appraising teacher performance.

Methods of judging teacher effectiveness have been subject to several kinds of difficulties. First, the various methods which have been utilized yield results which do not correlate highly with each other; hence they do not measure the same aspects. Second, the methods which appear most valid have often been perceived as difficult to administer. Third, and most important, the determination of teacher effectiveness depends to a large extent on the criteria used. In essence, if different methods and different criteria are used in measuring the factors which contribute to teaching success, the results will inevitably differ.

CRITERIA

Traditionally the appraisal of teacher performance has been related primarily to evaluation of teaching personnel per se. The various views, descriptions, and criteria of teaching behavior, used as bases for appraisal, have generally been assumed or inferred to relate to teaching effectiveness and, ultimately, to changes in pupil behavior. Such formulations have emphasized criteria which may be grouped under the broad rubrics of (1) *process,* (2) *teacher characteristics,* or (3) *product.* Of these three, product (or changes in pupil behavior) has been subject to systematic study since the 1960s.[2] The three criteria may be described as follows:

1. *Process.* Teacher behavior is appraised against some standard of performance or set of actions (overt teaching acts) assumed or inferred to be related to effective teaching performance. If the teacher performs certain specified acts, pupil behavior then can be predicted. In this view, teacher performance may be described, rated, or observed in terms of factors such as *(a)* how teachers

---

Harold E. Mitzell, "Teacher Effectiveness," in *Encyclopedia of Educational Research,* 3d ed., The Macmillan Company, New York, 1960, pp. 1481–1486.

Joseph Morsh and Eleanor Wilder, *Identifying the Effective Instructor: A Review of the Quantitative Studies, 1900–1952,* Lackland Air Force Base, San Antonio, Tex., Research Bulletin AFPTRC-T-54-44, 1954.

John D. McNeil and W. James Popham, "The Assessment of Teacher Competence," in Robert M. W. Travers (ed.), *Second Handbook of Research on Teaching,* Rand McNally & Company, Chicago, 1973, pp. 218–244.

David G. Ryans, *Characteristics of Teachers: Their Description, Comparison, and Appraisal,* American Council on Education, Washington, 1960.

2. Borich, op. cit.

structure learning situations (time and motion analysis), *(b)* extent
and kind of pupil-teacher and/or teacher-pupil responses, and *(c)*
analysis of teacher behavior by diverse systems, such as learner-
centered versus teacher-centered behaviors, or various "psychiat-
ric criteria" for assessing "good" or "bad" classroom pupil and/or
teacher behavior.
2. *Teacher characteristics.* A variety of characteristics such as intelligence, personality traits, personal appearance, verbal skills, quality
of speech, health, and other personal attributes of teachers are
assumed to be measures related to or predictive of effective teaching. Rating instruments, observation inventories, and reporting devices (containing indices assumed to relate to teaching ability)
have been used widely to assess teacher performance.
3. *Product* (pupil-behavior change). Appraisal of teacher performance (instructional behavior) is focused on assessing defined
changes in pupil behavior (on outcomes of teaching acts) rather
than on the act itself or on teacher characteristics assumed to relate to pupil behavior. Thus the act of teaching is viewed as that
which brings about a change in the learner. Appraisal of teaching
by this criterion is concerned with the degree to which defined
behavior or results are achieved by pupils instead of depending
upon a teacher's congruence to some hypothetical model.

The first two criteria for appraising teaching behavior (process
and teacher characteristics) were accepted as valid measures or descriptions of teacher performance for many decades, and they have
formed the basis of most schemes for appraising teaching effectiveness. However, relatively little evidence has been obtained to demonstrate that particular teaching acts or teacher characteristics assumed to relate to teacher effectiveness are associated consistently
with changes in pupil behavior—with pupil achievement. Numerous
studies using these two criteria as correlates of teaching performance
have not yielded significant levels of empirical or judgmental validity. In addition the schemes just described suffer from several apparent shortcomings:

1. Each implies a particular system of analyzation as well as acceptance of the objectives of the scheme without logical examination
of the extent to which the objectives relate to the purposes or
consequences of teaching.
2. Means become ends in such systems (e.g., "Good teachers are
warm and friendly," or "Effective teaching occurs when teachers
are permissive and nondirective").
3. Teacher performance is described and evaluated in terms of *infer-*

ence rather than in terms of *observed* results. Particular acts of teachers are inferred to relate to changed pupil behavior rather than to any observable and measurable effects on pupils directly.
4. The general focus is primarily on some acts of teaching—on the teacher as a performer—rather than on the direct consequences for the pupil.

The third of these criteria—*product,* or pupil-behavior change— is essentially a process of testing hypotheses about instruction.[3] [Interest in investigating product as a criterion for appraising instructional performance has resulted, in part, from (1) attempts of investigators to seek a solution to the criterion problem by shifting from studying what the teacher does to investigating what happens to learners as a result of instruction; (2) study and application of practices derived from performance-based programs in industrial and governmental organizations; and (3) development of accountability measures, new modes of evaluation, and performance-based educational programs in schools, resulting in large measure from actions and/or mandates of legislative bodies and state departments of education.] Teachers plan their teaching activities in terms of a set of hypotheses about how the educational objectives are to be achieved; that is, focus is on the product—pupil-behavior change. Teachers predict that under certain arranged instructional conditions pupils will change behavior in specified ways, and then collect evidence to support or deny their hypotheses.

We believe that when attention is primarily on attaining the goals of teaching, a number of value judgments about teaching acts or teacher competence can be reduced if not eliminated. If teaching is examined in terms of results, of changes teachers predict they can effect in learners, teaching competence is evaluated in a framework deemed more appropriate to teaching tasks. When teachers perceive the changes they want to achieve in pupils, they are dealing with the

3. See Borich, op. cit., chap. 3, "Applications of Performance Appraisal Systems," pp. 31–43.

Lesley H. Browder, Jr., William A. Atkins, Jr., and Esin Kaya, *Developing an Educationally Accountable Program,* McCutchan Publishing Corporation, Berkeley, Calif., 1973.

N. L. Gage and Philip H. Winne, "Performance-based Teacher Education," in *Teacher Education,* the seventy-fourth Yearbook of the National Society for the Study of Education, part II, Chicago, 1975, pp. 146–172.

J. Thomas Hastings, "Assessment of Learning Outcomes," in William H. Lucio (ed.), *The Supervisor: New Demands, New Dimensions,* Association for Supervision and Curriculum Development, Washington, 1969.

W. James Popham, "Performance Tests of Teaching Proficiency: Rationale, Development, and Validation," *American Educational Research Journal,* vol. 8, no. 1, pp. 105–117, January 1971.

essence of the teaching act. In our view, teaching creativity may be diminished when teachers do not know how to articulate desired changes in pupil behavior, or what they will accept as evidence that changes have occurred. Evaluative measures which are external, remote, or unrelated to appraising changes in pupil behavior decrease the possibility of teachers' determining explicit effects of teaching. Teachers whose attentions are directed to defining goals, to determining changes learners are to exhibit, and to appraising their teaching in terms of results will be more attuned to the central purposes of instruction.

PUPIL-BEHAVIOR CHANGE OR ACHIEVEMENT AS A MEASURE OF TEACHER PERFORMANCE

The product (pupil-behavior change) criterion discussed previously has been conceded to be one of the more effective measures of teacher performance. There is considerable evidence to indicate that indices of teacher performance, based on learner achievement, can be derived by (1) specifying the explicit changes desired in learners, (2) arranging instruction to produce the specified changes, and (3) appraising the extent to which learners achieve specified instructional objectives.[4] It is by comparing an individual's or a group's status before and after *instruction* that the kind and amount of learning *resulting from instruction* can be determined. And though various problems may be connected with using pupil-change criteria as measures of teacher performance, none of them appears insurmountable. Practical methods for assessing changes in learning that occur over any period of time in an individual or a group have been developed and are available to guide supervisors and teachers.[5] In general, measures of pupil gain require that only one teacher direct the specific learning contacts or that the effects of several teachers be controlled in some manner. Although in studies of pupil gain emphasis has generally been given to the measurement of subject-matter achievement

4. Morsh and Wilder, op. cit.

J. E. Morsh, G. C. Burgess, and P. N. Smith, *Student Achievement as a Measure of Instructor Effectiveness,* Lackland Air Force Base, San Antonio, Tex., Bulletin AFPTC-TN-55-12, 1958.

William H. Lucio, "Pupil Achievement as an Index of Teacher Performance," *Educational Leadership,* vol. 31, no. 1, pp. 71–77, October 1973.

John D. McNeil, *Toward Accountable Teachers,* Holt, Rinehart and Winston, Inc., New York, 1971.

5. Frederick B. Davis, *Educational Measurements and Their Interpretations,* Wadsworth Publishing Company, Inc., Belmont, Calif., 1964. See, esp., chap. 10, "Measurement of Change," pp. 234–252.

L. J. Cronbach, *Essentials of Psychological Testing,* 3d ed., Harper and Row, New York, 1970.

before and after teaching, it is reasonable to assume that application can be made to other aspects of learning as well. Areas sometimes thought to be difficult to assess, such as pupils' self-understanding, social attitudes, and similar behaviors, are equally open to assessment if they can be defined in discrete or measurable terms and formulated as desired outcomes from instruction. Research results have indicated that pupil-gain criteria, focused on the primary object of teaching—the task achievement of pupils—can be used to determine the outcomes of particular teaching acts with reasonable precision.[6]

In the past, appraisal of teacher performance has been dealt with in amorphous and diverse ways. Someone, in some fashion, remote or proximate to teaching, has been responsible for the appraisal of teacher performance. As a result, appraisals have been based upon every conceivable criterion, technique, and individual style imaginable. Because many appraisal procedures have had little relation to teachers' essential tasks, reasons for recurring criticisms by teachers and others are understandable. Research on problems of appraising and improving teacher performance has served to indicate shortcomings in past methods of appraisal and to suggest new and more effective approaches.[7]

Appraisal of teacher performance is an essential responsibility of teachers and supervisors, not that of others remote from the teaching process. The question is not *whether* appraisal should be done but *"How is it to be done most effectively?"* Appraisal is applicable to all teachers and supervisors regardless of length of service. It is our view that teachers should not be expected or allowed to consider the classroom their inner sanctum where they alone determine how and

6. Stephen M. Barro, "An Approach to Developing Accountability Measures for the Public Schools," *Phi Delta Kappan,* vol. 52, no. 94, pp. 196–205, 1970.

Lucio, op. cit.

McNeil, op. cit.

Harold H. Smithman and William H. Lucio, "Supervision by Objectives: Pupil Achievement as a Measure of Teacher Performance," *Educational Leadership,* vol. 31, no. 4, pp. 338–344, January 1974.

K. B. Start, "Establishing Children's Learning as the Criterion for Teacher Effectiveness," *Educational Research,* vol. 16, no. 8, pp. 206–209, June 1974.

Success in Teaching, University of California, Graduate School of Education, Teacher Education Project series, Los Angeles, 1967.

7. Borich, op. cit., chap. 1, "Toward Defining Teacher Competencies," pp. 5–12; chap. 2, "Measuring Teacher Performance," pp. 13–29; chap. 3, "Applications of Performance Appraisal Systems," pp. 31–43; chap. 9, "Selected Readings: Using Appraisal Procedures and Techniques," pp. 259–265.

W. James Popham, "Pitfalls and Pratfalls of Teacher Evaluation," *Educational Leadership,* vol. 32, no. 2, pp. 141–146, November 1974.

Robert S. Soar, "Teacher Assessment Problems and Possibilities," *Journal of Teacher Education* vol. 24, pp. 205–212, 1973.

what to teach and appraise their own performance. New teachers, particularly, need to know that their expertness will be appraised according to how effective they are in the classroom, and that they are not to be judged by how well they impress others with their social graces. Early concentration on teaching competence serves to focus new teachers' attentions on what they are hired to do. Reinforcement of good performance sets behavior in professional directions early. Supervisors want new teachers to be secure and happy, to be sure, but this is best done by helping them be successful in their teaching.

SUPERVISION BY OBJECTIVES
Appraisal and Improvement Strategy

Since the object of teaching is to produce learning—that is, change in behavior—a primary task of supervisors and teachers is to find out what is to be taught, when it is to be taught, and to whom it shall be taught. Jointly, supervisors and teachers need to:

1. Describe and define intended outcomes of learning (what pupils need to know—what terminal behavior is desired) and design the criterion-referenced measurement instruments to be applied after instruction.[8]
2. Preassess entry behavior of pupils—that is, their initial competence with respect to what is to be learned—and predict expected levels of achievement.
3. Select and program the sequence of learning contacts required to reach desired outcomes (what pupils are to learn).
4. Determine (posttest) the extent to which specified results are achieved (what evidence is acceptable to show that pupils have achieved the requisite behavior—they are able to "do this" or "say this"); administer criterion-referenced measurement instruments to determine the extent to which pupils can demonstrate the required behavior.[9]

In employing this instructional approach the following clues for supervisory-teacher behavior should be noted:

1. Teachers are helped to determine what they want learners in their class to do that they could not do before entering. Particular attention is given to individual requirements of learners, and, prior to

8. See W. James Popham, *Criterion-referenced Measurement*, Prentice-Hall, Inc., Englewood Cliffs, N.J., 1978.
9. Ibid.

teaching, determination is made of what will be accepted as evidence that pupil behavior has been changed.

2. Teachers, jointly with supervisors, know beforehand what will be accepted as criteria for evaluating results. Changes acceptable as indicators that teachers have achieved their goals are agreed upon before supervisory observations or postteaching conferences. There is clear understanding of the conditions under which goals or criteria may be revised as evidence dictates. Emphasis is placed on teachers' "becoming their own supervisor," able to state goals, program pupil learning, and appraise outcomes.

3. Observations or records of teaching focus on explicit problems identified by teachers and supervisors. Teachers, in applying propositions, such as "Pupils will have opportunity to practice the desired behavior," are helped to develop situations in which such practice may be appraised.

4. Observation data are recorded as facts observed without the injection of value judgments not relevant to classroom results. Suggestions suitable to specific situations are made, in terms of what outcomes were desired at the outset.

Sequence of Steps

An extension of these general propositions would include the following steps:

1. Specifying instructional objectives.
   a. Select specific instructional objectives (results to be achieved) and describe intended outcomes in terms of desired pupil behavior (what pupils need to know and do).
   b. Describe actions pupils are to perform to demonstrate that they have achieved desired changes in behavior.
   c. Specify conditions under which pupils are to demonstrate desired behavior.
   d. Specify minimum levels of acceptable pupil performance for each of the instructional objectives.
2. Preassessing instructional objectives and pupil entry behavior.
   a. Analyze and specify essential knowledge, skills, or attitudes which pupils need to acquire in order to succeed in reaching instructional objectives.
   b. Determine by appropriate formal and/or informal tests, observations, or analyses of prior records which of the specified prerequisites the pupil has acquired.
3. Evaluating instructional objectives.
   a. Throughout all instructional activity, determine the extent to which specified and predicted results were achieved—e.g.,

collect comprehensive evidence to sample pupil behavior required by stated instructional objectives in all situations in which behavior is expected to apply—give attention to both expected and unexpected behavior.

   b.   Determine by a variety of measures whether that learning which was intended did occur and, if not, why not; determine what steps toward refinement are required.

In hypothesizing about the effects of instructional contacts, the probability of achieving instructional objectives may be increased materially if teachers and supervisors will seek answers to the following questions:

1. Would greater opportunity to respond actively in learning situations have improved results?
2. Would more opportunity for pupils to practice both prerequisite and final behavior have changed outcomes of instruction?
3. Would greater provision for individual differences in interests, ability, or prior achievement have had an effect on learners' behavior?
4. Would more emphasis on the purpose of the instructional unit have changed learners' behavior?
5. Would modification of the rate of presentation and time allowed for response of learners have influenced performance?

The procedures just outlined are not intended to imply that informal or nonuniform attempts to teach are to be replaced or derogated. Certainly supervisors and teachers recognize that methods vary with particular objectives and with types of learners; they should keep in mind at all times that new objectives and different types of learners may require new, nontraditional, or unusual methods. Teachers must be encouraged to seek and experiment, for innovations result from inquiry. By defining, describing, and appraising teaching acts in some logical framework, teachers may be helped to account for efforts at a conscious rather than an intuitive level. If teachers know whither they are heading and why, their teaching strategies become replicable and open to others for examination and application.

Supervisors, then, in working out procedures for appraisal of teacher performance, start with the goal of committing teachers to defined and measurable tasks and establish the conditions by which teachers can succeed. Accordingly, supervisors place teachers in situations where (1) teaching objectives are defined and there is every reasonable probability of achieving them, (2) every effort and resource is applied to help teachers succeed in accomplishing defined objectives, and (3) quality of performance is judged in terms of how well defined and agreed-upon objectives are achieved. The three phases of this evaluation procedure are presented in Figure 11-1.

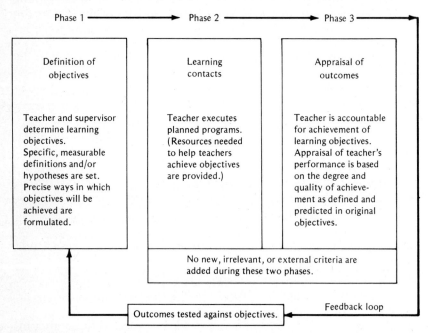

Figure 11-1   Appraising teacher performance by objectives.

Appraising by Objectives

Operationally, supervisors and teachers jointly define the objectives of instruction, specify the pertinent and necessary procedures required to accomplish these purposes, and determine in advance the evaluation measures to be applied. *They mutually predict the consequences of their proposals and work jointly to test their predictions.* If the objectives are not achieved by pupils, or only approximated, the reasons for lack of achievement are determined, objectives and hypotheses are restated, and a new attack is made. This procedure not only avoids the use of irrelevant criteria for appraising teacher performance but helps break the bonds of "alikeness." It reduces emphasis on uniform and sometimes mediocre standards of achievement. Teachers are directly responsible for designing and executing learning contacts to be used with their pupils. Teaching is targeted at what needs to be done for a specific group of pupils, based on long-term, carefully defined programs designed to achieve major objectives and uninfluenced by transient or irrelevant demands. Subsequently they are not appraised on the basis of brief observations, demonstration lessons for groups of visitors, special lessons requested by principals to see "how well they teach," or their behavior in staff meetings and social situations. When appropriate teacher behavior is defined as that which leads to the attainment of specified objectives, then many varieties of criteria can be employed. The appraisal procedure thus is focused on *explicit planning, specific requirements to be met, and predicted outcomes.*

We have presented a framework in which the expected accomplishments of teachers, whether directed at cognitive, conative, or affective behavior on the part of learners, can be defined. An important aspect of the proposal is that aid for the attainment of objectives will be made available to teachers. In addition it is expected that teachers will be provided with visible measures of where they succeeded or where they need to change. For example, if teachers have as an objective teaching four concepts concerning decimal integers which underlie work with decimal fractions, then appraisal of performance is the degree to which they are effective in achieving the development of these understandings as defined. If pupils are expected to acquire understanding of mathematics for use in daily living, this goal is recognized and made operational in the teaching design. It must be clearly understood that evaluation of a particular mathematical function does not preclude developing certain attitudes among pupils toward mathematics as well. But if attitudes are to be included among instructional objectives, they are explicitly defined. In any event, appraisal of teachers will be based upon the accomplishment of defined objectives.

Teachers must not find themselves in the position of having contracted to achieve particular instructional objectives only to discover that their appraisals, in reality, are to be based on objectives different from those originally specified. If appraisals are to include the number of parent council meetings attended, participation on school committees, or social relationships with peers, these variables should be incorporated in the original contract, not added after the fact. In general, teachers respond favorably to rational and systematic contractual modes of performance appraisal.[10]

In appraising teacher performance by objectives the following considerations apply:

10. Mildred M. Reynolds, "Performance Appraisal: The Educator Learns from Business and Industry," *Educational Leadership,* vol. 32, no. 7, pp. 465–468, April 1975.
     Smithman and Lucio, op. cit.

1. Supervisors and teachers agree on realistic, attainable objectives and set the criteria for appraisal. Teachers are provided with all necessary resources to help them reach objectives. Success in attaining instructional objectives should at least equal that attained by other teachers in relatively similar assignments. Persistent lack of success in achieving results within a specified period is faced by supervisors and teachers. New or probationary teachers unable to achieve results contracted for within a specified period are not continued on the job. Experienced and/or tenured teachers who are not achieving satisfactory results and who show signs of improvement in teaching after in-service training may be reassigned to other duties or counseled to leave teaching.
2. Once the sequence of appraisal events is clearly outlined and understood, no other performance criteria (ratings, inventories of attitudes, interviews, etc.) are added. Any threatening aspects of appraisal are lessened for both teacher and supervisor when negotiated instructional contracts are adhered to strictly.
3. Appraisal of teaching performance is based on proximity—those who are closest to setting instructional objectives have this responsibility.
4. Authority of expertness is agreed upon as the major consideration—the ability on the part of supervisor and teacher to determine instructional outcomes, select and arrange learning contacts, appraise results, and, above all, predict the consequences of particular acts upon the learning of pupils.
5. No teacher-appraisal program is legitimate unless it offers protection to pupils and evidence that it has the power to increase the educational progress of pupils. A prime responsibility of supervisors is to insure that appraisals of teacher performance are related to measures of pupil learning. The happiness and welfare of teachers is secondary to this objective. Supervisors who assign high ratings, not substantiated by evidence of performance, in attempts to keep teachers happy abrogate their supervisory responsibility and, indeed, may be guilty of professional malfeasance.

OPERATIONAL PLANS FOR PERFORMANCE-BASED APPRAISAL

To illustrate the strategy for appraising performance by objectives, a performance-based appraisal plan developed by the Newport-Mesa Unified School District (N-MUSD), California, will be described in this section.[11] The N-MUSD is a competency-based school district

11. Acknowledgement is made to Dr. L. E. Shuck, Assistant Superintendent, Research and Student Services, Newport-Mesa Unified School District, Newport Beach, Calif., for permission to use the materials describing the N-MUSD Staff Performance Improvement and Appraisal Plans for Teachers and Administrators.

which has employed performance-based appraisal systems for over a decade and has received recognition for its use of decentralized, school-site decision-making strategies.[12]

Appraising Teachers

The N-MUSD Staff Performance and Appraisal Plan for Teachers, developed to aid in both the *improvement* and *appraisal* of teacher performance, is based on the Role and Function Effect Model, reproduced in Figure 11-2. The major elements of the teacher-appraisal plan depicted in the N-MUSD model are as follows: (1) five "basic functions performed by a teacher" (shown on the horizontal axis), (2) five "populations with whom teachers work" (shown on the vertical axis), and (3) aspects of "maintaining and developing effective systems" (shown dimensionally). The five basic functions of the teacher are (1) identifying discrepancies (discrepancies defined as the differences between an existing set of conditions and an expected or desired set of conditions), (2) establishing objectives, requirements, and criterion measures (to obtain school district objectives), (3) designing and selecting processes, (4) executing processes to obtain results, and (5) executing processes for monitoring and evaluating. These five functions are discharged by teachers as they work with five populations: (1) individual pupils, (2) the consumer community (e.g., future employers of students), (3) the social community (e.g., neighborhood councils), (4) the school environment (e.g., fellow teachers), and (5) the professional self (e.g., self-improvement). The appraisal plan is designed to provide for the systematic collection of data regarding a teacher's performance with all five populations.

Operationally, the appraisal plan consists of two cycles, similar in sequences of activities but having different purposes, as follows: (1) The *Improvement Cycle,* an informal, formative-type appraisal providing teachers with the opportunity to practice instructional skills which need development or improvement. During an Improvement Cycle (one or more during each Appraisal Cycle), a teacher submits to a team of colleagues a plan for a lesson, including preassessment data on pupils, instructional objectives, and any evaluative measures to be used. The team observes a particular lesson, consults together to examine evidence to determine the extent to which the

12. For a comprehensive report on the development and implementation of the N-MUSD's competency-based program see *The Newport-Mesa Unified School District Four County Conference on Competency-Based Educational Systems,* Jan. 12, 1977, Newport-Mesa Unified School District, P.O. Box 1368, Newport Beach, CA 91663. (Mimeographed.)

See, also, Michael W. Kirst, "A Promising New Idea for Education," *Los Angeles Times,* Thursday, July 7, 1977, part II, p. 7.

Role and Function Effect Model
Use Tools – Procedures for

	Identifying discrepancies	Establishing objectives, requirements & criterion measures	Designing/selecting processes	Executing processes to obtain results	Executing processes for monitoring and evaluating
Of/for individuals	Determine if there are discrepancies between the current status of individuals and what is expected or desired.	Estab. object. & perf. rqmnts. to eliminate or reduce discrepancies that exist for individuals. Identify criterion measures for determining that object. & perf. reqmnts. for individuals have been met.	Design and/or select processes to enable individuals to achieve object. & meet perf. rqmnts. Design and/or select processes for the criterion measures established.	Execute the processes designed and/or selected to enable individuals to obtain results.	Monitor & evaluate results obtained by individuals. Revise or redesign processes as necessary to meet object. & rqmnts. & to eliminate or reduce discrepancies.
Of/for consumer community	Determine if there are discrepancies between the results currently being obtained and the results the consumer community expects or desires.	Estab. object. & perf. rqmnts. to eliminate or reduce discrepancies identified with respect to consumer comm. Identify criterion measures for determ. that object. & perf. rqmnts. for consumer comm. have been met.	Design and/or select processes to achieve the objective & performance requirements established for the consumer community.	Execute the processes designed and/or selected to obtain results for the consumer community.	Monitor & evaluate results obtained for the consumer comm. Revise or redesign processes as necessary to meet object. & rqmnts. & to eliminate or reduce discrepancies.
Of/for social community	Determine if there are discrepancies between the results currently being obtained and the results the social community expects or desires.	Estab. object. & perf. rqmnts. to eliminate or reduce discrepancies identified with respect to social comm. Identify criterion measures for determ. that object. & perf. rqmnts. have been met.	Design and/or select processes to achieve the objective & performance requirements established for the social community.	Execute the processes designed and/or selected to obtain results for the social community	Monitor & evaluate results obtained for the social comm. Revise or redesign processes as necessary to meet object. & rqmnts. & to eliminate or reduce discrepancies.
Of/for school environment	Determine if there are discrepancies between the current school environment and what is expected or desired.	Estab. object. & perf. rqmnts. to eliminate or reduce discrepancies identified with respect to school environment. Identify criterion measures for determ. that object. & perf. rqmnts. have been met.	Design and/or select processes to achieve the objective & performance requirements established for the school environment.	Execute the processes designed and/or selected to obtain results in the school environment.	Monitor & evaluate results obtained in the school environment. Revise or redesign process as necessary to meet obj. & rqmnts. & to eliminate or reduce discrepancies.
Of/for self	Determine if there are discrepancies between the current status of yourself, professionally, and what you expect or desire it to be.	Establish objectives & performance requirements for yourself, professionally, in order to eliminate or reduce discrepancies that exist.	Design and/or select processes to achieve the objectives & performance requirements established for yourself, professionally.	Execute the processes designed and/or selected to enable you to obtain results for yourself, professionally.	Monitor & evaluate results obtained for yourself, professionally. Revise or redesign processes as necessary to meet object. & rqmnts. & to eliminate or reduce discrepancies.

(Top face of cube: Maintain effective systems / Develop effective systems)

Figure 11-2 Role and function effect model. (Newport Mesa School District.)

instructional objectives were attained, and then confers with the teacher to discuss the results of their analysis. Their report is for the teacher's use only. (2) The *Appraisal Cycle* is a formal, summative-type appraisal of a teacher's overall performance. During an Appraisal Cycle (normally once a semester), a teacher submits instructional objectives covering two subject areas for the principal's approval. At the end of the semester, data are collated to document the extent to which instructional objectives were attained. Information for the Appraisal Cycle is used by the principal at the end of the school year in writing the teacher's formal, overall evaluation report.

The N-MUSD description of the purposes, elements, and operation of the appraisal plan for teachers follows:

N-MUSD STAFF PERFORMANCE IMPROVEMENT AND APPRAISAL PLAN FOR TEACHERS

The Newport-Mesa Unified School District has devoted staff time and other resources to the development of a District model for the improvement and appraisal of staff performance. The original intent was to provide the District with an overall model that could be implemented by various process plans. However, as the development of such a model was carried out it became evident that it would be necessary to also design a basic plan that could be used by those schools/operating units not wishing to develop their own plan. Schools/operating units choosing to develop their own plan must meet the same design requirements that the basic plan has met. The basic plan is described below:

Need for Both Improvement and Appraisal of Teachers

Repeatedly, the idea has been asserted that the goals of the schools are achieved from the behavior of teachers. Consequently, evaluation of teaching is essential in order to obtain information that teachers are contributing to the school's objectives. One aspect of evaluation—appraisal—deals with the performance of teachers on the basis of their ability to effect desired and desirable changes in learners. A second aspect of evaluation—improvement—deals with ways to help a teacher be more effective in advancing the progress of learners.

Evaluation of the individual teacher is necessary for making decisions about him and about the program of the school. It should be stated that the issue involved in teacher evaluation is not whether it should be done; the problem is one of how best to proceed.

Requirements for the successful operation of a Staff Performance Improvement and Appraisal Plan are:

1. The District's/Operating Units' objectives should be clearly stated and available upon request.
2. The appraisee/appraiser (the teacher and those evaluating the teach-

er) should agree on what should be appraised and how the appraisal is to be made.

3. Focus should be on the results obtained and not the processes used. Processes used by the teacher should be considered as factors in the improvement of instruction. They should be monitored and analyzed in relation to the obtained results. Methods are to be appraised, not prized.
4. The appraisal of Staff Performance should be conscientiously and systematically undertaken.
5. The plan must operate within the legal requirements of the Board of Education and/or State.
6. Adequate resources should be made available so that the plan's operational requirements may be carried out.

A central requirement is that the plan should provide data with which to make the following kinds of decisions:

1. How to effectively utilize teaching personnel (differentiated assignments, reassignments, etc.)
2. How to improve individual (teaching) performance
3. Whether to modify existing methods/means
4. Clarification of the assignment and/or results expected
5. Whether to continue or discontinue a teacher's services.

The evaluation of teachers is a vital function but it is of little value as an end in itself. Basically, it is a necessary step in the improvement of personnel and the results of District/Operating Unit programs.

Elements of a Staff Performance and Appraisal Plan.
The plan is based upon a Role and Function Effect Model. In accordance with this model, a teacher performs five basic functions:

1. Identifying discrepancies
2. Establishing objectives, requirements and criterion measures (to obtain school/district objectives)
3. Designing and selecting processes
4. Executing processes to obtain results
5. Executing processes for monitoring and evaluating.

The above functions are discharged by the teacher as he works with five populations: Individual pupils; the consumer community (e.g. future employers of students); the social community (e.g. neighborhood councils); the school environment (e.g. fellow teachers); and the professional self (e.g. self improvement).

Provisions for systematic collection of data regarding a teacher's performance with all five populations is a long term goal. An immediate priority is to establish means for identifying the teacher's performance in working with pupils.

**Appraisal as Carried Out in the Staff
Performance Improvement and Appraisal Plan**

1. By no later than the first day of the semester, the principal or his designee will notify the teacher of the area(s) to be appraised. (The designee can be another administrator, department head, or a team composed of teachers and administrators.) The area(s) can be in one or two subjects at the elementary level and for one or two classes at the middle and high school levels.

2. The teacher, during the first three weeks of the semester, will determine the discrepancies pupils have in the instructional area(s), the difference between what pupils can do and what they should be able to do. Using this information, the teacher will formulate his instructional objective(s), select appropriate criterion measures and state what the criteria for his acceptable performance will be (teacher criteria). These discrepancies, objectives, criterion measures, and teacher criteria are then to be presented in writing to the principal or his designee by the end of the third week. The objectives submitted are those to be attained by pupils at the end of the semester. The teacher need not specify daily instructional objectives believed necessary for attainment of the semester-long objectives. Neither need he describe the instructional process he might use in producing the intended changes in the learners at hand. The end-of-semester objectives are to be specific and should be written in terms of what students will be able to do, under what conditions, and the criteria for acceptable learner performance. There can be objectives in behalf of an individual pupil, or small group of pupils, as well as objectives for the class as a whole.

   First year non-tenured teachers, and any other teacher who did not realize his objectives during the previous semester, will submit an interim objective stating what they anticipate to accomplish by the end of the first quarter. The interim objective(s), criterion measure(s) and teacher criteria are necessary because the first year non-tenured teachers, and any other teacher who did not realize his objectives during the previous semester, are to be appraised at the end of the quarter. The purpose of this additional appraisal is to help the teacher and principal or his designee to determine what an appropriate instructional objective(s), criterion measures, and/or teacher criteria should be for that teacher for the group of students he is working with.

3. By no later than the end of the fifth week, the principal/designee, and the teacher will have recorded in writing their approval of the instructional objectives, criterion measures and teacher criteria that will serve to indicate the teacher's ability to get desired results. Teacher and principal modifications in the agreement for the semester can occur at any time before the end of the first week in the second quarter.

4. At the end of the first quarter of the semester, those teachers re-

quired to report will present to the principal or designee, the results obtained to this point in time.

5. First semester results for all teachers are to be reported to the principal or designee no later than the first week of the second semester. Second semester results are to be recorded no later than the last day of the school term. Teachers who did not achieve desired results at the end of the semester must report results attained at the end of both quarters of the next semester.

Instructional Improvement in the Plan

Thus far we have outlined appraisal procedures—means for assessing a teacher's ability to get results. Improvement of instruction follows a somewhat different procedure known as an improvement cycle. An improvement cycle is used to assist the teacher in accomplishing agreed upon semester objectives. The data collected in improvement cycles are not to be used in rating the teachers. Under the ground rules of an improvement cycle, the teacher feels free to reveal instructional weaknesses and to seek help in overcoming them.

1. During the period (quarter or semester) in which the appraisal is taking place, all teachers will complete at least one and not more than three improvement cycles. Each cycle is based upon one lesson.
2. Those teachers who reach their first semester objectives will be given at least one and not more than three improvement cycles during the second semester. All teachers who do not reach first semester objectives will receive at least one and not more than three improvement cycles each quarter the following semester.

An improvement cycle consists of a pre-observation conference in which the teacher submits pre-assessment data (information showing what pupils can and cannot do with respect to an instructional task), objective(s) for the forthcoming lesson, teacher criteria, and criterion measures. The conference is followed by an in-class observation, an analysis and strategy session, and a post-observation conference with the teacher. It is suggested that during the improvement cycle, the principal utilize other teachers to complete an observation team.

The parts of the improvement cycle are described below:

1. *The Pre-Observation Conference*
During the pre-observation conference the teacher presents to the principal and/or designee the instructional objectives he intends to use in the lesson to be observed. In addition, the teacher indicates the measurement (tests, product, situation, etc.) by which the learners will demonstrate whether or not they have acquired the skills, concepts, or pre-dispositions to be taught. The teacher establishes what will constitute a satisfactory level of pupil performance on the measuring instrument and what percentage of pupils are expected to reach this level before the lesson would be considered successful.

The pre-observation conference affords the teacher the opportunity to justify his selection of instructional objectives and to consider alternative instructional objectives that might be more appropriate. The principal/designee or members of the team (if one is used) and the teacher agrees on the attainability, appropriateness of the objective, criterion measures and teacher criteria.

In addition to clarifying instructional intents for both teacher and his peers, the pre-observation conference permits the other individuals who will be observing and analyzing the lesson to define their roles during the observation.

2. *The Observation*
During the observation, the principal/designee or members of the team (if one is used), collect data regarding the execution of the previously planned lesson. The observation team records both the verbal behavior of pupils and the teacher, (i.e., teacher questions, pupil responses) and non-verbal behavior which could be objectively described. The purpose of collecting data is to determine later if the processes used were appropriate for obtaining the desired results.

3. *The Analysis and Strategy Session*
Following the observation, the principal/designee or observation team, without the presence of the teacher who will continue instruction in the classroom, compare the results of the lesson as shown by pupil achievement with what the teacher had originally stipulated would be achieved.

The team reviews their observation and analyzes the teaching performance using such instructional techniques as appropriate practice and knowledge of results. In conducting the analysis session, the team members draw generalizations regarding the lesson; however, no generalization is to be made without presenting the data which led to the generalization. The team also plans the strategy for conducting the post-observation conference to be held with the teacher whose work is being reviewed.

4. *The Post-Observation Conference*
At this conference the teacher who taught the lesson and the other members of the team look at the results obtained by the pupil in the light of the intended instructional objectives. When results are unsatisfactory, the teacher is encouraged to try alternative instructional procedures based upon the findings derived from the analysis. Sometimes an analysis will indicate the need for changes in instructional objectives rather than in teaching procedures. In writing the original instructional objective the teacher may have presumed that the learners had mastered a prerequisite task when indeed they had not, or something may have been seen during the lesson which indicated a need for an additional objective. The suggestions given to the teacher come from interpretations which are drawn from factual data that the other members of the team have recorded during the observation.

Individual operating units, schools, or departments within a school have the option of developing their own improvement plan as a substitute and/or as an addition to the improvement plan described above. Before an alternate plan can be substituted for the improvement plan described above, it must be approved by the staff in the operating unit, the operating unit head, the Superintendent and the Board of Education.

Appraising Administrators/Supervisors

The N-MUSD has developed an appraisal plan for administrative personnel based on the Role and Function Effect Model shown in Figure 11-2, utilizing operational procedures similar to those described in the appraisal plan for teachers. Because the Appraisal Plan for Administrators provides an exemplary model clearly adaptable to appraising dimensions of supervisory performance it is presented here in its entirety. (Note: the reader is alerted to a series of descriptive statements which illustrate some specific elements for a principal's performance appraisal beginning on page 270.)

N-MUSD STAFF PERFORMANCE IMPROVEMENT AND APPRAISAL PLAN FOR ADMINISTRATORS
Rationale for N-MUSD Staff Performance Improvement and Appraisal Plan.

Repeatedly the idea has been asserted that the goals of the schools are achieved from the behavior of the personnel. Consequently, the evaluation of the performance of the District's personnel is essential in order to obtain some notion of how well performance of personnel is contributing to the District's objectives. Appraisal of the individual performance of staff members is necessary for making decisions about the individual and about the programs of the District. It should be stated that the issue involved in appraising performance is not whether it should be done; the problem is one of how it may be done most effectively.

Requirements for the successful operation of a Staff Performance Improvement and Appraisal Plan for Administrators are:

1. The District's and Operating Unit's objectives should be clearly stated and available upon request.
2. The appraisee and appraiser should agree on what should be appraised and how the appraisal is to be made.
3. Focus should be on the results obtained and not the processes used. Processes should be regarded as means, not to be prized but appraised in terms of results.
4. The appraisal of Staff performance should be conscientiously and systematically undertaken.
5. It must operate within the legal requirements of the Board of Education and/or State.

6. Adequate resources should be made available so that the plan's operational requirements may be carried out.

A Staff Performance Improvement and Appraisal Plan for Administrators should provide data for decisions on:

1. How to effectively utilize administrative personnel
2. How to improve individual performance
3. Whether to modify existing methods/means
4. Clarification of the assignment and/or results expected
5. Whether to continue or discontinue the Administrator's services.

Appraisal of personnel performance is a vital function but it is of little value as an end in itself. Basically, it is a necessary step in the improvement of personnel and the District.

Elements of a Staff Performance Improvement and Appraisal Plan for Administrators.

As depicted in the Role and Function Effect Model, on which the Staff Improvement and Appraisal Plan is based, there are five basic functions that an educator performs. These functions are:

1. Identifying discrepancies
2. Establishing objectives, requirements and criterion measures
3. Designing and selecting processes
4. Executing processes to obtain results
5. Executing processes for monitoring and evaluating.

The above functions are discharged by the administrator as he works with five populations:

1. Individuals (e.g., pupils and teachers)
2. The consumer community (e.g., future employers of students)
3. The social community (e.g., neighborhood councils)
4. The school environment (e.g., fellow administrators)
5. The Professional self (e.g., self improvement).

Provisions for systematic collection of valid data regarding an administrator's performance with all five populations is a long term goal. An immediate priority is to establish relevant means for identifying the administrator's performance in working with individuals (pupils and teachers).

1.0 Determine Probable Discrepancies

The determination of discrepancies is a never ending task in a dynamic organization. A discrepancy is the difference between an existing set of conditions and an expected or desired set of conditions. In the field of education, discrepancies change weekly, daily, or even hourly. As a school and District undertake to plan for the next instructional year, they must identify where individuals are most likely to be at the beginning of the instructional year and where they should be at the end of the instructional year, as defined by the District's/school's objectives and the student(s) capabilities. The discrepancies for an individual, or group of individuals, should be the basis for establishing planning objectives. What the discrepancies at the school/operating unit level will be, where the pupils compose the target population, is a question that can only be answered when the skills, knowledge, and attitudes of pupils in given areas are known. Individual or group performance during one instructional year, as determined by the school's and/or District's assessment program, and the District's/school's stated objectives should provide the personnel of the school/operating unit with sufficient data to establish discrepancies for the ensuing year by no later than June 30 of the present instructional year. A particular school will collect information beyond that found from a District-wide testing program and will have students with different capabilities. Thus the discrepancies identified for each school's/operating unit's students will most likely be different.

2.0 Establish/Submit Planning Objectives, Requirements and Evaluation Plans

Once the personnel of a school/operating unit has identified the probable discrepancies for the ensuing instructional year and the District's goals and/or objectives are known, planning objectives for the school/operating unit can be established.

A planning objective should contain the following:

1. The name of the individual(s) accountable
2. What will be accomplished
3. How well it will be accomplished (the criteria or standard)
4. The conditions under which it will be accomplished.

Planning objectives for the subsequent year should be established in all areas identified by the District by May 1st. Planning objectives in areas other than those set by the District should also be submitted if the school/operating unit would like District assistance in reaching the objectives.

The administrator should feel free to state the conditions which he expects the District to meet in order that objectives can be met. An example would be a request that the principal not be required to participate on more than X committees during the conduct of an instructional experiment.

The evaluation plan for each objective must also be established. The evaluation plan should include the tool or instrument to be used to determine if the planning objective has been reached. Also to be included is how the instrument or tool will be used.

The written report containing the discrepancies, planning objectives, requirements, and evaluation plans will be submitted to the superintendent and/or his designee by August 1st of each year. The designee could be an individual or group. If a group is used it may be made up of staff members with various assignments, i.e., administrator, teacher. Inasmuch as a group may constitute an appraisal team, the appraisee has the option to add additional persons, not to exceed two, as advisors to the team. Service as an advisor is voluntary.

3.0 Obtain Acceptances of Discrepancies, Planning Objectives, Requirements and Evaluation Plans

The superintendent and/or designee and the individual submitting the discrepancies, planning objective requirements and evaluation plans will indicate their acceptance by their signatures. Conferences between the superintendent and/or designee and the individual may be requested by either party. Acceptance is to be established by no later than September 1st.

4.0 Verify That Discrepancies Anticipated Actually Exist

If all students and teachers were to return and there had been no gain or loss of skill and/or knowledge, this would most likely be an unnecessary step. Since this will not be the case the administrator of a school will wish to verify that anticipated discrepancies identified still exist. The method for doing this will vary from school/operating unit to school/operating unit but it should be completed by the end of the third week of the instructional year (October 1st).

5.0 Modify/Submit Discrepancies, Accountability Objectives, Requirements, and Evaluation Plans

If there has been a change in the discrepancies, accountability objectives, requirements, or evaluation plans, they should be submitted to the superintendent and/or designee by October 15th for acceptance. The written acceptance established in 3.0, or as modified, will become the basis for appraisal of the administrator's performance with respect to individual (pupil and teacher) populations specified in the Model. Reaching the objective indicates that the administrator has succeeded with the target population. Appraisal of his performance with other populations in the Model (Social Community, Consumer Community, School Environment and Self) will be established in the traditional manner. Hopefully, procedures for systematic collection of information about these populations will eventually be established so that appraisal at these levels, too, may be more objective than it has in the past.

6.0 The Administrator Continues Selection/ Design/Execution of Processes to Reach Objectives

The administrator will establish and monitor processes to maximize his chances of getting the desired results. He should see that conditions considered as necessary to success are present, also, he probably will want frequent progress reports evidencing that the target population is changing in the directions desired.

7.0 The Appraisee Continues Monitoring and
Evaluation to Improve Programs and Obtain Data on Results

As established in the accepted evaluation plans (3.0 and 5.0) there will be instances when the appraiser(s) seeks to obtain data on the status of the program. These data may be for improving the program during the course of its development and verifying the results obtained.

8.0 Report Data on Results as Agreed in 3.0/5.0

Reports indicating the attainment of objectives must be submitted to the superintendent or his designee(s) as agreed in 3.0 or as modified. The superintendent and/or his designee is to indicate his acceptance of the results submitted.

9.0 Repeat 1.0–8.0 but Make Modifications
Based upon the Current State of Affairs

The following materials, provided by N-MUSD, are presented as a sample of performance requirements which might be formulated for (supervising) principals. The description statements refer to the basic functions performed by educators and the populations with whom they work (based on the Role and Function Effect Model, Figure 11-2). (Note: In two categories, Current Status of Personnel and Goals for Personnel; the statements are left open-ended for decision variations.)

DESCRIPTION STATEMENTS OF PRINCIPAL
ROLE AND FUNCTION EFFECT MODEL

Current Status of Student—The Principal has evidence of levels of performance, rate of progress, degree and kind of motivation and pattern of social interaction of individual instructional casualties. The Principal has evidence of progress of motivation and interactions of school population in terms of distributions.

Goals for Students—The Principal sees that maintenance levels and/or changes in kind and amount are specified for casualties and for school population.

Means and Plans for Students—Means and plans for students to meet goals specifies (1) personnel to be procured or reallocated training programs, (2) material to be acquired or reallocated, (3) strategies for grouping curriculum or alternatives and (4) changes in timing and placement, etc.

Monitoring and Evaluating Student for Maintenance or Change—The Principal determines the kind and amount of effects of student plans and means to meet specified goals through distributed observations, interviews, data devices, meetings and feedback mechanisms.

Current Status of Personnel—The Principal has evidence of the abilities, availability, values, plans and image of teachers and consultants, administrators, peers, aids and classified personnel in relationship to . . .

Goals for Personnel—The Principal specifies kind and degree of maintenance or change desired for particular teachers, consultants, administrators, aids, peers and classified personnel in relationship to . . .

Means and Plans for Personnel—The Principal specifies the method(s) employed to achieve the goals established for teachers, consultants, administrators, peers, aids and classified personnel status (abilities, availability, plans, image and interaction with the principal).

Monitoring and Evaluating Personnel for Maintenance or Change— The Principal knows in what amount and/or direction the desired effects have occurred through observation, interviews, data devices, meetings, feedback mechanisms and correspondence.

Current Status of Community—The Principal has evidence of demographic characteristics of communities.

Goals for Community—The Principal specifies by specific area the degree to which certain parents, agents and/or agencies are assessed, utilized and/or informed.

Means and Plans for Community—The Principal specifies the method in which the certain parents, agents, agencies are to be utilized, assessed and/or informed.

Monitoring and Evaluating Community for Maintenance or Change—The Principal knows in what amount and direction effects have occurred using observation, interviews, data devices, meetings, feedback mechanisms and correspondence.

Current Status of Self—The Principal has estimated, inventoried and described his abilities, values and image in each major administrative area (curriculum, guidance, personnel, prescription, etc.)

Goals for Self—The Principal specifies direction and amount of change desired in particular abilities, values and/or areas of reputation.

Means and Plans for Self—The Principal specifies the method, time and place for achieving the desired maintenance and changes.

Monitoring and Evaluating Self for Maintenance or Change—The Principal detects through observation, interview and feedback mechanisms the degree of specified maintenance or changes that have occurred.

In any organization where the attainment of goals and objectives is to be evaluated, some form of systematic evaluative system not only of programs but of personnel and other components is necessary. A smooth uniform system requires that supervisory performance be regularly appraised, since where supervisory problems or dysfunctions occur schools cannot be expected to accomplish the expected goals regardless of the quality of their curriculum and teachers. The appraisal plans, and the accompanying performance requirements, which have been presented provide an example of a systematic, comprehensive, and objective strategy for appraising the major decision-making and problem-solving functions of administrative/supervisory personnel.

Inadequate Teaching Performance

Over the years various procedures have been used to accommodate problems of inadequate teaching performance. Procedures have often been rule-of-thumb techniques to handle unpleasant decisions either because those concerned sought an easy way out or because thought was not given to examining more precise and rational ways to meet problems. A number of procedures have been practiced on teachers whose performance was considered to be inadequate, such as: (1) place them where they will do the least harm; (2) transfer them to another school for someone else to supervise; (3) move them to an administrative position; (4) send them to the kind of school from which it is hoped they will resign; (5) traumatize, shock, or embarrass them in the hopes they will perform better; or (6) wait for their retirement. None of these approaches fits in with accountability on the part of supervisors and teachers to pupils and purposes of schools. They degrade a profession which should pride itself on high standards of human performance, service to others, and a view that human talent can be cultivated. How many of us would like to be passengers in commercial airlines if we felt that pilot selection was based on such questionable personnel procedures? When focus is on the task to be done and its objective appraisal, we can apply more reasonable procedures to meet problems of inadequate performance.

Supervisors and teachers must face the facts of inadequate performance and accept the consequences of their review. Prospective teachers, in general, have experienced objective assessments overall during their collegiate training and expect them to continue after employment. The twofold nature of assessment is kept clearly in mind: (1) to help in the improvement of skills, essentially, but also (2) to evaluate accomplishment of requisite, agreed-upon purposes of schools. Careful review of accomplishment is the responsibility of supervisors. Teachers who, during a reasonable period of time, in varying situations, and after careful review, cannot set valid instructional objectives and attain their set purposes should not continue teaching. If what schools do with pupils has validity, what teachers do must be appraised in terms of what schools intend to accomplish.

Supervisors must give special attention to the improvement of permanent or tenured teachers whose performance is inadequate or who have "normalized" their teaching. Statesmanship is sometimes put to the most rigorous test in effecting desired changes. Supervisors' successes in working with experienced teachers may depend upon the model they present—on demonstration and exemplification of their expertness. Factors such as supervisory skill in human relations and ability to determine and evaluate objectives will be important in actions to change the behavior of others. Essentially, the purpose is to bring about changes in agreed-upon directions and not to punish or shock teachers into submission. Supervisors must face teachers with accountability to pupils and insist upon performance in accordance with objectives; but, in this process, it may be necessary to accept negative reactions without retaliation. Every possible resource should be employed to help teachers make changes in desired directions. In those instances where incontestable evidence has been accumulated to prove that a teacher is adversely affecting learning of pupils, this teacher must be removed from the classroom.

In positive terms attempts to improve the competence of permanent teachers should almost never lead to a graveyard. Teachers, with guidance, sometimes make enormous changes in their instructional behavior.[13] Supervisors are responsible for finding ways to improve teachers' competencies by practices which help teachers obtain new visions of teaching, define instructional objectives, select appropriate learning contacts, and determine the kind and quality of outcomes. Many teachers whose performance has lagged are simply "dying on the vine," and their inadequate teaching has resulted from years of technical neglect and from lack of opportunity or encouragement to try out new and valid procedures to help improve their teaching. Permanent teachers must be given the kind of help that accords with their values and experiences yet focuses on being able to describe the learning requirements of pupils, the ways to go about obtaining pupil achievement, and the ways to examine results of teaching.[14]

General institutes or workshops which are intended to be inspirational in nature but which are in reality latent window dressing are not effective mechanisms for providing teachers with substantive

13. Bruce Joyce, "Structural Imagination: The Creation of Alternative Learning Environments," General Session Address, the Forty-fourth Annual Claremont Reading Conference, Feb. 4–5, 1977. (Proceedings of the Conference published in the 1977 Claremont Reading Conference Yearbook, Claremont Graduate School, Claremont, Calif.)
14. Charles L. Hughes and Vincent S. Flowers, "Strategies for Effective Training," *Personnel*, vol. 53, no. 4, pp. 50–57, July/August 1976.
   Madeline Hunter, "Teacher Competency: Problem, Theory, and Practice," *Theory into Practice*, vol. 15, no. 2, pp. 162–171, April 1976.

content directly applicable to their in-school problems of teaching. Indeed, human talent is ill-used when teachers are expected to participate in activities remote from their particular and urgent professional needs. Only when in-service activities are carefully designed to benefit individual teachers can their existence be justified. Supervisors, working directly with individual teachers and directing efforts at particular in-school, in-classroom problems, have opportunities to achieve more substantial results. Careful organization of supervisors' time schedules and utilization of the expertness of other teachers should make this kind of individual attention possible. Supervisors get results by ignoring the idiosyncrasies of maverick teachers and by supporting teachers in their efforts to improve performance with more than words of inspiration or encouragement. In some cases, the more specific, systematic, and even directive a supervisor's proposals for change are, the greater the opportunity to pinpoint problem areas.

That dramatic changes can be effected in the performance of permanent teachers who have slipped backward or who have never been effective cannot be overemphasized. Changes may be slow in some instances, or they may occur only in limited areas of performance. Competent supervisors, especially those who may be new on the job, take the long view of change processes. They reinforce or reward each change but persist in seeing that overall performance continues to improve both in kind and in degree. As with a sick patient whose prognosis indicates an eventual cure, supervisors must be patient with ailing teachers when nursing them back to health. Teachers whose performance has not been satisfactory but who are attempting to improve must understand that they are actually taking steps toward reinstating themselves in their profession. Supervisors and teachers must have a clear understanding between them of the necessary steps that must be taken to improve performance. Questions helpful to both supervisors and teachers in determining the agreed-upon goals to be achieved would include:

Is there agreement on what is to be taught—have valid objectives been selected?
Have the procedures to achieve objectives been determined—is there a plan for ordering the presentation of learning experiences?
Have the measures which will be used to evaluate the results of instruction been formulated—tests, inventories, etc.?

Underlying instructional procedures are some larger questions concerning knowledge of skills and attitudes which might be considered by the teacher, such as: "Do I possess the requisite skills to accomplish the above tasks?" "Do I clearly understand the basic concepts and methodology underlying what is to be taught?" "If my knowledge is limited with respect to a particular problem, what investigations must I undertake?" "What self-study is necessary?" "What help is needed from the supervisor?" "What expert informants (other teachers, principals, parents) can I find to help in testing out proposals before embarking upon teaching?"

In implementing appraisal operations supervisors may ask:

1. "Have I helped teachers to view supervision as a technical resource designed to help them achieve objectives of the school?"
2. "Is there conscientious attention on the part of teachers to support the objectives of the school?"
3. "Have the motives which caused teachers to enter teaching and which currently sustain them emerged in our person-to-person relations? If these motives were assessed negatively (e.g., a temporary career interest), has teaching experience developed an awareness of professional responsibility on the part of these teachers?"
4. "Have I controlled my biases against those aspects of teachers' personalities which are at variance with my expectations but which do not relate to, or stand in the way of, competent teaching performance?"
5. "Have teachers met the agreed-upon criteria for achievement in spite of what might seem to others undesirable personality traits or the application of unique or 'different' classroom teaching procedures? In other words, do criterion measures show that the teacher's methods of instruction have resulted in positive educative experiences for pupils?"

Changes in school goals, programs, and practices and the development of alternative strategies for teaching affect the roles and responsibilities of all staff members in one way or another. Some of the conditions requiring professional accountability[15] on the part of supervisors and teachers, in performing their tasks, are these: (1) the school curriculum, defined in terms of pupil competencies and the school's educational objectives, will be stated clearly at both the in-

15. Harry S. Broudy, *The Real World of the Public Schools,* Harcourt Brace Jovanovich, New York, 1972.

Jo Ann Mazzarella, "Accountability and Testing," *School Leadership Digest,* 2d ser., no. 5. Prepared by National Association of Elementary Principals, ERIC Clearinghouse on Educational Management, Arlington, Va., 1975.

stitutional and classroom level; (2) teachers will be directly involved in defining instructional objectives and know what they are capable of accomplishing before engaging in teaching; (3) the extent of teacher accountability for pupil competency will be open to negotiations between appraisers and appraisees, since teachers are but one of several factors influencing pupil behavior; and (4) appraisals of instructional performance will include selected elements concerned with changes in pupil behavior.

CHAPTER 12

SCHOOL-BASED RESEARCH

DIMENSIONS OF RESEARCH IN SCHOOLS

An essential characteristic of any profession is the possession of expertness by its members. One dimension of expertness in teaching is the ability to predict the consequences of particular acts upon the learning of pupils. Supervisory expertness depends in part upon ability to define, analyze, and seek solutions to major educational problems. Throughout this chapter we stress the centrality of school-based research and the responsibility of supervisors and teachers alike to develop skills and apply expertness in conducting methodologically sound research relevant to educational practice in schools.

Although the term "research" has been used to describe varied educational activities, it can be defined broadly as a systematic method of inquiry directed toward the development of a science of behavior in education.[1] A brief review of the development of educational research will indicate some of the changes in purpose and emphasis which have occurred.

1. Robert M. W. Travers, *An Introduction to Educational Research*, 3d ed., The Macmillan Company, New York, 1969.

Development

At the turn of the century and in the years following, research was conducted in laboratories for the most part. Emphasis was on the selection of specific problems and was concentrated on studying isolated variables, maintaining controls of experimental procedures, and recording the results of findings as precisely as possible. Studies emphasized the psychological and physiological aspects of learning and behavior, ranging from eye movements in reading and perceptual factors to the measurement of various human skills and aptitudes. During the early part of the century considerable effort was expended on studies of child growth and development, and schools stressed the "child centered" aspects of curriculum and learning.[2] Some of the studies conducted initially in laboratories were repeated later in school settings, and the findings were used to change practices in these schools. Supervisors, teachers, principals, guidance specialists, and university staff members became involved in various research studies. Because many of these persons had been trained in laboratory research methods, the quality of educational research improved. Studies were expanded from controlled experimentation to operational research.

As classic laboratory studies on memorizing and learning (at one time called psychological research) were conducted more and more frequently in schools (or were shown to have implications for classroom teaching), the term "educational research" came into common use. Educational research has been shaped by a number of forces: (1) burgeoning school populations, (2) results of research conducted by researchers in the armed services, (3) demands for more extensive education, (4) development of courses in educational research in colleges and universities, and (5) establishment of such organizations as the National Society for the Study of Education, American Educational Research Association, and American Psychological Association, among others.

With the application of promising research findings in schools educational research increased and with it productivity of laboratory workers and workers in the field. Although educational research has been and will continue to be closely allied to psychological research, the need for more objective information about indigenous educational problems has formalized it as a distinct and necessary field of endeavor. Educational research increasingly has attracted researchers from other disciplines, i.e., behavioral scientists who (interested in

---

2. Peter B. Neubauer, M.D., "The Century of the Child," *The Atlantic* (Monthly), vol. 208, pp. 84–87, July 1961.

improving educational processes) have contributed procedures and techniques.

All fields of human endeavor have depended upon and profited from research. The mission of educational research may be stated thus: (1) to provide objective evidence to improve school learning, (2) to help place the work of the school on firmer ground with the consumers of education, (3) to controvert myths, and (4) to change beliefs and attitudes. Conclusive evidence, based on research, is necessary to ensure that proposed changes are not based on opinion, unexamined hypotheses, or proposals from power agencies outside the school. The controversies over school practices, ranging from such concerns as the most effective methods of learning to the specific qualities of teacher competence, may be traceable in part to lack of objective and scientific evidence. When relevant knowledge is absent, forces which are questionable may take over the decision-making function. Historically, research has expanded knowledge and has been used as a basis for combating ignorance (i.e., medicine), for the scientific assessment of human skills (i.e., airline pilot or astronaut selection), for the improvement of learning, and for the more adequate use of human talent.[3] In-school research, properly conceived and based upon well-defined theories of content, learning, and teaching, is a systematic way to develop justifiable learning programs. Supervisors and teachers have a responsibility to obtain objective evidence about existing programs and to communicate reasons for suggested changes.

Roles of Teachers and Supervisors
The idea that the teacher should have an active role as a researcher has not always been accepted by administrators, school boards, university professors, government agencies, or even teachers themselves. Samples of some of the views about teachers may help supervisors assess their own assumptions.

1. One view of teachers is that they are primarily practitioners concerned with improving teaching only as they are given prescriptions or means derived by others from the results of scientific inquiry. This view would see teachers as relatively untouched by basic constructs and comprehensive theories in daily work. They attend institutes, read what others have to say, and engage in a secondhand kind of participation. Since they deal only with practice or with application in restricted situations they are not re-

3. Frederick B. Davis, *Utilizing Human Talent*, American Council on Education, Washington, 1947.

quired to make use of sustaining theoretical constructs or to test educational goals against a set of hypotheses. They are constrained by the system to be no more than an implementer. As such they are not to be concerned with the development and understanding of structures, systems, or theories which will undergird and explain daily teaching. These tasks are to be left to the educational researcher outside the classroom.

2. Another view would see teachers as limited consumers of research findings. Here, the assumption is that teachers are sympathetic, supportive, and well-disposed toward researchers and their findings. This view casts the actors in two distinct roles: on one hand, educational researchers who formulate theories, test them, and arrive at generalizations; on the other hand, teachers who try to interpret as best they can the statements of the elite group.

3. Somewhere along this continuum is another view which places teachers at a point where they participate in research studies but are not provided much opportunity to become involved at the core of theory development or theory testing in their own classrooms. The teacher is envisaged as a kind of well-meaning amateur who can tackle some of the peripheral "hardware" but is not to tamper with the critical components.

Each of these three views places a limit, in varying degrees, on teachers' participation and involvement in research. For example, teachers may be supported strongly by a principal or supervisor as long as they implement a beginning reading program as outlined in a course of study. If, however, teachers raise serious questions about the premises on which the program is based (e.g., theories of readiness), they discover that such questions are to be left to others supposedly better qualified to answer them. Basic premises or fundamental questions of theory are not supposed to be within the purview of amateurs. Following a degree of participation in the formulation of hypotheses or questions, segments of the overall research are then parceled out so that the teacher may be involved in securing some small part of the data, administering tests, or compiling observational data. In general, the teacher is provided *limited* access to the total plan of the research, to the factors of the design, to the setting of hypotheses, to conduct of the study, and to formulation of conclusions.

It no longer can be assumed that teachers are not competent to engage in research, that they can be consumers only, and that their *imperative need to know* is not critical. Teachers as well as supervisors, acting within some defined or undefined framework, must have opportunity for the examination of problems from a systematic and scientific point of view. To set up dichotomies between the practitioner and the theorist, the classroom and the laboratory, is questionable. Research conducted in any one school can yield implications useful to other school systems, if it is based on accepted or universal theories. The classroom is the laboratory for learning, and it is here that theories may be tested and the results used in other classrooms.[4]

If the view is accepted that the task of the school is to teach wisely and systematically those things which cannot be learned elsewhere or by chance, then teachers and supervisors must be more than dispensers of existing programs. They must take on responsibilities (1) for new kinds of learning programs, (2) for precise analysis of content to be taught, materials to be used, and a program of presentation, and (3) for effective assessment of learning. Careful delineation and determination of objectives are needed at all times, since these are critical essences of teaching and supervision. Advances in learning occur in an atmosphere in which all persons involved are challenged to innovate, to test the choice of subject matter, to analyze teaching procedures, and to assess results.

Influences and Directions
Historically, a number of influences have shaped curricula and teaching-learning processes in schools. Among them have been (1) the influence of tradition—behavior expressed by "We have always done it this way, and we think we have been successful;" (2) the social values of the nation or of a particular community which determine the emphasis to be placed on curricula directed at teaching the fundamental skills to the exclusion of other areas, or on a particular type of physical education program, such as Little League baseball, or a girls' baton-twirling team; (3) the available types of instructional materials, including textbooks or locally prepared instructional guides or teaching materials; (4) the educational ladder and grade system which have constrained the program of the schools to certain fixed limits; and (5) teachers—their training, general cultural level, perceptions, and degrees of research-mindedness. These elements have to some extent determined the kind and quality of research and the extent to which it has been focused on the problems of what and how to teach.[5]

4. See Richard E. Schutz, "Research in Schools," *Educational Researcher,* vol. 5, no. 5, pp. 1–2, May 1976. This editorial discusses differences between academic research *on* schools and operational research *in* schools and stresses the need to expand the latter. The May 1976 issue of *Educational Researcher* inaugurated a new department, "R & D in Progress in Schools," in order to disseminate information concerning a variety of research activities in schools.
5. David H. Russell and J. Cecil Parker, "Using Research to Point the Way in Curriculum Change," *Educational Leadership,* vol. 12, pp. 269–276, February 1955.

The times are such that most intellectual disciplines, research agencies, corporate enterprises, and government bureaus are moving toward testing and examining fundamental propositions. Supervision cannot escape this trend. Curricula, teaching methods, learning theory, social and physical environment—all factors affecting people—must be subject to systematic study. It is well to recognize and take into account the range of forces that may influence the decision-making process and affect performance both negatively and positively, such as:

1. *Private opinion.* Experts who have a formula; organizations holding particular positions; private citizens who have developed unitary prescriptions.
2. *Public debate.* Manifested in discourse on radio and TV, in motion pictures, and in the press; corporate and agency documents; citizens' groups.
3. *Personal experience.* Akin to the perceptions expressed by the participants in 1 and 2. Rests on tradition, personal views, training, observation; practical thinkers and their personal points of reference. Teachers who depend in some degree upon this source for their rationale.
4. *Demonstration.* Exemplified by standardization on existing practices; by pilot studies conducted by organizations, study groups, and others. Purpose of studies may be to prove instead of to test a hypothesis.
5. *Operational research.* Studying a procedure as it occurs in its natural setting. Action does not necessarily follow in the sense of modifying classroom practices.
6. *Applied research.* Action-research in which techniques of research are applied to school problems, changes in current practices are introduced, and assessment is made of the effects of the changed practices.
7. *Basic research.* Experimental in nature, requiring the setting of special conditions to test carefully stated hypotheses.[6]

In general, each of these sources provides information which affects education. Communication media are emphasized in the first two. Many teachers and supervisors rely on the third. Foundations,

---

6. Adapted from Roger W. Russell, "Research in Education: A Neglected Question," American Psychological Association, Division 15, *Newsletter,* no. 1, pp. 15–21, December 1958.

lay study groups, citizens' committees, and other similar organizations have supported the fourth. And the last three sources are based upon a logical method for scientific inquiry.[7] Although any of these sources may be involved in educational decisions, it should be recognized that the first four tend to yield prescriptions and limited answers to questions. Teachers should be much more concerned with the last three, and in particular, applied research in their own classrooms. The criticisms sometimes voiced about operational research—that a lot of diffused action occurs, or that some studies are poorly designed—can be leveled at any poorly planned research. Well-conceived action-research if competently planned, can be as productive as research of a strictly experimental type.

It is true that supervisors are accountable to a variety of persons, but this only serves to point up the need for action at a professional level to ensure that support for educational programs will be based on sound findings. It would appear that "the general improvement of education results from the long-term, empirical study of problems using different kinds of research approaches. Such studies require continued support over a number of years and the involvement of many kinds of schools in different parts of the United States."[8] Seeking answers to pressing problems at an empirical and fact-finding level rather than at the level of tradition and practice alone is the responsibility of the school.

The kinds of research tasks which supervisors and teachers should undertake are those which revolve around the systematic long-range study of *what* (including how much) to teach (and to whom) and the determination of *how* (and when) to teach it most effectively. Research investigations which provide a basis for generalizations about causal relations between teaching and measured instructional outcomes are planned in terms of the objective sought. No one kind of research methodology should be prescribed for in-school research.[9] Nor is it necessary that one technique be considered better than another or be mutually replicable; each is chosen in terms of purposes. All research problems and techniques which are built upon carefully stated hypotheses for predicting expected data and which hold promise for providing answers about critical questions of teaching and learning have a place. In addition to attacking new problems and planning new approaches to problems, replication of prior studies is an important technique for adding to knowl-

7. Ibid., p. 15.
8. Ibid., p. 16.
9. Ronald G. Jones, "Research, Intuition, and Analysis," *Phi Delta Kappan*, vol. 42, pp. 263–265, March 1961.

edge.[10] For example, many promising studies concerned with elementary school mathematics have not been replicated. By replicating a variety of studies in many areas and school districts we should be able to provide some answers to persistent problems.

Problems concerned with such matters as managerial examinations or status certainly are not the responsibility of supervisors. Likewise, studies on plant construction, district population trends, comparative finance, organizational structure and operation, the number of teacher dropouts, ways to float a bond issue, or general status investigations of any type are the responsibility of others in the administrative system. Supervisors who commit themselves (and staff) to any of these types of studies are abrogating their responsibilities for helping the teacher. School districts, fortunately, in our view, appear to involve supervisors and teachers less and less in tasks primarily noninstructional or administrative in nature.[11]

PLANNING AND CONDUCTING RESEARCH

The general nature of educational research, the characteristics of its several fields, and the methodologies employed have been described as follows:[12]

> Educational research refers to the careful and thorough-going investigation of educational phenomena (observable facts or events) leading to the discovery of verifiable facts, principles, and relationships which are fundamental to the systematic explanation of these phenomena. It implies the orderly seeking of educational facts and their systematic connections by means of, first, selective observation of educational phenomena and, second, valid reasoning, applied to the data obtained through observation. . . .
>
> They [fields of research] range from school administration to child growth and development, from history of education to the psychology of learning, from curriculum to guidance. Although the key concerns of the researcher (having to do with sampling, reliability, validity, and significance of findings) are similar from area to area and approach to approach, the methods for obtaining data and the techniques for interpreting them vary considerably from field to field.
>
> In historical research in education the interest is to determine relevant and significant features of the past (with the hope of better understanding the present and suggesting guides for the future). In descrip-

---

10. Ellis Batten Page, "Educational Research: Replicable or Generalizable?" *Phi Delta Kappan,* vol. 39, pp. 302–304, March 1958.

11. Kenneth R. Howey, "Putting Inservice Teacher Education into Perspective," *Journal of Teacher Education,* vol. 27, no. 2, pp. 101–105, Summer 1976.

12. David G. Ryans, "The Preparation of Educational Research Workers," *Journal of Educational Research,* vol. 49, pp. 195–197, November 1955.

tive research the interest is in describing designated characteristics of an existing population (or in describing relationships between certain characteristics of a population, or in testing some hypothesis about some characteristic of a population) undertaken to accomplish classification, to suggest trends, to reveal "needs," or to make comparisons. In experimental research the interest is in the description of the effect of some "treatment" or "treatments" upon some characteristics of a population, or in the testing of some hypothesis about this effect.

In descriptive research and in experimental research statistical techniques loom particularly important, both in the design and the analysis stages of the investigation, as the researcher seeks to control relevant variables, to summarize the data, and to make the estimates of error that are basic to the determination of whether or not observed differences in data are differences due to grouping or treatment, on the one hand, or to sampling error or error introduced by the influence of extraneous factors, on the other. In historical research statistical techniques are of minor importance, but logical analysis and the logical comparison of data in determining their reliability, validity, and significance require a variety of related but somewhat different skills and techniques.

Educational research stresses an inductive or empirical approach to understanding educational problems, reasoning from observed facts and experience rather than from tradition, intuition, or dogma. The essential purpose of all educational research is to test hypotheses and not to prove a point of view.

The professional worker has three basic responsibilities in planning and conducting educational research:[13]

1. To raise pertinent questions—to ask "Why?" "Which?" "What if?" "For whom?" "How much?"
2. To arrange observations (design investigations) that will provide testable answers to questions.
3. To provide estimates of, or information about, the validity and reliability of the answers, i.e., the extent to which systematic and random error enter into the answers.

Outlining Research Proposals
Requisite criteria for any properly conceived research project should include:[14]

1. A clear-cut definition of the population or sources to be studied, including precise descriptions of the relevant characteristics of the

13. Ibid., p. 196.
14. Ibid.

population that will be sampled, experimented with, described, compared, or analyzed.
2. A description or estimate concerning pertinent aspects of the particular population to be studied.
3. Estimates concerning the reliability of the sample data and the methods or instruments used for obtaining those data.
4. Evidence concerning the validity of the data obtained, including *(a)* control of relevant variables or factors; *(b)* avoidance of bias in sampling, or, at least description of uncontrolled bias; *(c)* validity of instruments used to obtain data; and *(d)* the appropriateness of the statistical or other procedures used to tabulate, summarize, compare, and analyze the data.

All aspects of a research design should be considered in advance and clearly and precisely described (the study should be replicable by other competent researchers). Factors to consider in planning will be found in the following outline:

1. Statement of the problem and its setting
   a. Importance or significance of the problem
2. Related research
   a. What is known already about the problem
3. Basic hypotheses to be tested and/or questions to be answered
4. Dependent variable (criterion behavior)
5. Population description
   a. Universe population
   b. Sample population
6. Sampling technique to be utilized
   a. How the sample is to be derived
7. Description of the general procedure
   a. Ex post facto, projected, descriptive, genetic
8. Specific procedures
   a. Before-after, experimental and control groups, time sampling, polling, or others
9. Relevant variables to be controlled
   a. Sex, socioeconomic status, study habits, in-class learning
10. Control technique
    a. Precision control (pairing)
    b. Frequency-distribution control (matched means and variabilities)
    c. Randomization
    d. Analysis of covariance
    e. Training of observers or raters
11. Statistical tests or significance of results

    a. Chi square, *t* tests (means, correlation), *F* tests (analysis of variance and covariance)
12. Equipment
    a. Autoinstructional devices, laboratory equipment, tests, rating instruments, scales
13. Instruments
    a. How tests, questionnaires, interviews, or other instruments used to measure the dependent variable are to be developed
    b. How validity and reliability are to be determined
    c. Knowledge about the validity and applicability of any commercially prepared tests to be used in the study
14. Facilities
    a. Personnel required; qualifications for the task
    b. Subjects to be used—number, age, grade, schools
    c. Time required and duration of the study—in-school, out-of-school, length of sessions, number of sessions, spacing of sessions
    d. Space required
    e. Assistance of other personnel

Determining Standards and Responsibilities

As noted earlier, it is not difficult to find problems that need solving, and the objects of research concern can be fairly well defined. However, it is important for supervisors to have clearly in mind standards by which to judge whether or not a particular research proposal can be initiated and carried to a satisfactory conclusion. In thinking through a proposed research project, the following list of questions might be given consideration:

1. Is the project well designed, with appropriate criteria applied?
2. Are the persons who are to conduct the research technically qualified, or will they need assistance?
3. Can a high degree of objectivity be maintained, or is the study in a sensitive area where the accomplishment of genuine research is constrained?
4. What hypotheses will be used to predict data?
5. Have provisions been made for additional observations or replication?
6. Have value terms been excluded from the proposed design?
7. Are the variables well defined?
8. How can the particular behavior under study be measured?
9. Can the research be carried out on site?
10. Will demands on the time of affected personnel be reasonable?

11. Is the research a part of the long-term program of the school district, or is it a short-term study which nevertheless will make a contribution?
12. Can facilities be provided without unreasonable inconvenience or disruption of regular programs?

Although involvement and commitment on the part of all staff members are important, it is reasonable, and effective, to encourage the formation of small planning teams consisting of two or three representatives from the staff (trained in research if possible) who are interested in the major objectives of the school system and willing to take general responsibility for planning studies. Such representative teams can develop *with* and *for* the staff various aspects of proposed studies (1) by establishing criteria for their assessment, (2) by obtaining consultant help as required, (3) by setting up a slate of projects with priorities for action, (4) by planning training sessions, and (5) by helping to manage input systematically. A research planning team can be particularly effective in helping to plan or develop standards for long-term studies.

In large school districts with a central research office, research planning teams can operate in a subdistrict or among groups of schools. Autonomy for these teams within the organizational system and within the framework of major objectives is important. Research teams lose effectiveness if they are limited to certain kinds of research (e.g., administrative data gathering), or if they are to act merely as rubber stamps for proposals of central supervisory officers. The central office staff in a large school system, in determining general broad objectives, may suggest research topics for investigation at the classroom level, provide consultant help and in-service training, and encourage local research teams to take responsibility for specific problems. It is the latter who should be delegated responsibility for determining and finding solutions to questions with and for the teaching staff in particular situations. A research planning team (or teams) can be invaluable to the supervisor in defining and implementing objectives. The use of such units, no matter how large or small the school system, is consistent with the concept that supervisors multiply themselves through others to the end that as many persons as possible are involved in a variety of research projects. In the long run the most useful research will be accomplished by involvement of the teachers whose research concerns are closely related to their instructional tasks.

PROBLEMS AND QUESTIONS
The range of problems in education to which research can be directed is not only vast but complex as well. Every school system must

determine important questions requiring answers and devise a set of priorities for attacking its most urgent problems. There are three areas of research inquiry where the need for action would seem to be most evident: (1) the learner and the learning process, (2) improvement of instruction, and (3) social factors in learning.

The Learner and the Learning Process
All school programs are based upon some sort of assumption about the nature of the learner and the learning process. The most effective instrument to improve the child's learning environment is for teachers to be engaged in a balanced program of research which examines the problems of learners in degree and kind. Study of problems of the learner and the learning process may be approached in a variety of ways, some of which are represented in the following questions:

1. How adequately is the school examining assumptions and testing results of learning among, for example, *(a)* the mentally retarded, *(b)* the mentally superior, *(c)* the especially talented, *(d)* the emotionally maladjusted, *(e)* the physically crippled, *(f)* the sensorially handicapped?
2. How is knowledge of learning theory applied to classroom situations which may include many or all of the types of learners just mentioned?
3. What are the essential characteristics of a teaching program which will develop pupils' divergent abilities and aptitudes?
4. How can the rate for developing abilities among gifted pupils be increased to a maximum, and creativity nurtured among all pupils?
5. What effects do attitudes of pupils toward the various content fields—and the teacher—have on learning?
6. What are the differential effects of various teaching styles upon the learning and productivity of pupils?

Improvement of Instruction
Sometimes methods used in schools appear to be largely the result of tradition without evidence for their effectiveness. However, when the instructional process is viewed as a technology or set of technologies based on the findings of the sciences of human behavior, the following questions seem appropriate:

1. How can teaching materials be organized systematically into programmed sequences which pupils can understand step by step?
2. Do teaching programs using programmed sequences call for new types of evaluation or alterations in existing assessments of learning and the learner?

3. What evidence can be obtained regarding the validity of particular textbooks, films, and other materials for improving learning?
4. What particular content, at any level of schooling, can be introduced earlier or at different times than currently programmed?
5. How can the effectiveness of any system of instruction be tested, and what are the measurable effects on the achievement of pupils presently or later?
6. How can content and instructional procedures be adjusted to meet predicted future contingencies of societal change and new knowledge?
7. What traditionally favored content appears obsolescent, and what new emphases are appearing (e.g., second language teaching, new structures for the organization of mathematics, or the application of linguistic principles to native language instruction)?

Social Factors in Learning
While research continues on what to teach and how to teach effectively, there is a concomitant need to account for societal factors affecting learning. Questions illustrating the problems in this area might include the following:

1. What behavior patterns of pupils are to be changed—by whom—in what value direction—for what ends? Who is responsible for what?
2. What forces in modern society motivate pupils; that is, which constrain and which facilitate the mission of the schools?
3. To what extent are gifted students achieving their potential power and in what vocational careers?
4. What are the fundamental reasons why pupils of outstanding ability do not continue their education?
5. What influences in family structures affect the motivation and achievement of pupils?
6. What is the responsibility of parents in developing learning attitudes, how does this responsibility relate to teachers' functions, and what responsibilities are shared?
7. What are the perceptions of teachers, administrators, and parents which determine their thought and action in school affairs?

Information on these problems is to be found in educational and psychological research journals, in government, university, and school district studies. In the long run, those responsible for supervisory functions can make contributions to solving some of the complex problems by making them the focus of in-school research.

RESEARCH AS A METHOD OF LEARNING
Improving Technical Competence

It is well for the supervisor to keep in mind that the results of educational research are becoming the primary source of data for the implementation of objectives. If supervisors do not develop research skills, efforts to set and test educational objectives may result only in accomplishing useful, but not critically important, tasks. The ability to conduct research, and to help staff members in research, requires a spirit of inquiry, knowledge of content, and skills in the research process.[15] Supervisors who lack training in designing and executing research investigations are accountable for remedying this deficiency. Supervisors cannot be effective by living on their capital, or talking about research, but must know the what and how of it. Training in educational research at some point in past time is not enough. The imperative need to obtain answers to new and critical questions requires continued study throughout one's professional career. Technical learning does not end with the granting of a degree or a certificate to supervise.

Further, technical knowledge of research methodology cannot be obtained by an auditing or absorptive process, such as attending occasional conferences, listening to inspirational lectures, reading professional journals, or consuming the results of research accomplished by others. Valuable as these activities may be for keeping abreast of current issues and problems, it is necessary to participate actively and directly in research processes, basing one's actions upon sound, up-to-date technical knowledge. To become an expert leader in the research function means engaging in scholarly study, including some form of systematic instruction, and learning how to apply knowledge. Developing the kind of technical skill which will produce work at a rational, intellectual level (rather than depending upon tradition, personal intuition, or the untested proposals of every bystander at the scene) is an essential element in the supervisor's repertoire.

Supervisors (and teachers) who lack the requisite background in educational research might consider either or both of these steps: (1) engaging in advanced study of educational research at an institution of higher learning; (2) setting up a program of in-service seminars and obtaining an expert instructor to work with the staff. Since advanced study means the systematic study of research theory with

15. Harold A. Larrabee, *Reliable Knowledge: Scientific Methods in the Social Studies,* rev. ed., Houghton Mifflin Company, Boston, 1964.

related laboratory experience, taking short-term courses in how to interpret research studies or participating in a series of lectures on current trends in research is not sufficient. Two general areas of coverage are recommended as a minimum: (1) basic work in the fundamentals of research which treats the application of scientific method to problems in education, considers problems in the design of experiments, analyzes instruments and techniques for gathering data, and examines the ways to analyze and interpret data; and (2) specialized work in educational or psychological statistics which treats the ways of quantifying data and applying tests of significance and provides training in the development of skills necessary to present the results of studies in quantitative and scholarly form.

In setting up a program of in-service seminars with a qualified instructor to work with the staff, the same areas of content suggested for advanced study could serve as a basis for study here. Supervisors, while participant-learners along with other staff members, would be responsible for providing data and problems directly from the schools themselves as content for the study of research methodology. With such help from supervisors and staff, a skillful instructor can build the theoretical materials around realistic in-school problems. The study of the methodology of educational research is thus a profitable and realistic experience.

In-service seminars should be long-term, continuing for a year or longer and meeting regularly, and should be recognized by the administrative staff of the schools as a legitimate activity on the part of the participants. Staff members who have participated in long-term seminars should be interested volunteers selected to multiply their skills by helping others. As they attain insight and skill through training in seminars, they can be utilized to train others within schools or within a school system. The supervisor thus develops a cadre of trained persons who can help others to learn—and learn, be it said, in an organized fashion. It should be understood that seminars conducted during the school year become the major mission of an in-service program with few, if any, other tasks interjected, at least for those who are devoting major effort to these seminars. The complaints of teachers that they jump from one institute to another workshop without accomplishing any one task in depth should be sufficient reason for caution. Worthy in-service education hinges on a parsimonious selection of endeavors directly related to teachers' jobs so that they have long-term involvement and the satisfaction of completing one task and completing it well.

If it is not feasible to conduct seminars during the school year, supervisors should consider planning a summer seminar in the school district, preferably conducted by an in-service–trained teacher and/or the supervisor. In seminars or courses conducted by a university, or college, credit can be applied toward the school district's so-called hurdle credit on the promotional scale or toward a higher degree. Where in-school seminars, focused primarily on teachers' own classroom problems, have been tried, they have yielded dividends in terms of improved knowledge about the problems, along with improved skills and positive attitudes. Staff members engaging in the study of basic content use data from their own school system as bases for study and application, work closely with other staff members, relate their learnings to live problems, and develop a commitment to a task which has real meaning for them. Fringe benefits include the opportunity to live at home, to use facilities provided by the school system, and to obtain some visible status within the organizational system.

Supervisors who have the proper vision of educational research develop their own skills by participating in quality programs of study so that they, in turn, can plan and conduct study seminars for others. By teaching others, by recreating their understanding of research procedures and by applying their knowledge to in-school problems, they become even more proficient, contributing vis-à-vis to the learning of the staff.

Will such in-service learning on the part of supervisors and staff result in every member's becoming a technical specialist in research? Obviously the answer is "no"; but out of a staff which undergoes such exposure will come differentiated interests and skills. There will be those who display a high degree of insight and research skill, take major responsibility for continuing research efforts, and provide leadership for the less skilled or less motivated. There will be others who are interested in and know the nomenclature or the broad dimensions of research methodology, and have strong biases toward the research approach. All who participate will have a more catholic appreciation of the complexities inherent in designing research, determining the validity of data, testing ideas and results, and developing generalizations from findings. At first some teachers may find the concepts new and difficult, but through constant encouragement and consultative help from supervisors and other staff members they become dedicated to more systematic ways of studying the teaching process. Sometimes a "sleeper effect," not observable until long after the initiation of a program of study, emerges, and interests and skills which have been latent become manifest. The supervisor may have aroused this interest by reinforcing the initial exposure and continuously involving those who have not become skilled enough. Certainly, training in how to apply methods of research to educational problems cannot be a one-shot deal. There must be follow-up study, application, and continual assessment. The whole process of committing a staff to the research vision becomes a kind of wholesome contamination, followed by hearty reinforcement leading to improved technical skills and receptive attitudes toward systematic and scientific approaches to studying educational problems.[16]

Climate for Effective Research

It has been noted that one of the central problems in a democracy is the necessity to obtain from individuals as much participation in matters affecting their own destiny as possible. Teachers, after all, are professionally trained workers and responsible citizens. Teachers want to do a good job of teaching and are eager and willing to discover better ways to do the tasks to which they have committed themselves. They have enormous capacities to change behavior in new and worthwhile directions. While it may be true that intelligence, interest, and background of individuals may determine the limits of their technical performance, it is true also that if they are given training in research skills and the opportunity to participate in research projects directly related to their own interests and tasks, they are more likely to capitalize on their abilities. There are various

16. Fred P. Barnes, *Research for the Practitioner in Education,* Department of Elementary School Principals, National Education Association, Washington, 1964.

N. L. Gage, *Second Handbook of Research on Teaching,* Rand McNally & Company, Chicago, 1973.

Charles D. Hopkins, *Educational Research: A Structure for Inquiry,* Charles E. Merrill Books, Inc., Columbus, Ohio, 1976.

Fred N. Kerlinger, "Research in Education," in Robert L. Ebel (ed.), *Encyclopedia of Educational Research,* 4th ed., Collier-Macmillan International, Inc., London, 1969, pp. 1127–1144.

George J. Mouly, "Research Methods," in Robert L. Ebel (ed.), *Encyclopedia of Educational Research,* 4th ed., Collier-Macmillan International, Inc., London, 1969, pp. 1144–1152.

Travers, op. cit.

For a usable list of general research and evaluation task areas and related competencies required of personnel to conduct educational research (synthesized from a series of studies sponsored by the American Educational Research Association), see Blaine R. Worthen, "Competencies for Educational Research and Evaluation," *Educational Researcher,* vol. 4, no. 1, pp. 13–16, January 1975.

See, also, *Educational Leadership,* vol. 34, no. 3, pp. 163–209, December 1976, for a series of articles on various aspects of staff development; *Educational Leadership,* vol. 33, no. 6, pp. 403–455, March 1976, for a series of articles on the purposes and uses of teachers' centers in the United States and abroad; and James C. King, Paul C. Hayes, and Isadore Newman, "Some Requirements for Successful Inservice Education," *Phi Delta Kappan,* vol. 58, no. 9, pp. 686–687, May 1977, for a summary of the findings and recommendations of Phi Delta Kappa's Commission on Professional Renewal.

ways to set an atmosphere for research, encourage self-confidence, and secure widespread participation, and it is hoped that the following suggestions will be of help:

1. Supervisors who create an atmosphere for the free exchange of hypotheses, encourage the desire to seek answers to questions, no matter how these results may offend tradition, and stimulate divergent creative thinking cannot help but improve staff competence.

2. Supervisors encourage teachers to think broadly, to see all facets of problems, and to be open-minded. Supervisors make every effort to be aware of and control their own biases. Mistakes along the way are treated as means to seek other leads, not as failures or shortcomings.

3. Better researchers develop when teachers are encouraged to understand principles through the study of theories so that they move from abstract concepts to concrete applications. To start from experience or practice rather than from a theoretical basis or rationale for a particular problem is a "how to do it" approach, not a "why" approach, and may lead to studies which manipulate data but do not answer questions, since the studies were not cast in a theoretical framework to begin with.

4. Encourage the incubation of ideas, allowing time, and then more time. Ideas should not be rushed. By pushing ahead one may get across the tropical marshlands rapidly, but a slower journey would permit seeing some of the lilies which grow among the reeds. Investigating every avenue before finalizing a research proposal may take several months in some instances, time spent in surveying sources of data and consulting others who may have conducted similar studies.

5. Encourage personalized research ideas. That is, give individuals every opportunity to work out ideas on their own—alone, if desired, but at any rate at a personal level of commitment. Every research study does not necessarily call for a director and workers. What is desired is a group of interested people with ideas and the freedom to work them out, at times with others and at other times alone. Sometimes an individual is able to achieve results which slip the grasp of experts.

6. Tackle the idea front as if it were new and fair game. Avoid the attitude that all ideas have been used up, or that most major problems have been investigated already; for example, "After all, Dr. XYZ investigated children's concepts in arithmetic and the answers are all in." Encourage the replication of studies, and the

expansion or reassessment of old ideas, keeping in mind that such explorations are to be related to major purposes. New pathways along the main road may lead to rewarding surprises.

7. Encourage the long-term pursuit of problems. Remember that problems which are solved for one particular purpose during any one school year may not yield generalizations applicable to similar problems in the next year. The fact that conclusions have immediate use does not necessarily mean that they are fundamentally good or have long-term application. Isolate major critical tasks for long-term study whenever called for. Individual teachers should have complete freedom to spend several years on the study of a problem if this seems warranted, since there are few problems that can be neatly packaged year by year or topic by topic. Setting forth a theme or area of research for the year and then passing on to another, illustrates the kind of professional flitting about that is not in keeping with the criteria of competent research and can no longer be afforded.

8. Distinguish between purely administrative studies and those which test hypotheses for the purpose of prediction or validation. Both types have their place, but the supervisor's main concern is in conducting carefully formulated studies of teaching and learning behavior.[17]

9. Learn to treat other individuals as equal partners in a mutual endeavor. Reinforce positive attitudes toward research by rewarding others with overt recognition of their accomplishments. To treat teachers as if they were competent and interested students of research is to suggest the possibility that they will try to be such persons. The supervisor who accepts others as intellectually curious persons who also wish to find answers to questions is creating a climate in which a staff can move toward productive action. Keep in mind that the purpose of in-school research is to serve teachers in order that they may better serve pupils. Research is undertaken to seek approximations to truth, with emphasis on what works best and why, and not for purposes of surveillance to determine how well or how poorly tasks are being accomplished.

10. Set modest and reasonable levels of expectation regarding outcomes. If investigations yield greater values than might have been anticipated, motivation can be expected to provide a propellant toward further successful efforts.

---

17. See Jerome Bruner (ed.), *Learning about Learning,* U.S. Department of Health, Education, and Welfare, Office of Education, Cooperative Research Monograph No. 15, 1966.

Introducing Pilot Studies

Pilot studies of a small-scale or short-term nature (conducted by teachers with a class or several pupils) are often more desirable than large-scale studies which provide limited opportunities for teacher participation. Some of the advantages of pilot studies include:

1. Achieving gradual approximations of purposes and allowing for unanticipated consequences
2. Providing opportunities to examine positive and negative findings during the course of a study without serious risk or threat
3. Assisting persons to develop new skills for applying requisite knowledge, thus reducing the so-called resistance to change
4. Producing results useful for further study
5. Allowing opportunities for conflicting points of view or new evidence to be brought to bear on problems
6. Helping to initiate the implementation of innovations

The value of research in the classroom cannot be overemphasized and seems extremely propitious for two reasons: (1) by systematically monitoring classroom processes and products, individual teachers become more effective in producing desirable student outcomes, and (2) teachers learn to document and share technologies of teaching by various means, such as reporting their results at conferences or submitting them to publications.[18]

When supervisors plan research activities in terms of a consistent set of hypotheses about how educational goals are to be achieved, e.g., changes in behavior, they become models demonstrating how well-disciplined minds operate on objects of research concern. They take time occasionally for introspection to ensure that they do not become so engrossed or involved in urging some particular personal mission that they forget that the busy teacher is faced daily with a time-consuming, energy-draining task. Success in facilitating the teacher's own classroom research is an important measure of the supervisor's worth to a school system.

---

18. For a report on a two-year experimental program in teacher preparation that describes innovative concepts and methods of value in planning and carrying out instructional programs for a range of disadvantaged children, see Carolyn Lipton Ellner and B. J. Barnes, *Schoolmaking,* Lexington Books, D. C. Heath and Company, Lexington, Massachusetts, 1977.

See also Louis M. Smith and Pat M. Keith, *Anatomy of Educational Innovation: An Organizational Analysis of an Elementary School,* John Wiley & Sons, Inc., New York, 1971, for a description of events that make up the beginning of an innovative middle-class suburban school and for a model of educational innovation derived therefrom.

CHAPTER **13**

IMPROVING AND DEVELOPING CURRICULUM

The school cannot teach all things. A central task of the supervisor is to help others select wisely among possible instructional goals and objectives. Some supervisors aid in goal definitions and selections for entire districts at local, state, and federal levels. Others aid particular school communities—parents, teachers, students, others—in determining what shall be taught in a given institution. Still other supervisors assist individual teachers in determining more appropriate instructional objectives for the pupils in specific classrooms as a way to improve the curriculum. Regardless of the level—societal, institutional, classroom—for which goals and objectives are to be determined, the general procedures are the same, differing only with respect to the specificity of data to be employed. A primary purpose for this chapter is to lay out options in procedures available to the supervisor in deriving better goals and objectives than are now operating.

A second supervisory task of high priority is to aid in selecting and arranging the means—learning opportunities, activities, experiences, instructional materials—for attaining the objectives and advancing toward the goals. Hence, attention is given in this chapter to the criteria and procedures for guiding the selection and organization of learning activities and materials.

OPTIONS IN PROCEDURES FOR DETERMINING WHAT TO TEACH
Needs Assessment

Needs assessment is currently a popular way to determine curriculum goals and objectives. It is a process by which participants define educational needs and decide what their priorities are. In the context of curriculum, a need is a condition in which there is a discrepancy between an *acceptable* state of learner behavior or attitude and an observed learner state. The needs assessment approach is popular because (1) it appeals to those who are motivated by efficiency— those who want to identify and resolve the most critical needs so that resources can be employed in a cost-efficient manner; (2) it is an answer to social disorganization—some use the approach as a technique to effect shared values and mutual support. Discussion of possible goals and objectives by parents, students, teachers, and citizens at large is an educational activity in itself; (3) it is viewed by some as a way to get new value orientations into the school. Cultural pluralists, for example, use needs assessment to elicit and gain acceptance by the dominant culture of the subculture values held by blacks, Mexicans, and Chinese.

Steps for conducting a needs assessment are as follows.

FORMULATING A SET OF TENTATIVE GOAL STATEMENTS OR OBJECTIVES   (Goals are more general and encompassing than instructional objectives; hence, goal statements are used more frequently at societal and institutional levels while instructional objectives tend to be used with needs assessment at classroom levels.) Comprehensive sets of goals that reflect the dominant culture are available.[1] Such goal statements usually include the fundamental competencies for literacy, math, health, citizenship, and esthetics, as well as attributes of character, such as friendliness, respect, activeness, and independence.

Goals that reflect subculture values and values that are unique to a given community are more difficult to obtain. The participants must focus on their own perceptions of what they want their learners to think, feel, or be able to do as a result of school instruction. Perceptions are whetted by examining the life of pupils now and in the

1. See: Center for the Study of Evaluation, *Elementary School Evaluation Kit: Needs Assessment,* Allyn and Bacon, Inc., Boston, 1972; Phi Delta Kappa's *Educational Planning Model* (including Manual for Educational Goals and Objectives, Goals and Objectives Workshop Package, and Educational Goal Attainment Tests), Phi Delta Kappa, Bloomington, Ind., 1972.

foreseeable future. Supervisors, for example, may organize "concerns conferences" and "speakups" whereby groups of people—teachers, citizens, students—identify community problems and needs and suggest what curriculum goals should be in light of the identified problems.

ASSIGNING PRIORITY TO GOALS   Participants are given goal statements and asked to rank them in importance. The goals may be rated on a five-point scale. In order to rate many goals in a short time, samples of goals may be given to different individuals to effect average group estimates. Later, the combined ratings will reveal those goals considered very important, important, average, unimportant, and very unimportant.

It is helpful to ask those who are to rate goals or objectives to consider whether or not the goal will contribute to future learning and to fundamental needs like making a living, gaining respect from others, and whether the goal is teachable and not likely to be acquired elsewhere than in school.

The supervisor must also make clear whether the preferences of all participants or groups are to be treated equally or not. That is, student values may count as much as teacher values or they may be weighted.

DETERMINING DEGREE OF ACCEPTABILITY OF LEARNER PERFORMANCE IN EACH GOAL OR OBJECTIVE   The degree of acceptability can be estimated through either impression or by measurement. If the impression approach is taken, judges rate the acceptability of present learner status. No direct measure of learners is undertaken. Impressions might be gained by whatever the judges have observed or been led to believe by media and reports from children and neighbors. The judges' ratings become indices of need. When the measurement approach is used, the status of students with respect to each goal is determined by testing, observing, and student self-reporting. The measures are supposed to be congruent with the goals and objectives, of course. The appropriate measuring device is administered to representative samples of pupils. If the students' level of performance is less than acceptable, a need is indicated. The widest gap indicates a greater need. However, both the size of discrepancy and the preference ranking of the goal must be considered in determining the priority of the need.

TRANSLATING HIGH-PRIORITY GOALS INTO PLANS   Priority goals and objectives become the basis for new curriculum plans— new courses, materials, and arrangements. Learning activities, teaching strategies, and evaluation techniques must be changed accordingly.

Future Planning

Closely related to the needs assessment technique is future planning. A major difference between future planning and needs assessment is that under the former more attention is given to the study of research and trends likely to be important to society in the future rather than to the present status of learners and current social conditions. The following represent common techniques and phases in the approach:[2]

THE MULTIDISCIPLINARY SEMINAR   Supervisors and specialists from outside education—political scientists, economists, medical psychologists—meet for several days to discuss future developments likely to affect curriculum planning. Members of the seminar prepare papers examining research frontiers in their fields. The results of literature searches on educational innovations and goals are also presented.

JUDGMENT OF PROJECTED TRENDS   Major anticipated changes are ordered according to their importance to society and probability of occurring. The difficulty of bringing about these changes in terms of time, money, and energy is considered. A period of occurrence is estimated. The potential social effects of the changes are determined by consensus. Participants rate each change from very desirable to very undesirable.

EDUCATIONAL IMPLICATIONS   After the social consequences of trends have been established and rated, the supervisor and others in the school and community suggest how the schools should respond. They give consideration to whether or not the curriculum can effect the change or prepare students for it. The educational objectives thus formed are stated to support "good" futures and to resist "bad" ones. Those items in present curriculum that are inconsistent with future directions are marked for deletion.

SCENARIO WRITING   Members of the curriculum-developing team prepare two descriptions. One is a description of what learners will be like if action is taken on the decision in Phase Three and

2. Harold G. Shane, "Future Planning as a Means of Shaping Educational Change," *NSSE Seventieth Yearbook,* The University of Chicago Press, Chicago, 1971, pp. 185–217.

implemented by the school. The second iş a description of the necessary related changes in subject matter, activities, organization, and
methods.

Rational Curriculum Making

There are two well-known rational approaches.[3,4] Tyler's rationale for
curriculum making is the best-known model for curriculum development. The Tyler rationale suggests that educational objectives be
obtained, not by the simple preferences of individuals or groups, but
by a systematic search for information and knowledge that can serve
as a basis for wise decisions about objectives. Among the sources to
be considered are the following.

LEARNERS   Data regarding learners' deficiencies, psychological
needs, and interests should be gathered and then supervisors and
teachers must identify the implications of these data for educational
objectives. Inspection of a pupil's cumulative folder could reveal (1)
anecdotal accounts which imply need for approval; (2) analysis of
test results which show gaps in fundamental skills and understandings; and (3) descriptions of living conditions which are detrimental to health and attitude toward school. Observations and interviews with the pupil may reveal interests which warrant
encouragement and deliberate development. If the school controls
or can gain control of the variables which will fulfill the objectives
suggested by such study of the learner, it probably should do so.
Certainly it should—if these objectives can be undertaken without
detriment to other pupils and other priorities among instructional
responsibilities. Special guidance services testify to the school's good
faith in attempting to (1) change those behavior patterns of learners
which keep them from sharing in the values of society and (2) enable
them to make new contributions and new inventions and to stake
out new paths in keeping with their right to individuality. In order for
desirable practices in behalf of the individual learner to continue, we
must reward supervisors who (1) establish the means by which pertinent data about the learner can become available and (2) make it
possible for teachers to implement objectives derived from analysis
of these data.

It is a cardinal tenet of those responsible for vision in the devel-

3. Ralph Tyler, *Basic Principles of Curriculum and Instruction,* The University of Chicago Press, Chicago, 1950.
4. John I. Goodlad and Maurice N. Richter, Jr., *The Development of a Conceptual
System for Dealing with Problems of Curriculum and Instruction,* University of California Press, Los Angeles, 1966.

opment of instructional objectives that the learner be considered as an end or that the learner's personal concerns be considered as well as the demands of society and subject matter. This premise differs from the belief that social or subject-matter ends should first be established and learners studied primarily for the purpose of finding the best way for manipulating them and the classroom situation to predetermined ends. Conversely, instructional objectives in behalf of the learner can also be formulated with regard to society, subject matter, and the role of the school.

Supervisors and teachers at times talk past each other because of the term "needs." When some speak of the "needs of the learner," they refer to psychological and physiological needs, i.e., need for affection, need for activity, etc. Others use these same terms in the sense that learners had better match up to a normative standard of behavior if they expect to progress both in and out of school.

There are implications for teaching from a vast number of studies which generalize both kinds of needs. Much more is known about personality, emotional problems of learners, and the demands of the social context upon learners than we have been able to act upon. However, just because these needs exist does not mean the teacher should respond. The supervisor should help teachers to separate from scientific studies those implications for instructional objectives which are relevant to the school. It is probably desirable for a teacher, for instance, to know the reasons underlying many of the personal difficulties which a learner faces. But the teacher is not a therapist and must deal with the learner in a manner consistent with schooling rather than, say, psychopathology. Usually, the psychological and sociological factors affecting the learner have been taken into account, so far as the teacher is concerned, as means to the attainment of prior instructional objectives rather than as ends peripheral to the teacher's area of expertness. Knowledge of child growth and development will, of course, be useful both in arranging environments consistent with instructional goals and in reducing the number of sociopsychological problems aggravated by miseducative instructional methods.

CONTEMPORARY LIFE Data regarding activities, problems, and demands of contemporary life are collected with a view to inferring educational objectives. Critics have always protested the way objectives of the schools have lagged behind the actualities of life in society. For many, the content of the curriculum should be oriented to the demands of the present or to a speculated future. Often their efforts have been successful. During the war years, the vocational skills necessary to production of materials for defense received emphasis. In times of depression and change toward collective goals, outcomes were in terms of the learner's ability to participate in group deliberation and persuasion. At other times, demands for those who can attack problems with abstract models influenced selection of expected learnings at both elementary and secondary school levels, where instead of emphasizing concrete applications of mathematics, for instance, the structure of mathematics was given precedence.

Commencing in 1918 and continuing until the present, "activity analysis" has been a means of determining curriculum objectives.[5] One way of making such an analysis is to look at the community with respect to its health, leisure time, ethics, home membership, citizenship, and other categories important to a changing social order. Teachers are then asked to see what objectives would help fill these needs. This approach is appropriate when the content of the school is not relevant to the realities of life and when other agencies are not available for meeting new demands. Today, however, the responsibility for many aspects of problems like leisure time and health is shared among many other institutions, and the school is increasingly confining its obligations to the intellectual aspects of these problems—to those tasks which the school can discharge because it possesses the required means.

Studies are also made of the ways people fulfill their roles as citizens and employees. Data from these studies are used to suggest what should be taught. Limitations of this approach are seen when one recalls that current roles may be outdated by the time pupils are expected to fulfill them. Basing objectives on the limited roles of those in a particular community is miseducative in a society where pupils do not live out their lives in the same or similar community. Further, there is the philosophical position that practices current in a community should not set the standard. The teacher as a vicar should encourage pupils to fulfill ideals rather than follow existing practices. If, for instance, pupils from one side of the tracks have always gone into immediate employment rather than advanced schooling, it might be better for the school to foster objectives aimed at upsetting the predicted trend. This could be justified on the premise that it is the school's job to open doors rather than to preserve the *status quo*.

Although community analysis is inadequate as a single source of data for objectives, it is most valuable in revealing possible learning opportunities. Analyses of community situations suggest ways pupils might apply the theoretical systems which the school is teaching. While the community is an excellent laboratory for instruction, the

5. Franklin Bobbitt, *The Curriculum*, Houghton Mifflin Company, Boston, 1918, p. 42.

activity itself must be second to the outcomes sought from instruction. It is not so important, for example, that pupils succeed in bringing about better traffic conditions as a result of their survey and petitions. It is important that the survey result in the pupils' being able to define, explain, and illustrate the real nature of power as well as the skills for effecting social change.

Measuring rods of the good culture which may be helpful to supervisors seeking implications for instructional objectives from social conditions include:

1. How will attainment of the objective further subgroup communication? Will it relieve individuals with different interests from the waste of negative struggle, conferring upon them the positive understanding and common experience necessary for the climate which permits individuality? Does it lead to acceptance of the American canons of tolerance and does it call for illustrating the procedures for conduct of life in a multivalue society?

2. Will the objective help the learner reach aspirations rather than merely foster aspirations without providing means? The dangling of tantalizing prizes, such as the power of understanding, status position, wealth, grades, while closing off pathways to attainment is the way to create rebels and cynics. Enabling objectives must accompany those of a long-range nature. Consistency between the two is a necessity. Ends and means should agree with each other. There is, for example, little likelihood that learners will attain the skills of critical thinking for use in social situations when schools forbid treatment of controversial issues.

3. How will the objective help the learner effect a smooth transition from childhood to adulthood? Although ability to deal with developmental tasks, like coming to terms with one's body, relating to members of the opposite sex, and achieving economic independence, has been recommended as an important outcome for learners, schools have not been quick to build a curriculum upon such a basis. Consideration of this guideline by the social scientists might mean fewer instances of students being restricted in their opportunities to discharge responsibility of adulthood until graduation day and then being abruptly expected to perform as adults.

4. How will the objective help the learner adjust to the tempo of change? Teachers who have faced more change in their lifetimes than the changes faced by several generations of forebears recognize the importance of this criterion for personal and social adjustment. Too often, objectives have helped the learner learn about the known, a known which later turns out to be less certain than it

was supposed to be. Therefore, it is currently fashionable to say that in a world of change, teachers should select objectives by which the learner evidences ability to use a method of discovery. This method involves attitudes such as the habit of suspended judgment and recognition of the *probability* of truth and the tentative nature of explanation. It also includes the technique of inquiry in which the learner *(a)* uses formal patterns or mental structures in new situations and *(b)* invents new patterns or models for dealing with existing difficulties.

SUBJECT SPECIALISTS   Experts in different subject fields are asked what their respective fields can contribute to the education of given learners. By studying answers from the experts, the supervisor and others can infer objectives for the school. Subject matter and content are interchangeable terms. They stand for the thoughts and behaviors which are carried from generation to generation. The meanings of words and symbols, statements of principles, rules of conduct, as well as skills, constitute subject matter. Events and objects are not subject matter, but their interpretations are. So, too, are the cultural modes of thought or the processes by which the interpretations are formed. It is the business of the supervisor to select, from among vast cultural resources, subject matter which is consistent with the role of the school and to make this subject matter meaningful to learners, i.e., help them find "a tool to do something with."

Subject Matter Drawn from Personal Experience
In selecting subject matter, supervisors may draw from folklore, common sense, or wisdom derived from their own experience. It is likely, however, that this kind of information will reflect tradition and will lack a built-in method of self-criticism. The danger of obsolescence is especially acute under such circumstances.

Subject Matter Derived from the Specialist
The supervisor may, on the other hand, go to the master of a discipline and ask "What subject matter in your field will help learners choose among possible actions? Take more of their environment into account? Perceive new relationships?" (It is highly unlikely that supervisors will personally contact the scholar. They will, however, have ample opportunity to select from among recommended content and curriculum materials prepared by various scholars and promulgated through national science foundations, regional laboratories, and professional organizations such as the National Council of Teachers of

English).[6] There are at least two ways scholars may respond. First, they may review their disciplines, including outcomes from recent research, and indicate the contributions or conclusions each discipline offers to the education of all citizens. The physical geographer, for instance, might answer, "Earth movements of rotation and revolution are basic to understanding climate and time; rotation of the earth on its axis is a measure of time and causes night and day; seasons are caused by a combination of revolutions, inclinations, and parallelism of the axis." The political scientist might say, "In organizing government, it is essential to endow rulers with power and make provision for holding them responsible for its use." It is not anticipated, of course, that generalizations like these from the disciplines will be taught per se, but that they will become the content aspect of objectives, offering direction to instruction. Subgeneralizations, concepts, and factual data arising from these generalizations will be incorporated into a sequence of learning opportunities designed to make the terms meaningful to the student.

Second, the scholar within a discipline may feel that any "canned" notions given to the learner are limited and that these facts cannot be treated as self-existing givens. In science especially, the scholar may say, "Place more emphasis upon method or upon a systematic way of viewing situations." After all, it is method, including a set of processes, standards of performance, and ways of analyzing and testing solutions, which constitutes a discipline. The power of a discipline to increase the mental ability of the learner lies in its method rather than in its substantive aspects or formal content. Following this advice, the supervisor will then select from the discipline a kind of subject matter which relates to the way one trained in a field tries to subjugate or accept nature—what specialists observe, the way they frame their questions, the concepts they draw upon for, say explanation or prediction, and especially, the way they decide whether their performance and conclusions are sound. In transmitting this kind of knowledge to the pupil, the teacher, in turn, must afford an opportunity for the learner to challenge the truth of existing rules and laws and to engage in inquiry, formulating hypotheses about phenomena which the learner has handled, seen, heard, and puzzled over. Learners will help define the alternatives and examine views in light of supporting evidence which they collect. But in testing their hypotheses, they will be armed with the belief that there is a relationship or regularity to be found, for attitude, too, is an ingredient of a discipline.

6. See *The Link,* published by the Social Science Education Consortium, Inc., Boulder, Colorado 80302.

Let it be remembered, however, that method requires knowledge of the principles and conclusions as well as awareness of the structures by which these principles are organized (formal content). Formulation of a hypothesis to solve a problem will, for instance, require understanding of certain vocabulary or key principles with which to conceptualize the problem and to plan an attack upon it. In other words, method as content is not sufficient; formal content is also necessary: "We think topics and subjects, not thoughts."[7]

Considerations before Confronting the Specialist

Before turning to the scholar for advice about the selection of content (viz., before making a choice about which national curriculum to recommend for a school or district), supervisors have to be clear about their own expectations of how the subject matter is to serve the learner. First, supervisors may be interested in furthering communication between the specialist and the public. They may, for instance, expect the learners to be able to understand the writings of the specialist which appear as general articles in magazines and books to be read by those who are outside the scholar's community of discourse. They might desire learners to be familiar enough with a discipline to support the efforts of the specialist in the field because they (1) recognize the discipline's value as a human activity, (2) can define its domain of interest and authority, and (3) are able to compare its rules for asserting "truth" with the canons of other disciplines.

Although it is unlikely that supervisors will expect learners to be experts in a field as a result of common schooling, they may want to equip learners with the thinking patterns of several disciplines, so that they can raise questions important in their everyday life and be able to get at the answers.

Second, if supervisors believe that learners should be equipped with the power to add to knowledge in a field, they should make this known to the specialist. It may be desirable that learners be able to discover new facts and relate them to a discipline's particular scheme for classifying and ordering events, facts, laws, or theories. If so, it will be necessary to go beyond the selection of conclusions and include the grounds upon which these conclusions rest and the reason they were selected as relevant in the first place. The notion that certain studies more than others are best adapted to developing the intellectual and spiritual powers of the individual dies hard. Yet a

---

7. John Dewey, *Philosophy and Civilization,* G. P. Putnam's Sons, New York, 1931, p. 261.

particular discipline does not of itself make persons wise nor permit them to exercise good judgment in areas outside the specific field. There is no assurance that because physical scientists have acquired the thought processes for appropriate behavior in a peculiar field, they will contribute to the solutions of problems which are, say, essentially political or religious in nature. No subject matter is inherently intellectual or spiritual. As Dewey says, "Any subject, from Greek to cooking, and from drawing to mathematics, is intellectual, if intellectual at all, not in its fixed inner structure, but in its function—in its power to start and direct significant inquiry and reflection."[8]

The Supervisor and the Fields of Knowledge

We have said that the supervisor will find organized subject matter one of the most important sources of objectives. As a repository of knowledge, the disciplines offer arrangements of schemes and processes with which to solve practical problems and extend knowledge. It is also assumed that supervisors who possess knowledge about the logically organized subjects will be better able to maintain balance in the curriculum because they recognize the virtues of each. Further, supervisors who are able to indicate when any material becomes artistic, chemical, or psychological, or when it falls within the province of other disciplines in the esthetic, physical science, and social science fields, should be able to communicate with those teaching in the particular fields, for they will be familiar with their orientation. How, then, do supervisors attain such a vision of knowledge? In the seventeenth century, Comenius gave an answer: "If we know the fundamental conceptions and the modes of their differentiation, we shall know all things."[9] Modern educational philosophers such as Phenix[10] and Broudy[11] have continued to show how it is possible for supervisors to gain knowledge by which they can identify the key concepts, facts, and principles of a number of disciplines and master these ideas to the point that they can use them to explain the basic continuities and contrasts among subject-matter fields.

The supervisor will find it helpful to analyze disciplines in terms of elements such as the following:

1. *The sources used in different fields for the discovery and valida-*

8. John Dewey, *How We Think,* D. C. Heath and Company, Boston, 1933, pp. 46–47.
9. M. W. Keatinge (trans.), *The Great Didactic of John Amos Comenius,* A. & C. Black, Ltd., London, 1896, p. 34.
10. Philip H. Phenix, *Realms of Meaning,* McGraw-Hill Book Company, New York, 1964.
11. Harry S. Broudy, B. Othanel Smith, and J. R. Burnett, *Democracy and Excellence in American Secondary Education,* Rand McNally & Company, Chicago, 1964.

tion of knowledge. Supervisors will, for instance, be certain to notice that mathematics may be derived and validated by reason. They will recognize that valid conclusions in mathematics are rigorously drawn from basic assumptions, assumptions which themselves have no absolute validity and do not necessarily need to be confirmed in the everyday world. Because they can see that a logically consistent system of mathematics is timeless and not subject to improvement, supervisors will recognize that the demand for "new content" in mathematics is in response to social conditions rather than errors in earlier mathematical thought. On the other hand, supervisors will see how science requires *the direct appeal to nature* through experiment and objective observation of predicted consequences in order to obtain its truths. They will also find that, unlike mathematics, the new scientific truth is not taken as final but as hypothetical. As they look into the humanities, i.e., art, literature, religion, supervisors will notice the importance of the person's own *subjectivity and intuition* in the making of esthetic judgments and find that *revelation* is necessary in attaining knowledge from the divine.

2. *The kinds of objects, data, and systems of organization of importance to a discipline.* The importance of particular entities to a field suggests a basis for ordering the curriculum. Events in history, places in geography, molecules in chemistry are examples of entities associated with certain fields. The supervisor who knows the scheme by which these parts of a structure are arranged for efficient storage, application, and extension should be better able to help teachers arrange conditions by which the entities take their place in a larger system, thereby taking on greater value and meaning. Examples are seen in the two fields, history and grammar. In history, the schemes are aimed at interpretation and therefore attempt to relate events around such topics as *(a)* political forces and movements, *(b)* wars, *(c)* conflict among social beliefs, *(d)* institutions, or *(e)* individual persons. Grammar as a system for noting, classifying, and explaining distinctions in the pattern of language gives increased significance to words by relating them to such factors as form, order, and meaning.

In making a philosophical analysis of subject matter, the supervisors will seek the theoretical statements or concepts which are necessary for formulating questions in inquiry. As schools move from the transmission of general information and prescriptions which are static in time toward the teaching of statements which attempt to explain and predict, there will be fewer objectives, and the aspects of content included in these objectives will be the central concepts of the discipline. Cases in point are the modern school programs in (1) mathematics, whose cornerstones are the concepts of set, function, and logical thinking and (2) physical science, which features the powerful ideas of time, distance, motion, measurement, and atomic structure of matter.

A concluding illustration will point out the desirability of the supervisor's frequent examination of a field in light of the philosophical position which is to receive emphasis in the school and the importance of selecting a limited number of inclusive objectives. Let us take as an example the dimensions of literature. Teachers have reflected many of the different ways of conceptualizing literature. Some have seen it as a mechanical matter of form, a fine art, or an imaginative interpretation of human experience. To some learners, it has been a source of amusement, curious information, or answers to the momentous riddle of personal identification. At one time, teachers regarded it as a science in which the language and process of literary criticism, history, and versification were essential entities. Paralleling this emphasis pupils were assumed to have learned to appreciate literature when they demonstrated their saturation with information about specific authors, literary periods, and types of literature. At another time, the various forms of literary expression were used as handmaidens to factual sociological, psychological, and historical studies as well as personal problem-solving activities. As such, literary selections were expected to contribute to the objectives by stimulating an emotional feeling toward the situations under study. Currently, there are signs that the schools are regarding literature as a vehicle for helping pupils feel and reflect upon what it means to be a human being. In other words, the religious dimension in literature is becoming paramount. Literature is being used to raise crucial questions about the meaning of life and death, the nature and destiny of the human person and society, as well as the basis for our values. This point of view is not new; it has underlain age-old guidelines for selecting literary content: (1) that which has been most important to those who have been most influential in developing civilization; (2) that which raises ideas of permanent and universal concern, like friendship, family, conquest of self and nature.

Knowing the objectives inferred from the data drawn from the three sources which have been discussed (learners, contemporary life, subject fields), Tyler would select from among the proposed objectives those that meet the following criteria:

1. Consistency with other objectives
2. Consistency of objective with philosophy of school
3. Likelihood that the objective is attainable by intended learners

4. Appropriateness of objective to the age level of learners
5. Generalizability of the objective

Once the objectives are formulated and accepted, they are stated in an operational form indicating both what it is that the learner will do (behavior) and the content with which the learner will deal. Learning experiences or opportunities are then selected in order that the objective can be achieved.

One criticism of the Tyler rationale is that it gives the impression that objectives are *objectively* determined, that it downplays the value positions operating when one both goes to some particular source in lieu of others and sees particular implications in the data collected. Hence, Goodlad has proposed an approach that puts values first in the making of a curriculum. He would derive aims from values, educational objectives from aims, and learning opportunities from objectives. The procedures are as follows:

1. *Select given values as premises for the formulation of educational ends.* Beauty, health, intelligence, morals, etc.—the list of values is so great that one must accept values that appear to call for an educational effort and are within the context of the particular setting for which a curriculum is being planned.
2. *Select educational aims.* For example, education should develop respect for the rights of others, appreciation of the cosmos, potentialities of all, desire for continuing education, ability to enter world of work. Aims should be consistent with each other and with the functions of the particular school.
3. *Formulate educational objectives* by refining educational aims selected in accordance with data drawn from learners (interests, psychological needs, deficiencies); social conditions (facts about world, national, or local society and in such areas as health, economics, family, politics); subject-matter specialists—"What content would you suggest for learners in light of the aims presented?"
4. *Screen objectives stated.* Objectives are checked against the criteria of comprehensiveness (its capacity to provide for all aims adopted), internal consistency, attainability, and feasibility.

Our own experience with this approach has shown us that it is difficult to get participants to agree upon initial values and educational aims. Goodlad, himself, admits that rationality is impeded when responsible educational authorities are unable to resolve their own disagreements.

The Analytical Procedure

The chief function of the analytical procedure is to reveal what should be taught in order to prepare learners for given occupations. Steps to be taken are as follows:

1. *Study existing studies and plans revealing work force requirements in key occupational categories.* The annual Manpower Report of the President issued by the United States Department of Labor, for example, gives an overall employment picture. States and regional areas, too, have plans that take into account job market analyses, program reviews, curriculum resources, and local, state, and national priorities.

2. *Use advisory councils composed of parents, students, representatives from labor, and potential employers.* These persons help supply more information on both what will happen in the community and what kinds of employees employers are seeking. Further, they help inform the community about the forces affecting job economy.

3. *Make job descriptions and identify tasks.* A job description is a paragraph or two listing tasks involved and unusual conditions for carrying them out for a given position. Preparing the job description begins with a study of the particular job or jobs. The supervisor tries to answer these questions: "What tasks are required on this job?" "How frequently are they required?" "What skills and information is the graduate expected to bring to each task?"

   Task identification occurs through interviews, questionnaires, critical incidents, and examination on the job of the equipment which one must operate. Observation shows what the employees *do* while being observed. Questionnaires and interviews reveal what they *say* they do. Critical-incident reports may describe a specific work assignment which an employee carried out very effectively or very ineffectively. Reports of critical incidents are valuable in identifying contingencies, difficult tasks, and interpersonal aspects of a job. Each incident is interpreted for what it reveals about the need for teaching some skill, knowledge, or attitude, thereby suggesting objectives.

4. *Make a task analysis.* A task is a logically related set of actions required for a job objective. The first step in a task analysis is to list all the tasks for a job. Next, for each of these tasks an estimate is made of the frequency, relative importance, and relative ease of learning. Finally, there is a detailed listing of what the person does when performing each of the tasks.

   The job analysis and information about the status of intended learners is all that one needs in order to obtain course objectives.

Subtracting what students can already do from what they have to be able to do suggests what should be taught. However, one cannot go directly from a task analysis to the formulation of objectives for a course. It is necessary to decide which of the skills demanded by the occupation may be better taught on the job or in the course.

Negative features of this approach are that it tends to generate objectives more in tune with the way the marketplace *is* rather than as it *should* be. Similarly, it is more often associated with presentism than futurism.

Teachers' Planning Models

John Zahorik has studied what teachers actually do as they prepare to teach.[12] His investigation involved the cooperation of 194 teachers in listing the decisions they make prior to teaching and providing examples of their objectives and activities. Among his findings was the fact that objectives—decisions about goals, aims, outcomes, or purposes—are not very important to teachers. Other decisions are made more frequently and made before considering objectives. The objectives that are used, however, are almost always specific. Only about one-fourth of the teachers begin their planning with objectives. Also, almost none of the teachers begin to plan by identifying activities. Activities are decided on later in the planning process. Content is one of the most important planning decisions. Almost three-fourths of the teachers make this decision, and it is made first more often than any other decision. The most important question for these teachers is "What are the range and particulars of the subject matter of the lesson or unit to be taught?" Decisions about resources to be used—books, films, field trips, guest speakers—are made by over half of the teachers. However, decisions about evaluation, diagnosis, organization, and teaching strategies are made by only a third or fewer of the teachers.

The foregoing findings are disheartening to the rationalists who believe that content and other means should follow the selection of ends—goals and objectives. On the other hand, the findings do not support those who argue that teachers should begin their planning by deciding on the types of activities they will provide from which students choose their own learning experiences and pursue their own objectives.

---

12. John A. Zahorik, "Teachers' Planning Models," *Educational Leadership,* vol. 33, no. 2, pp. 134–139, November 1975.

One implication from the Zahorik study is that supervisors might exercise their power by emphasizing the content or curriculum domains that should be taught. Other implications are that supervisors should help teachers move from a low level of curriculum planning whereby the textbook determines content, activities, scheduling, and continuities to a somewhat higher level where the teacher is concerned about the interests, questions, and problems of children as they can be related to the textbook material or that the supervisors might even get some teachers to the point where they ask "What developmental concerns, purposes, questions, or problems do these pupils have that my expertise can address?"

Disjointed Incrementalism

Curriculum decisions about what to teach as made by school boards and top administrators are thought by Kirst and Walker to occur through a strategy called disjointed incrementalism, the fragmenting of decision making through compromise.[13] Accordingly, ideal reach is traded for program grasp. The major features of this strategy are:

1. *Propose only relatively small changes* in the existing situation. (Small changes are more likely to be supported than large ones.)
2. *Consider only a few options* or alternatives before making a selection or choice. (Consider changes that can be built upon existing practices. It is better to give more attention to options for which we have knowledge of the consequences than to options whose effects are unknown.)
3. *Adjust goals to means.* That is, reverse the rationalist's idea of starting with the goal and then finding the means to realize the goal. (After all, goals are governed by the availability of means.)
4. *Continue to change interpretations of data and all recommendations based on these interpretations.* Calculation is never finished. (Fudge the data in order to reduce conflict among different interest groups.)
5. *Do not try to "solve" a problem in the sense of eradicating it;* but rather simplify to make the problem situation somewhat better. (Accept poorly defined goals as they are given and try to formulate approximate ones that, although not the best, may still be better.)

In short, those practicing disjointed incrementalism realize that a great many people and institutions share in the work of policymak-

13. Michael W. Kirst and Decker W. Walker, "An Analysis of Curriculum Policy Making," *Review of Educational Research,* vol. 41, no. 5. pp. 479–509, December 1971.

ing. At least many persons have to support the decisions. The incrementalists are thus sensitive to what it takes to get general acceptance, preferring a modest curriculum change likely to be acceptable to many persons rather than a significant change for which conditions of acceptance are unfavorable. By way of example, Mann has pointed out that a disjointed incremental approach to the reading problem would not involve entirely new procedures and institutions but rather modifications in existing materials and processes that would only alter, not replace, existing efforts.[14] Disjointed incrementalism seems unduly cynical to some people. Remember, though, that it is a description of how curriculum decisions frequently are made, not a prescription.

CURRICULUM ORIENTATIONS AND THE SELECTION OF MATERIALS AND ACTIVITIES

A school system, individual school, or particular classroom can pursue one or more orientations toward curriculum. The most common orientation is an *academic* one whereby pupils are expected to acquire knowledge and thought processes and fundamental skills drawn from the disciplines and considered as being useful for all citizens. A second orientation is *humanistic* which holds that the curriculum should provide personally satisfying experiences for each individual. The new humanists are self-actualizers who see curriculum as a liberating process to meet individual needs for growth and personal integrity. A third orientation is *technological,* a rational means-ends conception whereby the technologist seeks the most efficient and effective means to whatever predetermined ends or objectives are operating. A fourth orientation is *social reconstructionism* whereby the curriculum is conceived as a vehicle for fostering critical discontent and for equipping learners with the skills needed for conceiving new goals and effecting social change.[15]

Each of the above orientations has its own guidelines and criteria for developing and choosing the material and activities to be used in classrooms. A major task for most supervisors is to give guidance with respect to materials and activities. We believe this can best be done when supervisors recognize the relationship between curriculum orientations and the criteria for developing and selecting learning opportunities. Armed with this recognition, supervisors can gain

14. Dale Mann, *Policy Decision-making in Education,* Teachers College Press, Columbia University, New York, 1975.
15. John D. McNeil, "Conceptions of Curriculum," *Curriculum: A Comprehensive Introduction,* Little, Brown and Company, Boston, 1977.

both acceptance and use of particular instructional material. Learning opportunities can be matched to the purposes to which they point.

Academic Guidelines for Selecting Materials

To the academician, learning opportunities are chiefly textbooks, films, teacher guides, and laboratory apparatus. Criteria of most importance in selecting among the materials available are:

1. *Valid content.* Concepts are those which are central to the comprehension and broadest application of the fundamentals of contemporary thought in the academic discipline.
2. *Active learner participation.* All learning opportunities should supply firm rooting for the growth of ideas by providing direct contact with relevant data. The student is expected to be an active participant, raising questions and performing experiments. The materials should make the students responsible for thinking out the nature and meaning of what they are to do.
3. *Logical organization.* There are two kinds of logical organization that should be present. One is the logical unit of the field itself. That is, the materials should faithfully represent the way scholars have organized the field, e.g., ideas about waves and particles are carried further in a higher synthesis of ideas in physics. Two, there is the logic of dependency—addition and subtraction are introduced before division. Note that the academician has not often attended to the logic of the child. Topics and concepts are determined by the subject specialist's task and are not necessarily in keeping with the learners' point of view.

Humanistic Guidelines for Selecting Materials

In contrast to other orientations, learning opportunities in the humanistic curriculum are not planned in the framework of a means-end continuum. Humanists emphasize the qualities of the teacher more than artifacts like plans, textbooks, and courses of study. In this perspective, the planning of opportunities, activities, and experiences should be a cooperative process by student and teacher, for the pupil's own purposes must be respected. The humanistic guideline focuses on the conditions of learning, attending to the characteristics, interests, and growth patterns of each child: a rich environment with many materials to manipulate; opportunities that stress wholeness, putting all senses to work; human relations; opportunities to wonder about and to be puzzled; and opportunities for the learner to feel independent by facing problems alone.

A bad learning environment for the humanist is one where

learners have to meet standards beyond their abilities, to endure too much tension, to face destructive criticism, to think in terms of canned solutions to problems, to conform to meaningless traditions, and, above all, to be denied choices.

Technological Guidelines for Selecting Materials

Most criteria used in formal evaluation of curriculum and instructional materials reflect the influence of the technologist. For example, recommendations by Tyler et al. contain the following, drawn from technologists' views as to what makes for effective instruction:[16]

1. Learning opportunities should be directly related to the behavior and content of the specified objectives. The means should be directly related to the ends.
2. Learning opportunities should be so arranged that the behavior of the student is developed. Prerequisites, if required, should be dealt with.
3. An evaluation package should be built in.
4. The technical manual should state in detail the objectives and cite sources of evidence about effectiveness and efficiency.
5. Objectives should be spelled out operationally; i.e., they should state behavioral responses desired of students.
6. The kind of student for whom the curriculum and instructional materials are designed should be specified—age, sex, socioeconomic class, and prerequisites.
7. Evaluation should be used both during development and tryout of the materials and after their completion. Effectiveness should be reported in terms of program objectives as well as unintended outcomes. The program's effects in relation to different types of students should be reported.
8. The technical manual must indicate the qualifications of the teacher needed in order to use the materials.
9. The conditions necessary to implement the curriculum must be specified.
10. The technical manual should indicate which materials are required and whether or not any of the materials can be revised.

Social Reconstruction Guidelines for Selecting Materials

Several criteria now used in choosing among materials reflect the political power of groups bent upon having the school join the battle

---

16. Louise L. Tyler, M. Frances Klein et al., *Evaluating and Choosing Curriculum and Instructional Materials,* Educational Resource Associates, Inc., Los Angeles, Calif., 1976.

against social injustice:

1. Teaching material must portray both men and women in the full range of leadership, occupation, and domestic roles, without demeaning, stereotyping, or patronizing references to either sex.
2. Material must portray, without significant omission, the historical role of members of racial, ethnic, and cultural groups, including their contributions and achievements in all areas of life.
3. Material must portray members of cultural groups without demeaning, stereotyping, or patronizing references concerning their heritage, characteristics, or life-style.

The following guidelines are for those planning activities for a social-reconstructionist curriculum:

1. *Select an idea.* Select a topic or problem—such as public opinion, elections, media, or conservation, which makes sense to the students. Issues and problems in the community should be considered.
2. *Explore the idea.* Students must consider what they can do about the issue or problem besides studying about it. The student must take responsible action.
3. *Plan for action.* Surveys, field trips, interviews are not what the social reconstructionists mean by action. Since the essence of the political act is carrying knowledge into action; a student activity that omits persuasion and decision making is not satisfactory. Planning means thinking of the action, such as organizing a public forum and indicating how students will carry it out.
4. *Test for realness.* Helping to get out a vote, campaigning, talking on issues is real. Mock trials, mayor for a day, taking straw votes are not real, only role playing to the reconstructionist. Learning activities must promise to contribute to the solution of the problem and be seen by students as important.
5. *Determine what will be learned.* Social skills and knowledge are valued. Instructional objectives should stress competencies, such as persuasion, getting information, arriving at valid conclusions, acceptance of responsibility, and knowledge of social instructions.
6. *Limit the scope of the activity* so that there is time for students to complete the action phase.
7. *Involve others* in the project.
8. *List needed information* and sources of information, select study materials, and plan for evaluating the gains and loses accruing from the project.

CONCLUSION

By way of conclusion, it seems clear that there are two ways to improve curriculum. One way is to have better—more defensible—intents or objectives. These objectives should represent inherent values and be instrumental to the learners attaining other more encompassing long-range purposes. We have seen that there are several approaches for determining warranted curricular ends. What must be said, however, is that different situations may make one or more of these approaches more appropriate than another. For example, the needs assessment approach is useful when a supervisor wants to gain public commitment to a program or curriculum. The rational approach, particularly as defined by Ralph Tyler, is best for generating novel objectives relevant to the times. The analytical approach has proven its worth in developing vocational curriculum at all levels of training and education. Disjointed instrumentalism fits in well with the desire to accommodate powerful political interests of different groups in shaping the curriculum. A major responsibility of the supervisor in the future is likely to be that of orchestrating the implementation of curriculum that represents the different approaches.

Similarly, the different sets of criteria for selecting and developing learning opportunities allow supervisors to do something that until now has been largely ignored: to match the quality of learning opportunities with the curriculum conceptions of participants. Too often the practice has been to impose one set of criteria for selecting materials regardless of the curriculum domain established by board, school staff, and individual teacher. Worthwhile educational materials and activities are not of universal value; their value is relevant to time, community, and individuals. Further, the justification of materials and activities will not necessarily spring from the same value premise.

For some people, the "transcendental" argument—justification of an activity on the grounds that it rises above mere partisan consideration—is valid. But when personal tastes and moral dispositions differ, we must appeal to a norm, and, if that does not suffice, appeal to expertise. There are people—supervisors—to whom we should listen because they have more experience than outsiders. Ultimately judgment about the worthwhileness of materials and activities is our own. Judgment should be tempered, of course, by the range of our impulses satisfied and by the extent to which it allows us to communicate with others.

NAME
INDEX

NAME
INDEX

SUBJECT INDEX

SUBJECT INDEX